Endorsements

I've known Ruth Schofield for over 30 years, living where she does in Washington DC at the center of the power base of the world and knowing and praying with the power brokers of the world. Ruth also knows the word of God and has an intimate relationship with the King of the Universe. The Power of the King Series, written by Ruth, comes from a life of walking with the King and praying and listening in intimate fellowship with Him. This series is like taking a university bible course.

–Bob D'Andrea, President, Christian Television Network, Largo, FL.

Over the years I have come to love and deeply respect Ruth Schofield as a friend and mentor. After reading the Power of the King Series I can see why she has triumphed in adversity and witnessed tremendous miracles throughout her life. The fruit of 35 years of determination to understand the fire and power of our mighty God pierces the heart of the reader as the Spirit of God ministers through every page. This book both challenged me to examine my life and ministry and caused a tremendous revelation of how GREAT the God of Israel is. If we heed the message revealed to her, we will be victorious in these last days and bring the glory and honor that will transform the lives of those around us. This book is a resource and wealth of heavenly information that will keep your eyes focused on Him.

–Annette Garcia, President Son Broadcasting, Santa Fe, NM

Ruth Schofield's Power of the King's Series transforms and empowers the reader through the immediate presence of God's Grace. It is inspirational and instructional in the highest sense. Every Christian should read this book series.

–Dr. Ted Baehr, Author and President of Movieguide ©, Hollywood, CA.

Most people have not gone to Bible school, but the information in this series would encourage and educate anyone to be a better disciple of Christ. When we diligently study the information presented in this series, we will be following Paul's admonition to Timothy in II Timothy 2:15: Study to show thyself approved unto God, a workman that needeth not to be ashamed, rightly dividing the truth (KJV).

–Norma Bixler, Co-founder Cornerstone Television Network, Pittsburgh, PA.

As I read the Power of the King Series it was obvious the years of study and research Ruth put into this significant work. This is not just another book about authority in Christ. This is a well-thought-out drill down about the potential each true Christian possesses to combat the very forces of Hell and find their

own personal destiny. What a strategic time in history for this book. As our country and world faces unprecedented challenges, we all need to re-visit the potential power in each of us for effective spiritual warfare. This book not only reminds me of the power of the Word of God and the power of prayer, but it gives me hope that regardless of what is happening in the world, we are still the victors through Christ.

–Shirley Rose, Author and Host of Aspiring Women, TLN, Chicago, IL.

The church is increasingly destitute of rich, biblical teaching that soars the heights and plumbs the depths of the Word of life. Ruth Schofield's book, The Power of the King's Fire, satisfies the thirst of all believers who yearn for fresh, living water from the Word of God. You will not be disappointed. Drink from a lifetime of prayer, meditation, and teaching. Read it now, as I am, along with the other books in her new Power of the King Series. Trust me – together we will meet at the throne.

–Rev. Jeff Farmer, Past President Open Bible Churches, Des Moines, IA.

Power of the King Series

Power of the King's Scepter

Keys to the Kingdom and Authority to Overcome

Ruth Schofield

"Your throne, O God, is forever and ever; a scepter of righteousness is the scepter of Your kingdom." – Hebrews 1:8

Power of the King Series POWER OF THE KING'S SCEPTER
Keys to the Kingdom and Authority to Overcome
by Ruth Schofield

Printed in the United States of America

ISBN 9781498406871

www.xulonpress.com

ACKNOWLEDGMENTS

I express great appreciation for my entire family and their commitment to love and accept one another in the Spirit of Jesus Christ. I also give thanks for my son Brad and his wonderful family.

I'm sincerely grateful to my precious brothers and sisters in Christ, who have added their endorsements to the *Power of the King Series*, and my dear friend Marie Roberts for her tireless support and editing skills. Special thanks to Gwendolyn Nelbach who tediously researched the scriptures for this volume.

The *Power of the King Series* has been compiled from 40-plus years of personal study notes in searching to unravel the mysteries within the Word of God. The revelation of how vital it is to release the power of God's Word in your own life will give you victory over the fiery trials you are now facing, and those yet to come. The series also proclaims a manifesto to the end-time Laodicean Church Era. Is the Church of Jesus Christ ready for the return of the Bridegroom? Does it accept the challenge of Christ to be prepared to rule and reign in His coming Millennial Kingdom?

This book is dedicated to my Lord and Savior Jesus Christ, Who is the living Word and the true Light of the world according to John, chapter one. It is by His authority that I have accomplished 35 years of dynamic ministry for His Glory!

Contents

Part Two
Empowering Prayer with Scripture

INTRODUCTION

Spiritual authority is basic; it comes through intimacy with Jesus Christ, not through works. I have personally learned the secrets of prayer by spending time worshiping Jesus, studying Scripture, and proclaiming God's Word. Sound doctrine and balanced teaching are necessary, but intimate worship is where we cross over into the glory of God, like Isaiah did in chapter six when he was enjoying fellowship with *Elohim* (God). Fellowship with Jesus is what the early believers understood. Intimate fellowship with Christ began with Pentecost in the Upper Room while the disciples waited upon the Lord Jesus and were baptized with Holy Ghost fire (Acts 1:4–5, 8). This is how the glory of God showed up with the power they needed to witness and walk in the miraculous. That anointing of His fire, His presence, made them witnesses of Jesus, and his signs and wonders accompanied them as they preached the Gospel message. Because of busy programs and activities, too many of today's churches are missing the glory of God in their midst. People's lives are only transformed when the glory of God is present.

Developing a deep love for the Word of God should be a daily experience. When we fall in love with Jesus, then it is natural to love His Word because He is the eternal Word. At a very young age, I had a keen interest in the Bible. As a child, I looked forward to every Sunday morning when our teacher would tell us stories about Jesus. Some of you can probably remember the fleece covered poster board on which the teacher would build a story from the Bible, and the paper characters would hold fast to the material.

My first Bible came from my Irish grandmother when I was a teenager. She had come to America as an immigrant at the age of sixteen, and I was always fascinated by the stories of her experience of going through Ellis Island. This branch of our family brought their strong Presbyterian faith from Ireland, and my grandmother would take us to Church when we would visit her seashore home near Ocean City, New Jersey.

Like most people, I found the New Testament easier to understand since it evolves around the life of Jesus Christ and the early Church. With my major in college being history, I later began an exhaustive research into the Bible and its people. When you get involved in studying about Israel, the Land of the Bible, you cannot help but develop a love for its people. Later, I was drawn to place my feet on the soil of modern Israel, and learn more about the roots of our Christian faith. Through numerous visits, my years of exhaustive Bible study turned into authentic experiences. It was much deeper than just putting your feet where the Savior walked. It was about looking into the faces of the people who are kin to the Messiah, and studying their lifestyles. Their customs, language, and culture are key to understanding the message that Jesus Christ spoke to His disciples. His parables must be seen through the kaleidoscope of the society that existed 2,000 years ago.

The Old Testament records the beginnings of the Hebrew people and focuses on God's ongoing covenant with Israel. The first five books are called the *Pentateuch,* or the books of Moses; which not only contain the laws given to Israel, but also the laws given to Adam, Noah, and Abraham. Our Lord Jesus Christ is the true treasure hidden within the Old Testament, being revealed as the Lamb slain from the foundation of the world, the *Redeemer*.

There was one time in my life when I became very angry at God, and threw away the Bible my grandmother had given me. I was broken-hearted over losing my husband who had gone missing in Vietnam, which forced me to start life over as a single mother and become the head of the household for our son. The grace of God soon drew me back, and I deeply regretted discarding the Bible my grandmother had given me. A short time later during a Sunday church service, I saw a paperback Bible in the pew which I glanced through and noticed how much easier it was to understand than the King James Bible. It was the "Good News for Modern Man" New Testament, and a note inside read: "If you would like to take this Bible home to read, you can keep it as a gift."

I excitedly took the Bible home and consumed the Scriptures into the wee hours of the morning for several weeks. One Sunday morning during a Communion service, I saw the heavens open up and I received the Baptism of the Holy Spirit. Soon afterward, another believer who had this experience, crossed my path and invited me to a Charismatic prayer group. Six months later, I enrolled in Bible College part time. After graduation and ordination, I began full time ministry in evangelism. These events positioned me into fulfilling the call of God that was upon my life for service; a destiny I believe had been foreordained from birth (Jeremiah 1:5-7).

When my son was very young, I had begun a daily altar time where we would read the Bible and pray together. He attended a Christian academy where he also learned the Bible, and eventually graduated from Bible College. He is now the father of five children, and I see him nurturing his own family in the same manner in which he was taught. Nothing fills my heart more than to have given them such a spiritual inheritance, worth much more than silver or gold (Acts 20:32-33). I rejoice that many of my family members are also sustained by a living faith in the Lord Jesus.

It is my sincere prayer that the *Power of the King Series* will offer some encouragement and depth as you pursue your visions and dreams in the Word of God through the power of the Holy Ghost. The entire series provides an intensive study on the Omnipotent power of the King of kings, giving foundational keys to equip the Church in the most challenging times in world history. Each book in this series has been compiled and condensed from portions of my Bible teachings, which aired for many years on radio and television into numerous countries across the 10/40 Window. This area is populated by people who are predominantly Muslim, Hindu, Buddhist, Animist, Jewish or Atheist. Many governments in the 10/40 Window are formally or informally opposed to Christian work of any kind within their borders.

The *Power of the King's Scepter* is the second book in the series, which focuses on the sword of the spirit; giving a deeper understanding of the power of God's Word, and the spiritual authority it carries. The central message reveals how much the God of the Bible desires to prepare His people to rule and reign over the nations with His Son, and that kingdom training must first begin in our everyday lives. As you study the Scriptures and assimilate them into your spirit, the Holy Spirit will give revelation, or Rhema. Hopefully, you will be stirred to serve the kingdom purposes of Christ with effectiveness and excellence by first laying a firm foundation in the Word of God.

May the Lord Jesus Christ, grant you great victory and success as you pursue His Kingdom to bring glory to God through your life! Be sure to look at the Prayer Guide included in Part Two, chapter three, which contains an exhaustive list of scriptures to pray for various needs.

Ruth Schofield
Ambassador to the Nations
Washington, D.C.

Part One

Keys to the Kingdom of Heaven

Chapter One

The King's Scepter

What does the scepter, or rod signify? The scepter is spiritual authority in a human hand. It was used by kings as a symbol of their authority and was ornate in design. The scepter also offered diplomatic immunity. Queen Esther received diplomatic immunity when the king extended his scepter toward her upon entering his court without prior permission. Psalm chapter two describes how, one day, the Lord Jesus, will stretch out His Kingly scepter and bring the nations into subjection to God's will. Christ will reign on David's throne as the Prince of Peace for 1,000 years. Presently, He sits upon the throne of grace in heaven; He is also the throne of power in the midst of His Church. *Yeshua* is the Messiah, the King of kings and Lord of lords, who will establish His kingdom and rule throughout the whole earth. "Your throne, O God, is forever and ever; a scepter of righteousness is the scepter of Your kingdom" (Hebrews 1:8). He will not rule alone–the saints will reign with Christ for 1,000 years:

> And I saw thrones, and they sat on them, and judgment was committed to them. Then I saw the souls of those who had been beheaded for their witness to Jesus and for the word of God, who had not worshiped the beast or his image, and had not received his mark on their foreheads or on their hands. And they lived and reigned with Christ for a thousand years (Revelation 20:4).

> The Messiah's Scepter, His Sword and Rod of Iron, represent His authority to rule the nations: "All the ends of the world shall remember and turn to the Lord, and all the families of the nations shall worship before You. For the kingdom is the Lord's, and He rules over the nations" (Psalm 22:27-28).

> Psalm two is called the Psalm of Messiah the Prince: "Ask of Me, and I will give You the nations for Your inheritance, and the ends of the earth for Your possession. You shall break them with a rod of iron; You shall dash them to pieces like a potter's vessel" (vv. 8-9).

Psalm, chapter two, describes Jesus Christ as a threefold King: His enemies' King, His saints' King and His Father's King. He is King over all kingdoms, all nations, all governments, all powers, and over all people (Isaiah 9:6). Having been given all authority in heaven and on earth, Jesus Christ passed the scepter of His authority and power to the Church. The Son of God is seated at the Right Hand of the Throne of God extending His royal scepter of authority to His Bride–the Church. This scepter was initially passed to Peter and the disciples. If we were to envision this scene, we would see the King of kings extending the Scepter to His Church; His Body, His Army, His Bride:

> .....thou art Peter, and upon this rock I will build my church; and the gates of hell will not prevail against it. And I will give unto thee the keys of the kingdom of heaven: and whatsoever thou shalt bind on earth shall be bound in heaven: and whatsoever thou shalt loose on earth shall be loosed in heaven (Matthew 16:18-19).

Jesus was referring to Peter's solid confession to be the "rock" on which the Church will be established. Peter had just recognized Jesus as the Rock, "thou art the Christ, the Son of the living God" (Matthew 16:16). Peter's name is interpreted "small stone" in Greek. It is never stated in Scripture that he should be the head of the Church with future successors who would represent Christ and function as the official monarch leader over all the Church. Jesus is the Rock, the first and great foundation of the Church (1 Corinthians 3:11). Peter states in his first letter that Jesus is the "living stone.....Rejected indeed by men, but chosen by God and precious, you also, as living stones, are being built up a spiritual house, a holy priesthood, to offer up spiritual sacrifices acceptable to God through Jesus Christ" (1 Peter 2:4-5). Peter is saying that all Christians are living stones who become part of the structure of the spiritual house which God is building. Jesus gave the "keys to the kingdom" to His Church, giving His disciples authority over His Kingdom work on earth (Matthew 16:19). It is foretold in Psalm 2:9, that the Messiah has placed His "rod of iron" in their hands to deal with the nations. As Jeremiah (1:10) who was commissioned to pluck up and plant, the Church has been given authority to pull down strongholds with the Messiah's rod of iron (2 Corinthians 10-4-5).

The Church broadly represents a partial truth when teaching that the Messiah's rule over the earth is a loving, peaceful scepter; while Scripture also states He will ultimately crush and overthrow all his foes. Christ loves the Body of Christ, but His rod of iron represents God's judgment. The message to the seven churches in

John's Revelation indicates how He will judge the House of God when necessary. Born-again believers who are baptized in the Holy Spirit have been given Christ's scepter of authority to break through the evil spirits, and the principalities of darkness that would like to hold their family, community, and nation in captivity. Those who accept this responsibility are the overcomers who will rule and reign with the Messiah during His Millennial reign on earth and for all eternity.

The greatest power in the universe stands behind the believer. Jesus was addressing the Church when He said, "All authority has been given to Me in heaven and on earth" (Matthew 28:18). He was saying, "I have the authority and I delegate that authority to you." God Himself is the power behind the authority, which is a power greater than our enemy possesses. Christ's spiritual authority exercised upon the earth has to be demonstrated through the Church. Believers are responsible for holding up the standard of the Cross against false gods; as Elijah did when he stood against Ahab and Jezebel's prophets of Baal.

The Church of Jesus Christ is God's extension of His Kingdom on earth, and it has always been His plan to operate through the Church. Since the Church is commanded to do spiritual warfare against the devil, James says this applies first to the believer: "Therefore submit to God. Resist the devil and he will flee from you" (James 4:7). Again in Luke 10:19, we see Jesus passing His scepter of power to the Church: "Behold, I give you the authority to trample on serpents and scorpions, and over all the power of the enemy, and nothing shall by any means hurt you." In Matthew 16:18, Jesus said the gates of hell shall not prevail against His Church, and in Matthew 18:18, "Assuredly, I say to you, whatever you bind on earth will be bound in heaven, and whatever you loose on earth will be loosed in heaven." This refers to the second heavenly and our spiritual activity in relation to angels. Angels respond to the faith of the believer in Christ.

Who is the King of Glory and His Kingdom?

> I watched till thrones were put in place, and the Ancient of Days was seated; His garment was white as snow, and the hair of His head was like pure wool. His throne was a fiery flame, its wheels a burning fire; a fiery stream issued and came forth from before Him..... (Daniel 7:9-10).

Daniel's vision describes the King of Glory as the "Ancient of Days" who is sitting upon His fiery throne. In Deuteronomy 4:24, Moses heard *Yahweh* describe Himself: "For the Lord your God is a consuming fire, a jealous God." *Yahweh* spoke to Jeremiah, "Is not My word like a fire?" (Jeremiah 23:29). Daniel's "Ancient of Days" is the Almighty God, whose eternal throne rules over all other thrones, and the fire coming from it is judgment. Further on in Daniel's vision he describes the Son of Man, coming as the Messiah, to establish God's rule on earth:

> I was watching in the night visions, and behold, One like the Son of Man, coming with the clouds of heaven! He came to the Ancient of Days, and they brought Him near before Him. Then to Him was given dominion and glory and a kingdom, that all peoples, nations, and languages should serve Him. His dominion is an everlasting dominion, which shall not pass away, and His kingdom the one which shall not be destroyed (Daniel 7:13-14).

The Prophet Isaiah foretold of the Messiah's birth and His reign forever upon the throne of David:

> For unto us a Child is born, unto us a Son is given; and the government will be upon His shoulder. And His name will be called Wonderful, Counselor, Mighty God, Everlasting Father, Prince of Peace. Of the increase of His government and peace there will be no end, upon the throne of David and over His kingdom, to order it and establish it with judgment and justice from that time forward, even forever. The zeal of the Lord of hosts will perform this (Isaiah 9:6-7).

This particular prophecy from Isaiah speaks of great hope during a time of gloom for God's people. The hope is in the imminent reign of Christ, which will bring freedom from all enemies of the Kingdom of God. Isaiah also describes the universal rulership of the house of David and speaks of how God is in control and even pledges justice on behalf of His faithful. Going forward into the New Testament, in Acts, chapter two, Peter preaches about the Messiah's triumphant deliverance from the power of Death. He speaks of King David's prophecy of the Messiah's reign as second-in-command to *Yahweh* himself. Peter referenced David's words:

> The Lord said to my Lord, "Sit at My right hand, till I make Your enemies Your footstool." The Lord shall send the rod of Your strength out of Zion. Rule in the midst of Your enemies! (Psalm 110:1-2).

> The Lord is at Your right hand; He shall execute kings in the day of His wrath. He shall judge among the nations, He shall fill the places with dead bodies, He shall execute the heads of many countries. He shall drink of the brook by the wayside; therefore He shall lift up the head (vv. 5-7).

Finally, we look at Daniel's vision, which reveals how the Lord's redeemed bride will rule and reign with Him forever when all dominion is taken away from the antichrist, along with all beast nations throughout all the earth. This is when the redeemed–those true believers in Christ–will rule and reign with the Messiah in His Kingdom:

> Daniel 7:27 describes how the saints will rule and reign with Him: "Then the kingdom and dominion, and the greatness of the kingdoms under the whole heaven, shall be given to the people, the saints of the Most High. His kingdom is an everlasting kingdom, and all dominions shall serve and obey Him." (Also read Revelation 11:15; 20:4)

This spiritual reign of Christ will begin with the destruction of the antichrist and will last until the end of the Millennium; and after that his people will reign with Him throughout all eternity (Revelation, chapters 21 and 22). What one does to fulfill their "Call" to advance the Kingdom of God on earth will determine their inheritance with Christ (Revelation 11:15). The word describes divine rewards given to believers for the moral quality of their actions; while taking note that quality is always better than quantity. There are also rewards in this present life during one's earthly walk. For instance, obedience to Christ's commandments gives the believer a Oneness with the Father, Son, and the Holy Spirit; as Jesus taught His disciples in John chapter fifteen and seventeen! This is an awesome revelation to understand that the presence of the King of kings resides within your spirit (John 17:21). His presence is where that still small voice whispers the direction of your destiny. It speaks to each of us:

> Before I formed you in the womb I knew you, and before you were born I consecrated you..... (Jeremiah 1:5, 10).

We should not reason with the calling of God upon our lives–only say yes, and remember that whom God calls, He also trains and equips. Can we find anyone in the Bible who actually felt they were qualified to step into the "call" of God? Since we do not always fully grasp God's plan when He asks us to obey, then each moment is a step of faith. Ask the Lord to show you His perfect timing and give you His heart in all you do, and understand that He sends you out in the power and might of the Holy Spirit (Zechariah 4:6). Discern and shut out the opposing voices that bid you to compromise your destiny, which is the will of God. Revelation of whom the King of Glory is in the Word brings humility into your heart while serving His Kingdom, as David worshiped:

> For the Lord is the great God, and the great King above all gods. In His hand are the deep places of the earth; the heights of the hills are His also. The sea is His, for He made it; and His hands formed the dry land (Psalm 95:3-5).

This is one of the keys to the Kingdom of God: "Seek first the kingdom of God and His righteousness, and all these things shall be added to you" (Matthew 6:33). Christ warned the disciples about the danger of slipping into lethargy and complacency in the end times:

> But take heed to yourselves, lest your hearts be weighed down with carousing, drunkenness, and cares of this life, and that Day come on you unexpectedly. For it will come as a snare on all those who dwell on the face of the whole earth. Watch therefore, and pray always that you may be counted worthy to escape all these things that will come to pass, and to stand before the Son of Man (Luke 21:34-36).

In John's Revelation, Christ confronted the church of Laodicea, which represents the Church of the end times. This warning reaches out across the centuries to speak to us today: "So then, because you are lukewarm, and neither cold nor hot, I will vomit you out of My mouth" (Revelation 3:16). What an appalling indictment! What is the crime, the unbelievable sin committed by this Church, which appeared to be thriving?

> Because you say, "I am rich, have become wealthy, and have need of nothing"—and do not know that you are wretched, miserable, poor, blind, and naked—I counsel you to buy from Me gold refined in the fire, that you may be rich; and white garments, that you may be clothed, that the shame of your nakedness may not be revealed; and anoint your eyes with eye salve, that you may see (Revelation 3:17-18).

Burning faith asks with boldness and sees the heavens open. It moves God's heart and His hand and gives us unlimited access to miraculous and supernatural resources. This is the faith that moves God! It releases His power and obtains His favor!" Our cynical and skeptical world needs to see the faith that pleases God! Jesus is clearly crying out to this lukewarm Church, "Let Me in! Repent!"

> John records His appeal: "Behold, I stand at the door and knock. If anyone hears My voice and opens the door, I will come in to him and dine with him, and he with Me" (Revelation 3:20).
>
> At the end of each message to the seven Churches, Christ mentions rewards for overcomers. For example: "To him who overcomes I will grant to sit with Me on My throne, as I also overcame and sat down with My Father on His throne" (Revelation 3:21).

Messiah's Rod of Iron

You shall break them with a rod of iron; You shall dash them to pieces like a potter's vessel. –Psalm 2:9

The rod of iron, which the Messiah judges and rules the nations with is different from the rod of chastisement seen throughout Scripture. God's chastisements are a discipline for correction and the refining of His people, but the rod of iron signifies final judgment. Every believer should desire and endure the Lord's chastening to avoid being judged with the entire world. The scriptures are clear:

> For if we would judge ourselves, we would not be judged. But when we are judged, we are chastened by the Lord, that we may not be condemned with the world (1 Corinthians 11:31-32).

> My son, do not despise the chastening of the Lord, nor detest His correction; for whom the Lord loves He corrects, just as a father the son in whom he delights (Proverbs 3:11-12).

> He who spares his rod hates his son, but he who loves him disciplines him promptly (Proverbs 13:24).

> If you endure chastening, God deals with you as with sons; for what son is there whom a father does not chasten? (Hebrews 12:7).

The chastisement of the world is far more severe than God's loving chastisement. For example, the ancient Romans used the *cat of nine tails* as a punishment tool to scourge, causing a much worse result than ordinary whipping. The *cat of nine tails* is a flagellum, a whip with several strands weighted with lead balls, so it will lacerate into the flesh. Christ took the chastisement for our sin upon Himself. Iniquities are literally wickedness and rebellion. He suffered not for Himself, but for mankind's sins and sicknesses. Spiritual and bodily healing are provided in the atoning work of Christ through the scourging of the 'cat and nine tails,' and salvation through His death on the Cross. The Atonement is a fulfillment of prophecy:

> Surely He has borne our griefs and carried our sorrows; yet we esteemed Him stricken, smitten by God, and afflicted. But He was wounded for our transgressions, He was bruised for our iniquities; the chastisement for our peace was upon Him, and by His stripes we are healed (Isaiah 53:4-5).

> Peter describes Christ's example to all Christians: "For to this you were called, because Christ also suffered for us, leaving us an example, that you should follow His steps: "Who committed no sin, nor was deceit found in His mouth"; who, when He was reviled, did not revile in return; when He suffered, He did not threaten, but committed Himself to Him who judges righteously; who Himself bore our sins in His own body on the tree, that we, having died to sins, might live for righteousness—by whose stripes you were healed." (1 Peter 2:21-24).

Role of the Rod of Iron in the Church Today

The Church has a mandate of stewardship from the Lord Jesus to occupy until He returns (Luke 19:12-13). At this present time in the United States, many Christian legal groups are filing lawsuits against our oppressive government which has put religious liberty and First Amendment rights on the chopping block. Christian legislators in the U. S. Congress and across the nation are working to reinforce the First Amendment rights of every citizen. According to the Beckett Fund, in the past four years 94 lawsuits with over 300 plaintiffs were filed against the Obama Administration over the HHS Abortion Mandate. These Christian attorneys are using Christ's rod of iron in performing the kingly (judicial) role of the Church against the leaders of tyranny who would like to strike down the U. S. Constitution and replace it with International Law. The legal teams are resisting the increased effort to remove all vestiges of our heritage in the public arena. You do not always hear it reported in the news; how Christians serving in public offices are taking bold stands to preserve America's Judeo-Christian heritage across the land. The kingly role of the Church should ensure that this great land will always be "one nation, under God, indivisible, with liberty and justice for all." As the Church goes, so goes the nation!

Rod of Iron Signifies God's Final Judgment of the Nations

> She bore a male Child who was to rule all nations with a rod of iron. And her Child was caught up to God and His throne (Revelation 12:50).

The rod of iron mentioned here signifies the severe judgments the King of kings will inflict on all those who resist his authority. It is associated as a weapon of war; yet, it is much different from the royal scepter of sovereignty the Son of God will rule with during His millennial kingdom. A scepter is an emblem of sovereign power, while the rod of iron is an instrument of correction and punishment. The Messiah's judgment of the nations of the world with the rod of iron will be final. The judgment of nations began in Egypt with a different rod of authority. Moses' rod was what he used to shepherd the flocks at Sinai. Once anointed by "I Am, that

I Am," Mose's rod represented and displayed *YHWH's* divine power over Pharaoh, bringing Egypt to her knees with God's judgments. In early wars, the rod was a short club used as a weapon of defense or discipline. With spiritual application, the rod symbolizes God's strength, power and authority (Exodus 21:20; Job 9:34).

The shepherd's staff David used was a long slender stick with a wide hook on one end, used to draw a sheep close to the shepherd, or rescue it from trouble. In Psalm 23, David gives this comforting thought about the Lord, His Shepherd: "...Thou art with me, thy rod and thy staff they comfort me." God's rod and staff reassure us of God's love and guidance in our lives. Through the prophets Isaiah, Jeremiah and Ezekiel, *Yahweh* compares Himself to a shepherd in order to illustrate His great love for His people. The Lord Jesus Himself adopted the same metaphor to express His relationship to His people, who are like sheep (John 10:11-16).

God selected Aaron's rod from an almond tree to prove that he was chosen to head the priesthood over the other tribes of Israel. Aaron's rod miraculously became a living branch, budded, and blossomed, and yielded almonds. In some places, there were buds, in other's blossoms, in other's fruit, at the same time. This was a plain indication to the people that Aaron was chosen to the priesthood, and not any other of the princes of the tribes. He was a type and figure of Christ and His priesthood: for he is the man, the branch, that is to be a priest upon his throne as spoken of in Zechariah 6:12; and he was to grow up before God, as those before the ark, like a tender plant, and as a root out of a dry ground (Isaiah 53:2).[1]

Why do the Nations Rebel against God?

> Behold, I will make Jerusalem a cup of drunkenness to all the surrounding peoples, when they lay siege against Judah and Jerusalem. And it shall happen in that day that I will make Jerusalem a very heavy stone for all peoples; all who would heave it away will surely be cut in pieces, though all nations of the earth are gathered against it (Zechariah 12:2-3). ("In that day" refers to End of the Age).

Biblical prophecy today majors on the Epicenter, which is Israel, the Middle East, and Jerusalem. A Middle East peace plan between Israel and the Palestinians, in which Jerusalem is considered a major stumbling block, is literally taking place today (Daniel 9:27). Billionaire George Soros says, "The main stumbling block is Israel." Why? A proposed New Jerusalem Covenant that would make Jerusalem an International Capital has been floating around for some years. In 2003, former Israeli foreign minister, Shimon Peres dropped a bombshell by suggesting a solution for Jerusalem could be achieved by placing United Nations stewardship over Jerusalem. The plan called for declaring a holy area of sites sacred to Jews, Christians and Muslims in Jerusalem's old walled city as a "world capital," with the U.N. Secretary-General serving as mayor..... Shimon Peres, the head of Israel's opposition Labor Party, has suggested resolving Israeli-Palestinian conflict over Jerusalem by putting its holy sites under U.N. stewardship, a spokesman said on Tuesday.[2] The Obama Administration continues to pressure Israel to concede and release the West Bank as a Palestinian State. Jerusalem has not been negotiated in this process because Israel's Prime Minister Netanyahu is holding out for an undivided Jerusalem.

What does *Yahweh* say about Jerusalem and the land of Israel? In Leviticus 25:23, He says, "The land, moreover, shall not be sold permanently, for the land is Mine: for you are but aliens and sojourners with Me." The Land of Canaan was given by *Yahweh* to Abraham, and his descendants based on an unconditional covenant from God Himself. It was renamed Israel by the Lord, which is an everlasting possession:

- In Genesis 12:7, we read: "The Lord appeared to Abram and said, 'To your descendants I will give this land.'"
- In Genesis 12:7, we read: "The Lord appeared to Abram and said, 'To your In Genesis 13:15, He repeated His promise when He said, "for all the land which you see, I will give it to you and to your descendants forever."
- In Genesis 15:18, we read: "To your descendants I have given this land."

Almighty God has declared in His Word the rights of Israel and the Jewish people to the Land, which He deeded to them by His covenant with Abraham and his seed. The Land of Canaan was not given to the descendants of Ishmael, the ancestor of the Arab peoples; it was deeded to the descendants of Isaac, Jacob and his descendants. Scripture foretells how the resurrected Christ will judge the nations that have warred against *Yahweh's* very own nation Israel. During his 1,000 year reign on earth, Jerusalem will be the eternal capital of the world. Psalm chapter two is referring to rogue nations, which will not be included in Christ's Kingdom Age, and will receive eternal punishment. It describes how the rogue nations are rebelling against God Himself:

> The kings of the earth and the rulers have conspired and have taken counsel together against the Lord and against his anointed, saying "Let us break their bands asunder, and let us cast away their yoke from it.' He that dwells in heaven shall laugh, and the Lord shall mock at them" (Psalm 2:2-4).
>
> You shall break them with a rod of iron; You shall dash them to pieces like a potter's vessel (Psalm 2:9; Revelation 2:27).

- **Pray for America:** O Lord, please help America to stand with Israel as she faces her enemies in the Middle East. "For the day of the Lord is near upon all nations. As you have done, it shall be done to you; your dealings will return upon your own head" (Obadiah 1:15)

- **Pray for Israel,** that her enemies would fall into their own evil traps, like when God intervened, and Haman tripped himself up (Esther 7:9-10). Pray that the LORD God would hear the cries of His people once again, like He heard Abraham's seed cry out in Egypt. Amen.

The eternal Father promises to give His beloved Son, the ultimate inheritance of the nations, and to defeat all who oppose His rule. This promise will be completely fulfilled when Christ comes to earth at the end of the age and destroys the enemies of God. No earthly king was ever given this promise of the nations as an inheritance. It was a promise only to be fulfilled by the Messianic King, Jesus (Zechariah 9:9-10). The resurrected Savior speaks in John's Revelation about a promise that all faithful believers will share in His reign over the nations:

> And he who overcomes, and keeps My works until the end, to him I will give power over the nations—"He shall rule them with a rod of iron; they shall be dashed to pieces like the potter's vessels"—as I also have received from My Father..... (Revelation 2:26-27).

In Matthew 25:31-46, we have a description of the last judgment of the nations. In this parable, Jesus separates the sheep and the goat nations:. "And all nations will gather before him, and he will separate them one from another, just as a shepherd separates the sheep from the goats; and he will set the sheep at his right hand and the goats at his left." This judgment occurs after the tribulation and Christ's return to earth, but before the beginning of His millennial reign. The judgment involves the separation of the wicked from the righteous. The wicked will not be allowed to enter Christ's kingdom, but will go into eternal punishment. The righteous will inherit eternal life and the kingdom of God.

Spoiling the Nations with the Rod of Iron

The rod of iron is God's judgment, and without God's grace, we are in a position of being vulnerable to His judgment being levied upon us. God always offers grace before pronouncing judgment, for without grace, there is no mercy. I want us to take a very brief look back into the Old Testament before discussing the use of the rod of iron in the Church Age. When it was time for Abraham's seed to be delivered out of bondage in Egypt, Moses had been sent to offer *YHWH's* grace to Pharaoh, but he mocked Moses and Aaron. In their future audiences with Pharaoh, God pronounced judgment against Egypt. Moses' shepherd's staff demonstrated the authority of God's rod of iron. Ten times Pharaoh refused God's grace and hardened his heart. Years later, we see the prophets dealing with the nation of Israel, which hardened its heart against God, time after time. Elijah the prophet held up the rod of iron against King Ahab and Queen Jezebel in judgment when he slayed their 450 prophets of Baal. Afterward, *Yahweh* personally judged Ahab and Jezebel. Throughout Israel's history, God's prophets warned the people of the consequences of judgment, but still they hardened their hearts. The LORD told Jeremiah:

> Therefore you shall speak all these words to them, but they will not obey you. You shall also call to them, but they will not answer you (Jeremiah 7:27).

When the LORD chooses to judge a nation for its heinous deeds, there are occasions when He uses qualified representatives within His Church Body to be an instrument. In modern times, Rees Howells was one of the most effective intercessors known to the 20th Century. Howells and his student intercessors in Wales were chosen to intercede with God for the well-being of Britain during the Second World War. The Holy Spirit trained and anointed Howells to use Christ's rod of iron against Hitler, Mussolini and Stalin as their armies advanced to plunder Europe and North Africa. Howells and his intercessors prayed in England for the defeat of these diabolical forces as they marched against the free world. The rod of iron goes into action when anointed intercessors and watchmen proclaim the Word of God. The Name of Jesus, the Word of God, and the Blood of Jesus are the secret weapons Howells and his students used to stop this affront against the nations of the free world. Spiritual warfare is explained in Scripture when Isaiah said, ".....When the enemy comes in like a flood, the Spirit of the Lord will lift up a standard against him" (Isaiah 59:19). When a violent enemy assails the Church, or in this case the entire free world, and it comes in formidable force with allies, then it is like a flood.

There is only one entity on earth that can lift up a standard against Hell's agents, and that is the Church of Jesus Christ. The Holy Spirit gave Howells spiritual revelation on where the enemy troops were headed next, so they could conduct spiritual warfare; praying Scripture and praying in the Holy Spirit. While these warriors interceded, the Lord Jesus fought the battle with His heavenly army–giving the free world the victory. In Isaiah 11:4, we learn that the Spirit of the Lord rules over evil: "He shall strike the earth with the rod of His mouth, and with the breath of His lips He shall slay the wicked." Christ's first coming accomplished this in Colossians 2:15, and He will complete it in the natural at the end of the age (Revelation 19:11-16; 20:11-15). Until that happens, the Church has been given His scepter and some are given the authority of His rod of iron. Our prayer is this: "Let God arise, let His enemies be scattered; let those also who hate Him flee before Him" (Psalm 68:1). God will only arise through His Church! As the church goes, so goes the nation!

In 1995, the LORD instructed me to hold up Christ's rod of iron to the Middle East countries, beginning first with Iran. The LORD gave me the keys to one of Iran's former embassy buildings (the ambassador's residence) for our ministry headquarters in Washington, D.C. This building is front and center on famous Embassy Row on Massachusetts Avenue. It has always humbled me to know the Lord chose me for this strategic mission–"But God has chosen the foolish things of the world to put to shame the wise, and God has chosen the weak things of the world to put to shame the things which are mighty….." (1 Corinthians 1:27). It was truly Jesus, who opened the door for me to lease one of Iran's ambassador's residence from the U. S. State Department. It was in this 19,000 square foot building that Iran set up their first official chancery, until a larger chancery was constructed next door. I turned this site into a prayer tower with the theme, "From the Prince of Persia to the Prince of Peace."

The Lord confirmed this call by having me pass the State Department's qualification process within four weeks' time. The Lord divinely spoke to a Christian couple who were obedient to answer the call to partner financially and launch this great mission. The open door to Iran's former embassy complex was a divine appointment, which took 21 days fasting and praying to seek God's will. I entered the leasing process with the U. S. State Department for the Iranian property with fear and trembling, as Esther did when she went before the king on behalf of her people. I committed the entire outcome to God's will–"These things says He who is holy, He who is true, 'He who has the key of David, He who opens and no one shuts, and shuts and no one opens'" (Revelation 3:7). We glorify Jesus!

Upon moving into Iran's embassy complex, the Lord instructed me to "spoil Iran." The Islamic religion considers it a curse to be defeated by a woman, and the intercessors and watchmen who joined with me helped to breach the wall of militant Islam with the "breaker anointing." Some of those who prayed on-site during those years have observed that the Middle East has never been the same. The ancient gates of brass in Persia began opening up to the gospel of Jesus Christ, an absolute fulfillment of Scripture (Isaiah 45:2).

Occupying one of Iran's diplomatic buildings was like the repossession of Canaan for the Church. We named the mission, *Embassy of the Prince of Peace*, and Pat Robertson conducted the dedication ceremony with these words: "From the Prince of Persia to the Prince of Peace." This former Muslim stronghold was now being used as a spiritual military fortress against Islamic terrorism. It also became a crossroad for the leaders of the Church. Unfortunately, some Church leaders only saw it as a facility for their gatherings, and when it was time to shut down this mission after seven years, many of them interpreted it as a failure on my part. Although, we hosted thousands of saints with their church leadership meetings, the primary mission was conducting spiritual warfare to demolish the enemies of the free world and the Cross of Jesus Christ. Hundreds of prayer warriors visited us from across the nation and around the world, helping us to transform a site that promoted violence into one that promotes international peace.

Christian Arabs, Lebanese, Iranians, Egyptian Copts, Latinos, Africans and many other nationalities came to pray at the *Embassy of the Prince of Peace*. In describing our diversity; a unique prayer group met at the embassy every week called the Sons of Abraham, a mixture of born-again Jews, Europeans, Arabs, and a Greek brother. As an embassy, we were always concerned about the unreached countries, and we prayed regularly for numerous hotspot countries behind the Islamic Veil. These areas are now experiencing the greatest harvest of souls—millions are supernaturally coming to Jesus Christ as Lord and Savior from behind the Islamic Veil.

Since a few Christian leaders misinterpreted our mission, I must clarify that we love Muslims and our warfare is only directed against militant Islam–the Jihadist terrorists and their radical leaders. Our prayers of compassion are always directed toward bringing freedom to Muslims who are living under the tyranny of radical regimes and Middle East Christians who are under fire for their faith. We pray for Muslims to have the veil of Islam rolled off their spiritual eyes, and Jesus has answered this prayer by appearing to them supernaturally in dreams and visions. I recommend you read the book by Tom Doyle, "Dreams and Vision," describing some of these personal testimonies. We have had underground church leaders from the Middle East speak at our embassy who shared that Jesus is even appearing to Muslims during the annual Hajj in Mecca.

In 2002, the U. S. State Department pressed me to move from Iran's embassy complex, seven months after the 9/11 terrorist attack on our country. During that year, there was 500 million dollars' worth of judgments won against the Islamic Republic of Iran and their assets by the 1980 American hostages at the United States Embassy in Tehran. For several years, I was caught in the crosshairs of the ongoing struggle between the U. S. Congress and the State Department for Iran's embassy buildings. Since we were not sure if we could remain in the building, our attorney had the rent frozen during the time these judgments were being won in court. Our funding was also frozen amid these uncertain incidences. The State Department did offer to expunge the pending frozen rent if I would just get out of the way and move. After prayer, I believed the Lord wanted me to continue my effort to negotiate with members of the Congress for the release of Iran's buildings. The State Department chose to evict us with only one week's official notice. During this time, our attorney had been communicating with the State Department's legal counsel and received inside reports that this was nothing more than a political eviction. Our attorney is a brother in Christ, who stood on the wall with us to see God's will fulfilled. Iran's buildings continue to remain empty to this day, and we give God the glory for the testimony that came out of this seven-year mission in the heart of Embassy Row—fulfilling the prophecy to the nations.

State Department officials had told me earlier that Iran's embassy complex has always been a "crown jewel" for the State Department, and now they were speculating it could be a bargaining tool to negotiate with Iran's mullahs during the "War Against Terrorism." Since the early 1970s, the U. S. government has used Iran for their own advantage. Iran-Contra was a covert operation under Presidents Reagan and Clinton. The State Department is always seeking to normalize relations with

Iran, even with the current mullahs. There is just one problem: the days of the Shah are over, and we are seeking to normalize with the worst terrorist regime in today's world. The present diplomatic negotiations being forged with Iran are influenced by Iranian Valerie Jarrett, a Senior Advisor to President Barack Obama. Israel understands that the Islamic Republic of Iran is their number-one enemy, and they know you cannot negotiate with terrorists. The U. S. State Department does not take Iran's mullahs seriously when they call the United States the great Satan.

Since moving out in the spring of 2002, some of our intercessors believe that Iran's empty buildings are a sign and confirmation that we possessed the land for the Lord Jesus Christ. The Holy Spirit assured me that we achieved our spiritual mission and succeeded in repossessing this Persian territory for the sake of the innocent victims of Islamic terrorism. Missionaries are reporting that the underground church in Iran is the fastest growing church in the world. The entire Middle East has benefited from our mission, since we included all Islamic countries, even Indonesia, the world's largest populated Muslim country. Our testimony is Revelation 11:15: "The kingdoms of this world have become the kingdoms of our Lord and of His Christ, and He shall reign forever and ever!" While the full manifestation of this success is laid up in heaven for the King of kings, and Lord of lords (Revelation 19:6); the Middle East has been visibly transformed since 2001, and the Church of Jesus Christ is flourishing behind the Islamic Veil. Besides, there are praying saints across the Body of Christ, who have taken up the prayer effort to pray for the Muslim world.

One note of interest about Iran's former embassy buildings is, they sit on legal Iranian soil in Washington, D. C., because the title deed is being held in a treaty in The Hague, along with eight billion dollars of Iran's assets. No one can buy them, or sell them. In 1979, the evil Ayatollah Ruhollah Khomeini stood on the front steps of Iran's ambassador residence (the building we occupied) to tell the world the Iranian monarchy was being abolished in favor of an Islamic Government–the Islamic Republic of Iran. It was a dark day for the world when the warfare tactic called "terrorism" was birthed and spread throughout the Middle East aimed at the Free World. The LORD Almighty will avenge the blood that has been shed from Iran's terrorist armies–the Quds, Hamas and Hezbollah. Rogue nations are chastised and warned until the cup of their sin is full, when final judgment is imminent–Scripture says He removes that nation from power (Daniel 2:21; 4:17; Leviticus 18:24-28). Some ask today about America: How much time remains until its cup of sin full?

We give the Almighty Lord God all the glory for any success that we are privileged to share in for His Kingdom. The above defines how we can possess the nations using the authority of the Messiah's rod of iron. While we have not stopped Iran's tyrannical government, we opened up the door for the gospel to save many souls. The success of this mission confirms a prophetic word that was spoken to me during the years I occupied Iran's embassy building: "The Lord has placed an establishing anointing upon you and you will unravel that which is even holding nations.

The Lord says you will discern the gathering of nations that are occurring in dark places, and as you discern the gathering of those nations, you will be capable of telling those nations what direction to take. You will be used in such a way that you will be anointed to dismantle darkness—even dismantle ungodly tensions that are occurring throughout the nations, saith the Lord."[3] Note: I did not make this happen. How this prophetic word manifested was beyond my imagination, and this word is still actively being walked out.

When the Holy Spirit leads, I continue to operate with the authority of the rod of iron "for the gifts and the calling are irrevocable" (Romans 11:29). How you use the gifts is a serious matter! A personal prophecy is given to confirm what the Lord has already spoken to you, or to confirm a vision the Holy Spirit has given you. Too often, when a believer receives a personal prophecy, they will go out and make it happen. This is dangerous and certainly not Biblical. We are to act on the instruction the Lord Himself has given us, and test all spirits:

> Beloved, do not believe every spirit, but test the spirits, whether they are of God; because many false prophets have gone out into the world (1 John 4:1).

Kingly Role of the Believer

These will make war with the Lamb, and the Lamb will overcome them, for
He is Lord of lords and King of kings; and those who are
with Him are called, chosen, and faithful.
–Revelation 17:14

Scripture entitles Jesus as the Lord of lords and King of kings, describing His kingly (judicial) role (1 Timothy 6:15; Revelation 19:16). The kingly anointing judges between right and wrong. It makes war against the enemies of God's kingdom with the rod of iron. Therefore, Christ expects His believers to raise up resistance when evil comes to demolish the harvest field. Christ presented the kingly role to His disciples in Matthew 16:19, when He explained to Peter that His disciples would have the authority to judge between good and evil. Jesus said, "And I will give you the keys of the kingdom of heaven, and whatever you bind on earth will be bound in heaven, and whatever you loose on earth will be loosed in heaven." This is the kingly anointing. Also in John 20:23 Jesus said, "If you forgive the sins of any, they are forgiven them; if you retain the sins of any, they are retained."

Many in the Church community today are well-acquainted with the priestly role of the believer, but few personally identify with the kingly (judicial) role. The reason the judicial role for the believer is not preached from most pulpits is because a social gospel is preferred over hearing about the Jesus who returns (in His kingly role with fire in His eyes) to judge the churches (Revelation 2 and 3). The Baptism of Fire empowers the Church to overcome and advance the Kingdom of God in this evil world. 2 Thessalonians 2:7 describes the Holy Spirit in the Church as the restrainer of evil until the end of the Church Age when Christ snatches His Bride from this world. We read in 2 Peter 3:10:

> But the day of the Lord will come as a thief in the night, in which the heavens will pass away with a great noise, and the elements will melt with fervent heat; both the earth and the works that are in it will be burned up.

The Book of Acts records how believers in the New Testament Church stepped directly into their kingly (judicial) role once they received the Baptism of Fire on the Day of Pentecost. The fire anoints the believer to overcome, yet, the modern Church of today is slow to represent the judicial (kingly) role of Christ, and this is why there is little or no fear of God within the nation. Today's culture implosion demands the Church's kingly fire. If we are going to save even a part of our nation from social implosion, we need fire in the Church for the kingly role to be made visible with spiritual authority. When the government demands that the people condone immorality for the sake of tolerance, then the Church must stand up and be the conscience in the land. We cannot endorse laws that condone homosexuality, or the murder of innocent children through abortion. This also must be achieved with the gospel of truth, demonstrating love and grace, and not a message of hate. The loving kindness of the priestly role must balance the judicial fire of the kingly role.

Christ's disciples are called to demonstrate Christ in the earth by growing into His kingly anointing. The nine gifts of the spirit have a kingly manifestation just as much as the priestly role. The Baptism of Fire is the only way the Church can successfully witness the gospel and overcome a demonized, determined enemy. The Church without fire is also without power! One of the signs Jesus promised to the Church is fire. Where is the fire in the Church? Where is the fire to be released upon the enemy? Where is the fire to bring Kingly rule from heaven to earth? Man's religious tradition has robbed the Church of its fire.

The Church has already been baptized with judicial fire! When the Holy Spirit was first poured out in Acts 2:1-4, a rushing, mighty wind filled the house where they were sitting and divided tongues of fire sat upon each of them. There was not a person who received the Holy Spirit that did not experience the wind, the fire and prayed in another language. It is vital for believers to understand that this act initiated judicial fire within the Church for advancing the Kingdom of God, and to stand up and become a conscience for society with the fire of God's Word. If we refuse to be that witness, then the Kingly Jesus will remove His candlestick–His light will go out in those churches who refuse to exercise justice! Ichabod is written over the door-post of all dead churches who have lost their true witness.

There are signs occurring today, which indicate we are entering into the time frame when God's righteous judgment will be poured out upon all of mankind. Jesus said in Luke 17:26, "And as it was in the days of Noah, so it will be also in the days of the Son of Man....." What about the righteous? The God who is, and has always been, is in control. The Church will fulfill her destiny, her calling, and her assignment; but beware, this is an hour to be sober. It is not an hour to be distracted by the cares of life:

> But the end of all things is at hand; therefore be serious and watchful in your prayers (1 Peter 4:7).
>
> For the time has come for judgment to begin at the house of God; and if it begins with us first, what will be the end of those who do not obey the gospel of God? (1 Peter 4:17).
>
> Watch therefore, and pray always that you may be counted worthy to escape all these things that will come to pass, and to stand before the Son of Man (Luke 21:26).

Understanding the Kingly Anointing

> ....To Him who loved us and washed us from our sins in His own blood, and has made us kings and priests to His God and Father, to Him be glory and dominion forever and ever. Amen (Revelation 1:5-6).

In this scripture, we see the present tense reference which Christ made about His redeemed saints already being kings and priests. These dual offices are not political, but serve to equip the Church with spiritual authority to carry out its duty in advancing the kingdom of God. The offices of king and priest are clearly a function for each believer to perform on behalf of the Church during their season on earth. Born again believers are not destined to sit in the church pew and wait until they are promoted to heaven. The redeemed are to be *proactive* representatives of Jesus Christ, in whom God has delegated authority to extend and administrate the powers of His rule. (A proactive person creates or controls a situation by prevention or responding to a crisis.) Those who are a faithful witness for the gospel and give faithful service to humanity in the love of God are proactive. Success will always involve confrontation against the dark powers of hell with prayer warfare, and performing the miraculous works of Christ. Ruling with Christ in the kingly role is only effective when the priestly mission is operating in one's life; after developing the spirit of praiseful worship and the call to obey the Word.

Worship is foundational to kingdom advancement, since the anointing within the believer comes while worshiping the Lamb before God's throne. Pure worship demolishes Satan's power when the redeemed celebrate the triumph of the Lamb of God (Colossians 2:15). Worshiping the Lamb is natural when we are grateful for His Redemption, His Resurrection, and the Holy Spirit who is ever present in us. In their priestly office, the saints reign on earth as Christ's ambassadors. The Apostle Peter explains: ".....You also, as living stones, are being built up a spiritual house, a holy priesthood, to offer up spiritual sacrifices acceptable to God through Jesus Christ" (1 Peter 2:5). "But you are a chosen generation, a royal priesthood, a holy nation, His own special people, that you may proclaim the praises of Him who called you out of darkness into His marvelous light...." (v. 9). The worship of the saints here on earth is connected to the ongoing praise in progress, in heaven, and on earth at the same time:

> Now when He had taken the scroll, the four living creatures and the twenty-four elders fell down before the Lamb, each having a harp, and golden bowls full of incense, which are the prayers of the saints. And they sang a new song, saying: "You are worthy to take the scroll, and to open its seals; for You were slain, and have redeemed us to God by Your blood out of every tribe and tongue and people and nation, and have made us kings and priests to our God; and we shall reign on the earth" (Revelation 5:8-10). (It is interesting to note that "incense" represents the prayers of the saints which are offered to the Lamb by the twenty-four elders.)
>
> Christ's kingly role is a fulfillment of Daniel 7:9-14 where reference is made to the "Ancient of Days" also mentioned in Revelation 1:13-16 with the "One like the Son of Man."

In conclusion, fervent, effectual prayer moves the Hand of God to open iron gates and set captives free (Isaiah 45:1-3). Once prayer has reached the Throne of God, the believer is prepared to go out in action. One living example of such faithful action can be seen in the *Annual March for Life* which has been conducted for 41 years on the anniversary of Roe vs. Wade. The participants convene in Washington, D. C. several days ahead of the march to hold prayer vigils and conduct mass in several areas of the nation's capital. After their priestly role is performed, they move into their kingly role and march from the White House to the U. S. Supreme Court, upholding the pro-life message and demonstrating their opposition to abortion. Religious leaders hold press conferences to address government leaders and educate the general public on the vital biblical message of a pro-life culture, not a culture of death, in our society. Similar rallies are also being conducted simultaneously across the country, and the sanctity of life message is reinforced all year long by various anti-abortion organizations.

Proactive movements such as this certainly give the Body of Christ an invitation to stand up and be counted for Jesus Christ. Typically 150,000 Catholics, Pentecostals and Evangelicals join together in Washington, D. C. during the January frigid cold weather to conduct the annual March for Life, with about half being youth. They are united and agree with the same basic fundamental doctrines of the Church establishment. Even though they may differ over techniques and other superficial things, Christians must unite and work together by emphasizing areas of agreement. When this happens, the Church becomes a supernaturally powerful force.

Every genuine move of God throughout history has resulted when men and women pray and fearlessly act in faith. This is the essence of the "salt and light" message for the Church. Activists within the Church become a model of the Kingly role in the Body of Christ. Fervent, effectual prayer moves the Hand of God to open iron gates and set captives free (Isaiah 45:1-3). The key is found in Exodus where we see an example of Moses exercising the priestly role of intercession before he took action:

> Then Moses said to the Lord, If Your Presence does not go with us, do not bring us up from here. For how then will it be known that Your people and I have found grace in Your sight, except You go with us? (Exodus 33:15-16).

In Acts 12:7-11, we find it was the fervent prayers of the disciples that freed the Apostle Peter from Herod's prison. This deliverance was due to their constant, fervent prayers. They did not know if Herod had already killed Peter and were still praying when Peter showed up at the gate to announce his miraculous release, but did not believe the report that Peter was at the gate.

Joint Heirs with the King of Kings

> The Spirit Himself bears witness with our spirit that we are children of God, and if children, then heirs—heirs of God and joint heirs with Christ, if indeed we suffer with Him, that we may also be glorified together (Romans 8:16-17).

The kingdom belongs to the Son of man, but the Church shares with His rulership—"The saints of the Most High shall receive the kingdom and possess it for ever and ever" (Revelation 11:18). The saints are those who are holy because they are sanctified by the indwelling of the Holy Spirit, and they have separated themselves from sin and the corrupt world and consecrated themselves instead to the service and worship of God. The saints are the Bride of Christ who will rule with Christ during the Millennium. The rod of iron is for the judgment of the nations during the Day of the Lord, yet I have experienced using the rod of iron during times of intercession for rogue nations. The believer's inheritance of the nations begins on earth with converting souls:

> Ask of Me, and I will give You the nations for Your inheritance, and the ends of the earth for Your possession (Psalm 2:8).
>
> When Christ returns to judge the nations the believer's inheritance will be revealed: The kingdoms of this world are become the kingdoms of our lord, and of His Christ; and he shall reign for ever and ever! (Revelation 11:15).

We have each been given a short span of time on earth as a period of testing to determine if we will be faithful to advance God's Kingdom. In Psalm 39:4-5, David prays that the Lord will help him realize the days of his life on earth:

> Lord, make me to know my end, and what is the measure of my days, that I may know how frail I am. Indeed, You have made my days as handbreadths, and my age is as nothing before You; certainly every man at his best state is but vapor. (Also James 4:14).

What is the Kingdom of God?

The word translated "kingdom" throughout the New Testament is the Greek word *basileia*, which denotes "sovereignty, royal power, [and] dominion."[4] A careful examination of the Bible reveals that the next phase of the Kingdom of God is nothing short of a world-ruling monarchy that God will establish on this earth through Jesus Christ for 1,000 years, or the Millennial reign of Christ on Earth (Revelation 20:2-5). Christ will reign with the resurrected saints in peace and righteousness, with Jerusalem as the religious center of the world, as Isaiah prophesied:

> For Zion's sake I will not hold My peace, and for Jerusalem's sake I will not rest, until her righteousness goes forth as brightness, and her salvation as a lamp that burns. The Gentiles shall see your righteousness, and all kings your glory. You shall be called by a new name, which the mouth of the Lord will name (Isaiah 62:1-2).

Until his final destruction, Satan (and his satanic world system) will be bound in the bottomless pit for 1,000 years during the Millennium, so he will not deceive the nations anymore (Read Revelation 18:1-24 and Revelation 20:1-3).

Keys for Approaching the King's Presence

The secret of the Lord is with them that fear him; and he will show them his covenant. –Psalm 25:14

The fear of the Lord unlocks the treasure of knowing God and the requirements of His covenant with mankind. God reveals His secret counsel with those who draw near to Him. This is seen in the lives of the Old Testament patriarchs and the New Testament apostles. Hidden sin cannot hide in the light of His Glory. Adam and Eve hid themselves from God's Glory after they disobeyed. Jesus explained this in John 3:20, "They stay away from the light for fear their sins will be exposed." God has a bigger plan than just saving your soul — He wants you to be transformed from the world's image into His likeness. We have to be born again, to be delivered from the world, but we must not stop there; we are called to enter into His kingdom. Our desires must come through a healthy fear of the Lord, which is the beginning of knowledge (Proverbs 9:10; 111:10). Purity and holiness come from spending time with the Lord as Moses did (Exodus 34:29). A heart after God has a sincere desire to know the Lord of Glory, the one seated at the Right Hand of God, not the imagery of Jesus created by this world, which only satisfies our selfish desires. The Apostle Paul warned:

> And do not be conformed to this world, but be transformed by the renewing of your mind, that you may prove what is that good and acceptable and perfect will of God (Romans 12:2).

We have been conformed (fashioned) by the world's image, and we are transformed into God's image by a desire to enter His Glorious Presence (John 3:3, 5). This change happens by spending time in His Presence. God's true image is revealed through His living Word on the mountaintop with Him. If you go to the mountain like Moses did, you will be changed into Christ's character. If you stay at the foot as Aaron did, your image of Christ will be fashioned by the society in which you live. Aaron did not know God intimately because He chose to only worship *Elohim* at the foot of the mountain, which reduced God's image to Aaron's surroundings. Today, we ask God to come down into our situation; rather than going deeper into His Presence with the help of the Holy Spirit. This simply produces a veneer of Christianity. Our flesh needs to be retrained through the Spirit man, which has been renewed in Christ; and the Word of God alone has the power to transform our carnal thinking and actions.

The Apostle Paul declared in Romans 1:20-23, ".....Although they knew God, they did not glorify Him as God, nor were thankful, but became futile in their thoughts, and their foolish hearts were darkened." They know Him, but give Him far less honor than He deserves. Our modern-day society worships self, which is corruptible man. Too many Christians serve a Jesus in the image they have made, and they still call Him Lord. This type of idolatry is a false religion which is a very convenient form of worship, which satisfies the inborn need to worship a higher being. An idol gives its creators what they want: the satisfaction of their own hearts. Clearly, this form of idolatry is rebellion (1 Samuel 15:23). The Apostle Paul expresses his concern for the believers being deceived:

> But I fear, lest somehow, as the serpent deceived Eve by his craftiness, so your minds may be corrupted from the simplicity that is in Christ. For if he who comes preaches another Jesus whom we have not preached, or if you receive a different spirit which you have not received, or a different gospel which you have not accepted—you may well put up with it! (2 Corinthians 11:3-4).

If we persist in going against God's authority, and continue to serve our own image of Jesus, then without realizing it, we are serving a false deity. It is a subtle deception in which we comfort ourselves saying, "Jesus is my friend," or "God knows my heart." Thus, we justify our actions that contradict His covenant. The fear of the Lord is an attitude of the heart. You choose to obey, or not to obey. When you love the Lord, you want to please Him with Holy living.

Ruling and Reigning with Christ

In Revelation 5:5-10, we discover that the Jesus, who is the Lamb in the Gospels, has now become the Lion in the book of Revelation. The resurrected Jesus in Revelation is the Lion, and the Lion of the tribe of Judah prevails by opening the book and loosing the seven seals– "Do not weep. Behold, the Lion of the tribe of Judah, the Root of David, has prevailed to open the scroll and to loose its seven seals" (Revelation 5:5). Believers who do not understand the kingly role of the Church have never transitioned from the Lamb to the Lion. Even though the Church will not officially rule and reign with Christ until the Millennial Age, it is still vital that believers possess the biblical knowledge that they need to understand their future role. Kingdom training begins on earth by winning souls throughout the nations of the world, which will one day become the "kingdoms of our Lord and of His Christ, and He shall reign forever and ever!" (Revelation 11:15).

Hundreds of thousands of missionaries have gone forth since the Day of Pentecost to demolish the works of Satan in the nations, by going and living among the people. I have been privileged myself to go on many mission trips into Third-World countries as an evangelist and Bible teacher. In 1985, during an extended time of fasting and prayer, the Holy Spirit gave me a vision of multitudes of souls entering the gates of Heaven. Joel 3:13-14 was quickened to me: "Put in the sickle, for the harvest is ripe. Come, go down; for the winepress is full, the vats overflow—for their wickedness is great. Multitudes, multitudes in the valley of decision! For the day of the Lord is near in the valley of decision."

The Kingly Role is not a Safety Zone

As we deepen our faith and learn how to exercise spiritual authority, we will be confronted with testing and trials like we read about in the Word of God. For example, I have personally gone through similar mini-trials like Abraham, Job, and Joseph. We can only possess our inheritance in the Kingdom by being open to having our faith tested. On one occasion, the Lord Jesus spoke this to me at a time when I was shrinking back in fear: "You can only get to where I want to take you by going through a Gethsemane experience." This is the scripture the Holy Spirit gave me:

> Now the just shall live by faith; but if anyone draws back, My soul has no pleasure in him (Hebrews 10:38). The Amplified translation says, ".....If he draws back and shrinks in fear."

It has never been one of my ambitions to rule and reign with Christ in His Kingdom; this only becomes a reality as you move forward in your faith walk. My greatest aspiration has always been what the Apostle longed for in Philippians 3:8-9:

> Yet indeed I also count all things loss for the excellence of the knowledge of Christ Jesus my Lord, for whom I have suffered the loss of all things, and count them as rubbish, that I may gain Christ and be found in Him, not having my own righteousness, which is from the law, but that which is through faith in Christ, the righteousness which is from God by faith.....
>
> Verses 10-11, ".....that I may know Him and the power of His resurrection, and the fellowship of His sufferings, being conformed to His death, if, by any means, I may attain to the resurrection from the dead."
>
> Verses 13-14, "Brethren, I do not count myself to have apprehended; but one thing I do, forgetting those things which are behind and reaching forward to those things which are ahead, I press toward the goal for the prize of the upward call of God in Christ Jesus."

Promotion will happen when we have died to any desire to make a name for ourselves. God's promotion comes to those who have a wholehearted longing to be one with the LORD, Who is the prize of the upward call of God in Christ Jesus. For example, God had destined David the shepherd boy to be King over God's nation, Israel. David did not have dreams about being King over Israel one day; his heart's desire was to give his devotion to his God. This was expressed through his devoted worship. David even had to run for his life from the Kingdom of Saul while serving the king. The great Prophet Jeremiah was chosen, in his youth, to speak the uncompromising truth to the backslidden leaders of Judah. Jeremiah saw the destruction of Jerusalem and the holy Temple after he had persistently warned his people to repent of their ways before it was too late. Jeremiah was born into the priesthood, but in Jeremiah chapter one, *Yahweh* confirms his divine appointment as a prophet.

Then there is Ruth, a Moabite woman, whose devotion to her mother-in-law Naomi led with her marriage to the prominent Boaz of Bethlehem in Judah. Through this marriage, Ruth inherited the lineage of King David and ultimately that of the Messiah, Jesus Christ. The Book of Ruth is read in synagogues on the Feast of Pentecost, known as Shavuot, the Jewish Harvest Festival. The story of Ruth shows that God's love is open to both Christian and Gentile as He blessed the Moabite woman who chose *Yahweh* as her God (Ruth 1:16), and placed her life under his wings (v. 12). The lineage of King David in the last lines of the book (Ruth 4:17-22) are repeated in the genealogy of Christ in Matthew 1:4-6.[5]

You may be saying, "I'm just the average Joe or Suzie working to support my family and exercising a simple daily faith." Perhaps you are a work-at-home mom or dad and the best you can do is be loyal to your local church. The truth is the Lord is mostly concerned about whether your heart is devoted to Him, and if you are faithful to serve where you are planted. God has a way of placing intrinsic value on what many consider to be the small things in life, like caring about our family and loving our neighbors. Then there is always the sacrificial offering to support missionaries who are advancing the Kingdom in the inner cities or foreign lands. When you partner with missionaries then you become a co-laborer with them–you share with their inheritance in God's Kingdom. Prayer is another way of offering your service to advance the Kingdom of God in the earth.

Jesus explained stewardship in Matthew 25:14-30: When you are faithful in small things, He will make you ruler over many things. When we are faithful with the spiritual gifts that God has given us, He will give us His true riches (Luke 16:10-11). Christ expects all believers to be a faithful "witness" which means "testimony" in the Greek translation. All are not expected to preach the gospel, but sharing our testimony will have a great impact on those around us who are lost. Our testimony must be backed up by a life that testifies to the gospel's reality, so it will impact the lost souls. This is being salt and light to the world around us. The testimony of Christ's lordship in our lives backs up the gospel we preach. Why do we not see a true witness of "salt and light" in our city or across the country? It is obvious the Church needs a gospel with a testimony behind it! Christians cannot live the gospel when worldly sin is prevalent in the churches of America—idolatry, fornication, adultery, alcoholism, drug abuse, pornography.

A lukewarm gospel, which falls away from the truth, has resulted in widespread apostasy, and we wonder why society is ridiculing and mocking God's testimony across the country. Christ's living tabernacle, the Body of Christ needs to be cleansed before it can be effective in permeating the nation with "salt and light." The Holy Spirit is moving mightily where the full gospel message is being preached in many churches, and we are personally responsible for seeking out those living wells where the truth of the gospel is presented in the power of the Holy Spirit. The Word will bring conviction to our spirit where we find the fire of the Holy Spirit flowing. The Word is alive because it is God-breathed, it is not a book written by humans. John 8:35 indicates it has the message of God's salvation and Matthew 5:18 verifies the Word is prophetic truth.

I offer these keys which have proven to be helpful for achieving balance and recognizing the real truth in my own personal walk:

1. Commit to a personal study of the scriptures, and ask the Holy Spirit to give you the sevenfold spirit as listed in Isaiah 11:1-5, so that the Holy Spirit becomes your teacher and revelator.
2. Choose to learn from teachers who are certified with institutions that offer a sound biblical foundation. Are they lone rangers teaching their own doctrine? On the other hand, are they credentialed through denominations based on sound foundational doctrine? Where they have studied will influence whether their teaching is sound.
3. False teachers seek to go against biblical jurisprudence, or actual Christian truths as found in the Bible. They rebel against sound doctrine. Teachers of heresy always have a different twist on Scripture. They display a spirit of independence, arrogance and rebellion against leaders and teachers within the Church establishment. False teachers are lone rangers that are not accountable to any leadership and operate in a cult-like fashion by putting down other churches, building themselves up, and appear to have all the answers. A cult is when a certain group feels it is exclusively different from the rest of the Church. They alone have the truth, and consider that the mainstream operates in error.
4. Listen to the quiet nudging of the Holy Spirit's guidance which reveals and discerns truth against heresy. The Word of God, for the most part, is pretty forthright–it means what it says! You don't have to twist it and give it a hidden meaning. While background and history give us further knowledge; God has communicated His own Word so that His children could understand it as it has been written!
5. Listen to the voice of the Great Shepherd. Jesus said in John 10:27, "My sheep hear My voice, and I know them, and they follow Me." The entire tenth chapter of John's gospel is a powerful truth about the trust we can

place in the care and guidance of the "Good Shepherd." Those who spend his or her life's energy tearing down unity in the Church operates as sheep in wolf's clothing.

Rod of Iron Rends the Islamic Veil

Biblical scholars believe the rending of the Islamic Veil is the final mission of the Church. Al Qaeda has networks in 80 countries and its goals are to control the world and take down Israel, the little Satan, and America, the Great Satan. Although the general public has had difficulty understanding the war against Jihadist terrorism; the wars in the Middle East have been about bringing our (the eternal God's) enemies to justice. God has divinely used America to make the world safe from tyrants like Stalin, Hitler, Mussolini, Osama bin Laden and Saddam Hussein. As a Christian nation, we are our brother's keeper. When President George W. Bush engaged the nation in the war against terrorism, it was a war to liberate the innocent people who are under the captivity of Islamic dictators and regimes. I personally don't support war, but we understand from history that some wars have been necessary for world stability. Today's disengagement of America's military under President Barack H. Obama is destabilizing the nations.

Christian and Jewish persecution has exploded with the shaking of the nations, and the blood of the saints cries out from Islamic soil! Open Doors USA recently released its widely cited 2014 World Watch List—a report that highlights and ranks the 50 worst nations around the globe persecuting Christians. The report cites that Muslim persecution of Christians today exists in 41 nations as part of a continuum that started nearly 14 centuries ago. Raymond Ibrahim documents in his book *Crucified Again: Exposing Islam's New War on Christians*, that the very same patterns of Christian persecution prevalent throughout the Muslim world today are often identical to those from centuries past.

It is time for the Church to wake up and take its place on the wall as watchmen similar to Rees Howells and his intercessors during the Second World War. I mentioned him earlier, and I highly recommend reading Norman Grubb's book, "Rees Howells Intercessor." Our enemy, Satan, has always been at work trying to lead the Church into apathy, a comfortable life without struggles. After all, intercession is hard work! It is vital that God's intercessors continue to stand in the gap and restrain the conflict that presses at the door of Israel until prophecy is fulfilled. I believe we live in the time which precedes the major Middle East war described in Ezekiel, chapters 38-39, when Russia leads the Arab countries against Israel. Currently, Russia's Vladimir Putin has broken international treaties to reclaim parts of Ukraine. The world has a new czar to keep its eye on!

Synopsis for Chapter One
THE SCEPTER AND THE CHURCH

The Church of Jesus Christ is God's extension of His Kingdom, and it has always been His plan to operate through the Church. Jesus explained stewardship in Matthew 25:14-30, that when we are faithful in small things He will make us a ruler over many things. During our short span of time on earth, we have each been given the opportunity to advance God's Kingdom. Our faithful service is being tested and we will receive rewards in heaven for sharing in Christ's rulership. He passed His scepter of power onto the Church to anoint the believer for his kingly and priestly role. Those who accept this responsibility are the overcomers who will rule and reign with the Messiah during His Millennial reign on earth and for all eternity. The greatest power in the universe stands behind the believer who has become God's spiritual temple. Jesus was addressing the Church when He said, "All authority has been given to Me in heaven and on earth" (Matthew 28:18).

Question?

What are you doing to offer your gifts and talents to advance God's Kingdom on earth? Are you conducting your own personal study of the scriptures, asking the Holy Spirit to give you the sevenfold spirit as listed in Isaiah 11:1-5, so the Holy Spirit becomes your teacher and Revelator?

Visit the Prayer Guide in Part Two, Chapter Three, which Includes a list of scriptures to pray for numerous needs.

Chapter Two

The Sword

From the beginning of time, God's sword represents His judgment. We first hear of a sword in the Bible in the Book of Genesis when the Garden of Eden was sealed. "So He drove out the man; and He placed cherubim at the east of the garden of Eden, and a flaming sword which turned every way, to guard the way to the tree of life" (Genesis 3:24). We move forward to King David, who was threatened by God's sword of judgment several times. It fell upon David's family for his sin of killing Uriah, Bathsheba's husband: "Now therefore, the sword shall never depart from your house….." (2 Samuel 12:10). His children, Amnon, Absalom, and Adonijah all fell by the sword. Even though the sword did not depart from David's house, God promised that his mercy should not depart from him and his house (2 Samuel 7:15). King David and all Israel came under judgment when the warring angel stood over Jerusalem with the sword of death. David sinned in numbering the people; a direct disobedience to *Yahweh's* command not to number them. Why? The eternal, living God expected the Hebrew nation to trust in Him alone. Here is David's repentance:

> Then David lifted his eyes and saw the angel of the Lord standing between earth and heaven, having in his hand a drawn sword stretched out over Jerusalem. So David and the elders, clothed in sackcloth, fell on their faces. And David said to God, "Was it not I who commanded the people to be numbered? I am the one who has sinned and done evil indeed; but these sheep, what have they done? Let Your hand, I pray, O Lord my God, be against me and my father's house, but not against Your people that they should be plagued" (2 Chronicles 21:16-18).

In the days of the Prophet Jeremiah, the rebellious Hebrew people received this warning: "I will scatter them also among the Gentiles, whom neither they nor their fathers have known; and I will send a sword after them till I have consumed them" (Jeremiah 9:16). The Prophet Ezekiel delivered the message of *Yahweh's* judgment against Israel because they had not accepted His chastisement. *Yahweh* had no choice but to deliver them over to the sword. This is the Word given to Ezekiel for the Hebrew nation:

> Son of man, prophesy and say, "Thus says the Lord!" Say: "A sword, a sword is sharpened and also polished! Sharpened to make a dreadful slaughter, polished to flash like lightning! Should we then make mirth? It despises the scepter of My son, as it does all wood..... Cry and wail, son of man; for it will be against My people, against all the princes of Israel. Terrors including the sword will be against My people; therefore strike your thigh" (Ezekiel 21:9, 10-12).

The only reprieve the world has from the Almighty's judgment is to return to Him with repentance. 2 Chronicles 7:14 is a prayer which has been offered throughout many generations for the Hebrew people, the Church, for the nation, and for the people:

> .....If My people who are called by My name will humble themselves, and pray and seek My face, and turn from their wicked ways, then I will hear from heaven, and will forgive their sin and heal their land.

Word of God: A Spiritual Sword

The revelation of the Word gives the believer spiritual authority, which is a sword in the hand of the believer for advancing the Kingdom of God around the world. The Word of God assures that what is declared in the power of the Holy Spirit will not return void, but will accomplish what the Father pleases and will prosper in the thing for which it was sent:

> So shall My word be that goes forth from My mouth; it shall not return to Me void, but it shall accomplish what I please, and it shall prosper in the thing for which I sent it (Isaiah 55:11).

The Holy Spirit is the author of the Holy Bible, and it is best understood by His guidance. When you read the Scriptures, be sure to ask the Holy Spirit to give you revelation. The Bible is called the Book of books, which was written for our admonition and direction (1 Corinthians 10:11). It is also called the Holy Book because it was written by holy men, under the inspiration of the Holy Ghost, making it perfectly pure from all falsehood and corrupt intention. It gives revelation of the Triune God and their individual roles to develop and advance the Kingdom of God in the earth. Scripture reveals that Jesus was prophesied as the Messiah in the Old Testament, until His appearance in the flesh in the New Testament. It is natural to develop a personal love for Jesus, when we recognize Him as the eternal Word. The Apostle John describes Jesus as the Word:

> In the beginning was the Word, and the Word was with God, and the Word was God. He was in the beginning with God. All things were made through Him, and without Him nothing was made that was made. In Him was life, and the life was the light of men. And the light shines in the darkness, and the darkness did not comprehend it (John 1:1-5).

> And the Word became flesh and dwelt among us, and we beheld His glory, the glory as of the only begotten of the Father, full of grace and truth (v. 14).

The eternal Word is God Who creates and speaks to man through His Word. The Word is Jesus Christ, Who clothed the Word in his flesh. In the Old Testament, God spoke the world into existence, and in the gospel, God spoke His final word through the living Word, His Son. The expression "the Word was with God" attributes deity of the Word without defining all the Godhead as "the Word."

Knowledge of God's Word is one of the keys to spiritual authority when accompanied with obedience. The believer who desires to be victorious in every circumstance will need to seek more depth in their spiritual life through the Word. Spiritual authority only increases when we spend time studying and digesting the Word of God. The LORD told Joshua, "Keep this Book of the Law always on your lips; meditate on it day and night, so that you may be careful to do everything written in it….." (Joshua 1:8). It is important to distinguish the difference between Christian meditation and Eastern meditation. It is becoming more popular to practice yoga meditation these days. What if you're a Christian? Should Christian's practice the same sorts of things as Buddhist, Hindu's and New Agers? Followers of Jesus Christ are not to practice yoga methods to seek the "God within" like pagans do. They are never to go into a trance-state and focus on a false entity. The Bible teaches that when Christians meditate, their minds are to be fully engaged upon the Word.

Christ's Sword of the Spirit

Jesus passed the authority of His sword onto the Church. When we increase our understanding of the Word, then we are sharpening our sword. This is how we put on the whole armor of God; so that when we do face the enemy, we are ready to defeat him with the weapons Jesus gave the Church. This is how we can refuse to become a victim of our circumstances, and arise to declare God's truth:

> The Word of God is quick, and powerful, and sharper than any two edged sword, piercing even to the dividing asunder of soul and spirit, and of the joints and marrow, and is a discerner of the thoughts and intents of the heart (Hebrews 4:12).

> And they overcame him (Satan) by the blood of the Lamb, and by the word of their testimony; and they loved not their lives unto death (Revelation 12:11, Emphasis added).

When the resurrected Christ appeared to John on the Isle of Patmos, He had a sharp two-edged sword coming out of his mouth. The Apostle John's life was miraculously preserved by the Lord, not just to live safely in exile in Ephesus, but to receive and communicate the apocalyptic conclusion for the Church, and the final judgment of the nations described as the Day of the Lord. The Revelation of Jesus Christ was written during a period of extreme Christian persecution prior to the destruction of Jerusalem in A.D. 70. John's Revelation gives all Christians hope and courage knowing that Christ has already overcome, and they can and will be overcomers. Believers undergoing persecution need to know their sufferings are not meaningless, and ultimately, they will be vindicated. The absolute sovereignty of the Lord God Who is the Lamb guarantees the ultimate doom of sin and evil. I would like to address the supernatural power of the sharp two-edged sword in John's vision of the triumphant Lamb of God:

> He had in His right hand seven stars, out of His mouth went a sharp two-edged sword, and His countenance was like the sun shining in its strength (Revelation 1:16).

Again, we read of the two-edged sword appearing in John's vision of Christ leaving heaven with His saints and angels to destroy Satan's forces, who are ruling with destruction on the earth:

> Now out of His mouth goes a sharp sword, that with it He should strike the nations. And He Himself will rule them with a rod of iron. He Himself treads the winepress of the fierceness and wrath of Almighty God (Revelation 19:15).

> The Book of Hebrews explains the supernatural power of the two-edged sword.....

> For the word of God is living and powerful, and sharper than any two-edged sword, piercing even to the division of soul and spirit, and of joints and marrow, and is a discerner of the thoughts and intents

> of the heart. And there is no creature hidden from His sight, but all things are naked and open to the eyes of Him to whom we must give account (Hebrews 4:12-13).

The Hebrew writer describes the Word of God as living and powerful, *Logos* and *Rhema*. This indicates that the scriptures are *Rhema,* a spoken word, to you, which becomes a weapon of the Spirit (Ephesians 6:17). The word powerful in the Greek is "energes" (en-er-gace), which is comparable to the English word "energetic," that denotes something at work, active, and effective.[1] I like this commentary on the double-edged sword by Bible Study Tools: "The sword goes out of His mouth in agreement with all the creative acts of God which were spoken forth by the Word of God (Gen. 1:3, Gen. 1:6, Gen. 1:9, Gen. 1:11, Gen. 1:14, Gen. 1:20, Gen. 1:24, Gen. 1:26; 2Pe. 3:5). It is for this reason that Jesus is the Word (λόγος [logos]). The speaking forth of God's will can bring creation or destruction. Isaiah informs us that the mouth of the Messiah is "like a sharp sword" (Isa. 49:2) and with His lips He will "slay the wicked" (Isa. 11:4). The Word spoken through the prophets is a weapon in the hand of God (Hos. 6:5). It is the only offensive weapon of the Christian (Eph. 6:17). Its power as a sword is seen in its ability to pierce "even to the division of soul and spirit" and discern "the thoughts and intents of the heart" (Heb. 4:12). The Word of God has already slain His enemies because it sets forth their impending doom in words "which cannot be broken" (John 10:35). That which is prophecy today, will be accomplished history tomorrow. It is in this sense that Jesus slays His enemies with the sword of His mouth (2Th. 2:8; Rev. 2:12+, Rev. 2:16+; Rev. 19:15+). The sword signifies His judicial power which will be in accordance with His Word (Mat. 25:31-32; John 5:22; Acts 10:42; Acts 17:31; Rom. 2:16; Rom. 14:10; 2Cor. 5:10; 2Ti. 4:1; 1Pe. 4:5; Rev. 20:12+)."[2]

A perfect example of the power of the living word, is seen when Christ entered the wilderness to fast for forty days, and He spoke the Word to defeat Satan's temptations. He disarmed Satan, who had never confronted a Man anointed in God's Word with such authority. Matthew records it this way:

> Then Jesus was led up by the Spirit into the wilderness to be tempted by the devil. And when He had fasted forty days and forty nights, afterward He was hungry. Now when the tempter came to Him, he said, "If You are the Son of God, command that these stones become bread." But He answered and said, "It is written, 'Man shall not live by bread alone, but by every word that proceeds from the mouth of God" (Matthew 4:1-4).

When we speak and declare Scripture to Satan, then it strikes him as a sharp two-edged sword which demolishes his power; because the Holy Spirit moves in power whenever the Word is spoken by those who have a covenant relationship with the

Lamb of God. Of course, we must be full of the Word, which is why Jesus explained that man does not live by bread alone. We live in a time of apostasy today when the Word of God is being distorted and watered down. New-Age principles are commonly being used to redefine Scripture. Believers must fill up their spirit with the Word and be ready to use it as a weapon during a time of temptation or oppression. This is why the enemy can disarm so many Christians. Jesus gave the Church the scepter of His power, but the believer needs to be strong in the Word:

> Behold, I give unto you power to tread on serpents and scorpions, and over all the power of the enemy: and nothing shall by any means hurt you. Notwithstanding in this rejoice not, the spirits are subject unto you; but rather rejoice, because your names are written in heaven (Luke 10:19-20).

Spiritual warfare is not engaged against physical forces, but against the invisible powers of darkness. The Apostle Paul teaches how Christians have spiritual armor to shield them against spiritual attacks the enemy would design against them in their daily life (Ephesians 6:10-18). The sword of the spirit is mentioned as part of the armor, which is the greatest weapon of defense against any invisible attack. There are two more weapons not mentioned, which are the Name of Jesus and His Blood. The armor of God provides protection, while the sword of the Spirit is an offensive weapon to be used against satanic forces, which come to rob and steal. Why are spiritual weapons necessary? The believer must be empowered with the Baptism of Fire and armed with spiritual weapons to overcome the enemies of the Church. Proactive Christians are a threat to Satan's advancement. Christ has commissioned His Church to overcome and advance His Kingdom until His Return, which is a hefty assignment with no room for passive wimps. Christ would not send His disciples, unless they were equipped. All the power of Heaven is with us:

> And Jesus came and spoke to them, saying, "All authority has been given to Me in heaven and on earth. Go therefore and make disciples of all the nations, baptizing them in the name of the Father and of the Son and of the Holy Spirit, teaching them to observe all things that I have commanded you; and lo, I am with you always, even to the end of the age. Amen" (Matthew 28:18-20).
>
> What the prophet Isaiah said about the Messiah's mission also describes the corresponding mission for the Church: "The Spirit of the Lord God is upon Me, because the Lord has anointed Me to preach good tidings to the poor; He has sent Me to heal the brokenhearted, to proclaim liberty to the captives, and the opening of the prison to those who are bound....." (Isaiah 61:1).

Christ fulfilled this prophecy by bringing Heaven to earth. When He read this portion of Isaiah's prophecy in the Temple, the people rejected the idea that Satan's yoke over mankind was now broken by the appearance of the Messiah. Later, after His resurrection, Christ commissioned His Disciples to spread the good news of salvation, deliverance, and healing. Fulfilled prophecies are one of the most significant ways that proves we know God's Word is true. The New Testament explains and fulfills the Old Testament Covenant, while the Old Testament prophecies confirm the New Testament Covenant. This is showing us Jesus Christ is the same yesterday, today and forever. However, the preaching of the word without the glory is dry, and it can even kill as the letter of the law! The Apostle Paul preached of the spirit and the glory in 2 Corinthians 3:4-6:

> And we have such trust through Christ toward God. Not that we are sufficient of ourselves to think of anything as being from ourselves, but our sufficiency is from God, who also made us sufficient as ministers of the new covenant, not of the letter but of the Spirit; for the letter kills, but the Spirit gives life.

There is a spiritual key here, which tells us to embrace trust and faith in the LORD. Jesus said in John 14:12, "Most assuredly, I say to you, he who believes in Me, the works that I do he will do also; and greater works than these he will do, because I go to My Father." Without faith, it is impossible to please God. Scripture builds our inner faith to act on God's Word: "So then faith comes by hearing, and hearing by the word of God" (Romans 10:17). Faith cannot become perfected by watching the works of God being performed, but it must come by hearing and doing the Word of God. Too often, believers merely mimic the power of God with an intellectual knowledge of the Word. The Apostle James taught how we must heed the Word of God:

> For if anyone is a hearer of the word and not a doer, he is like a man observing his natural face in a mirror; for he observes himself, goes away, and immediately forgets what kind of man he was (James 1:23-24).

An Undrawn Sword is Worthless!

I want to share a ministry experience which demanded a precise action on the Lord's instruction. It required bold faith, even though it was a small beginning in my works for the Lord. In 1978, the Lord moved me from Orlando over to Central Florida (the heart of Florida) to pioneer a youth shelter for abused girls. In seeking out the location for this youth ranch, the Holy Spirit instructed me to believe for a property that was already occupied. I was led to a 180-acre ranch owned by a local

Bible College, which housed a young men's drug rehabilitation program, but they were not open to any type of partnership. I had formed a nonprofit corporation for this youth ranch, and one of the board members was an 82-year-old retired architect from my home church. He was a renowned architect who had assisted with the Lincoln Memorial during his very young days. He agreed to draw the blueprints for the youth ranch, according to the vision the Lord had given me. He and his wife were of Swedish descent, and the wife had been an evangelist in Sweden before they married. The Holy Spirit told me to invite them to go with me and stand in the middle of this Bible Colleges' ranch and proclaim Genesis 12:14-17 over the land. When we arrived at the ranch, I knocked on the office door and asked permission to go out in the field to pray. Permission was easily granted, and we stood in the middle of the land praying the Scripture the Lord had instructed:

> And the Lord said to Abram, after Lot had separated from him: "Lift your eyes now and look from the place where you are—northward, southward, eastward, and westward; for all the land which you see I give to you and your descendants forever. And I will make your descendants as the dust of the earth; so that if a man could number the dust of the earth, then your descendants also could be numbered. Arise, walk in the land through its length and its width, for I give it to you," (Genesis 12:14-17).

I fasted and prayed for 21 days, seeking God's open door for the youth ranch, but the heavens seemed like brass. Six months after proclaiming the scripture on their property, the Bible College called and asked if I was interested in leasing their 180-acre youth ranch. Their drug rehabilitation program had run out of Federal grants, and the college could not afford to keep the program any longer. Miraculously, I moved in within two weeks into this beautifully furnished, two-year-old Spanish style facility, which would accommodate 20 people. The main house was completely supplied with linens, towels, kitchen utensils, and cans of food in the pantry. It was the fulfillment of a scripture the Lord had given me six months earlier:

> So it shall be, when the Lord your God brings you into the land of which He swore to your fathers, to Abraham, Isaac, and Jacob, to give you large and beautiful cities which you did not build, 11 houses full of all good things, which you did not fill, hewn-out wells which you did not dig, vineyards and olive trees which you did not plant—when you have eaten and are full— (Deuteronomy 6:10-11).

When we moved into the ranch, the main house had been fully cleaned and was in perfect condition; although, we soon discerned the land needed spiritual cleansing of some demonic giants. I learned that the Bible College had not provided adequate management over their rehabilitation program, and drugs were being smuggled to the young men from the lake on the far side of the property. This sin allowed demonic principalities to inhabit the property, and it took several weeks to cleanse the land. Our worship team that went into prisons with me came out each week and helped bring heaven to earth. They joined with me in taking spiritual authority over the demonic inhabitants. We give the Lord all the glory for His miraculous ways to work through his clay vessels. My burden for souls was now stretching out to shelter, spiritual children (Isaiah 54:1).

It is important to explain that this miracle for the youth ranch did not happen just because we possessed the land with Scripture. The Lord who knows the beginning to the end already knew the Bible College would run out of funding before they even knew it. They lost God's favor because they were poor stewards, and it was God's divine plan for our youth ranch to be birthed and established on this land. Our prayer to possess the land did not run off the Bible College; and the Holy Spirit was simply prompting us to put our "dibs" on this soon-to-be vacant land. Christ's rod of iron was shutting down this corrupt rehabilitation center: "For if we would judge ourselves, we would not be judged. But when we are judged, we are chastened by the Lord, that we may not be condemned with the world" (1 Corinthians 11:31-32). There is very little mention in Church circles about the Lord using His chastisement against the Church, but the Apostle Peter clarifies this:

> For the time has come for judgment to begin at the house of God; and if it begins with us first, what will be the end of those who do not obey the gospel of God? (1 Peter 4:17).

During the 1970s, there was a great void in the nation to help rehabilitate girls within a Christian setting, and our Good Shepherd Youth Ranch and Academy of Central Florida did just that. The mission was faith-based without government money, believing God for all needs without any formal fundraising methods. A good portion of the funding was donated by the citrus industry, and since the ranch was nestled in the middle of the citrus groves, the Lord led me to present the project to their local organizations. As the word spread of our girls' ranch, young women were referred to us from many states, from Florida to Boston. The girls called me their preacher, teacher, mama; and many times they went along with me when I preached in churches. The mission stayed open for five years until Teen Challenge recognized the needs of young women and opened a center in Central Florida that would accommodate 100 girls. Since they wanted to move into our area, the Lord instructed me to merge the Good Shepherd Academy with Teen Challenge.

During the years while directing the youth ranch, I taught the Word on radio and television every week and eventually the television outreach expanded to Atlanta, Georgia to cover five states in the southeast on CBN's Network. After releasing the youth ranch, which had become a part of my DNA, the Lord commissioned me to teach the Word of God full time, moving the ministry to Atlanta. Overseas missions also opened up, giving me the opportunity to win souls for the Kingdom of God in India and East Africa. Numerous mission trips were made into these regions to teach Bible training to pastors who could not afford to enroll in Bible College. After teaching all day, I would preach a crusade in the evening. Over the years, many souls were saved, along with many miraculous healings and deliverances.

In 1985, while praying in the early-morning hours on a train trip from Nairobi, heading to a crusade at the seacoast city of Mombasa, the Lord called me to reach all the nations. Some months after returning to the States, the Lord directed me to move to Washington, D. C. and minister healing to the nation. This was a promotion into the kingly role within the Church, being sent to help rebuild the walls of my own country. The assignment in Washington, D.C., expanded my weekly television broadcasts, which once featured Bible teaching and healing for the individual, and now gave focus for the healing of our nation according to 2 Chronicles 7:14. The programs were produced at CBN's News Bureau in Washington, and CSPAN in the U. S. Congress. Through the media, I have been able to stand on the wall and blow the trumpet to the people!

In due time, the Lord established the ministry at the nation's capital by providing a headquarters on Embassy Row. I shared earlier in chapter one, that the location the Lord chose happened to be one of Iran's former embassy buildings. For years, the Holy Spirit had revealed to me that the greatest harvest of souls was yet to come out of Islam – Ishmael's seed. Seventeen years earlier, the Holy Spirit imparted the call of Esther upon my life, but it was not until now, that I could understand how this would manifest through my ministry. A quick reminder that we should not make a prophecy happen – the Lord's ways are perfect. The end-time mission of the Church is to carry on the same work of Esther, to stand in the gap so that people of all nations will not perish. During the assignment in Iran's embassy property, we interceded that a nation of people would not perish under Islam, and we included all the seed of Ishmael throughout the Middle East. We can fulfill God's call to be a "light" to the world without physically visiting a country. Of course, we were standing on Iranian soil when we operated from their embassy property in Washington, which gave us legal authority in the Spirit.

The total success for all this ministry is due to intercession and seeking God's divine will. I show great appreciation to all those who have stood with me over the years with their intercession and financial funding. When walking through the corridors of Congress, visiting office to office, and through the House and Senate galleries; I pray for cleansing, revival, and restoration. The past thirty years, I have worked to bridge the gap between Church and State meeting with legislators and praying at the U. S. Supreme Court, the U. S. Congress, and the White House. We are presently standing with the Body of Christ, believing the LORD for another great spiritual awakening in America.

Christ's Two-edged Sword has Heaven's Power Behind it!

In the Book of Revelation, chapter one, the Apostle John tells, "I was in the Spirit on the Lord's Day, and heard behind me a great voice, as a trumpet" (v. 10). Unlike earthly rulers and leaders who would hold a scepter, the Resurrected Jesus appeared to John with a sharp two-edged sword coming out of His mouth (v. 10). The sword represents His justice, and His Word. The Word reveals to the sinner all that is in his heart. He is the living Redeemer and Mediator; the believer's advocate with the Father.

Although Isaiah called *Yeshua* the Prince of Peace, Jesus declared that His Gospel would bring division: "Do not suppose that I have come to bring peace on earth; I have not come to bring peace but a sword" (Matthew 10:34). *Yeshua's* title, Prince of Peace, will be fulfilled in His future Millennial Reign. There can only be true peace when God's grace is fully present over the earth. During the Church Age, faith in Christ separates the believer from the sinner and the world, and the proclamation of God's Word and its truth will cause opposition, division, and persecution. As I mentioned earlier, the sword of the Spirit, which is the Word of God, is the believer's weapon to be used in his war against spiritual opposition:

> Stand therefore, having girded your waist with truth, having put on the breastplate of righteousness, and having shod your feet with the preparation of the gospel of peace; above all, taking the shield of faith with which you will be able to quench all the fiery darts of the wicked one. And take the helmet of salvation, and the sword of the Spirit, which is the word of God..... (Ephesians 6:14-17).

The writer of Hebrews gives a vivid description of God's two-edged sword and its spiritual authority. The two edges have two purposes: one to purge us and redeem our lives, or one to judge us into everlasting destruction:

> For the word of God is living and powerful, and sharper than any two-edged sword, piercing even to the division of soul and spirit, and of joints and marrow, and is a discerner of the thoughts and intents of the heart (Hebrews 4:12).

A personal revelation of just how much the Word of God is a powerful weapon is received when we discover insights into the Word. Being grounded and rooted in God's Word places a reservoir in our spirit that enables us to speak out the Word of God in power as it is proclaimed from our lips. Anything we can say or imagine will not compare to the authority and the power of His Word. Only the Word can release God's power and authority within the spirit of man to overcome circumstances. Prayer warriors are skilled and anointed to be engaged in fierce, spiritual battle against Satan, and all evil forces warring against his or her spiritual, physical, financial and social well-being. A prayer warrior understands what scripture says about spiritual warfare. Consequently, like Jacob of old, he wrestles until victory is totally won (Genesis 32:26-28; Luke 22:44; Hebrew 5:7). Jesus' disciples noticed that He was a man of prevailing prayer and asked Him, "Lord, teach us to pray" (Matthew 6:5-14; John, chapter 17).

Jesus won the victory over the cross in the Garden of Gethsemane when He prayed, persevered and prevailed to obey the Father's will. He was pressing on to His own cross while in the Garden of Gethsemane when He said to the disciples, "My soul is exceedingly sorrowful, even to death. Stay here and watch with Me" (Matthew 26:38). "He went a little farther and fell on His face, and prayed, saying, "O My Father, if it is possible, let this cup pass from Me; nevertheless, not as I will, but as You will" (Matthew 26:39). The cup Jesus agreed to drink of was God's wrath poured out upon sinners.

Prayer warriors strive and struggle, physically, morally, mentally, emotionally and spiritually in prayers, until the victory is obtained. They agonize in prevailing prayer. No man can do a great and lasting work for God, if he is not a man or woman of prayer. Prayer warriors do not see prayer as just a duty. They are completely devoted to praying on matters of urgency and will pray like their lives depend upon it. In Acts 6:4, the apostles sought that administrators be appointed to manage over church business because they desired to spend more time in prayer. The Holy Spirit within the believer has to take over the intercession, for He gives us the power to intercede for others (Romans 8:26-27). Scripture teaches that every believer should be "continually filled with the Holy Spirit" (Ephesians 5:18).

The Sword Means Authority and Obedience is the Price

Before His ascension, Jesus said in Matthew 28:18: "All power is given unto me in heaven and in earth." Jesus is saying that all authority descends from God the Father through Jesus the Son into every situation on earth. In Ephesians 1:22, the Apostle Paul states that God gave Jesus to be "head over all things to the church." Jesus has given authority to His believers, so they can carry out His will in every nation. According to the Scriptures, disciples do not pursue their own personal goals. Whatever word a king issues becomes the absolute authority for the subjects under their rule, likewise, when a Christian submits to Christ's authority, then His disciples are subject to His commands. This concept has often repelled the spirit of those who prefer to work independently, because they rebel against accountability. The teachings of Christ indicate that when His disciples willingly submit to spiritual authority, it creates a concerted movement in which they work together as members of one body, the Body of Christ.

Jesus warned His disciples that, at the end of the present age, there would be an upsurge of lawlessness. "And because iniquity (lawlessness) shall abound, the love of many shall wax cold" (Matthew 24:12). Such lawlessness will cause people's love for God and His people to grow cold. While the general population operates without a fear of the LORD, yet there are many Christians who would never believe they could deny Christ, but rejecting His authority will result in a hardened heart. Lawlessness is fundamentally a rejection of authority, which is ever-increasing in today's modern culture. The foundation of our faith begins with unreserved obedience to the authority of Jesus Christ, the author and finisher of our faith. First of all, we must bear in mind that we are not bond slaves to Christ, but love slaves to the Savior of our soul. Jesus said in John 14:23-24, "If anyone loves me, he will obey my teaching. My Father will love him, and we will come to him and make our home with him. He who does not love me will not obey my teaching." When we are madly in love with Christ, then we will honor and obey His word, but if we try to obey with our own strength, then it is merely legalism. The good deeds of religion are in vain if we do not submit to obeying God's Word.

Christ will return to earth, and He will sit upon the throne of His glory in Jerusalem. Until that time, Jesus is seated at the right hand of God (Mark 16:19), which is a throne of grace, to which believers may come boldly; it is a throne of government, the throne of his forefather David; He is a priest upon that throne: but then He will sit upon the throne of glory, the throne of judgment.[3] In Daniel 7:9-10, He is called the Ancient of Days, or the Eternal One, who is the 'Judge of all the earth.' The Hebrew name is 'Ah-teek Yo-meen.' The description of God in this verse reveals His holiness: ".....His garment was white as snow, and the hair of his head like pure wool, His throne was like a fiery flame, its wheels a burning fire....."

Spiritual warfare is not an exercise we decide to take up; the battle must first be seen through the lens of the Holy Spirit for clarity and strategy. Elisha prayed for the LORD to open the eyes of his servant Gehazi, so he could see the battle being engaged in the heavenlies, over the battle in the natural (2 Kings 6:17). Since the armies of heaven are constantly doing battle on behalf of God's children, then why are so many engaging in the battle on their own ability? Oftentimes, we should be declaring the powers of heaven into the battles we face, rather than just swinging the sword. David spoke in Psalms 35:5, ".....And let the angel of the Lord chase them, let the angel of the Lord persecute them." Actually, verses 1-8 of this psalm are powerful to pray for any enemies who are engaged against you.

When believers place their trust in the LORD, then their faith is coordinated with the activity of the angels of God in heaven. We read in Revelation 12:7-11, God's angels are working with believers in the casting down and defeat of Satan and his angels. In verse seven, Michael and his angels cast Satan down. In verse eleven, "And they overcame him by the blood of the Lamb and by the word of their testimony, and they did not love their lives to the death." The testimony of the believer is powerfully used in overcoming the devil. This portion of Scripture in Revelation indicates that when believers start moving in the plan of God, following the principles of Scripture in terms of spiritual warfare, then angels are released to fulfill the plans and purposes of God. The angels move on our behalf against the powers of darkness when the Church begins to recognize its authority and take the position God ordained for it to take.

The Old Testament gives a revelation of how angels are commissioned in response to man's actions on earth. Too often, modern-day teachers say that we have a new covenant under Jesus Christ, and the Old Testament ways of moving in the spirit are different from the Church Age because of the greater authority which Jesus gave to the believer. This is only partially true. Even though Jesus passed His scepter of power to the believer, God's order of how heaven and earth work together has not changed. So, it is important to learn from the Old Testament the order that has been established by God the Father for the angelic hosts, and for the believers on earth to work with each other.

One example is Daniel, who began a time of fasting and prayer concerning the deliverance of his Hebrew people from Babylonian captivity. In Daniel 10:12, the messenger angel Gabriel delivered this message: "Do not be afraid, Daniel. Since the first day that you set your mind to gain understanding and to humble yourself before your God, your words were heard, and I have come in response to them." The angel had been immediately sent when Daniel began to pray and remind *Yahweh* of His promised deliverance in the Word. The messenger angel was sent in response to the words of Daniel. As he began to pray the inspired Word of God, those words were instantly heard at the Throne of God. Then Gabriel was dispatched to Daniel with a message from the LORD. Gabriel had been sent the first day of Daniel's prayer, but he was intercepted for twenty-one days by an evil power called the prince of the kingdom of Persia. The archangel Michael had to be sent to free Gabriel so the message could get through to Daniel.

Whenever Gabriel is mentioned in Scripture, he is a messenger angel; and Michael is a warrior archangel assigned to guard over Israel. Daniel exercised the principles of spiritual warfare correctly. With prayer, he held the prophetic Word before the Throne of God to call the Hebrew people into their destiny. Daniel's continued prayer for twenty-one days was the key to Gabriel's completing his mission from *Yahweh* to answer his prayer. The Prince of Persia, which resisted Daniel's prayer was powerful. Israel and the Church face the same prince today. The Apostle Paul mentions in Ephesians 6:12 that we wrestle with principalities, "For we wrestle not against flesh and blood, but against principalities...." This is how the battle becomes the Lords: When the believer prays the Word of God, the angels respond with spiritual warfare.

Israel's King Jehoshaphat is another Old Testament example showing the heavenly angels will begin to cooperate with God's people in spiritual warfare. In 2 Chronicles, chapter twenty, the Hebrew nation faced an invasion by three armies. Jehoshaphat's response is an example of how the battle is won in the spiritual realm with prayer before there is a physical victory on earth. Jehoshaphat began seeking *YHWH,* and proclaimed a fast throughout all Judah. He offered a great prayer before the people, and the spirit of prophecy spoke through Jahaziel, a Levite, which outlined the strategy for the next day's battle. The plan of attack was for the Levites to lead the army into battle. Now, the Levites were professional musicians in the temple, and they were being sent in advance before the armies of Israel, praising and worshiping the LORD. Their worship of the LORD would supernaturally become weapons against the three armies which were prepared to annihilate the Hebrew nation.

As soon as the Levites obeyed the LORD's instructions, their praise loosed the angels who set ambushes, which confounded the enemy, and they destroyed themselves. Their obedience to God's instructions placed the battle in the hands of the heavenly hosts of the Lord. The angels of God did not overcome the invading enemy until they had exercised the principles of spiritual warfare as instructed. Then, the angels confounded the enemy, and they destroyed themselves.

Yahweh also instructed Joshua with a similar strategy when the children of Israel marched around the walls of Jericho. The wall collapsed when they blew their trumpets, and all the people gave a loud shout. Because they obeyed their God's instructions, there was a supernatural miracle which occurred collapsing the great walls of Jericho. David also knew how the LORD worked on his behalf in Psalms 35, when he spoke against his enemies, "Let the angel of the Lord chase them." In the Book of Acts, we find examples of how prayer and praise engaged angels on behalf of the apostles. In chapter twelve, Herod had just killed James and Peter, who was still in prison, was going to die next. The Church immediately began to intercede without ceasing, believing for Peter's release. In answer to their prayers, the angel of the LORD came to Peter in prison, delivered him, and set him free from jail. This demonstrates the connection between the prayer of God's saints and the activity of angels:

> Now behold, an angel of the Lord stood by him, and a light shone in the prison; and he struck Peter on the side and raised him up, saying, "Arise quickly!" And his chains fell off his hands. Then the angel said to him, "Gird yourself and tie on your sandals"; and so he did. And he said to him, "Put on your garment and follow me." So he went out and followed him, and did not know that what was done by the angel was real, but thought he was seeing a vision. When they were past the first and the second guard posts, they came to the iron gate that leads to the city, which opened to them of its own accord; and they went out and went down one street, and immediately the angel departed from him (Acts 12:7-10).

In Acts, chapter sixteen, Paul and Silas were exercising spiritual warfare when they praised the Lord during their imprisonment, and an earthquake shook the foundations of the prison. They were not praising the Lord to see if they could be released; instead of getting into a depression over their shackles, they continued to give glory to their God. The powers of darkness were broken in heaven when they started praising, and the angels were loosed to perform exploits on their behalf. It was Paul who passed on the spiritual insight of what happened when he later wrote in Colossians 2:15, explaining what Christ accomplished through His sacrifice on the Cross:

> Having disarmed principalities and powers, He made a public spectacle of them, triumphing over them in it.

Behind the authority possessed by the believer is a power greater than your enemy. God has delegated authority to the Church, and He expects the Church to exercise what has been delegated to her. Paul was stating in Colossians 2:15, we can believe that God has already done it.

Identifying our Enemy

Before we engage in winning over Satan's spiritual attacks, it is necessary to understand his origin and background. It appears Lucifer was present at the creation of the earth, "To what were its foundations fastened? Or who laid its cornerstone, when the morning stars sang together, and all the sons of God shouted for joy?" (Job 38:6-7). The morning stars are the angels who worship in heaven. Ezekiel describes Satan's devices: "You were perfect in your ways from the day you were created, till iniquity was found in you" (Ezekiel 28:15). In chapter fourteen of his book, the Prophet Isaiah was given prophetic insight about Satan. He is called the fallen angel Lucifer, which means "day star" or "son of the morning." Isaiah describes Lucifer's fallen state: "Your pomp is brought down to Sheol, and the sound of your stringed instruments; the maggot is spread under you, and worms cover you" (Isaiah 14:11). Lucifer was a master musician and was certainly involved as an anointed Cherub covering the glory of God with the music of heaven. As a fallen angel, he has corrupted music on earth to distract humans from worshiping the One Creator God, in order to draw worship to himself.

Isaiah's chapter fourteen tells the story of Lucifer's fall and how sin entered into his heart: "For you have said in your heart: 'I will ascend into heaven, I will exalt my throne above the stars of God.....'" (v. 13). Lucifer was filled with pride when he took his eyes from the glory of God and focused on his own beauty and brilliance. Instead of offering worship to God, which he was created for, he began to desire worship for himself. Isaiah describes how Lucifer and one-third of the angels were cast out of God's presence. The gift of music was not taken away from him. When Lucifer fell, his gift fell with him. His ability to create worship through music was perverted in the same way his nature was perverted and turned against God. Secular music has become a tool Satan uses to turn people in rebellion against God because it appeals to the lower nature of man.

Satan desires to be worshiped by mankind and uses his false anointing in secular music, directing worship to himself. In his feeble attempt to be like God, he must divert the worship of mankind to himself. He offers young talented musicians the kingdoms of this world, alluring them with fame, popularity, and money. He influences the music of our generation as an act of worship to himself while turning souls against God. The secular music world recognizes the power of the supernatural, and some of these musicians have pronounced themselves as Messiah, even leading others into covenants with Satan in altar calls at the end of concerts. Some rock and roll music contains backward Satanic messages aimed at brainwashing the listener. There are occult music groups whose devil worship contains their formal backward messages, which sing an ode to the devil. There are also subliminal messages that encourage everything from homosexuality to marijuana use.

Satan tried to get the Son of God to worship him when He entered the wilderness for prayer and fasting. In Matthew 4:8-10, Satan tempted Jesus: "Again, the devil took Him up on an exceedingly high mountain, and showed Him all the kingdoms of the world and their glory. And he said to Him, 'All these things I will give You if You will fall down and worship me.'" Then Jesus said to him, "Away with you, Satan! For it is written, 'You shall worship the Lord your God, and Him only you shall serve.'" Satan knew that if Jesus fell down to worship him, then he would be like God himself, which was his original ambition.

Praise and worship are Essential in Spiritual Warfare

There is ongoing music in heaven, all directed at worshiping the glory of God, and likewise, the created are to worship God in the earth. We should bring heaven to earth by worshiping God the Father, the same way it exists in heaven. We can see from the Old Testament to the New Testament that music is an important part of the relationship between God and His people. In 1 Chronicles 6:31-32, David appointed the priests and Levites in the house of the Lord to conduct worship. They were to minister to God day and night with singing and instruments. They were full-time ministers of music, salaried by the tithes of the people. In 2 Chronicles 7:6, David designed instruments for the exclusive purpose of worshiping God.

The Psalms are a celebration of God. They emphasize the importance of sensitivity to the Holy Spirit in the area of worship. They help us enter into a spiritual place where the Holy Spirit can use us with great power through worshiping the Father–then we will achieve spiritual warfare the way God wants it conducted. God will possess the kingdoms of this world with those who will commit themselves to praise and worship. God still requires the praise that is due to Him, and He has designed to get His praise and worship through the Church of Jesus Christ. The worship leaders of the Church need to be just as anointed as the preachers, and their worship should always be based on the Word of God in music, as much as the preacher.

Synopsis for Chapter Two
CONDUCTING SPIRITUAL WARFARE

The revelation of the power and authority of God's Word is a spiritual key for gaining victory in our lives. The Word gives the believer spiritual authority, the key for success in your personal walk and for advancing the Kingdom of God in your community and the nation. God Himself is the Surety of His Word. When we declare His Word it will not return void, but shall accomplish what the Father pleases and shall prosper in the thing for which it is sent. Developing a spiritual knowledge of God's Word is one of the keys to spiritual authority. Since we all want to be more than conquerors, and victorious in every circumstance, most believers want to seek more power and authority in the area of their spiritual lives. Still, spiritual authority only increases when we spend time studying and digesting the Word of God. Jesus gave the authority of His sword to the Church, and we sharpen the sword with the help of the Holy Spirit.

Question?

What are you doing to overcome spiritual adversity? Are you filling up your spirit with the Word daily, so you can be ready to use the Word as a weapon during times of temptation or oppression? The enemy will disarm many Christians when they are not full of the Word.

Visit the Prayer Guide in Part Two, Chapter Three, which Includes a list of scriptures to pray for numerous needs.

Chapter Three

Keys to Spiritual Authority

> And to the angel of the church in Philadelphia write, "These things says He who is holy, He who is true, He who has the key of David, He who opens and no one shuts, and shuts and no one opens: I know your works. See, I have set before you an open door, and no one can shut it; for you have a little strength, have kept My word, and have not denied My name." –Revelation 3:7-8

The 'key of David' is one of the basic truths in the entire Bible, yet remains a mystery to most Christians who have not spent time studying and meditating on the Book of Revelation. The 'key of David' symbolizes authority. In the culture of that time, a key was a symbol of authority representing government. When transferring any governmental authority to another (such as the authority over a city or kingdom), a large key was laid upon the shoulder of the person. Furthermore, when a father was about to die, he would put a coat of heir-ship upon his firstborn son, which symbolized the authority the son would have over the household after the father's death. This heir-ship included a set of keys to everything in the father's household, which was set upon the shoulder of the eldest son, signifying that all the authority of the father's household had been transferred to the him. By possessing the keys to a household or city, one possesses the authority to open up to anyone; likewise, they possess the authority to lock people out. What they open, no man can shut, and what they shut, no man can open.

The 'key of David' message in Revelation, chapter three, adds a kingly dimension to the Church. It is the royal gospel of Jesus Christ — a message about mere human beings who will share the throne of David with Christ during the Millennium. In Matthew 16:18-19, Jesus promised to build His church on a solid foundation that would never be destroyed: "And I also say to you that you are Peter, and on this rock I will build My church, and the gates of Hades shall not prevail against it. And

I will give you the keys of the kingdom of heaven, and whatever you bind on earth will be bound in heaven, and whatever you loose on earth will be loosed in heaven."

Christ is the only one who has the 'key of David,' and all who are destined to rule and reign with Him will need to understand this is the authority behind the keys of the Kingdom of God! Christ has shared these keys with His Church, and He expects His people to walk with this authority in the world. Jesus told Peter, "And I will give you the keys of the kingdom of heaven, and whatever you bind on earth will be bound in heaven, and whatever you loose on earth will be loosed in heaven" (Matthew 16:19). The Church is where the 'key of David' message is, and where you find this message, you will find the faithful Bridal Church which is exercising stewardship to advance the Kingdom of God. The resurrected Christ appeared to John as the overseer of the churches. We either belong to the faithful Philadelphia Church or the lukewarm Laodicea Church. Here are a few tips that will help you qualify and share in the keys to the kingdom:

1. Why the power of Christ's authority rests in the 'key of David'

Isaiah had prophesied of an ideal king from David's lineage who would combine the power with goodness (Isaiah 11:1, 10). Christ is the Lion, who is the greatest member of the tribe of Judah (Genesis 49:9-10; Revelation 5:5). King David was a man after God's own heart (Acts 13:22), and God wants us to realize that David is a type of all mankind. The fact that He named this key to the Kingdom after a person is a clue that He wants every single human being that has ever lived to identify with this message. God's plan is to teach every person to submit and repent like David—so they can be born into His Kingdom!

2. All authority belongs to God alone

Jesus Christ is the living God who holds the key of David. The power of the key involves two branches: legislative power and forgiving power. The revelation of the key of David gives the believer understanding of the authority to bind and loose; to forbid or allow, or what is lawful and unlawful, which specifies a governing role rather than the general use of binding or loosing the devil. When Jesus Christ speaks in Revelation 3:7 to the Philadelphia Church, He speaks as the Head of His Church: "These things says He who is holy, He who is true, He who has the key of David, He who opens and no one shuts, and shuts and no one opens." Notice that the Church in Philadelphia is the sixth of seven churches described in the early chapters of John's Revelation. The Philadelphia church has a remnant of faithful saints who will not deny Christ's name! As a result, they have the power of God, and an open door that no man can shut! They are clinging to Jesus Christ's key of David message regarding the Second Coming of Jesus Christ, when Christ will rule this Earth! The next church is Laodicea (vv. 14-22), which represents the era of apostasy, the lukewarm Church. Today, we live in the days of apostasy, and Christians are either part of the faithful Philadelphia church, or the lukewarm Laodicea church.

3. Spiritual authority is only received by faith

"I know your works. See, I have set before you an open door, and no one can shut it; for you have a little strength, have kept My word, and have not denied My name" (Revelation 3:8). Christ has opened the door for His Church to deliver the key of David. It is all Gods doing, not man. Christ gives the kingdom's 'key of David' message to His people today, so they will deliver it to the world. Most Christians only have a surface knowledge of this magnificent truth, with the mission to expand the Kingdom of God. This is not a hidden message; it is being broadcasted and published through the miraculous door of satellite media and the Internet. God has provided the miracle of cable and social media to enable His Church to proclaim the gospel to the world. Without God's power, we would never be able to deliver His message to advance the Kingdom of God.

4. Faith only works when submitting to authority

As we just read, Revelation 3:8 gives the key to understanding the power of the key of David. God opens the door for His very elect when they keep His Word and have not denied His name. In these last days, when most of God's people are turning further away from obeying God's Word, the Philadelphians remain true. They keep God's Word even as others are casting the truth to the ground. They come under Christ's authority and His rule over His Church. Denying Christ's name means denying His government under the key of David. The Philadelphians are unlike the Laodiceans who deny God's government and refuse to let Christ rule them. They want to go their own way, the way of apostasy. As a result, Christ cannot give them His power and cannot open a door for them. He will not do those things, unless we submit ourselves to Him! Within ourselves, we do not have any power over Satan. The "synagogue of Satan," mentioned in Revelation 3:9 was a foothold Satan had inside the Church. Many call today's present Church Age the Laodicea Era. The people had become blind (vv. 18-19), and now Jesus is knocking on their door, trying to get in so He can turn them back to Him (v. 20). He keeps pleading for His people to return to Him so that they can understand and attain their promise of David's key!

5. Why the Key of David, and not the Key of God or Key of the Kingdom?

> For to us a child is born, to us a son is given, and the government will be on his shoulders. And he will be called Wonderful Counselor, Mighty God, Everlasting Father, Prince of Peace. Of the increase

> of his government and peace there will be no end. He will reign on David's throne and over his kingdom, establishing and upholding it with justice and righteousness from that time on and forever. The zeal of the LORD Almighty will accomplish this (Isaiah 9:6-7).

God established His Kingdom with David because of his heart for God, which meant David would advance God's kingdom on earth, not his own. He sought out a servant king instead of one like King Saul, who ruled as his own sovereign:

> After removing Saul, he made David their king. He testified concerning him: 'I have found David son of Jesse a man after my own heart; he will do everything I want him to do (Acts 13:22).

Thus, the Lord established His kingdom with David, for he saw that it would be established on earth through the obedience of David. This was ratified in 2 Samuel, chapter seven, and finds final fulfillment in Christ. Saul himself even acknowledged this, for after David spared his life, Saul said to him, "I know that you will surely be king and that the kingdom of Israel will be established in your hands" (1 Samuel 24:20). David knew the meaning of absolute surrender, submission, obedience, and worship and intimacy with God (2 Samuel, chapter six). However, Jesus is the supreme model of a "man after God's own heart." He said, "For I have come down from heaven not to do my will but to do the will of the one who sent me" (John 6:38). Because Jesus only sought to do his Father's will, "the will of the LORD prospered in his hand" (Isaiah 53:10). Whatever Jesus did; it was the Kingdom of God being manifested on earth. Wherever Jesus went, it was the Kingdom of God advancing on earth.

The Kingdom of God is a realm in which everything operates in perfect submission to the authority of the King of kings, a realm in which everything operates in complete accordance with his will, his heart and his ways. The Kingdom of God, in a theoretical sense, is the manifested expression of God's heart. We must, therefore, understand that the authority we possess is only the authority of the Father God and our Lord Jesus Christ, who is working within us. The Apostle Paul explained: "..... For it is God who works in you to will and to act according to his good purpose" (Philippians 2:13). Christ Himself said, ".....Indeed, the kingdom of God is within you" (Luke 17:21).

We are steadily advancing toward the consummation of all things in Christ (Ephesians 1:9–10), when the full manifestation of the Lord's rule over heaven and earth is eternally established. Born-again Christians have the tremendous privilege of playing a part in God's establishment of his kingdom here on earth. Christ himself desires to establish and outwork his kingdom inside each believer (Galatians 2:20). Jesus wants to use his believers as vessels to advance and establish his kingdom here on earth! (Revelation 11:15) It is the ultimate goal of what Jesus taught us to pray in Matthew 6:10: ".....Your kingdom come; your will be done on earth as it is in heaven." Mighty is the power of the Church which can pray in the Name of her Lord Jesus Christ!

Proclaiming and Prophesying God's Word

Death and life are in the power of the tongue, and those who love it will eat its fruit.
—Proverbs 18:20-22; James 3:5

You are probably acquainted with the common saying, "What you say, is what you will get!" Scripture reveals that the words we speak have power once released into the atmosphere, either for good or evil. Teachers within the faith movement have expounded on the power of the tongue by teaching, "You can have what you say!" This theory exaggerates the original meaning of the Scriptures, for example, Jesus told the disciples that with faith, they could perform the miracles He demonstrated:

> So Jesus answered and said to them, "Assuredly, I say to you, if you have faith and do not doubt, you will not only do what was done to the fig tree, but also if you say to this mountain, 'Be removed and be cast into the sea,' it will be done. And whatever things you ask in prayer, believing, you will receive" (Matthew 21:21-22).

The faith movement has been called, "the name it and claim it movement." This borderlines on the psychic and soulish realm. When a basic truth is expanded beyond its original meaning, it misleads many within the Body of Christ, leading believers into the dangerous realm of deceptive spirits. The missionary, Watchman Nee, explains the difference between soul power and spiritual power in his book, "The Latent Power of the Soul." The secret to the believer's power and authority in Christ are to understand in Scripture how Jesus empowered His Church, which is the message I aim to convey in the *Power of the King's Scepter*. Since the tongue is such an uncontrolled member of the body, the gift of speaking in other tongues enables believers to communicate directly with God. We read in Acts 2:4 how this supernatural gift was imparted upon the early Church: "And they were all filled with the Holy Spirit and began to speak with other tongues, as the Spirit gave them utterance."

Most likely, every one of us can recall bad consequences from wrong words that were spoken about us. In my younger years, I bought a small sports car, and my mother used to tell me that my car was so small that someone was going to run right over me. Her words of fear came to pass. An older over-sized Buick demolished my sports car because the driver didn't see me on the freeway. Another experience happened many years later, in Washington, D.C. when a disgruntled ministry leader put a curse on me with evil commands, which caused me to fall extremely ill with bronchitis. A men's prayer group that met at our embassy building brought healing into my feverish body when they anointed me with oil and prayed for healing.

These are just two examples when negative words have had an evil impact upon my life. There were also opposite motives behind each incident. For instance, my mother's negative words were spoken out of her inner fears because she did not know how to pray against a danger upon my life that she was sensing in her spirit. She proclaimed the problem rather than praying against any danger that could come against me. The motives of the disgruntled ministry leader were based on a spirit of hatred and animosity, which come from an evil heart. We must see how vital it is to ask the Lord to examine our hearts as David did, and be willing to ask the Holy Spirit's help to correct whatever His searchlight reveals:

> Search me, O God, and know my heart; try me, and know my anxieties; and see if there is any wicked way in me, and lead me in the way everlasting (Psalm 139:22-24).

On the other hand, there have been hundreds of times when favorable words of encouragement have been spoken into my life. My parents were both very positive in rearing their four children. They always set the bar high and were very determined that all of their eaglets would soar like powerful eagles once they were ready. They did this with love, encouragement, and sometimes tough love. This would lead me one day to adopt this testimony in my own life: "I can do all things through Christ who strengthens me" (Philippians 4:13). Throughout my life's journey, I have been blessed to be surrounded by people who were there to reinforce my destiny. We all need edification when we face impossible challenges. At times, I have been aware the Lord has graciously positioned earth angels to be there for me at the right time.

There is another key issue we must face if we are to be free in our spirit: that is, not just our words, but our thoughts have power. Our thought life hides secret sin: "For as he thinks in his heart, so is he" (Proverbs 23:7). This is a dangerous trap, because we become what we think! Secret sin leads to condemnation, which builds a wall of fear around our spirit. Scripture tells us, if you have given your life to Jesus, you don't have to be hammered away on the inside by condemnation. Repenting of secret sins, bitterness and unforgiveness, is essential for the heart to be cleansed. The precious Blood of the Lamb washes away all sin when you become a new creature in Christ Jesus, and you are reconciled to God the Father through the Son (2 Corinthians 5:17). Satan uses condemnation to harass you, so he can make you a captive again, while the Word states: "Therefore if the Son makes you free, you shall be free indeed" (John 8:36). Standing firm in your own faith becomes a weapon:

> Therefore, if anyone is in Christ, he is a new creation; old things have passed away; behold, all things have become new (2 Corinthians 5:18).

> There is therefore now no condemnation to those who are in Christ Jesus, who do not walk according to the flesh, but according to the Spirit (Romans 8:1).

Proclaiming Scripture is Powerful

I not only pray specific scriptures out loud; I also play the Word on CDs into the atmosphere where I live, and whenever on a mission trip. The demons and principalities over regions need to be addressed and are only dispelled by the sword of the living Word. This is how you can create an "open heaven" over your home and neighborhood. The Word of God brings restoration, healing, and victory when it is released through the lips of Gods anointed. It only becomes active when proclaimed from our mouth. Praying the Word of God will help thrust it into action, as you speak restoration into the life of your family, community, and the nations. The Word builds a wall, a shield of protection, around them. This is why Christian media is so powerful when the Word of God is sent across the airwaves: the Internet, radio and television. This is much different from "positive confession" methods, which use Scripture to control and manipulate circumstances.

Why is it appropriate for the believer to proclaim God's Word? Scripture tells us that God used the words of His mouth to create the world, and His prophetic Word must be proclaimed in prayer for it to be fulfilled. By proclaiming His Word, both written and prophetically spoken, we bring God's Will to be done on earth as it is declared in Heaven! For instance, Daniel brought the nation of Israel out of captivity by praying the words of the prophet Jeremiah. He understood that according to Jeremiah's prophecy that the desolation of Jerusalem was to last seventy years, and the time of deliverance was now at hand. The appearing of the Messiah was preceded by prophetic prayers in the Temple by Anna and Simeon, who were alive to see the fulfillment of this in their generation (Luke, chapter two). When we proclaim God's Word out loud in prayer, we let our own voice join in harmony with the voice of Christ, ".....Who is at the right hand of God, who also makes intercession for us" (Romans 8:34). In Psalm 35:28 we read:

> And my tongue shall speak of Your righteousness And of Your praise all the day long.
>
> My tongue shall speak of Your word, for all Your commandments are righteousness (Psalm 119:172).

In Joshua 1:8, *Yahweh* commanded the Israelites to meditate on His Word, or the Pentateuch. We think of meditation as a silent reflection. Strong's definition of the Hebrew word for "meditate," is "hagah," which means to speak, talk, or utter. The instruction to Joshua meant he was to *hagah*—to say over and over again—the Book Of The Law out loud to God. The men would stand with Joshua and learn the Word, and then they would go home and recite it audibly to their family members. They prayed the Word of God aloud back to God until the law took root in their hearts. This supernatural work is only possible when we study the Word and digest it into our spirit. The whole counsel of God's written word balances our Biblical perspective. Bits and pieces of scripture are only part of the counsel of God. Studying the entire Word gives a complete understanding of the whole counsel of God. It is also our responsibility to train our children in the ways of the Holy Scriptures, since we are accountable for teaching them the entire truth.

Communication with God Should Come Naturally

> God created man in His own image; in the image of God He created him; male and female He created them (Genesis 1:27).

> And the Lord God formed man of the dust of the ground, and breathed into his nostrils the breath of life; and man became a living being (Genesis 2:7).

Both Adam and Eve were distinct from the rest of creation, having God's image and likeness. They were created as triune spiritual beings, having a body, soul and spirit. They were destined for kingship over the Earth. Their intelligence and perception far exceeded that of any other earthly being. They communed with God out of their spirit and were connected to God through their spirit. This divine fellowship was drastically changed after the Fall, and God has been working to restore mankind's relationship and kingship for thousands of years. This has been fulfilled with the Atonement of His own Son. Once sin entered the Earth, Adam and Eve's soul died, because their disobedience was a sin before God. Romans 6:23 explains, "For the wages of sin is death." They were now enslaved to sin instead of remaining love-children to God. They became disconnected with the Spirit of God, living out of their souls instead of their spirits. The soul is the mind; the center of our will, intellect, reasoning, imaginations and emotions. They were now led by their five senses instead of their spirits.

The Bible indicates that during the time period from the Fall until the appearance of the Second Adam (the Son of God) on earth, the Creator only communicated with mankind on special times and occasions. God called upon Adam's oldest son Cain after he murdered his brother Abel: "Then the Lord said to Cain, "Where is Abel your brother?......And He said, "What have you done? The voice of your brother's blood cries out to Me from the ground" (Genesis 4:9-10). Later, it is recorded in the Pentateuch that the Creator communicated to Noah, Abraham, Jacob, and Moses. With the help of the Holy Spirit, the Temple priests communicated to the

Living God. In the New Testament, prayer becomes the prominent communication with the spiritual God as seen in Jesus Christ, the Son of God, who communicated through prayer with His heavenly Father. The Holy Spirit was the connector. Jesus openly demonstrated to his disciples how he was in constant communication with the Father in prayer. He also used the present tense when talking to the Father "who is in heaven." He even taught his disciples how to pray to the Father: "Our Father who is in heaven. Hallowed be your name...." (Matthew 6:9-13).

Prayer is the bridge between Heaven and Earth. It is the conduit through which the spiritual realm is brought into our everyday lives. Prayer is the way our spirits breathe. Just as our lungs require oxygen and are designed to seek it out, so our spirits require the presence of God and are designed to seek Him out. Without His presence, we are left gasping for meaning and desperately seeking our purpose in life. We find ourselves trying our best to pray because it is as needful as air for our lungs. Prayer is the method God uses to answer our requests, but it also brings comfort, strength and guidance. The late E. Stanley Jones, missionary and preacher, wrote: "Prayer is the opening of a channel from my emptiness into His fullness."[1] (Abundant Living)

For sincere Christians, prayer is communion with the Creator, which builds a relationship with the Father. The quality of one's prayer life determines the quality of the relationship with God. Prayer is talking with God; it is listening to God, and enjoying the presence of God. Humility in prayer gets God's attention. His ear is deaf to the proud. There is a humble prayer which originated from the time of the Desert Fathers. These simple three or four phrases the Desert Fathers chose to pray were mentioned by Jesus in the parable of the Pharisee and the publican: "God be merciful to me a sinner" (Luke 18:13). This humble prayer has changed the lives of untold numbers of praying people and has ultimately reached the Throne of God. The early apostles understood the importance of humility:

> God resists the proud, but gives grace to the humble (James 4:6).
>
> Humble yourselves in the sight of the Lord, and He will lift you up (v.10).

Jesus told a parable of the proud Pharisee, who was self-righteous before God when he prayed. He thought he was righteous because of his own good works, and he was not conscious of his constant need for God's mercy and grace. Then Jesus told of the humble publican who was deeply convicted of his sin and guilt, and in true repentance turned to God for forgiveness and mercy. Are you finding that your prayers are not working? Perhaps you need to focus on being closer to the Lord Jesus. Since "prayer works in the context of our relationship, then once the relationship is established, you will find that prayer becomes a natural expression. It is simply speaking and listening to your Heavenly Father. God wants to answer our prayers. Answered prayer is how He manifests Himself in our life and makes this relationship personal."[2]

> For the eyes of the Lord run to and fro throughout the whole earth, to show himself strong on behalf of them whose heart is perfect toward him (2 Chronicles 16:9).

God the Father distinguishes between those Christians whose hearts are completely His and those hearts which are divided between Him and the world. This reality is seen in Christ's message to the seven churches in Revelation, chapters two and three, where the Lord praises the faithful overcomers and censures the lukewarm members of His churches. The heart that seeks God's heartbeat waits to hear His voice for direction; even so, we see the majority of Christians seeking after counselors and psychologists. The book and social media industry are a multi-billion-dollar business funded by people hoping to hear from God, instead of waiting for His voice to direct them. Overall, the "herd" wants a leader to follow, an advisor that will help plan their future or solve their problems. Christian counselors and psychologists are successful in helping mend a broken life and repair the breach for a family, because they use biblical principles with their advice. The writer of Proverbs 15:22 recommends: "But in the multitude of counselors they are established. There is wisdom in the multitude of counselors." For the most part, God expects His people to be led by His Spirit. This requires wisdom by hiding God's Word within your heart, which becomes a resource for guidance and direction as you endeavor to live a spirit-led life. While you wait upon the Lord, a word of confirmation might be spoken through a best friend or even a stranger, who is completely unaware of the direction you are seeking. Sometimes it is a matter of your stepping into your answer. I call this by-the-way faith; it happens during your daily activity. Most frequently, Jesus performed miracles when He was on his way to somewhere.

God Commands us to Pray, Meditate and Recite His Law

> So then faith comes by hearing, and hearing by the word of God (Romans 10:17).

For thousands of years, godly men and women have used the model of praying the Scriptures—out loud—to God every day. This does not mean that silent prayer is not recommended, but when you pray and seek God's direction, it is more effective when you have a leading or confirmation from Scripture to guide you while you wait for His answer. We learn in Hebrews 12:25, "See that you do not refuse Him who speaks." The Lord Jesus cried out to the last church, the Laodicea church: "Behold, I stand at the door, and knock: if any man hear my voice, and open the door, I will come in to him, and will sup with him, and he with me" (Revelation 3:20).

The Word of God is not just for digestion into the intellect, but it is meant to be quickened (made alive) by the Holy Spirit as you speak it forth. This is a supernatural work of the Holy Spirit. Praying the Word of God out loud will transform your life and the atmosphere around you! Prayer is the Christian's lifeline to God. Prayer is not just for women; it is also a "guy" thing and a "kid" thing too! I love to read the Bible with my grandchildren and see how it catches fire as they receive it into their spirit. When children are taught to memorize Scripture, it has eternal value.

The Covenant of Grace

Faith Comes by Grace–Not by Works

"The Apostle Paul taught about the Covenant of Grace in Romans. He denies that there is any corporate salvation, any offer of corporate salvation, or corporate election to salvation, as the unbelieving Jews of that day commonly thought. They were falsely assured of their favor with God and of their salvation because they were children of Abraham, in solidarity with the patriarch with whom God had made the covenant. The Apostle Paul denounces that assurance in Romans 2 and declares the Jews are guiltier before God than the Gentiles….."[3]

> Indeed you are called a Jew, and rest on the law, and make your boast in God, and know His will, and approve the things that are excellent, being instructed out of the law, and are confident that you yourself are a guide to the blind, a light to those who are in darkness, an instructor of the foolish, a teacher of babes, having the form of knowledge and truth in the law. You, therefore, who teach another, do you not teach yourself? You who preach that a man should not steal, do you steal? You who say, "Do not commit adultery," do you commit adultery? You who abhor idols, do you rob temples? You who make your boast in the law, do you dishonor God through breaking the law? For "the name of God is blasphemed among the Gentiles because of you," as it is written (Romans 2:17-24).

God's Grace Circumcises the Heart

> For circumcision is indeed profitable if you keep the law; but if you are a breaker of the law, your circumcision has become uncircumcision. Therefore, if an uncircumcised man keeps the righteous requirements of the law, will not his uncircumcision be counted as circumcision? And will not the physically uncircumcised, if he fulfills the law, judge you who, even with your written code and circumcision, are a transgressor of the law? For he is not a Jew who is

> one outwardly, nor is circumcision that which is outward in the flesh; but he is a Jew who is one inwardly; and circumcision is that of the heart, in the Spirit, not in the letter; whose praise is not from men but from God (vv. 25-29).

When we study the teachings of the Apostle Paul, we hear the message of "circumcision of the heart." A clear explanation for this circumcision, Paul mentions, is simple: put no confidence in the flesh (Philippians 3:3). Circumcise your past by cutting it off! Your past is polluted; you cannot fix it, so cut if off! Instead of dwelling on the past, desire to know Christ more than anything else (Philippians 3:10). Seek a personal relationship with the LORD, rather than trying to be holy. God's first desire is to make us one with Himself. Personal perfection is the byproduct of a relationship with the LORD. Believers who have not allowed their hearts to be circumcised of the old life, or flesh, are acting out their faith under the law, which is of the flesh. Merely hearing God's Word cannot move us into acting by faith, submission, and obedience to Christ. A circumcised heart is tender toward the direction of the Holy Spirit, while people who are apostate have no conscience of their sin. Their actions are unconscionable:

> For circumcision is indeed profitable if you keep the law; but if you are a breaker of the law, your circumcision has become uncircumcision (Romans 2:25).

> For he is not a Jew who is one outwardly, nor is circumcision that which is outward in the flesh; but he is a Jew who is one inwardly; and circumcision is that of the heart, in the Spirit, not in the letter; whose praise is not from men but from God (vv. 28-29).

Christ is the new Circumcision of Grace

> Jesus Christ was a minister of the circumcision for the truth of God, to confirm the promises made unto the fathers (Romans 15:8).

Progress in our faith depends upon keeping the new covenant truths about Christ. False teachers water down the gospel by saying there are many different ways to get to heaven; or, all you need is God's love and grace. This is only partial truth and is merely lowering the bar, rather than proclaiming the full message of the gospel. For instance, in a recent television appearance, I was on a panel with several ministry people who were discussing whether Halloween is an event Christians should participate in. The Satanic association for Halloween was documented by one guest who warned about the evil history of this popular fall holiday. Another shared that his family participates in Halloween because it is an opportune time to show Christ's love and acceptance to everyone. Their family dresses up in costume and decorates their home to welcome all, showing great love and acceptance. My response, was that Scripture instructs Christians to be separated from the evil ways of this world, while we should hate the sin, not the sinner. I endorsed the fall festivals which many churches have adopted as an alternative to Halloween, and serve as a time of invitation for souls to enter the Kingdom of God.

Halloween is celebrated by millions of people as a fun time for kids, putting on costumes, and going door-to-door to get candy. However, it is also known as a time of witches, ghouls, goblins, and ghosts. On one hand, some see Halloween as a harmless time of fun and on the other, a ghastly and demonically inspired night to be avoided. History indicates that Halloween is dedicated to celebrating the demonic trinity of the Luciferian spirit, the Antichrist spirit, and the spirit of Belial. The Wiccan New Year begins on October 31st, which is a witch's coven day dedicated to the underworld when curses are released by witches and warlocks. Halloween is an old pagan festival of the dead celebrated by witches all over the world. Since there are ancient pagan and occult connections, what is the Christian to do? Here is what *Yahweh* instructed His people in Deuteronomy, chapter 18:

> When you come into the land which the Lord your God is giving you, you shall not learn to follow the abominations of those nations. There shall not be found among you anyone who makes his son or his daughter pass through the fire, or one who practices witchcraft, or a soothsayer, or one who interprets omens, or a sorcerer, or one who conjures spells, or a medium, or a spiritist, or one who calls up the dead. For all who do these things are an abomination to the Lord, and because of these abominations the Lord your God drives them out from before you. You shall be blameless before the Lord your God. For these nations which you will dispossess listened to soothsayers and diviners; but as for you, the Lord your God has not appointed such for you (vv. 9-14).

Halloween has to be treated with your own personal conviction. Even though it has pagan origins, many Christians enjoy dressing up in costumes and going door-to-door saying, "Trick or Treat." I still recommend the fall festival theme that many modern-day churches are adopting, which offer a great opportunity to reach out to the community with the gospel of Jesus Christ. In this way, Halloween can be turned into a night of evangelism. Neighborhoods welcome this type of church activity since it is unsafe for children to go door-to-door with today's high crime rates. The gospel of Christ is not about legalism, but about being salt and light within our communities. The Apostle Paul warns in 1 Corinthians 10:20-22:

> Rather, that the things which the Gentiles sacrifice they sacrifice to demons and not to God, and I do not want you to have fellowship with demons. You cannot drink the cup of the Lord and the cup of demons; you cannot partake of the Lord's table and of the table of demons. Or do we provoke the Lord to jealousy? Are we stronger than He?

God's Law and Grace are Totally Separate

> For sin shall not have dominion over you, for you are not under law but under grace (Romans 6-14).

Not at any time in this life can we say that we are free from all sin (James 3:2; 1 John 1:8), but we also should never feel completely defeated by our weaknesses. The power of Christ's resurrection at work within us is greater than the power of our weaknesses, and all the more reason for our reliance on the help of the Holy Spirit to help us overcome sin that hampers us. To be under the law is to be under a system of trying to earn salvation in our own strength by obeying the law. To be under grace is to be justified and to live by the indwelling resurrection of Christ. We can die to sin through all the resources that grace provides. This does not mean that we can disobey God's commands. In Matthew, chapter five, Jesus explains that He came to fulfill the Law:

> Do not think that I came to destroy the Law or the Prophets. I did not come to destroy but to fulfill. For assuredly, I say to you, till heaven and earth pass away, one jot or one tittle will by no means pass from the law till all is fulfilled. Whoever therefore breaks one of the least of these commandments, and teaches men so, shall be called least in the kingdom of heaven; but whoever does and teaches them, he shall be called great in the kingdom of heaven. For I say to you, that unless your righteousness exceeds the righteousness of the scribes and Pharisees, you will by no means enter the kingdom of heaven (vv. 17-30).

Jesus was constantly confronted by the religious Pharisees who thought they had to perform good deeds in religion and keep the laws and commandments of *Yahweh* with all their strength in order to please Him. They were trying to earn their holiness. Their beliefs created friction and conflict for Jesus, who had brought the message of God's grace, which is totally different from the rituals and ordinances under the Law of Moses. Jesus' parables revealed that the law and grace cannot be mixed together–they are absolutely separate. One example is in Matthew 9:16: "No one puts a piece of unshrunk cloth on an old garment; for the patch pulls away from the garment, and the tear is made worse." Verse 17: "Nor do they put new wine into old wineskins, or else the wineskins break, the wine is spilled, and the wineskins are ruined. But they put new wine into new wineskins, and both are preserved."

The word garment in the Bible is symbolic of our righteousness before God. It points to the external work of the gospel, which is visible to men. New wine refers to the internal work of the gospel, for it is invisible to men. The Law patches up the old sinful life, while the gospel of God's grace gives the sinner a brand new robe of righteousness. The key to unlocking such unmerited grace is to repent and change from the old sinful life, and accept the covenant of grace through Jesus Christ as Lord and Savior. Since none of our good deeds will redeem us from sin, then we must by faith throw away the old garment altogether and put on the new garment. The law of grace requires that we fully trust in Christ's completed work of redemption on the cross; the work of redemption was completed when Christ said, "It is finished!" Having been crucified and resurrected, He has already satisfied the righteous demand of the Father. The new robe is the righteousness of God; it is new and whole. Sinful mankind is wearing an old filthy, torn garment. A new robe of righteousness awaits those who will accept redemption through Jesus Christ, the Son of God. Herein is the gospel of God's grace:

> No one has ascended to heaven but He who came down from heaven, that is, the Son of Man who is in heaven. And as Moses lifted up the serpent in the wilderness, even so must the Son of Man be lifted up, that whoever believes in Him should not perish but have eternal life. For God so loved the world that He gave His only begotten Son, that whoever believes in Him should not perish but have everlasting life. For God did not send His Son into the world to condemn the world, but that the world through Him might be saved (John 3:13-17).

One does not get saved by works, good deeds of love, or trying to keep God's commandments. Salvation has been provided by God's covenant of grace, and man must receive it through faith. The Apostle Paul explains in Ephesians, chapter two:

> All the unsaved are spiritually dead, and under the dominion of Satan. They are enslaved to sin, and under the condemnation of God (vv. 1-2).
>
> Therefore remember that you, once Gentiles in the flesh—who are called Uncircumcision by what is called the Circumcision made in the flesh by hands—that at that time you were without Christ, being aliens from the commonwealth of Israel and strangers from the covenants of promise, having no hope and without God in the world. But now in Christ Jesus you who once were far off have been brought near by the blood of Christ (vv. 11-13).

Grace and the Commandments

If you love Me, keep My commandments. And I will pray the Father, and He will give you another Helper, that He may abide with you forever— the Spirit of truth, whom the world cannot receive, because it neither sees Him nor knows Him; but you know Him, for He dwells with you and will be in you. I will not leave you orphans; I will come to you (John 14:15-18).

Although obedience is a choice, it is still not a work of the flesh, and must be considered a gift from God. ".....For it is God who works in you both to will and to do for His good pleasure" (Philippians 2:13). Such spiritual gifts are only manifested through a surrendered life accepting God's gift of obedience. We are free to refuse to desire the life of obedience, and to draw near the Father through Christ. Too often, believers bypass the first step of learning how to walk a surrendered life and desire gifts for ministry. Before we can go out into works and service, the fundamental understanding of achieving a righteous life must be realized. This is God's desire: that believers know His will according to His Law, or His Word. Anyone who is seeking the secret for walking in God's great power will find the answer by walking in childlike obedience to the known Will of God. It is really easy: Desire to pursue His heart, His will and His kingdom. Obedience from your heart in response to the Father's Will releases the power of God to become manifested within your life. Jesus Christ, the Son of God was a perfect example of walking in simple obedience to the Father's Will: "For I came down from heaven, not to do mine own will, but the will of him that sent me" (John 6:38).

Keys for obeying God's Word:

1. Incline your ear to God's Word, it will keep your heart (Proverbs 4:20-23).
2. His Word must abide in you if you are going to succeed (Joshua 1:8; John 15:7)
3. Verbally profess God's Word (Matthew 12:34-37; Deuteronomy 6:6-12).
4. Righteousness will speak out of your mouth (Romans 10:6).
5. "Know that the Lord, He is God" Fear Him! (Psalm 100:3).

Keys for Being Accepted Before the Lord:

1. Put your offenses on the altar as incense.
2. Hold onto the "horns" of the altar with prayer.
3. Leave whatever is not pleasing to God on the altar.
4. A hardened heart is softened by offering the incense of worship to God.
5. Give what little bit of incense you have before God, because everyone's incense is great before Him.
6. The smell of incense upon you tells others that you spend time in the Presence of God, like the woman who anointed the feet of Jesus.

The Carnal Spirit Blocks Grace

The soul is the decision-making element within a person which manifests itself in the will—that power of self-assertion. Countless saints are blind to the latent carnal spirit within every individual who needs to be harnessed by the Holy Spirit. Ask the Lord to open the eyes of your understanding to operate in the sevenfold spirit and the fullness of these seven gifts: The Spirit of the LORD, the Spirit of wisdom, understanding, counsel, might, knowledge, and the fear of the LORD (Isaiah 11:2-4). Pray for the Lord to lift all veils off the eyes of your understanding (Ephesians 1:15-19). Examine your intentions when praying and repent of any impure motives. Do you have enough compassion to pray genuinely for souls? Is there darkness in your own heart that will block the effectiveness of your prayers? The Lord grows weary of double-minded hearts, and the heavens become like brass. Ask the Holy Spirit to shine a light on your heart and cleanse you. Ask Him to search your thoughts to see if there are any wicked ways, and lead you in the path of His righteousness (Psalm 139:23-24).

Here is a quick review: The soulish, or carnal realm consists of the will, the emotions and the intellect; it is linked to the choices we make in our thinking. "For as he thinks in his heart, so is he" (Proverbs 23:7). We have control over our thinking, and the key to disciplining our thought life is to allow the Word of God to renew our thinking. The Word has much to say about our responsibility for how we think. "And do not be conformed to this world, but be transformed by the renewing of your mind, that you may prove what is that good and acceptable and perfect will of God" (Romans 12:2). Christians are responsible for choosing to live by the principles of the kingdom of God. This involves forsaking old mindsets whose standards are aligned with the ways of the world (1 John 2:15-17). Since thoughts control our lives, here are some keys to overcome:

- "Keep your heart with all diligence, for out of it spring the issues of life" (Proverbs 4:23).
- "For to be carnally minded is death, but to be spiritually minded is life and peace" (Romans 8:6).
- The remedy is to be cleansed by the Word of God, which is the powerful sword of the Spirit (Hebrews 4:12).

Trusting God's Grace

I have learned that we will be tested by every word of Scripture that is sown into our heart. Have you often wondered why some people never change under the teaching of the Word? The heart of the disobedient carnal Christian grows harder as they hear God's Word preached on Sunday, because they are not sincerely seeking to be transformed. Rather than being humble with a genuine hunger for the Word, they go to church services with the wrong motive; thinking that this is what a Christian is supposed to do to be righteous, but the Word only hardens their heart. Jeremiah the prophet spoke about this to *Yahweh's* people in Jeremiah 23:29: "Is not My word like a fire?" says the Lord, "And like a hammer that breaks the rock in pieces?"

We can guard against confusion in finding God's will by taking time to stop, look and listen to the Holy Spirit's instruction. Compare it to mapping an upcoming trip. We cannot always rely on S.O.S. prayers to bail us out! Panic prayers keep us in a survival mode. Rely and trust the Lord to guide your future by declaring that Jesus is the One who ".....Opens and no one shuts, and shuts and no one opens" (Revelation 3:7-8). Ask the Lord to show you the doors He has opened and do not try to break down the doors He has shut. Jesus teaches us that carrying out the will of His Heavenly Father is a condition for entering the Kingdom of Heaven. Scripture declares that we must continually pray for His grace, which enables us to choose obedience in accepting God's will, which is His law. For example, in Psalm 40:8, David connects God's will with His law: "I delight to do Your will, O my God, and Your law is within my heart." Again, we see a parallel in Romans 2:17-18, when the Apostle Paul teaches that knowing the law of God is synonymous with knowing the will of God. In His law, God instructs His people in the way they should live; therefore, the law may be appropriately called "the will of God." The law means "instruction" and includes the whole Word of God.

God's first purpose for the believer is to know His will according to His Word. Too often, believers bypass the essential first step of learning obedience in the Word and prefer to move over into spiritual gifts. Obedience is truly basic: Mary, the Mother of Jesus, told the disciples at a wedding in Cana, "Whatever He says to you, do it" (John 2:5). You can run from God's Will like Jonah, or you can choose to obey it as Abraham, Moses, David, Daniel, Nehemiah, and the list goes on. Scripture declares that Abraham's faith was accounted as righteousness: "Abraham believed God, and it was accounted to him for righteousness" (Romans 4:3).

Remain committed: The psalmist of Psalm 143:10 asks, "Teach me to do Your will, for You are my God; Your Spirit is good. Lead me in the land of uprightness." If these are your prayer and commitment, then you can be assured that your present and future are in the protective care of your heavenly Father. However, if there is a deliberate sin in your life and rebellion against His Word, then, you must realize that His plans and purposes are hindered. We cannot expect God's Will to be done on earth as it is declared in heaven, unless we are choosing to do His Will in our lives. I mentioned earlier that the key for responding to the Will of God requires yielding to the Holy Spirit by opening up to the grace of God working in your life. Once you receive the understanding of God's Will for your life, then commit to do what He tells you. Perhaps you have never stopped to consider seeking God's Will for your life, which can only come through a commitment to Christ's lordship.

Even though, I had a serious relationship with Jesus early in my life, there came a time when the Holy Spirit convicted me of how much I was living more for myself than for the Father's plans and purposes. I was not living under Christ's Lordship. This was during a time when I was devouring the teachings of the Apostle Paul, and the Holy Spirit was convicting me as the Word was being absorbed into my heart. Conviction reached such an intensive level within my spirit that I knelt beside my bed and surrendered my will and asked Jesus to become the Lord of every area of my life. This had the impact of what we describe as a "born again" experience. As soon as eternal life from God Himself is imparted into a person through the Holy Spirit, he becomes a child of God (John 3:16), no longer conformed to this world, but re-created after God's righteousness.

A Heart after God Desires to Please Him!

> Trust in the Lord, and do good; dwell in the land, and feed on His faithfulness. Delight yourself also in the Lord, and He shall give you the desires of your heart. Commit your way to the Lord, trust also in Him, and He shall bring it to pass. (Psalm 37:3-5).

I believe the Lord is not a hard taskmaster, and He wants His children to serve Him from a position of love. Therefore, the desire of our heart should be to please Him. This is only possible with a regenerated heart that hates to sin. Jesus told a parable of the prodigal son who was eventually sickened of his sin and came to himself. When we place our personal faith in Jesus Christ as Lord and Savior, forsaking the old life of sin, we enter a new life of obedience to Jesus Christ. Jesus explained it this way to one of the Pharisees, named Nicodemus, who had secretly come to Jesus in the night seeking the keys to the kingdom of God:

> Most assuredly, I say to you, unless one is born of water and the Spirit, he cannot enter the kingdom of God (John 3:5).

The natural mind has a major stumbling block for keeping a commitment to God's Will and needs to be transformed by the Word of God. During the many years, I have been conducting intensive studies in the Word, my mind and heart have been submitted to a cleansing work being performed by the Holy Spirit. I am aware of the changed thinking that has expanded my life into being influenced by the sevenfold spirit. In Titus 3:5, Paul speaks of this cleansing process as: ".....The washing of regeneration, and renewing of the Holy Ghost." The carnal way of thinking must be changed and placed under the control of the Holy Spirit, so the bondage of sin can be broken. One who is born of God does not desire for sin to be a habitual practice in his life. This is accomplished only through the grace given to the believer by Christ, through a sustained relationship with Christ, and through dependence on the Holy Spirit (Romans 8:2-14). *Yahweh* called His people to this same transformation through the Prophet Isaiah:

> Let the wicked forsake his way, and the unrighteous man his thoughts; let him return to the Lord, and He will have mercy on him; and to our God, for He will abundantly pardon. "For My thoughts are not your thoughts, nor are your ways My ways," says the Lord. "For as the heavens are higher than the earth, so are My ways higher than your ways, and My thoughts than your thoughts" (Isaiah 55:7-9).

The Lord's Prayer, which Jesus taught His disciples in Matthew, chapter six, expresses the fear of the Lord. It helps the believer put sin to death daily, so he can walk in the Father's will in purity of heart. Believers should pray for God's Will to be done, and sincerely desire His perfect will with the intention of fulfilling it in their personal lives and in their families. Purification is also necessary for following God's Will. The Apostle Paul explains to the Thessalonians that they must follow the Will of God by abstaining from fornication, and living a purified life with honor (1 Thessalonian 4:3, 4). This requires that:

- Sinful ways of the flesh must be abandoned.
- Old habits of the human spirit must be changed.
- Old mindsets must be abandoned and new mindsets adopted.

The Apostle Paul prayed for the Colossae church to understand God's Will, in order that they "might walk worthy of the Lord unto all pleasing, being fruitful in every good work" (Colossians 1:9, 10). Believers are called to spiritual separation from the world. Loving the world defiles our fellowship. It is impossible to love the world and the Father at the same time. The world's system opposes God, His people, His Word and His righteous standards. The Word of God discloses that believers are strangers and pilgrims in this world. Each generation is called to be "keepers of the flame" which is passed on from generation to generation. Simply said, we have a mission for the Kingdom of God, and then we are out of here! All are called to win souls for God's kingdom. Scripture teaches that believers must come out of the world and not adopt the world's ways. They are not to love the world, but overcome the world; hate the world and die to the world; and be delivered from the world. (Study: Hebrews 11:13; 1 Peter 2:11; John 15:19; Romans 12:2; 1 John 2:15; 1 John 5:4; Hebrews 1:9; Galatians 6:14; Colossians 1:13-14)

Paul was adamant in his teachings for believers to be separated from the world. It is impossible to do the Will of God and live under the influence of the world's system. This causes a spiritual tug with the corrupt, carnal desires within; and against ungodly, pleasures of the world and invites temptations of every kind. All Christians are involved in this spiritual battle that can only be won with the help of the Holy Spirit (Ephesians 6:11). Some just struggle with the physical circumstance, and do not know how to define the conflict as a spiritual battle. This is why believers are instructed to separate themselves from the ways of the world:

> Do not love the world or the things in the world. If anyone loves the world, the love of the Father is not in him. For all that is in the world—the lust of the flesh, the lust of the eyes, and the pride of life—is not of the Father but is of the world. And the world is passing away, and the lust of it; but he who does the will of God abides forever (1 John 2:15-17).

Not everyone will choose to follow God's calling and instructions: "Many are called, but few are chosen" (Matthew 24:14). What are you willing to surrender to the Lord? When the Lord assigned me to move my television program to Washington, D.C. in 1988, there was a cost involved. It required giving up my Bible teaching programs on television in the Southeast. I loved teaching the Word on radio and television, but this would now become history on my resume. It also meant I would not return to the churches in Africa, until nine years later in 1995 when the Lord gave me an embassy in Washington, D.C. to the nations. From there, He sent me as an ambassador on numerous diplomatic mission trips, meeting with heads of State, government officials, and ambassadors in Israel and Africa. Long before I had died to myself, but now this assignment at the nation's capital required forsaking the old ministry. The bonus was the great opportunity to interview national Church leaders and Members of Congress at the U. S. Capitol.

During my years of ministry as an evangelist, miracles occurred in every meeting, which was exhilarating and humbling to experience the Holy Spirit moving through you. The Holy Spirit's miraculous signs and wonders were now to be manifested on a governmental level; the healing of the nations was the mission. This was to be a silent covert work without human recognition. It was a service that solely ministered to the Lord's purposes. "He must increase, but I must decrease" (John 3:30). The gifts belong to the Lord Jesus, and we must be willing to submit them to His instructions. Obedience to this high level mission in the nation's capital has certainly brought a greater reward in the Kingdom of God. Our human nature wants to hold onto the old, but if I had held onto Ishmael (the old mission), I would have missed the greater promise of Isaac. My commitment to the Lord Jesus is the same as Isaiah, who also heard the voice of the Lord, saying: "Whom shall I send, and who will go for Us? Then I said, 'Here am I. Send me!'" (Isaiah 6:8-9).

Do you Know your own Motives?

The primary motive for a Christian should be to please the LORD. Moses' first commandment tells us that embracing God Himself must come first. Father Abraham was called to sacrifice and give up his beloved son Isaac, the seed for future generations. If he had held onto Isaac, that is all the inheritance that Abraham would have had. Because he was willing to sacrifice his only son, God multiplied his inheritance beyond what most high-tech calculators can count. Who can count all the stars?

Christ expects us to bear fruit and demonstrate His character. Today, believers are more interested in the gifts of the Spirit than in manifesting the nature and character of the Savior, which will bear fruit. The Son of God explained this principle to His disciples in John, chapter 12: "The hour has come that the Son of man should be glorified. Truly, truly, I say to you that unless a grain of wheat falls and dies in the ground, it will be left alone; but if it dies, it produces much fruit" (vv. 23-24). We are all trees that are the planting of the Lord Jesus, and we are destined to bear fruit. This knowledge is very important, and it is covered several times in this book. Believers are to bear fruit in their personal lives and then in their works for the Kingdom of God. Fruit is different from the gifts of the Spirit. Most people think of the gifts, and overlook the fruit which is essential to the value of any tree.

Jesus cursed the fig tree that did not bear fruit, and it dried up and died: "Now in the morning, as they passed by, they saw the fig tree dried up from the roots. And Peter, remembering, said to Him, "Rabbi, look! The fig tree which You cursed has withered away" (Mark 11:20, 21). John the Baptist also taught that the tree that does not bear good fruit will be cut down and cast into the fire (Matthew 3:10-12). Fruit is not always publicly visible to others. Some people are hidden in their service to the Lord, and their fruit is recognized in heaven; while those who are called to public service for the Lord carry a greater accountability to show good fruit. Jesus spoke of the faithful and unfaithful servants: "..... For everyone to whom much is given, from him much will be required; and to whom much has been committed, of him they will ask the more" (Luke 12:48).

Synopsis for Chapter Three
Keys to Spiritual Authority

The 'key of David' message in Revelation, chapter three, adds a kingly dimension to the Church. It is the royal gospel of Jesus Christ; a message about mere human beings who will share the throne of David with Christ during the Millennium. All who are destined to be part of the Kingdom of God will want to understand the keys of the Kingdom of God! Christ is "he who has the key of David." He gave it to His Church, and He expects His people to share it with the world. God's true Church is where the 'key of David' message is, and where you find this kingdom message, you will find the faithful Bridal Church. David's heart for God, his absolute surrender and his desire to see God's kingdom established on earth (rather than his own 'kingdom') are what qualified him to be a vessel through whom God could have powerfully advanced His kingdom. The Lord's Prayer expresses reverence and the fear of the Lord; it helps the believer put sin to death daily, so he can walk in the Father's will in purity of heart.

Question?

What is the motive of your heart? Do you have a heart for God, or do you seek position and spiritual authority for your own selfish desires? Examining one's own heart is vital for spiritual purity. "Search me, O God, and know my heart; try me, and know my anxieties; and see if there is any wicked way in me, and lead me in the way everlasting" (Psalm 139:23-24).

Visit the Prayer Guide in Part Two, Chapter Three which Includes a list of scriptures to pray for numerous needs.

Chapter Four

A Burning Faith Overcomes

Now faith is the substance of things hoped for, the evidence of things not seen. For by it the elders obtained a good testimony. By faith we understand that the worlds were framed by the word of God, so that the things which are seen were not made of things which are visible (Hebrews 11:1-3).

Scripture reveals how God is always searching for men and women of faith that can be used as instruments of revival and restoration in society. He is not raising up armies to enforce His will upon the people; He uses vessels who have faith to believe in prayer and His Word to bring revival and restoration with the good news of the Gospel. The Holy Spirit searches the hearts of His people to see who will take up the hedge, and stand in the gap so His plans and purposes will be fulfilled on earth. You may be one of those who shares the Lord's burden over your nation's backslidden condition. Biblical history shows there were such men and women who lamented over their broken Hebrew nation. For instance, Nehemiah spent his time praying, fasting, and mourning over Israel–he was a man with God's burden on his heart. The walls of Jerusalem were in complete ruins, and worse, there was absolutely no witness to the existence of their Hebrew God. What did *Yahweh* do? He met the broken heart of Nehemiah, and commissioned him to be His emissary to restore the broken walls of Jerusalem.

Israel's spiritual walls were also restored under Nehemiah and Ezra the scribe when a revival of holiness swept the land. "Then the priests and the Levites purified themselves, and purified the people, and the gates, and the wall" (Nehemiah 12:30). Nehemiah also had the house of God purged of all filth and idolatry (Nehemiah 13:8-9). Where did Nehemiah get his great faith and spiritual authority, which defeated his enemies and restored godly fear to the temple? The king of Persia, who authorized the restoration of Jerusalem did not give it to him. He got his authority on his knees, interceding for the sins of his people. Nehemiah is just one of the many faith heroes God used for preserving the nation of Israel. He is called the James of the Old Testament, challenging God's people to show their faith by their works in rebuilding the walls of Jerusalem. Nehemiah's name means "*Yahweh* comforts." Nehemiah recruited the help of Ezra, the scribe, who led a spiritual revival by renewing *Yahweh's* covenant and restoring the people into obedience of God's Word. This was all achieved by fervent prayer and obeying God's will:

> And I said: "I pray, Lord God of heaven, O great and awesome God, You who keep Your covenant and mercy with those who love You and observe Your commandments, please let Your ear be attentive and Your eyes open, that You may hear the prayer of Your servant which I pray before You now, day and night, for the children of Israel Your servants, and confess the sins of the children of Israel which we have sinned against You. Both my father's house and I have sinned. We have acted very corruptly against You, and have not kept the commandments, the statutes, nor the ordinances which You commanded Your servant Moses." (Nehemiah 1:5-7).

In 1 Samuel, we again see God at work to preserve the posterity of Israel. The priesthood was corrupt, and the priests could not hear from the LORD on behalf of the people. *Yahweh* was seeking for a new prophetic voice that would replace the old corrupt priesthood and speak on His behalf to the people. Hannah, the beloved wife of Elkanah, was barren and cried out to *Yahweh* for years to have a son. Scripture says that God had shut up her womb, and when she prayed she vowed to dedicate a son to *YHWH's* service if He granted her request. Hannah's barrenness was not only her condition, but her nation was also spiritually barren. Hannah had faith in the sovereign LORD; but she never imagined her intense intercession was moving in concert with God's plan for the Hebrew nation. What she was personally praying for would bring restoration for herself and her people.

Yahweh answered Hannah's cry for a son and also advanced His larger plan through her. Her son, Samuel, restored Israel's corrupt priesthood and returned the prophetic voice of God to the people. Samuel means "God hears." He was Israel's first prophet and the last of Israel's judges. He was also a counselor to its first two kings, Saul and David. Samuel is listed in the LORDs "Faith Hall of Fame" in Hebrews 11:32, along with the other great patriarchs. Hannah also had faith to pray for years, believing for a child when most of us would have given up. She was a devout, persistent woman, and *Yahweh* finally answered her prayers. Hannah became an example for all praying people to never give up, and believe that God will honor your vow to Him.

From examples like these in Scripture, we too can serve God's plans and purposes through intercession and understand that we can be instruments to stand in the gap on behalf of the people, confessing sin and praying for mercy for the nations. This requires dedicating our works and accomplishments to the LORD, along with enabling others who are striving to advance the Kingdom of God. When we pray according to God's Will in faith, believing that He will intervene on our behalf, then we will experience our prayers being answered. It involves some spiritual warfare, so be prepared to stand and be faithful to defend others who are under attack.

Without Burning Faith – it is Impossible to Please the LORD

> But God has chosen the foolish things of the world to put to shame the wise, and God has chosen the weak things of the world to put to shame the things which are mighty..... (1 Corinthians 1:27).

The LORD gets all the glory when weak human beings become instruments of His mighty power. The Apostle Paul describes how this works in 2 Corinthians 4:7-10:

> But we have this treasure in earthen vessels, that the excellence of the power may be of God and not of us. We are hard-pressed on every side, yet not crushed; we are perplexed, but not in despair; persecuted, but not forsaken; struck down, but not destroyed—always carrying about in the body the dying of the Lord Jesus, that the life of Jesus also may be manifested in our body.

Paul was saying, in the midst of these perils, they were experiencing the life of Jesus within their spirit, strengthening and sustaining them in their present weakness. Their faith is in the future resurrection, not their dying flesh. It is interesting to see in today's society the over-emphasis on preserving the body to look younger and live longer. Genuine disciples gain their strength from their faith in Jesus, the "true vine" (John, chapter 15). When we become lukewarm, we become a dead branch; there is no life in us. The fire of God helps us develop a *burning faith* which ignites our spirit when we receive the gift of the Holy Spirit. *Burning faith* requires being single-minded, placing our complete trust in the Lord Jesus Christ. Without this confidence, we will shrink back in fear (Hebrews 10:38), like King Saul's army ran from Goliath. The youthful shepherd David was sent to the battle front with lunch for his brothers, and when he heard Goliath's taunting, he testified:

> This day the Lord will deliver you into my hand, and I will strike you and take your head from you. And this day I will give the carcasses of the camp of the Philistines to the birds of the air and the wild beasts of the earth, that all the earth may know that there is a God in Israel. Then all this assembly shall know that the Lord does not save with sword and spear; for the battle is the Lord's, and He will give you

> into our hands (1 Samuel 17:46-47). Verse 50 says, ".....there was no sword in the hand of David."

God often chooses the weak to prove His strength. David was certainly the least of the least standing there among Israel's well-trained soldiers on the front line facing Goliath of Gath, and the Philistine army (1 Samuel, chapter 17). He knew he was no physical match for Goliath, yet within his spirit; he knew the battle was not his, but it was God's battle. We face battles on many fronts; but remember, Christ has already overcome our enemies (Colossians 2:15). We possess an authority no demon can stand up to, and we must remember the battle is the Lords! The weapons which are available to every believer are the Word of God, the Name of Jesus Christ, and the Blood of the Lamb! Spiritual victory comes through Jesus Christ our Deliverer, and the Holy Spirit: "Not by might nor by power, but by My Spirit," Says the Lord of hosts (Zechariah 4:6).

What mountains do you face, and how are you reacting? Lay down your weapons and quit trying to be self-sufficient and strong on your own. Allow Jesus Christ to become your strength, and utilize the Word as your weapon. You cannot save yourself, so rely on the finished work of the cross by faith and follow these steps for how to walk by faith:

1. Ignore false signals in your circumstances. Trust the LORD with *burning faith*. (Numbers 13:30).
2. Follow divine wisdom in His Word and trust the leading of the Holy Spirit (Isaiah 11:2-5).
3. Quiet your feelings and emotions (2 Corinthians 10:5).
4. Trust God's guidance and rest in Him (Hebrews 4:10).
5. Have confidence in Christ's strength, not your own (Philippians 4:13).

Faith Gives us the Courage to Take up our Cross and Follow Jesus

> For I through the law died to the law that I might live to God. I have been crucified with Christ; it is no longer I who live, but Christ lives in me; and the life which I now live in the flesh I live by faith in the Son of God, who loved me and gave Himself for me. I do not set aside the grace of God; for if righteousness comes through the law, then Christ died in vain (Galatians 2:19-21).

If we could earn salvation by obedience to the Law, then the Cross would not have been necessary. The Apostle Paul states that the believer who has been united by faith to Christ in His death has also died to the old life and has risen to a new life. Paul is saying the Law gave him no power to overcome sin, so he turned from the Law as a means of acceptance by God. One of the first choices we all must make is to resist temptation and then draw closer to Christ. Our confession should be, when I am weak, Christ is strong! How do we take up our cross and follow Christ?

Here are a few ways in which we will personally experience our own cross?

1. Suffering (1 Peter 2:21; 4:13)
2. Shame (Hebrews 12:2)
3. Ridicule (Matthew 27:39)
4. Rejection (1 Peter 2:4)
5. Self-denial (Matthew 16:24)

Christ can only live through us when we are willing to die to our self-will. This is a great challenge—enough to make any sensible person run away fast! However, if you truly love the Lord, and are committed to becoming His disciple, then there will be times in your faith walk when you will suffer death in many areas of your life. Too many preachers and teachers avoid the message of the cross and the personal cost. They teach that Jesus paid the full price for the believer, and therefore, we do not have to suffer. This is only a partial truth. Jesus did pay the price for our sins, but every believer has a cross to bear as they walk out their salvation to completion (Philippians 2:12). Such preaching is pulling many away from the cross and the crucified life. This is a betrayal of Jesus, who said, "If any man will come after me, let him deny himself, and take up his cross, and follow me" (Matthew 16:24).

About thirty years ago I discovered Roy Hession's book, "Calvary Road," which changed my life after reading it through several times. "Calvary Road" spells out the cost of discipleship in no uncertain terms. It is wrong to believe that we can just pray to be like Jesus and expect it to happen. We only reflect His image when we take up our cross and follow Him. Fear of the unknown holds back many believers from taking up their cross. It is natural to shudder at the thought of suffering, but the Word of God gives us this assurance:

> No temptation has overtaken you except such as is common to man; but God is faithful, who will not allow you to be tempted beyond what you are able, but with the temptation will also make the way of escape, that you may be able to bear it (1 Corinthians 10:13).

Christ is the Good Shepherd, and He knows how to care for His sheep (John 10:6-15). The many trials we go through make us humble; they strengthen and fortify our faith and confidence in Him. For instance, patience is a by-product of tribulation (James 1:2-8). The refiner's fire will expose and purge any impurities within the heart: pride, bitterness, resentment, anger, greed, and impure motives must be removed. When we are willing to withstand the fiery furnace then trials bring us forth as precious gold, so we are worthy of being used as God's conduits in this earth. The Lord only chooses vessels that will be steadfast. Just 300 courageous, God-fearing soldiers were chosen out of Gideon's army of 3,000. The Holy Spirit could see into the hearts of those who would not shrink back in the heat of the battle. They were already refined by the fire of God in their personal lives. And so it is with Christ's disciples who are representative of Gideon's army, who were handpicked by the Lord Himself.

In Matthew 28:18-20, Jesus Christ commanded His followers, ".....Go and make disciples of all nations, baptizing them in the name of the Father and of the Son and of the Holy Spirit, teaching them to observe all things that I have commanded you; and lo, I am with you always, even to the end of the age." Amen." Yet the Church in America has demonstrated a vacuum in producing disciples. Most Christians do not know what discipleship means. More pastors need to involve their congregations in training up disciples after the teachings of Jesus Christ.

Faith and Obedience are Inseparable

> Now faith is the substance of things hoped for, the evidence of things not seen (Hebrews 11:1).

Walking with a *burning faith* changes our perspective on life and eternity. For instance, Abraham was not poor but wealthy, yet, by faith he lived in a tent. Abraham was not a vagabond without a home; he viewed himself as a pilgrim headed home. It takes faith to launch out and start life over:

> By faith Abraham obeyed when he was called to go out to the place which he would receive as an inheritance. And he went out, not knowing where he was going (Hebrews 11:8).

Abraham serves as an example to all of God's people who should recognize that they are pilgrims traveling through this world on their way to their heavenly home. Trust and obedience develop into loyalty and devotion, which equate into a faith that says, ".....But as for me and my house, we will serve the Lord" (Joshua 24:15). For the New Testament believer, *burning faith* includes obedience to Jesus Christ and His Word. Faith in Christ involves repentance; turning from sin with true sorrow, and accepting salvation through the blood atonement. Faith without works is dead:

> What does it profit, my brethren, if someone says he has faith but does not have works? Can faith save him? (James 2:14).

The Apostle James was speaking to those in the Church who professed faith in Christ and His blood atonement, yet they believed this was all that was necessary for salvation. James says that such faith is dead and will not produce salvation and an obedient relationship with Christ as Lord. The grace of God, the indwelling Holy Spirit, and the intercession of Christ (Hebrews 7:25) work in our lives to enable us to walk by faith. "The just shall live by faith" (Romans 1:17). Faith will die if we do not rely on God's grace and the leading of the Holy Spirit. God has a divine plan and purpose for each believer's life, and we need the Baptism of Fire to walk out His Will.

When Faith Fails!

The Bible reveals that many of God's greats were overwhelmed by adverse situations, and their faith failed. For example, the great Prophet Elijah ran for his life after killing 450 prophets of Baal at Mount Carmel. King Ahab and Queen Jezebel had massacred the prophets of the LORD and now Jezebel was seeking to kill Elijah who took refuge in a cave. The voice of God called out to him:

> What are you doing here, Elijah?" So he said, "I have been very zealous for the Lord God of hosts; for the children of Israel have forsaken Your covenant, torn down Your altars, and killed Your prophets with the sword. I alone am left; and they seek to take my life" (1 Kings 19:14).
>
> Then the Lord answered Elijah: "Yet I have reserved seven thousand in Israel, all whose knees have not bowed to Baal, and every mouth that has not kissed him" (v. 18).

Another example is Joseph, and how severely his faith was tested! *Yahweh* had given Joseph dreams about his future, but they did not include being thrown into a pit by his jealous brothers, and then being sold to a slave caravan headed for Egypt. I have always been amazed how the Lord does not show us the severe trials that precede the fulfillment of His splendid promises. This is the reality: The greater our dream for God's work, the larger our trial. The truth is, drastic faith will throw us into a pit almost every time. Have you been saying, "Lord, I will gladly go wherever You want me to go"? Perhaps you are one of those who are crying out, "Lord, there has to be more to this walk. I don't just want to warm up a church pew. I offer myself as a living sacrifice, so I can impact Your Kingdom." When you desire to live a life that reflects God's glory, then expect to be tested almost beyond your limits. If we want God to use our lives, then we better prepare ourselves for trials and testing. However, here is the good news: We will see victory and can say what Joseph could testify to his brothers fifteen years later; when they came to Egypt during the seven-year famine:

> Do not be afraid, for am I in the place of God? But as for you, you meant evil against me; but God meant it for good, in order to bring it about as it is this day, to save many people alive (Genesis 50:19-20).

The writer of the Book of Hebrews tells us in chapter eleven that it is our faith that gives us the victory. This epistle was written to encourage all wavering Judaic believers to stand fast in their faith. Many were turning back to Judaism because of the extreme persecution and death of many Judaic Christians. This message is relevant to all Christians throughout the Church Age who need to be spared from apostasy in the end time. This epistle emphasizes that we all need to reach out to Christ with a consuming hunger, and thirst, which is the key to our victory. Another key is to never justify weakness, resist giving into it, and do not accept it as part of life. Christ's salvation tells us that He alone has the power to free us from sin's power, each time we fail Him. Repentance and the Cross mean that sin's bondage is broken. We are all weak children of God, needing the strength of Jesus. When we commit all to Him, then we will surely come forth as pure gold tried in the fire. Of course, we cannot sin willfully and expect to be exonerated endlessly:

> For if we sin willfully after we have received the knowledge of the truth, there no longer remains a sacrifice for sins, but a certain fearful expectation of judgment, and fiery indignation which will devour the adversaries (Hebrews 10:26-27).

Trusting Christ to become our strength is not an achievement, but rather a willingness to allow Christ's power to sustain us in difficult challenges. Leaning on the Lord gives us the ability to rise above suffering and trials. We most likely will not be delivered out of our trials, but Christ's strength will carry us through. So, let your faith arise and believe for Christ to be your sufficiency in every circumstance. Of course, such faith is only possible when we are anchored in the Word of God, which makes us steadfast because our trust is in Christ alone. The Apostle Paul testified:

> I can do all things through Christ who strengthens me (Philippians 4:13).

> The Prophet Isaiah spoke of what happens when we are willing to wait for the Lord to become our strength:

> But they that wait upon the Lord shall renew their strength; they shall mount up with wings as eagles; they shall run, and not be weary; and they shall walk, and not faint (Isaiah 40:31).

With renewed strength, we can run the spiritual race without tiring. We can walk steadily forward toward the goal without fainting when we encounter delays. We are able to rise above every difficulty like the eagle that soars into the sky high above the storm. Waiting on the Lord demands our trust, looking to Him as our source of help and grace. We are promised the strength of God to revive us in the midst of weakness. God promises that if we faithfully trust in Him, He will provide whatever we need to sustain us. The Apostle Peter explains:

> Blessed be the God and Father of our Lord Jesus Christ, who according to His abundant mercy has begotten us again to a living hope through the resurrection of Jesus Christ from the dead, to an inheritance incorruptible and undefiled and that does not fade away, reserved in heaven for you, who are kept by the power of God through faith for salvation ready to be revealed in the last time (1 Peter 1:3-5).

> The righteous shall live by faith; and if any man draw back, my soul shall have no pleasure in him (Hebrews 10:38).

The Amplified translation states: "if he draws back and shrinks in fear." We will never possess our inheritance by looking through blades of grass like grasshoppers! When one's spiritual life is dwarfed, then you stand as a helpless grasshopper running from giants.

> It is He who sits above the circle of the earth, and its inhabitants are like grasshoppers….. (Isaiah 40:22).

> Faith is the substance of things hoped for, as it was the substance of things which have come to pass; and it is the evidence of things not seen (Hebrews 11:1).

Faith and obedience are inseparable, just as unbelief and disobedience are inseparable:

- By faith Abraham obeyed God. The works by which Abraham was justified were not "deeds of the law," but works of faith and love for God.
- By faith Moses returned to Egypt and set God's people free.
- By faith Rahab the harlot helped the Hebrew spies search out Jericho.
- By faith David, Samson and Barak conquered kingdoms.

As I mentioned earlier, the Apostle James said, "Faith without works is dead" (James 2:20). The term "works" used here by James has a different meaning than it did for Paul in Romans 3:28, "it is by faith a man is justified and not by the works of the law." "Works" denotes our obligation to God and man which are commanded in

Scripture and must proceed from a sincere faith and desire to please Christ. This is faith at work. Paul teaches that "works" seek to gain merit and salvation by obeying the law rather than through repentance and faith in Christ. The grace of God, the indwelling Holy Spirit, and the intercession of Christ works in our lives to enable us to respond to God by faith. Faith is fruitless whenever we withdraw from being receptive to God's grace and the leading of the Holy Spirit.

Only Burning Faith Bears Fruit

I Am the true vine, and my Father is the laborer. Every branch in me that does not bear fruit, he cuts off; and the one that bears fruit, he prunes so that it may bring forth more fruit. –John 15:1-2

Jesus instructs His disciples on how to keep their faith and be fruitful: "Abide in Me, and I in you. As the branch cannot bear fruit of itself, unless it abides in the vine, neither can you, unless you abide in Me" (v. 4). The word "abide," means to stand for, or remain. Christ knew the disciples would be tempted to leave him, and return to the Law of Moses again. He tells them how necessary it was that they should continue to be steadfast to follow him, and to love one another. Christ was preparing them to endure in the midst of severe temptation. He did not want them to shrink back under persecution, and fall. When the Word becomes our constant guide, in our hearts and in our homes, then we are living in Christ, and He is ever-present with us. This is the benefit for those who abide in Him:

> If you remain with me, and my words remain with you, whatever you ask shall be done for you (v. 7).

Believers are branches of the vine, and Christ is the root of the vine. The root is hidden, and so our life is hidden with Christ; the root feeds the tree and distributes sap to the branches, so it will flourish and bear fruit. We cannot bear fruit without getting life from the vine, Jesus Christ. The failure to abide in Christ results in fruitlessness, removal from Christ, and destruction. When a branch breaks off, it dies without life from the vine. The Father is the gardener of the vineyard who will separate those who stop abiding in Christ. The branches that bear fruit the Father prunes so they might become more fruitful. He removes from their lives anything that would divert or hinder the vital life of Christ flowing into them.

The fruit of the Spirit is produced when we allow the Holy Spirit to purge the power of sin and the works of the flesh in our lives, so we can walk in fellowship with God. One of the signs of life on a tree is that it bears fruit. In John 15:1-8, Christ tells His disciples that they must be fruitful. We expect to see a vine bear grapes; likewise, we look for spiritual fruit in a Christian, which is a Christ-like temper and disposition, a Christ-like life and conversation, and a commitment to Christ-like devotions and witness. We must honor God and demonstrate the purity and power of the religion we profess; this is bearing fruit. The disciples are told to be fruitful in righteousness and good works.

Plans, goals, and ambitions must be reset to God's will by intentionally applying God's Word to your life. The Holy Spirit resides within the believer to help him resist evil and love what is righteous. With the help of the Holy Spirit, we can resist greed, selfishness, humanistic ideology, political maneuvering for power, envy, hate, revenge, impurity, filthy language, ungodly entertainment, sensuality, immodesty, immorality, drugs, alcohol, and worldly companions. Even so, the mind must be renewed so that a new way of living is attained. The Atonement provided for redemption from sin, but the mind (man's thinker) still needs to be conformed to God's way of thinking, which is achieved by reading and meditating on His Word. The Hebrew word for "meditate" denotes an active recitation, a repeating of God's word out loud; thus, they shall not depart from your mouth. *Yahweh* instructed Joshua:

> This Book of the Law shall not depart from your mouth, but you shall meditate in it day and night, that you may observe to do according to all that is written in it. For then you will make your way prosperous, and then you will have good success (Joshua 1:8).

When we remain close to Christ with our meditation and study of the Scriptures, then our prayers will line up with His will, and become more effectual. Those who make Christ their heart's delight will have their heart's desire. If we abide in Christ, we shall not want anything that is not good for us. When we abide in Christ and His Word, then our interest will be in securing God's favor. Disciples must show that they abide in his love because it is the love for the world that causes our love for Christ himself to grow cold. To sustain their love for him, they are told to keep his commandments:

> If you keep my commandments, you shall abide in my love. Christ states his own walk as an example: "Even as I have kept my Father's commandments, and abide in his love" (Joshua 1:10).

The believer's responsibility after salvation is to generate new life daily in the Holy Ghost; otherwise, he will eventually die. Jesus warned His disciples in John 15:6 that it is indeed possible for true believers to fail to abide in Him and be cast into an everlasting fire:

> If anyone does not abide in Me, he is cast out as a branch and is withered; and they gather them and throw them into the fire, and they are burned.

How do we know if we have the Fruit of the Spirit?

In John 15:8, Jesus said: "By this My Father is glorified, that you bear much fruit; so you will be My disciples." It pleases the Father when we bear fruit, and we are able to fulfill our mission in Christ. We are only able to bear fruit when there is nothing hindering the spirit of Christ from flowing through our life. Jesus gave us the key in verse three, "Now ye are clean through the word which I have spoken unto you." With our permission, the Word of God will bring light to every dark hidden thing. This purging removes all hindrances. The Scriptures reveal how the manifestation of the Spirit is given to every believer in order to benefit the Body of Christ. However, the gifts are a by-product of our prayer life. They also come forth after the "fruit of the Spirit" is developed in our spirit. To lack "the fruit of the Spirit" is to lack the fullness of the Spirit:

> But the fruit of the Spirit is love, joy, peace, longsuffering, kindness, goodness, faithfulness, gentleness, self-control. Against such there is no law. And those who are Christ's have crucified the flesh with its passions and desires. If we live in the Spirit, let us also walk in the Spirit. Let us not become conceited, provoking one another, envying one another (Galatians 5:22-26).

Scripture makes it clear; one must turn from all known sin and develop a daily reliance on the Holy Spirit if he is to walk in the fullness and the fruit of the Holy Spirit. Developing the fruit of the Spirit in your life will pave the way for the gifts of the Spirit for the gifts come through a sanctified spirit. The nine fruits of the Spirit are manifested in believers who walk in fellowship with the LORD, and are willing to allow the Spirit to sanctify their lives and destroy the power of sin, the works of the flesh. (Study: Romans 8:5-14; Ephesians 4:2-3; 5:9; Colossians 3:3:12-15; 2 Peter 1:4-9)

Each of the nine fruits of the Holy Spirit reflect the condition of the inner soul:

1. **Love** (agape) is not the romantic, sensual type of love seen on the big screen in Hollywood movies. It is the divine love that is "poured out in our hearts by the Holy Spirit who was given to us" (Romans 5:5). Agape love enables us to love mankind: the poor, the needy, and the outcast. It removes racial bigotry and jealousy. It is no respecter of persons (Acts 10:34).
   Agape love was missing in the church of Corinth. They were competitive and zealous for spiritual gifts, which is why Paul said in 1 Corinthians 13:1-3: "Though I speak with the tongues of men and of angels, but have not love, I have become sounding brass or a clanging cymbal. And though I have the gift of prophecy, and understand all mysteries and all knowledge, and though

I have all faith, so that I could remove mountains, but have not love, I am nothing. And though I bestow all my goods to feed the poor, and though I give my body to be burned, but have not love, it profits me nothing."
The Holy Spirit produces agape love, which helps us to love the whole Body of Christ. "Beloved, let us love one another: for love is of God….." (1 John 4:7). We learn more about this supernatural love in 1 Corinthians 13:4-7: "Love suffers long and is kind; love does not envy; love does not parade itself, is not puffed up; does not behave rudely, does not seek its own, is not provoked, thinks no evil; does not rejoice in iniquity, but rejoices in the truth; bears all things, believes all things, hopes all things, endures all things."

2. **Joy** is not the superficial happiness that springs from sports or television; for fleshly happiness, depends on self-satisfaction. Instead, this is the joy of the Lord, which gives strength and brings contentment in times of suffering, sorrow, and even death (Nehemiah 8:10). Peter said, it is a "joy unspeakable and full of glory" (1 Peter 1:8). Hebrews 12:2 speaks of Christ and His joy of saving men and of sitting at God's right hand: "…..Looking unto Jesus, the author and finisher of our faith, who for the joy that was set before Him endured the cross, despising the shame and has sat down at the right hand of the throne of God."
3. **Peace** also fills the minds and hearts of those who are Spirit-led. This is not the peace that accompanies salvation (Romans 5:1), but it is the "peace of God, which surpasses all understanding, will guard your hearts and minds through Christ Jesus" (Philippians 4:7). This peace produces a calm heart and mind in spite of every disturbance, or adverse condition and glorifies God before an unsaved world.
4. **Longsuffering** within a believer is a quality that only the Holy Spirit can produce. It is the opposite of impatience. It cannot be produced within our human nature; for it is the nature of the living God who described Himself to Moses as: "The Lord, the Lord God, merciful and gracious, longsuffering, and abounding in goodness and truth….." (Exodus 34:6). This is why *Yahweh* is called the God of a thousand chances Who gives countless opportunities for the unrighteous to be saved, for: "The Lord is not slack concerning His promise, as some count slackness, but is longsuffering toward us, not willing that any should perish but that all should come to repentance" (2 Peter 3:9). These same attributes are imparted into the believer's spirit from God the Father Who "…..Has delivered us from the power of darkness and conveyed us into the kingdom of the Son of His love, in whom we have redemption through His blood, the forgiveness of sins" (Colossians 1:13, 14).
5. **Gentleness** is a true gift from God, for "…..Wisdom that is from above is first pure, then peaceable, gentle, willing to yield, full of mercy and good fruits, without partiality and without hypocrisy. Now the fruit of righteousness is sown in peace by those who make peace" (James 3:17, 18). Backbiting,

fighting, complaining church members are ignorant of the Scripture, "and a servant of the Lord must not quarrel but be gentle to all, able to teach, patient, in humility correcting those who are in opposition, if God perhaps grants them repentance, so that they may know the truth, and that they may come to their senses and escape the snare of the devil, having been taken captive by him to do his will" (2 Timothy 2:24-26).

6. **Goodness** is produced at salvation and matures when the believer is filled with the Holy Spirit. However, it is the Holy Spirit within that produces real goodness toward others. Jesus said: "Why do you call Me good? No one is good but One, that is, God" (Luke18:19). The Apostle Paul said, "There is none righteous, no, not one; there is none who understands; there is none who seeks after God. They have all turned aside; they have together become unprofitable; there is none who does good, no, not one" (Romans 3:10-12).
7. **Faith** is essentially faithfulness. Speaking about *Yahweh*, Lamentations 3:23, states: "Through the Lord's mercies we are not consumed, because His compassions fail not. They are new every morning; great is Your faithfulness." This same faithfulness in a Christian becomes a daily reality. Believers should not be up and down spiritually. God's faithfulness, living within a Christian by the Spirit will make him faithful every day. "For in Him we live and move and have our being, as also some of your own poets have said, 'For we are also His offspring'" (Acts 17:28).
8. **Meekness** is the most difficult fruit to possess, for as soon as we think we have it, we have deceived ourselves. Since the flesh cannot generate meekness, then we must avoid the trap of pride, pretending to be more than we really are. Only the Holy Spirit can help us to walk in meekness as required by Scripture: "Therefore, as the elect of God, holy and beloved, put on tender mercies, kindness, humility, meekness, longsuffering; bearing with one another, and forgiving one another, if anyone has a complaint against another; even as Christ forgave you, so you also must do" (Colossians 3:12).
9. **Temperance** is self-control. God gives the gift of self-control to those who have the fullness of the Spirit. Since God demands a holy standard of life for His children, then He has also provided the means to produce it–"Walk in the Spirit, and you shall not fulfill the lust of the flesh. For the flesh lusts against the Spirit, and the Spirit against the flesh; and these are contrary to one another, so that you do not do the things that you wish. But if you are led by the Spirit, you are not under the law" (Galatians 5:16). The key is to seek the fruit instead of gifts. Gifts are for all, but the fruit may not be produced within those who "grieve the Holy Spirit of God" (Ephesians 4:30). Scripture instructs: "Do not quench the Spirit" (1 Thessalonians 5:19), and "Walk in the Spirit, and you shall not fulfill the lust of the flesh" (Galatians 5:16).

Building a Holy Character

> Redemption brings the Holy Spirit into our lives so that we can be transformed into His image: "If any man be in Christ, he is a new creature; old things are passed away; behold, all things are become new" (2 Corinthians 5:17).

We can only become a new creature with the help of the Holy Spirit, which is received in a measure at the time of salvation. Redemption delivers a person from the old life; however, it does not include deliverance from the human nature, which is a work of the Holy Spirit. This is why it is best for a person to be baptized in the Holy Spirit at the time of salvation. There are two steps that help a new Christian walk out his salvation: Baptism in water and the Baptism of the Holy Spirit. Being baptized in water buries the old nature and the Baptism of Fire brings the fullness of the Spirit (Acts 1:8). Baptism in water is following Christ's obedience to be baptized, even though He did not have a sinful nature. Transforming the natural life into a spiritual life also requires the individual's cooperation; in making the correct moral choices. God does not make one holy in the sense of character through the gift of eternal life, which delivers a person out of darkness, and brings them into the light. A holy character is developed through applying biblical principles in our choices. Mindsets from our old natural life must be demolished by the Word of God; so the glory of God can be exalted through us. Old habits have been formed within the human nature which must be abandoned with the help and strength imparted by God's Spirit. Our warfare is not against sin. The Atonement of Jesus Christ dealt with sin through Redemption, but the first step in moving toward holiness is to move out of our old thinking:

> For though we walk in the flesh, we do not war according to the flesh. For the weapons of our warfare are not carnal but mighty in God for pulling down strongholds, casting down arguments and every high thing that exalts itself against the knowledge of God, bringing every thought into captivity to the obedience of Christ, and being ready to punish all disobedience when your obedience is fulfilled (2 Corinthians 10:3-6).

Our reasoning is darkened until it is enlightened by God's word and then the Holy Spirit can guide us. Rather than relying on your personal judgment, pray for God's wisdom and will in all your decisions. Otherwise, you are limiting God with your own thinking. When we live in close relationship to the Lord for His counsel; God promises to direct all our paths and lead us into His will for every area of our life. This also allows Him to remove all obstacles, so we can make the right choices.

Forming these habits will give you a firm foundation for developing a Holy Character:

1. Keep God's Word continually before your mind and within your heart.
2. Keep in close communion with Christ in order to draw strength and grace from Him.
3. Keep His commandments by abiding in His love, and loving one another.
4. Keep your life clean through the Word, resisting all sin, and yielding to the direction of the Holy Spirit.
5. The firmest foundation is when we allow the Lord to break our hearts. "The sacrifices of God are a broken spirit, A broken and a contrite heart—'These, O God, You will not despise'" (Isaiah 51:17).

Revealing False Images of God

God is who He says He is, not whom we think He is. When we pray to God according to how we perceive Him to be; we envision a God that is smaller than He really is, and not as He has revealed Himself to be in the Word. We are praying to an image of our own thinking. Oftentimes, Christians fantasize God through their pastor and idolize a man instead of learning to revere the Almighty God. This is also done through hero worship toward superstar ministers. Christians do wrong to place these leaders on pedestals as false gods. It equals idolatry!

Praying with the revelation of who God is in Scripture will keep you from praying through an extension of your own darkened mind. Your faith will reach a whole new spiritual level when you repeatedly pray with the revelation of God as revealed in the Bible. Your faith will take on prophetic proportions as you see through the Word of God that a different world exists beyond the terrestrial earth on which we live. The Bible shows many times when God supernaturally made Himself known to men and women. By studying these, we see how intricately God is involved in the affairs of His created, and how much He desires to direct their path. This knowledge of God's nature leads the saints into developing intimacy and communion with the Son of God as savior.

Faith Brings Heaven to Earth

In Job 1:6 and 1 Kings 22:19-22, we learn that *Yahweh* has a heavenly council that convenes to discuss affairs on earth. There are multiple ranks of angels with magnificent powers, who surround God in heaven. All of these awesome beings have the capacity for independent thought and action. They offer their counsel and volunteer for service. They exist in a host of distinct levels with different functions, beauties and strengths. In Daniel, chapter 10, we learn how this other world intersects with our world; how it impacts it, moves it, changes it and communicates with it. The greatest holy men of history had personal encounters with Almighty God, or the glorified Christ with their eyes and wrote down what they saw. Studying these accounts of "divine encounters" gives the believer a new revelation of who He is. These encounters were experienced by Moses in Exodus chapters 24 and 34; Isaiah in chapter 6; Ezekiel in chapters 1 and 10; Daniel in chapters 7 and 10; Peter in Matthew, chapter 17; John in Revelation chapters 1, 4, 9, 21.

The occurrences recorded in Scripture show us glimpses of where God lives and who is around Him and, to some extent, what He is doing. For instance, God walked and talked with Adam and Eve in the cool of the day in the garden (Genesis 3:8). He visited Abraham as one of three traveling strangers (Genesis 18:1, 13). He showed himself as an awesome King to Isaiah (Isaiah 6:1-4). Jacob saw a ladder from heaven to earth, with angels descending and ascending, and the Lord standing above it (Genesis 28:10-22). In each example, the people who witnessed these things experienced the reality of the Divine One up close and personal. They then prayed to God as He had revealed Himself. That is why these revelations from the Word of God are vital to your prayer life today, so you can also pray to God as He has revealed Himself.

The promise of God's power coming to live in his sin-bound people was prophesied by Ezekiel: "Then will I sprinkle clean water upon you, and ye shall be clean: from all your filthiness, and from all your idols, will I cleanse you. A new heart also will I give you, and a new spirit will I put within you: and I will take away the stony heart out of your flesh, and I will give you an heart of flesh" (Ezekiel 36:25-27). The vision God gave Ezekiel of the dry bones, was an illustration of what He would do. God was telling Ezekiel that He will put His very own Spirit within sin-bound people. And His Spirit will cause them to fulfill every command He gives them. They are dead to any ability to overcome, but God's Spirit is going to empower them to turn away from their sin. Jesus fulfilled Ezekiel's prophecy of God's spirit living within mankind with His New Covenant.

In Ezekiel 37:9-10, the prophet was told to prophesy to the wind, the Holy Ghost: "Also He said to me, 'Prophesy to the breath, prophesy, son of man, and say to the breath, thus says the Lord God: 'Come from the four winds, O breath, and breathe on these slain, that they may live."' Since the Holy Spirit was under oath to fulfill God's Word, the prophet spoke the word of the Almighty God. This is what happens when believers under Christ's New Covenant speak God's Word to the Holy Spirit.

Faith Sees Through the Eyes of the Holy Spirit

> And Elisha prayed, and said, Lord, I pray thee, open his eyes, that he may see. And the Lord opened the eyes of the young man; and he saw: and, behold, the mountain was full of horses and chariots of fire round about Elisha (2 Kings 6:17).

We gain a deeper understanding of the eternal God when examining the visions of Daniel. For instance, in Daniel 7:9-10, God appears to him as the "Ancient of Days" sitting on His throne, judging in a courtroom setting. In verse 13, God appeared to Daniel as the "one like a son of man." Daniel was a monotheist who only knew "The Lord our God, the Lord is one!" (Deuteronomy 6:4). Daniel says in 12:8, "Although I heard, I did not understand." Such examples in Scripture show us that God is not just removed and far off but close and personal. Your relationship with God will change when you familiarize yourself with the descriptions of heaven in the Word, and you will understand just who it is you are talking to. You can have confidence in recognizing that when you are addressing the sovereign God Almighty, who has all the power to answer prayer; He is also your Abba Father Who wants to hear your need. Intimacy and communion flow as the Holy Spirit brings you closer to the Father and the Son, and then you will begin to discern that still small voice within your spirit as Elijah did:

> Then He said, "Go out, and stand on the mountain before the Lord." And behold, the Lord passed by, and a great and strong wind tore into the mountains and broke the rocks in pieces before the Lord, but the Lord was not in the wind; and after the wind an earthquake, but the Lord was not in the earthquake; and after the earthquake a fire, but the Lord was not in the fire; and after the fire a still small voice" (1 Kings 19:11-12).

Yeshua Gives the Believer a Personal Relationship with God

Jesus modeled a relationship with *Yahweh* that was radical for His day. Up to that time, no one in history had ever addressed the Lord God Almighty in the way Jesus did. Devout Jews were afraid of even using God's name, *Y*, for fear of taking it in vain. Elaborate systems were set up so Jews could refer to *YHWH* (or *Yahweh*) without actually saying His name. Rather than pronounce the sacred name, Jews would say, "Adonai," which means "my Lord." It was quite a shock for Jesus to address God as "Abba Pater" or "Dear Daddy" (Mark 14:36). Never had a Jew addressed God in such a familiar way. Jesus was opening the door to a higher degree of intimacy when He instructed His disciples to pray, "Our Father in heaven" (Mark 6:9). Jesus introduced a closer relationship with God, one between a father and his child; which gives all believers intimacy with God as His children. We also glorify the Father when we walk in the revelation of being one with the Father and Son:

> And the glory which You gave Me I have given them, that they may be one just as We are one: I in them, and You in Me; that they may be made perfect in one, and that the world may know that You have sent Me, and have loved them as You have loved Me (John 17:22).

Therefore, we too should glorify the Father with our lives as Jesus did with His (John 17:1). All believers can pray with the same boldness that Jesus did in John, chapter 17, when He prayed for His Church. Jesus is our model and example. The Apostle Peter said, "To this you were called, because Christ suffered for you, leaving you an example, that you should follow in his steps" (1 Peter 2:21). The life of Christ is the pattern for our lives.

What was Jesus praying for His Church in John, chapter 17?

- He prayed to be glorified so He may glorify the Father (John 17:1-5).
- He prayed for His disciples to be protected and united (John 17:11-12).
- He prayed for joy in the midst of a hostile world (John 17:13-16).
- He prayed for practical holiness grown by the Word of truth (John 17:17-19).
- He prayed for God's Will to be done (Matthew 26:39-42; Luke 22:44).
- He prayed to forgive His enemies (Matthew 27:46; Luke 23:33-34, 46).

Christ prayed that His disciples would have the identical oneness that He has with the Father. They share the like purpose, plan, and power: "For I have come down from heaven, not to do My own will, but the will of Him who sent Me" (John 6:38). Likewise, our unity is dependent on sharing the priority of seeking and doing the Lord's will. Our desire should be the same as Christ, to glorify the Father, who will not share His glory with another (Isaiah 42:8). We must not take this responsibility lightly and should always consider what God requires. If we get in God's way, we face disqualifying ourselves; or even worse, we bring chastisement upon ourselves and/or our family.

Faith Glorifies God in Your Life

When we reflect His Glory, He will choose to use us as His instrument. Believers are called to sacrifice the members of their bodies for His service. Believers are called to sacrifice the members of their bodies for His service by living a life of holiness, acceptable unto God. This requires forsaking the principles of the world and adopting God's biblical perspective. This means giving up those social activities that steal the time we should be spending with God. "Abraham believed God, and it was accounted to him for righteousness" (Romans 4:3). He was called to leave his decadent, idolatrous culture and start a new nation of people that would worship the One True Living God. Abraham's life is an example of faith being tested by fire; which deepened his devotion to the God of Heaven and Earth. He maintained a loyal and devoted commitment to his God by believing in His promises and responding with obedience.

When we thirst after God's Presence, the Holy Spirit moves us into the "secret place of the Most High." This is more than spending time "reflecting" on His

Presence; it is "entering" into His Presence. The Holy Spirit works to strengthen the inner man, so we can be grounded in sincere love for God. Fear must be conquered because it hinders our love for Christ. Drawing closer to Jesus is what removes fear from our lives:

> There is no fear in love; but perfect love casts out fear, because fear involves torment. But he who fears has not been made perfect in love. We love Him because He first loved us (1 John 4:18-19).

A Surrendered Life is the Highest Offering to God

The act of consecrating our lives to God is the act of becoming a living sacrifice on the altar of surrender. If you truly want to be used as God's instrument, then you will need a passion to see God's will to be done in your life. Outward expressions of spirituality do not always mean we are ready to be used of God; however, we are developing an intimate relationship with the Father, Jesus the Son and the Holy Ghost. When we are victorious in our hearts, minds, and emotions, then we are led into victory from the inside out. Many step into the ministry without developing this inside relationship, and without developing the right foundation; they fall away from their first love and enter into the bondage of works. Unfortunately, many will watch their works burn up when they are tested at the judgment day of Christ:

> For no other foundation can anyone lay than that which is laid, which is Jesus Christ. Now if anyone builds on this foundation with gold, silver, precious stones, wood, hay, straw, each one's work will become clear; for the Day will declare it, because it will be revealed by fire; and the fire will test each one's work, of what sort it is. If anyone's work which he has built on it endures, he will receive a reward. If anyone's work is burned, he will suffer loss; but he himself will be saved, yet so as through fire (1 Corinthians 3:11-15).

The First Thing we must Surrender is our Mind

We cannot surrender our lives until we win the battle for the mind. Earlier, I introduced the need for renewing our mind with the Word of God, since the battle for the mind is spiritual. Being born-again is not enough to experience a complete transformation of the mind. There are spiritual strongholds over the mind that have built a fortress which struggles against your freedom. There are mindsets of poverty, sickness, abuse, low esteem, self-pity and intimidation. Psychiatrists have determined that some people have darkened minds; causing them to think and do evil. Pedophiles, rapists, murderers, and terrorists are definitely influenced by a veil of darkness over their conscience. Such people are usually beyond rehabilitation;

unless they experience a miraculous transformation by the Holy Spirit, which delivers them from Satan's hold on their psyche. Jesus demonstrated this when He delivered the demoniac of the Gadarenes (Mark 5:1-20).

Carnal believers in Christ often do evil deeds because a darkened area still remains within their mind; deep where the conscience is buried. This type of Christian commits unconscionable sin. It is not as bad as being reprobate, but it is a sinful way of life, and very un-Christ-like. We often marvel at how a Christian could act with such ill behavior, or thinking. The Apostle Paul describes the unsanctified human nature's struggle with the law of sin:

> I find then a law, that evil is present with me, the one who wills to do good. For I delight in the law of God according to the inward man. But I see another law in my members, warring against the law of my mind, and bringing me into captivity to the law of sin which is in my members. O wretched man that I am! Who will deliver me from this body of death? I thank God—through Jesus Christ our Lord! So then, with the mind I myself serve the law of God, but with the flesh the law of sin (Romans 7:21-25).
>
> And this is God's response to the sanctified believer: "There is therefore now no condemnation to those who are in Christ Jesus, who do not walk according to the flesh, but according to the Spirit. For the law of the Spirit of life in Christ Jesus has made me free from the law of sin and death" (Romans 8:1-2).

The battle for the mind is the greatest challenge for our spiritual life! Only the Word of God and the Holy Spirit can penetrate the hidden darkness within a person's mind and spirit. Even after one is born-again, a believer still has old areas of carnality that need to be demolished. As long as the understanding is darkened; that individual is blocked from discerning the truth. Darkness within the understanding distorts any spiritual awareness from breaking through. There is a place of darkness in everyone's soul, which needs to be filled up with the Word of God. Many times believers cannot understand why resentment, fear, discouragement, rage, lust and depression arise from within their inner man and control their behavior. These are areas that need to be surrendered and sanctified. Once a Christian experiences sanctification that does not mean they will never make a mistake again; only they can take comfort that God's grace is available when we fall short of the glory of God (Romans 3:23). Until we are delivered of the sin nature within, no one escapes the temptation to sin:

> "For to be carnally minded is death, but to be spiritually minded is life and peace. Because the carnal mind is enmity against God; for

> it is not subject to the law of God, nor indeed can be. So then, those who are in the flesh cannot please God" (Romans 8:6-8).

The Word of God is the only light that will transform any darkness within the human spirit. Satan seeks to inhabit the darkness of a person's understanding, so he can control the emotions and the will of the human nature. When the eyes of our understanding are enlightened, we are able to discern and determine what is right or wrong. Peter describes Scripture as a "light that shines in a dark place" (2 Peter 1:19). The Word of God turns a light on in the understanding so revelation, wisdom and true knowledge can be received. You most likely have loved ones who need to have a veil removed from their understanding so the light can transform their thinking. Make Isaiah 11:2-3 a prayer request, asking the Holy Spirit for the sevenfold spirit to come into your life, and others you are praying for. This is a prophetic act of standing in the gap; to help enlighten their way of thinking, which ultimately affects their actions.

The Battle for the Intellect is Endless

The 21st Century has appropriately been called the Age of Information. If we are not careful, the knowledge within our mind will exalt itself against the (true) knowledge of God. We must continually surrender our thinking and submit ourselves to the thoughts of the Holy Spirit. Every idea and purpose must lead us to the obedience of Jesus Christ, the Messiah. Our mind must not get in the way of hearing the Holy Spirit's commands (2 Corinthians 10:5). I tell some people to stop thinking; their mind is running like a train racing down a railroad track. Until we are dead to self; our life is controlled by carnal thoughts. Repent of those thoughts that exalt themselves against the knowledge of God. It takes a lot of dying to the flesh to come under the influence of the Holy Ghost. In Romans, chapter eight, the Apostle Paul taught that we can bypass the intellect when we pray in tongues; which is the heavenly language received with the Baptism of the Holy Spirit:

> Likewise the Spirit also helps in our weaknesses. For we do not know what we should pray for as we ought, but the Spirit Himself makes intercession for us with groanings which cannot be uttered. Now He who searches the hearts knows what the mind of the Spirit is, because He makes intercession for the saints according to the will of God (Romans 8:26, 27).

How do we Bring Carnal Emotions under Control?

Your life will change when you change your thinking! You are what you think; so, get out of your own way. The author of Proverbs gives a powerful key for controlling our thoughts:

> Trust in the Lord with all your heart, and lean not on your own understanding; in all your ways acknowledge Him, and He shall direct your paths (Proverbs 3:5-6).

Masses of people are addicted to their past emotions, and many of them suffer from depression; becoming captive to their past or a present disappointment. Many Christians even re-enact and rehearse guilt or disappointment every day of their lives. This can be overcome by applying the Word of God to all emotional thoughts, which will speak hope into the inner man. Jesus said, "No man, having put his hand to the plough, and looking back, is fit for the kingdom of God" (Luke 9:62). Instead of rehearsing the past, each day, we should renew our mind with the Word of God. When we submit to Christ's lordship, then we renew our mental and physical ability. At times, people who are amazed at my accomplishments, have called me a superwoman. My answer is this: I lean upon Jesus, Who has become my strength!

God has given us a free will to choose, and we can choose how we think. The brain is a muscle, and the mind is your soul; your thinker. In disciplining myself to ward off wrong thoughts, I declare: I'm not going to go there! And, the battle begins. Your flesh will fight against your spirit; however, the spirit will win with the help of the Holy Spirit. Romans 6:13-14 instructs:

> And do not present your members as instruments of unrighteousness to sin, but present yourselves to God as being alive from the dead, and your members as instruments of righteousness to God. For sin shall not have dominion over you, for you are not under law but under grace.

Our body hears every thought in our mind, and this is why we become what we believe. The Apostle Paul explains: "So then faith comes by hearing, and hearing by the word of God" (Romans 10:17). The Word of God will change our thoughts and bring discipline to the flesh when we obey the Word of God: "But be doers of the word, and not hearers only, deceiving yourselves" (James 1:22). The Word helps us to make the right choices and take responsibility, as Paul instructed in 2 Corinthians 10:4-6:

> For the weapons of our warfare are not carnal but mighty in God for pulling down strongholds, casting down arguments and every high thing that exalts itself against the knowledge of God, bringing every thought into captivity to the obedience of Christ, and being ready to punish all disobedience when your obedience is fulfilled.

Through faith in Christ, we receive not only mercy and forgiveness, but also the power and freedom to obey the law of God (Romans 3:31). God's moral laws are not abolished by the gospel of Christ. Christ obeyed the Law for us and died to pay the penalty for our breaking the Law. The Apostle James explains that the Word of God is the perfect law of liberty: "But he who looks into the perfect law of liberty and continues in it, and is not a forgetful hearer but a doer of the work, this one will be blessed in what he does" (James 1:25). Liberty must never be mistaken to be a privilege to violate the commandments of Christ, but rather the freedom and power to obey them.

Opening the Eyes of our Understanding

> .....That the God of our Lord Jesus Christ, the Father of glory, may give to you the spirit of wisdom and revelation in the knowledge of Him, the eyes of your understanding being enlightened; that you may know what is the hope of His calling, what are the riches of the glory of His inheritance in the saints..... (Ephesians 1:17-19).

The Apostle Paul explains, there is a darkened area of the mind, which has veils covering it. He calls it the "eyes of your understanding." Only the Word of God and the Holy Spirit can do the supernatural work of removing veils. Unquestionably, some people have enlightened minds, and some have darkened minds. The Holy Spirit draws a soul to salvation, at which time a veil is removed from their eyes, and the means to enlightenment begins. Jesus taught that the eye is the lamp of the body:

> The lamp of your body is your eye; when therefore your eye is bright, your whole body will also be lighted; but if it is diseased, your whole body will also be dark. Take heed, therefore, lest the light which is in you be darkness. If your whole body is lighted and there is no part in it dark, the whole of it will give light, just as a lamp gives you light with its shining (Luke 11:34-36).

When the heart is so very hardened, the ears are dull of hearing; they cannot hear the gentle whispers of the Holy Spirit; even the loud calls of the Word. Although the Word of God is available for these hard-hearted souls, they reject it by "shutting up their ears." Jesus made this observation of a sinners' willful blindness and hardness:

> For the heart of this people has become hardened, and they hear with difficulty, and their eyes are dull; so that they cannot see with their eyes and hear with their ears and understand with their hearts; let them return, and I will heal them (Matthew 13:15).

Pharaoh willingly hardened his own heart (Exodus 8:15, 32), and afterwards God hardened it (Exodus 9:12; 10:20). We should fear sinning against the divine grace of God and hardening our heart against His Word. It is not enough to hear the gospel message; it also needs to reach our inner heart so the transformation can happen. It is vital that we respond with repentance to the Holy Spirit's conviction. God will take away the light from those who shut their eyes against it; allowing them to live in ignorance. When the evil heart of man embraces secret sin, the righteous hand of God will inflict chastisement to work purification.

Scripture says, they ".....Loved darkness rather than light, because their deeds were evil" (John 3:19). However, there is good news for those who have an ear to hear: "But as for you, blessed are your eyes, for they see; and your ears, for they hear" (Matthew 13:16). God's grace changes the heart by opening the eyes, and turning the sinner ".....From the power of Satan to God, and from darkness to light" (Acts 26:18). Seeing, hearing, and understanding are signs of conversion; for the unredeemed person is blinded by Satan of their lost and perishing condition. Only preaching the gospel of Christ Jesus, in the power of the Holy Spirit, will open their understanding. All those without Christ come under Satan's control and are enslaved to his power. Scripture speaks of Satan's spirit at work in the "children of disobedience" (Ephesians 2:2). Only preaching the gospel, empowered by the Spirit, will deliver a soul from Satan's captivity and bring them into the Kingdom of God.

Unveiling the Mind and Heart

The Holy Spirit releases revelation to our mind once we practice living according to His Word. James 1:8 says, "A double minded man is unstable in all his ways." How can we know if we are double minded? Ask yourself this question: Do my present circumstances control my life, or do I trust God's Word as the truth in my life? God has promised to write His Word on our heart and mind, ".....Not on tablets of stone but on tablets of flesh, that is, of the heart" (2 Corinthians 3:3). This is only possible by the Spirit of the living God. Our spiritual heart becomes strong and healthy when we feed on God's Holy Scripture. The opposite is also true. Our spiritual heart dies and grows weak and sick without feeding on God's Word. True prayer, fasting, meditation on the Scripture, and obedience train our hearts; and then, we can freely receive God's revelation. How?

> But He answered and said, "It is written, 'Man shall not live by bread alone, but by every word that proceeds from the mouth of God'" (Matthew 4:4).

> This is the covenant that I will make with them after those days, says the Lord: I will put My laws into their hearts, and in their minds I will write them..... (Hebrews 10:16).

In regard to the salvation of a soul, Jesus Christ, our High Priest, is the only one that can go beyond the veil of a person's body, soul and spirit. The Word of God is the spirit of truth that will lift the veil. A soul cannot be born-again until the veil of darkness is lifted by the Holy Spirit. Only the Holy Spirit can bring light to the dark cells of our carnal mind. No one can walk in the spirit consistently without a continual unveiling of the carnal areas of the flesh. For example, the Jewish people can only come to know Christ as their Messiah when the veil of darkness and spiritual blindness are removed.

> But their minds were blinded. For until this day the same veil remains unlifted in the reading of the Old Testament because the veil is taken away in Christ (2 Corinthians 3:14).

Since veils are strongholds over a person's life, then unveiling the hidden darkness within a soul requires the revelation and supernatural work of the Holy Spirit. In the Old Testament, we see that the tabernacle had an inner room called the Holy of Holies. A thick curtain, known as the veil, stood before the Holy of Holies, and only the sanctified High Priest could go beyond the veil and enter the Holy of Holies. Ordinary man was barred from entering the Holy of Holies into the presence of God. When Jesus died on the Cross, there was an earthquake and the veil of the temple was torn in half. The renting of the veil signified the way was now opened to enter into the presence of the Father. With the sacrificial death of Jesus Christ, the curtain was removed; the way into the holiest place of God's presence was opened for all who believe in Christ and His saving word (Hebrews 9:1-14).

Scripture describes three types of veils:

1. Veils over the unbeliever: 2 Corinthians 4:3-4, tells us about the veils over the understanding of the unbeliever. They are the people we just described who live in total darkness.
2. Veils over Jewish people: 2 Corinthians 3:13-16 and Romans 11:7-8, explains the veils over the eyes of the Jewish people.
3. Veils over carnal Christian: Romans 8:5-8, describes the veils over the carnal believer (a Christian, who takes comfort in his natural, human nature).

The Apostle Paul instructs the believer how to get the victory over these veils in 2 Corinthians 10:3-6:

> For though we walk in the flesh, we do not war according to the flesh. For the weapons of our warfare are not carnal but mighty in God for pulling down strongholds, casting down arguments and every high thing that exalts itself against the knowledge of God, bringing every

> thought into captivity to the obedience of Christ, and being ready to punish all disobedience when your obedience is fulfilled.

Intense intercession is necessary when praying for others to be set free from strongholds that have been set up in their mind. Praying Scripture for them will demolish any strongholds that have taken their mind captive. This is not to be confused with mind control or manipulation, as long as the intercessor is reliant on the Word and the Holy Spirit to achieve it. When the Word of God is spoken, this becomes the powerful labor of spiritual warfare, and the King's scepter of power will set the captives free. Here are a few keys on how the believer can walk in victory:

1. There are certain veils over the mind that must be surrendered:

a. Imaginations: Reasoning, logic, and natural wisdom (2 Corinthians 10:5).
b. Pride: It exalts itself against the knowledge of God (1 John 2:16).
c. Temptations: Submit to God and resist the devil (James 4:7).
d. Thoughts: Taken captive by declaring the Word of God. (Proverbs 3:5-6)

Spiritual veils can be canceled with the Word of God and permanently removed with the help of the Holy Spirit. Strongholds that hold on to the imaginations are selfish, prideful, vain thoughts. The Word admonishes us to resist these carnal ways and submit to God's ways. A stronghold is a fortified position Satan seeks to attach and exalt himself against the knowledge and the purposes of God. Satan builds strongholds with the purpose of binding people from the truth of the gospel (2 Corinthians 4:3-4). The battleground for the souls of men is primarily the mind. Satan gains control over people through sin, traumatic experiences and thought patterns. We have been given weapons mighty through God for pulling down these strongholds; they are, authority in the Name of Jesus Christ and power with the Blood of the Lamb! (Matthew 26:36-44; Revelation 12:11)

2. Jesus must become Lord over every area of our life:

Lordship is a process! Obedience is indeed an ongoing condition for salvation, and it is also a "grace" for entering God's kingdom. The only way to escape being deceived is to be totally committed to the truth in God's Word. The temptation to succeed in ministry must be avoided at all cost. Success is a blessing which comes through our personal relationship to Christ; but when it is acquired with wrong motives, it is possible to miss the benefits of God's grace:

> Not everyone who says to Me, "Lord, Lord," shall enter the kingdom of heaven, but he who does the will of My Father in heaven. Many will say to Me in that day, "Lord, Lord, have we not prophesied in

> Your name, cast out demons in Your name, and done many wonders in Your name?" And then I will declare to them, "I never knew you; depart from Me, you who practice lawlessness!"

3. We are to pursue holiness first:

A person might boast in wisdom, strength, or wealth, and although useful, these things are just temporary. Only knowing and understanding God will produce any life-changing eternal value. The challenge of holiness is to walk in God's ways in the midst of both overt and subtle pressures to sin. Even when the sin appears to be major or trivial, we are enabled to resist and walk in holiness by the grace and power of God. In all our decisions, God calls us to remain faithful to walk in His ways. Hold to what you know is right, regardless of the circumstances. Godliness starts with redemption, the process in which God's grace and mercy bring about transformation: ".....Old things pass away, and new things come to pass; behold, all things have become new" (2 Corinthians 5:17). Our lives should reflect what kind of intimacy we have with Christ, for instance:

a. Know that the Lord loves you unconditionally.
b. Ask God to write His laws on your mind and heart.
c. Receive His forgiveness, recognizing that He removes your iniquity and sin.

4. Walk with the understanding that Jesus is the resurrection and the life!

Jesus healed the sick on many occasions and raised many from the dead. His own resurrection testifies to the fundamental truths of the gospel and verifies the accuracy of Scripture. Faith in Christ's identity as the Son of God is the key to experiencing spiritual authority here on earth. In John 11:25-26, Jesus said to Martha: "I am the resurrection and the life. He who believes in me will live, even though he dies, and whoever lives and believes in me will never die. Do you believe this?" We must comprehend the significance of the resurrection of Jesus from the dead.

During the early 1980s, I prayed for a woman that I found dead in her home. She had been addicted to drugs and alcohol, but after going through rehabilitation, she was now back home with her husband. We had been meeting to study the Bible, and her husband asked me to check on her at home while he was off on a business trip for several days. I visited her every day and on one, occasion, I found her on the kitchen floor, looking stiff and lifeless. When I checked her breathing and pulse, I could not find any sign of life; she looked like a dead holocaust victim lying there, with her limbs all twisted. I called for an ambulance and prayed for her while waiting for the medics to arrive. I prayed, asking the Lord Jesus to put life back into her dead bones and took authority over the spirit of death. After a few minutes of travailing prayer, I heard her give a sound like a death rattle as she began to struggle to breathe. The Holy Ghost was breathing new life back into this woman. Her eyes suddenly flew wide open, and she regained consciousness, but she could not move.

When the paramedics arrived, they concluded she was not going to make it this time. They had come for her on many other occasions, and one commented: "Well, Judy has done herself in this time!" She had overdosed on alcohol and prescription drugs, which were spread all over the kitchen counter. At the emergency room, they pumped her stomach, but it had been too many hours and all the chemicals had gone into her system. They put her in ICU where she remained unconscious. The doctors did not expect Judy to pull through, but I sat by her bedside praying the Word of God. After several hours, she suddenly opened her eyes and regained consciousness. She was now sober and alert. The resurrection power of God's Word woke up Judy, just like when Jesus was at the bedside of the young girl whom He woke up from the dead (Luke 8:26). When I explained to her what had happened, she understood God had spared her life, and she praised the Lord. I had led her in the sinner's prayer several months earlier, and she was growing in the Word, but with her husband out of the house, the enemy came in as a flood and tempted her. At the hospital, they were all amazed of her recovery, and she was released within 24 hours. Her husband came home and was grateful for the outcome. To God be the Glory!!

I had many similar experiences at home, and abroad—when the blind were healed, the lame walked, and the dead were resurrected several times. Let me add a little humor here: A stray dog showed up at our girl's youth ranch which suddenly died. The girls were extremely maternal with the animals at the ranch, and they called me to pray this dog back to life. They had seen me minister many miracles, and they were confident that I could resurrect this dog, which was now showing signs of "rigor mortis." Its muscles had stiffened up, and its legs were sticking out straight. Out of respect, I prayed a half-hearted prayer asking the Lord Jesus to resurrect the dog. To my utter surprise, the dog began breathing and woke up. The girls were jumping around rejoicing as the dog stood up very alive. It wasn't too long until the dog wandered off; however, the girls experienced one more miracle, building their faith in the resurrection power of Jesus Christ.

Ministry Offices and Gifts for the Church

> And he gave some, apostles; and some, prophets; and some, evangelists; and some, pastors and teachers.... (Ephesians 4:11).
>
> Paul states why these offices are given: "For the perfecting of the saints, for the work of the ministry, for the edifying of the body of Christ: Till we all come in the unity of the faith, and of the knowledge of the Son of God, unto a perfect man, unto the measure of the stature of the fullness of Christ..." (vv. 12-13).

These five ministry offices are gifts that Christ gave for the development and equipping of His Church. Paul teaches that these offices help unite the Body of Christ in the Holy Spirit. This is the oneness Jesus prayed for in John, chapter 17. When the leaders of the Church are united together a spiritual impartation occurs; they become one in the Spirit, a "Church without walls." This common slogan applies to the Church: "United we stand, divided we fall!" The Church is responsible for selecting godly and faithful leaders, so believers will be nourished in the words of faith and sound doctrine (1 Timothy 4:6-7). The Church must be taught to persevere in the teachings of Christ, and the apostles, ensuring redemption for itself and those who hear (1 Timothy 4:16).

Church leaders must protect the flock of God, regarding false doctrine and teachers who arise within the Church. They function as under-shepherds following the model of Jesus as the good Shepherd (John 10:11-16). This is the only way believers will grow in grace and advance toward spiritual maturity, being no longer children who accept every wind of doctrine; who instead, have knowledge of the truth by which to reject false teachers.

Faith Produces Personal Spiritual Gifts for the Believer

> In 1 Corinthians 12:7-11, the Apostle Paul lists a variety of the gifts that the Holy Spirit gives to believers: "But the manifestation of the Spirit is given to each one for the profit of all: for one is given the word of wisdom through the Spirit, to another the word of knowledge through the same Spirit, to another faith by the same Spirit, to another gifts of healings by the same Spirit, to another the working of miracles, to another prophecy, to another discerning of spirits, to another different kinds of tongues, to another the interpretation of tongues. But one and the same Spirit works all these things, distributing to each one individually as He wills."

The Holy Spirit is manifested through these gifts for the growth and sanctification of the Church. These are different from the five ministry offices which are also spiritual gifts mentioned in Ephesians chapter four, where a believer receives the power and ability to minister in a more official role in the Church. Scripture tells us that the believer should have a desire for more than one gift (1 Corinthians 12:31; 14:1). Spiritual gifts are imparted to believers who prove to be responsible, and numerous gifts are often present depending on the demand for certain situations like healing and deliverance. Spiritual gifts should be distinguished as being very different from the fruit of the Spirit which relates more directly to the development of Christian character and sanctification. Believers are expected to be fruitful, and develop a divine character:

> "But when the Holy Spirit controls our lives, he will produce this kind of fruit in us: love, joy, peace, patience, kindness, goodness, faithfulness, gentleness, and self-control. Here there is no conflict with the law. Those who belong to Christ Jesus have nailed the passions and desires of their sinful nature to his cross and crucified them there. If we are living now by the Holy Spirit, let us follow the Holy Spirit's leading in every part of our lives. Let us not become conceited, or irritate one another, or be jealous of one another" (Galatians 5:22-26).

The Greatest Gift

> Though I speak with the tongues of men and of angels, but have not love, I have become sounding brass or a clanging cymbal. And though I have the gift of prophecy, and understand all mysteries and all knowledge, and though I have all faith, so that I could remove mountains, but have not love, I am nothing. And though I bestow all my goods to feed the poor, and though I give my body to be burned, but have not love, it profits me nothing (1 Corinthians 13:1-3).

The Apostle Paul emphasizes that to possess spiritual gifts without having love amounts to nothing. Our deeds are just a fruitless religious activity. The more excellent way is the exercise of spiritual gifts in love. Love must be the governing principle of all spiritual manifestations. Believers must desire the things of the Spirit because they sincerely want to help, comfort, and bless others in this life. Unfortunately, over the decades, some have manifested the gifts of the Spirit in a showmanship manner, entertaining their audiences. I questioned the Holy Spirit about this a number of years ago while sitting in a meeting where this was being done. I received a quick answer: "Do not turn the manifestation of the gifts into a circus performance!" This meeting reminded me of the tumbling acts you see in a carnival performance.

Use Caution in Seeking Spiritual Gifts and Manifestations

Seeking the supernatural requires wisdom. Jesus addressed this issue by pointing out that His Father in heaven is the one who promotes. Matthew records how the mother of Zebedee's sons asked, "Grant that these two sons of mine may sit, one on Your right hand and the other on the left, in Your kingdom." Jesus answered, ".....But to sit on My right hand and on My left is not Mine to give, but it is for those for whom it is prepared by My Father" (Matthew 20:21-23). Subsequently, Peter was confronted by Simon the sorcerer in Samaria, who had earlier been converted, and was now attempting to purchase the Baptism of the Holy Spirit with money. He was seeking the "power" of God to perform miracles, and Peter rebuked him because his heart was not right; he was still under the evil influence of sorcery. When he saw the apostles performing signs and wonders he wanted to purchase this gift, and Peter said to him, "Your money perish with you, because you thought that the gift of God could be purchased with money!" (Acts 8:20). Discernment is a precious gift of the Holy Spirit:

> Believe not every spirit, but try the spirits whether they are of God (1 John 4:1).

The miraculous can very well be counterfeited by Satan through false workers who misrepresent themselves as servants of Christ (Matthew 7:21-23). The believer must discern all spiritual manifestations because many false prophets are gone out into the world (1 Thessalonians 5:21). Any supernatural demonstration that occurs in a person who continues to follow their sinful ways of the flesh is not of Christ; but has a counterfeit baptism influenced by demonic gifts and powers. Beware when observing others using occult-type, or strange methods in prayer and spiritual warfare. We must be very cautious in seeking an impartation from another person, no matter how anointed they may appear.

Christ's covenant includes healing for the body as well as for the soul; so we see the Kingdom of God being manifested through supernatural healing, miracles, and casting out demons. Christ gave gifts of healing in His Church and commanded His followers to heal the sick as part of their proclamation of the Kingdom of God. During Jesus' earthly life, His threefold ministry was teaching God's Word; preaching repentance and the blessings of God's kingdom, and healing every kind of sickness, disease, and infirmity among the people (Matthew 4:23-25). The primary healing for any individual is the redemption of the soul. God's provision of salvation includes: forgiveness for sin, eternal and resurrection life, and healing for sickness. This is the complete covenant through Jesus Christ! Some debate that Jesus healed during His ministry only to demonstrate His deity; however, Scripture reveals that He healed out of compassion for the suffering multitudes. His great commission includes the promise: "They will lay hands on the sick, and they will recover (Mark 16:18). Christ extends this commission based on His atonement, His compassion, and His promise of power and authority (Isaiah 53:4-5; Matthew 28:18-20).

Satan's Spiritual Conflict Against the Believer

> Having disarmed principalities and powers, He made a public spectacle of them, triumphing over them in it. –Colossians 2:15

It is Jesus Christ who disarmed the evil powers and authorities of wickedness, led captive a host of captives, and redeemed the believer from Satan's dominion (vv. 13-15). His triumph was achieved because of the Cross, which provides for full reinstatement with God the Father. Even so, all Christians are engaged in a spiritual conflict with evil, whether they want to admit it or not. Clearly, the believer's life in the world encompasses standing firm against Satan's assaults; however, they can be confident that their victory is assured by Christ Himself. The battle demands some warring against the invisible works of hell behind the scenes, utilizing Christ's authority over evil so the will of God can be advanced. The Apostle Paul describes the believer's spiritual armor using the metaphor of a first-century Roman soldier equipped for conflict:

> Put on the whole armor of God, that ye may be able to stand against the wiles of the devil, for we wrestle not against flesh and blood, but against principalities, against powers, against the rulers of darkness of this world, against spiritual wickedness in high places (Ephesians 6:11-12).

"Standing" means we boldly battle against our spiritual enemies. To do this, the Apostle Paul declares that every believer must put on the full armor of God, which is made up entirely of spiritual weapons: truth, righteousness, the gospel of peace, faith, salvation, the Word of God, and prayer. By learning to wear these powerful armaments, we can overcome the sinister plans of the devil. We are taking a stand in the mighty Name of Jesus, who has been given <u>all</u> authority in heaven and on earth; because we are seated with Him in heavenly places, "...Far above all rule and authority, power and dominion, and every title that can be given, not only in the present age but also in the one to come" (Ephesians 1:21).

Here is a brief summary describing the believer's authority:

1. The believer's victory has been secured by Christ Himself through His death on the cross. Jesus waged a triumphant battle against Satan and disarmed the evil powers and authorities of wickedness (Matthew 12:29; Luke 10:18; John 12:31). "When He ascended on high, He led captivity captive, and gave gifts to men" (Ephesians 4:8). (Now this, "He ascended"—what does it mean but that He also first descended into the lower parts of the earth? He who descended is also the One who ascended far above all the heavens, that He might fill all things.)" (vv. 9-10).
2. This conflict is called spiritual warfare, which should only be waged by the power of the Holy Spirit (Romans 8:12-14). What is the war the believer is waging?

   a. The corrupt desires within themselves (1 Peter 2:11; Galatians 5:17).
   b. The ungodly pleasure of the world and temptations of every sort (Matthew 13:22; Galatians 1:4; James. 1:14-15; 1 John 2:16).
   c. Satan and his forces work to thwart God's will in the believer's life (Ephesians 6:12).

3. Christian soldiers must wage war against all evil, not in their own power (2 Corinthians 10:3), but with spiritual weapons (vv. 4-5). In their battle of faith Christians are called upon to:

   a. Endure hardships as good soldiers of Christ (2 Timothy 2:3)
   b. Suffer for the gospel (Matthew 5:1-12; Romans 8:17)
   c. Fight the good fight of faith (1 Timothy 6:12; 2 Timothy 4:7)
   d. Do not war according to the flesh (2 Corinthians 10:3)
   e. Persevere (Ephesians 6:18)
   f. Conquer (Romans 8:37)
   g. Be victorious (1 Corinthians 15:57)
   h. Triumph (2 Corinthians 2:14)
   i. Defend the gospel (Philippians 1:27)
   j. Not be alarmed by opponents (Philippians 1:28)
   k. Put on the full armor of God and stand firm (Ephesians 6:14)
   l. Destroy Satan's strongholds (2 Corinthians 10:4)
   m. Take captive every thought (2 Corinthians 10:5)
   n. Become mighty in war (Hebrews 11:3)
   o. Contend for the faith (Jude 3)

"Wrestling" means to resist against, not shrink back in fear! The believer will face spiritual conflict with Satan and his host of evil spirits during his entire walk. The powers of darkness are the spiritual rulers of the world who frequently confront and attack believers. The enemy will do everything to undermine the believer's faith and confidence in the Word, but they are to draw their strength from the Lord and His power. Paul gives this encouragement, "Be strong in the Lord, and in the power of His might" (Ephesians 6:10). The Amplified Bible translates it this way: "Be empowered through your union with Him; draw your strength from Him—that strength which His might provides." Now this is the armor of a heavy-armed soldier, which God Himself provides:

1. Belt of Truth (God's Truth and Justice).
2. Breastplate of Righteousness (Integrity, moral rectitude and right standing with God).
3. Feet shod with the Gospel (Readiness and firm-footed stability).
4. Shield of Faith (Covers you from Satan's flaming missiles).
5. Helmet of Salvation (Redeemed by the Blood of the Lamb).
6. Sword of the Spirit (The Word of God).

"If you have run with the footmen, and they have wearied you, then how can you contend with horses? And if in the land of peace, in which you trusted, they wearied you, then how will you do in the floodplain of the Jordan?" (Jeremiah 12:5)

Indeed, we face a formidable enemy, "but the battle is the Lord's!" (1 Samuel 17:47; 2 Chronicles 20:15).

The equipped believer needs this insight:

1. Realize that every Christian faces a spiritual conflict with Satan's demons and evil spirits: Demons are members of Satan's kingdom and enemies of God and His created (Matthew 12:43-45). Working under Satan's authority, they are vicious, and malicious (Matthew 4:10). Demons are the ruler of this age, and Christians must wage continual warfare with them.
2. True believers have authority over Satan and his cohorts. As we confront them, we can break their power by waging intense spiritual warfare through the weapons: The Word God, the Blood of Jesus, and His Name. These are the weapons Jesus gave the Church so they can stay free from the powers of darkness. We no longer have to be a victim, of the devil, when the power of the Holy Spirit dwells within us. In Ezekiel 34:22-25, 28, 30, the prophet foretold how the Messianic Covenant would bring a new promise of freedom from Satan's rule.
3. To be successful in casting out demons (Luke 10:17), we must live a holy life before God, fully dedicated to obeying His truth and righteousness (Romans 12:1-2; Ephesians 6:14). We must walk confidently in faith, knowing that Satan's power has already been broken in any sphere of his domain (Acts 26:18; Ephesians 6:16; 1 Thessalonians 5:8). Possess the revelation in God's Word of why the believer has been given powerful spiritual weapons for the destruction of Satan's strongholds (2 Corinthians 10:4-5). Here are just three ways to use these weapons:
   a. Preach the gospel of the kingdom in the power of the Holy Spirit (Luke 1:16-17; Acts 1:8; 2:4; 8:12; Romans 1:16-17).
   b. Encounter Satan and his power directly in the Name of Jesus (Acts 16:16-18).
   c. Pray for the Holy Spirit to convict unbelievers concerning their sin, and lead them into further truth in God's Word (John 16:7-11).
4. The believer's spiritual weapons are the:
   a. Word of God (Ephesians 6:17)
   b. Name of Jesus (Mark 16:17)
   c. Blood of the Lamb (Revelation 12:11)
   d. Fasting will empower the above weapons (Matthew 6:16; Mark 9:29).
5. Desire and pray for the gifts of the Spirit with the manifestation of healing, tongues, miracles, signs, and wonders (Acts 4:29-33; 10:38; 1 Corinthians 12:7-11).

No Shrinking Back!

Fear must be overcome so we can walk in victory and conquer the Father's promise. During my early years in ministry, there was a time when I absolutely grew weary in the battle. While I persisted to gain the victory within myself with fasting and prayer, my spirit was fighting off abandonment and fear. Such lack of faith offended the LORD, and the Holy Spirit directed me to look up a scripture I had read in the Amplified Bible which spoke about "shrinking in fear." This turned out to be a hard word that I received from the Holy Spirit:

> Now the just shall live by faith: but if any man draw back, my soul shall have no pleasure in him." The Amplified translation says, "....if he draws back and shrinks in fear, My soul has no delight or pleasure in him (Hebrews 10:38).

I was anticipating a word of comfort and encouragement; however, this certainly served as a wake-up call. The message to my spirit was: "Get a grip! You're squirming around like a worm!" I was never a quitter and had always been the runner in the race who endured to get to the finish line first. Even so, this race could not be handled with my natural ability or strength, and I was sinking in my own efforts. My survival could only be secured by complete dependence on the LORD. How many times have I read the history of Moses and the Israelites in the wilderness; and now, I was going through the same experience. I did not want to spend forty years learning their lessons! It suddenly seemed sensible to learn quickly what God expected of me on this faith journey. During one of my prayer times, the Lord spoke so clearly to me and settled this issue of feeling overwhelmed. I know I disappointed the Father's heart with my inner desire to quit; telling Him "I'm just a woman." The Lord's answer came in two Scriptures: First, the call of God was confirmed in Jeremiah 1:5, "Before I formed you in the womb I knew you; before you were born I sanctified you; I ordained you a prophet to the nations." Second, this was His answer to the woman question:

> Say not, I am only a youth (woman); for you shall go to all to whom I shall send you, and whatever I command you, you shall speak (v. 7, Emphasis added).

The Father desires that we obey His will so that His plans and purposes can be fulfilled in our lives, even when living according to His plan involves suffering and hardship. Recognizing how God promises to be with you, and that He has empowered you to accomplish His will, helps you to stay unwavering in your faith, recognizing His abiding love sustains you:

> "There is no fear in love; but perfect love casts out fear: because fear involves torment. But he who fears has not been made perfect in love. We love him, because he first loved us" (1 John 4:18-19).

The Holy Spirit gives us Strength to go Forward

The enemy would love to bring you down from your place on the wall; so rely on the Holy Spirit to help you maintain the level of victory the Lord has already given you, and resist turning back to the past ways. There are many biblical examples, which help us gain victory in our spiritual walk, so we can make that transition to die to the old ways. One powerful example is Nehemiah, who had to resist the pressure to come down off the wall to address his enemies. God has formed a beachhead from your obedience, so do not go backwards and be recaptured by the enemy into your past. Submit to the Holy Spirit, who is working to help you make a transition from the past. When we allow the perfect love of God to take away all fear; then we can walk through the valley of death with the fragrance of life upon us. Each testing of our faith brings us into a place of communion so Jesus can reveal Himself in a new way. The Holy Spirit will help us recover from setbacks when we believe in God's ability to restore:

> And I will restore to you the years that the locust hath eaten, the cankerworm, and the caterpillar, and the palmerworm, my great army which I sent among you. And ye shall eat in plenty, and be satisfied, and praise the name of the Lord your God, that hath dealt wondrously with you and my people shall never be ashamed (Joel 2:25-26).

Because the conflict of evil against light never ceases, many grow weary and drop out. Jesus said, ".....The kingdom of heaven suffers violence, and the violent take it by force" (Matthew 11:12). Christ has anointed you to pursue and recover what the enemy has stolen from you. Do not shrink back in fear when you face obstacles that are overwhelming; the Lord will remove those hurdles as you keep moving forward in faith. Let go of your past failures. Do not look back, but look ahead to the victory line:

> And Jesus said unto him, "No man, having put his hand to the plow, and looking back, is fit for the kingdom of God" (Luke 9:62).

David moved forward after being banished by King Saul. He assembled an army of supporters who helped him to spoil God's enemies across the land. On one occasion, he returned home from the battlefield and found that his evil neighbors had stolen everything he owned. The Amalekites burned David's camp city of Ziklag, and carried off the inhabitants and flocks, which included his two wives. David sought the LORD for direction:

> And David inquired at the LORD, saying, Shall I pursue after this troop? Shall I overtake them? And he answered him, Pursue: for thou shalt surely overtake them, and without fail recover all (1 Samuel 30:8-18).

David pursued his enemy based on the Word the LORD spoke to him: Pursue and recover! He went into the enemy's camp, killed all the thieves and recovered all. Because David went with God's power, the victory was assured. Likewise, Jesus Christ went before us and assured the victory (Colossians 2:15). Scripture offers these guidelines to pursue and recover:

1. We demolish Satan while fulfilling the purposes of God (Luke 4:18, 19).
2. Before entering Satan's camp (his strongholds), overpower him by prayer and proclaiming the Word; this destroys his weapons of demonic deception and temptation (Revelation 12:11).
3. Proclaim deliverance for those who have been taken captive by Satan's wiles and restore them to God (Luke 11:22; Acts 26:18).

Be Scriptural with Spiritual Warfare

Many prayer groups have interpreted the role of the intercessor and the watchman to be like something out of Star Wars, slaying all the "Darth Vader's" they come up against. We need to guard against the influence of Hollywood in relation to spiritual warfare and avoid reacting in the flesh. We have all learned some wrong methods in church and prayer circles; nevertheless, we can rely on the scriptures for balance. Although Jesus gave us full authority over Satan and his demons, he did not assign us as His earthly swat team to get into the second heavenly and aggressively pursue demonic principalities (Jude 9). During one of my visits to Israel, I met a prayer leader who had engaged in spiritual warfare against a Buddha idol whom the people worship in Malaysia. When she began to rebuke the false god, lightning struck her and damaged her back. She has severe pain to this day; even after receiving frequent prayer for healing and seeking doctors for remedies.

There is one fundamental truth, which gives us the victory over Satan's attacks; rely on your spiritual weapons, not your own strength. Follow the example of what Jesus did when Satan tempted Him in the wilderness: Lift up the standard of the Word of God, which is truth and righteousness. Here are a few keys for declaring righteousness in prayer:

- Declare scriptures of God's LOVE toward His children.

- Declare scriptures of PEACE, not war.
- Speak scriptures of LIGHT into the darkness.

Oftentimes, intercessors visit Washington, D.C. with a mission to conduct an "operation clean sweep" in the heavenly realm. They endeavor to remove the demonic principalities over the U. S. Capitol, so the government will come into alignment with Godly principles. This is not only dangerous for the intercessors; it also stirs up the spiritual atmosphere over the entire region. Scripture indicates that such transformation occurs when righteous leaders rule; and in America, that comes down to the responsibility of, "We the people." God-inspired leaders bless the land and the people: "When the righteous are in authority, the people rejoice...." (Proverbs 29:2). The Prophet Isaiah declared that when Messiah rules, ".....The government is upon His shoulder..." (Isaiah 9:6). This speaks of Christ's entitlement to rule, and His reign will bring freedom from Satan's domination (vv. 4-5). We spiritually achieve Christ's rulership within our government when we place God-fearing righteous people in public office. Such a transition of the country's leaders would increase the presence of the Kingdom of God over the government and the land.

For instance, in the early 1990s, we prayed for evil, corrupt leaders in the U. S. Congress to be removed and replaced by righteous leaders. Every time I walked through the halls of the U. S. Congress to conduct my television interviews for the *Washington Report,* I prophesied this transformation by praying Scripture. I asked the Lord to remove the legislators with corrupt hearts and replace them with God-fearing men and women. We watched this transformation happen in 1994 with a complete turning of the tide in both houses of Congress.

Revitalization in America will only occur when such transformation takes place inside the hearts and minds of the masses across the nation. Many Church leaders across the nation are currently conducting campaigns to ignite a great spiritual awakening. Numerous ministries have often gathered Christians to pray on the national mall in Washington, and our *Embassy for World Peace* has helped host many such events for various organizations like: Washington For Jesus, Promise Keepers, Annual March for Life, Africa For Jesus, National Juneteenth Observance, USA Solemn Assembly, and countless smaller groups. During the 1980s and 90s, these gatherings on the national mall served to unite the Church of Jesus Christ. Evangelist Luis Palau's DC Festival united over 400 church leaders and conducted community improvement projects for several years in the nation's capital. While many national events have produced unity, they have not yet succeeded to ignite a national revival. We continue to believe the LORD will rain down a Third Great Awakening, before the nation loses God's grace. The Holy Spirit has shown me that America needs a Nineveh-type revival!

It would be great if we could conduct a spiritual clean sweep over regions and cities to ignite transformation; however, Church history indicates that revival is the result of travailing prayer. For instance, in 2 Kings 23:15-24, King Josiah followed

Yahweh's instructions to tear down every site where the people worshiped false gods in Israel; even so, they reverted to their idolatry because their hearts and minds were not transformed. When Nehemiah rebuilt the temple, he had Ezra read the Word of God to the people; sowing the principles of God into their hearts to renew their Covenant with God. In the New Testament, we read how the apostles would disciple converts with kingdom principles after they were delivered from darkness by the Gospel. Otherwise, new Christians fall away and are worse off than they were before conversion. Jesus spent valuable time with the disciples by sowing the Kingdom of God into their hearts.

Harvesting Nations with Intercession

> The Lord answered Abraham, "If I find in Sodom fifty righteous within the city, then I will spare all the place for their sakes" (Genesis 18:26). Abraham began to negotiate with the Lord and asked, "(If) there shall lack five of the fifty righteous: wilt thou destroy all the city for lack of five?" (v. 28). Abraham then asked, "Or, what if there are only ten upright people who seek you? If only ten call on you, will you spare the city?" God answered Abraham, "I will not destroy it for ten's sake" (v. 32).

This passage tells us how much the heart of God searches to find just one praying believer who will stand in the gap, so He can spare an entire society. In Ezekiel's time the LORD spoke, "I sought for a man among them, that should make up the hedge, and stand in the gap before me for the land, that I should not destroy it: but I found none" (Ezekiel 22:30). Without someone who is willing to stand in the gap, darkness invades societies and the destruction of people occurs. Intercession will cost time, energy, sleep, and a much greater faith than most other things we do. What great reward there is by responding to the call to intercede for the nations? Let us give it priority time.

Transformation in People's Lives will Change an Entire Region

Christ's ministry reached out to the poor, disabled, and the oppressed (Isaiah 61:1-3; Luke 4:18-19). The gospel was, and still is the good news to the poor. Defeating demonic strongholds will result when lives are transformed by the Gospel. Spiritual awakening in the people will change the entire atmosphere over a city or region. The Church in Philippi was established when Paul and Silas delivered a possessed woman. The occult practice of fortune telling was a stronghold that held the people in bondage to this form of idolatry. Paul and Silas went on preaching the Gospel with a demonstration of signs and miracles, which would replace the demonic thirst for the supernatural. In Acts 16:16-30, we read the account where there was a slave girl possessed by an evil spirit of fortune telling. Her masters made a lot of money for her services, which were in much demand. The girl followed Paul and Silas, irritating them for many days. When Paul delivered her of the evil spirit, her masters had them whipped and imprisoned. As Paul and Silas praised God in the midnight hour, an earthquake shook the jail, which brought about a tremendous revival and the fear of the Lord fell on the city. I believe the coming revival in America will be one of fire; with demonstrating great miracles.

Transformation in a Person's Life is a Two-Step Process

First, salvation is a move of the Holy Spirit convicting people of their sin. Inviting Christ into one's life brings about the transformation from darkness to light. Second, there needs to be a daily transformation through the Word of God being sown into the heart of the new convert. Otherwise, they will be worse than they were before salvation. Jesus explained in Matthew 12:45, "Then he goes and takes with him seven other spirits more wicked than himself, and they enter and dwell there; and the last state of that man is worse than the first. So shall it also be with this wicked generation."

During the 1980s, my home church in Orlando, Florida sponsored "Jesus Rallies" which were held in a cow pasture next to Disney World. Each year, approximately 25,000 youths would come for a three-day Christian rock concert on the order of the old Woodstock concerts in New England. Popular Christian rock stars would come and minister to the young people day and night. There was also powerful preaching by well-known evangelists who could connect with the youth. Thousands were converted every day, and they would have a huge bonfire at night; where the youth would burn up their secular music and drugs. We always took the young people from my youth ranch, and I volunteered each year to help counsel at the altar invitations. Those who were ready to receive Christ as Savior were directed to a large tent; which would accommodate several thousand souls that responded to each altar call.

I especially recall the transformation that was seen during the altar calls with David Wilkerson, the founder of Teen Challenge. I would stand at the back of the platform behind Pastor Wilkerson while he led them in the "Sinner's Prayer." Before the prayer, the crowd looking up at him were like a "lost sea" of humanity, with hopelessness and despair on their faces. Afterward, their faces were suddenly transformed. This transformation was so overwhelming that I was flooded with tears, weeping for joy. You can sense the same joy that heaven celebrates when just one sinner enters the Kingdom of Heaven. God and the angels in heaven have such love, pity and grief for those who have fallen into sin and spiritual death, and when only one sinner repents there is great rejoicing. Jesus explained the value of one saved soul:

> I say to you that such will be the joy in heaven over one sinner who repents, more than over ninety and nine righteous who need no repentance (Luke 15:7).

Where do we find the gospel preached today with such a fiery conviction? Too often, what we hear is the voice of compromise in the Church crying for more contemporary methods for reaching the lost without an emphasis on repentance. This message appeases the flesh and has nothing to do with the cross. Such false teachers rob Christians who end up living empty, unfulfilled lives, having never been exposed to the gospel of separation from the lusts of this world. Here is what the Apostle Paul advised his protégé Timothy:

> Preach the word! Be ready in season and out of season. Convince, rebuke, exhort, with all longsuffering and teaching. For the time will come when they will not endure sound doctrine, but according to their own desires, because they have itching ears, they will heap up for themselves teachers; and they will turn their ears away from the truth, and be turned aside to fables. But you be watchful in all things, endure afflictions, do the work of an evangelist, fulfill your ministry (2 Timothy 4:2-5).

False teachers are skillful orators who speak with flattering words and empty rhetoric. They reject true Bible doctrine, and they do not rely on the Holy Spirit to guide what they are teaching. Today, many are embracing the false theology of universal reconciliation, which asserts that, everyone will ultimately be restored to a right relationship with God in Heaven. This is untrue heresy, and those who teach or believe such apostasy have created their own religion. A great falling away from sound biblical truth is growing in leaps and bounds. The explosive growth of apostasy is a significant sign prevalent in the Western Church. The "falling away" that Paul taught about describes the apostasy of the Church in the end times:

> Let no one deceive you by any means; for that Day will not come unless the falling away comes first, and the man of sin is revealed, the son of perdition, who opposes and exalts himself above all that is called God or that is worshiped, so that he sits as God in the temple of God, showing himself that he is God (2 Thessalonians 2:3-4).
>
> Jesus said to His disciples, "You are the salt of the earth; but if the salt loses its flavor, how shall it be seasoned? It is then good for nothing but to be thrown out and trampled underfoot by men" (Matthew 5:13).

Keys for Moving in the Spirit and not the Flesh

> Beloved, do not believe every spirit, but test the spirits, whether they are of God; because many false prophets have gone out into the world. By this you know the Spirit of God: Every spirit that confesses that Jesus Christ has come in the flesh is of God, and every spirit that does not confess that Jesus Christ has come in the flesh and is not of God (1 John 4:1-3).

Ask the Holy Spirit to confirm what spirit you are hearing. Test the spirits which are instructing you. If we accept every idea or opinion without discernment, then we open ourselves up to error. The Holy Spirit will teach us the truth. While the gospel message is one of love, we must not compromise the truth. Learn between truth and error by testing what you hear by the Word of God and the Holy Spirit. When you are well grounded in God's Word, then your spirit will discern between truth and error. The Apostle Paul warns believers to be tough-minded in discernment, yet loving to all, and fearless in the face of judgment (Philippians 2:5-11; 17-18). Building a firm foundation in God's Word comes by developing more depth in the scriptures with a systematic Bible study; then when you hear someone teaching heresy you can check it out.

This is the challenge: How can we know which voices to follow? There are many voices calling out to believers in the modern Church. In John 10:4, Jesus describes the good shepherd, "…..And the sheep follow him: for they know his voice." God's heavenly voice speaks clearly to us today through His Son Jesus Christ, who is seated at the right hand of the Father. He is the promised Messiah, Who has a mystical body, His Church, fulfilling His mission in the earth. Consider these words from Hebrews 12:25-29, which speaks of what happens to those who reject His heavenly voice:

> See that you do not refuse Him who speaks. For if they did not escape who refused Him who spoke on earth, much more shall we not escape if we turn away from Him who speaks from heaven, whose voice then shook the earth; but now He has promised, saying, "Yet once more I shake not only the earth, but also heaven." Now this, "Yet once more," indicates the removal of those things that are being shaken, as of things that are made, that the things which cannot be shaken may remain. Therefore, since we are receiving a kingdom which cannot be shaken, let us have grace, by which we may serve God acceptably with reverence and godly fear. For our God is a consuming fire.

If severe punishment fell upon those who rejected the revelation of Sinai, how much more will be the severe penalty upon those who disregard the fuller revelation they have experienced in Christ.

Keys for Seeing and Hearing by the Spirit

First, rather than following movements and popular teachings within the Church, believers must be diligent to hear and obey the still small voice of the Holy Spirit. Christ has placed many trustworthy under-shepherds over His flock who will feed His sheep with love. Every believer should seek the Lord's direction to come under the tender care of a good shepherd who is leading his congregation in the right direction. Local churches should reflect the leading of Christ to be separated from the world and fulfill the evangelistic mission of the Church. The heartbeat of God is souls, and Christ gave His followers authority and power to proclaim the gospel throughout the world (Matthew 28:18-20). If we are unable to go to reach the lost; then we must send and support missionaries, and be faithful to undergird them with prayer.

Second, since it is Satan's scheme to resist the advancement of the gospel; then, the first work of the Church must be prayer. Christians should seek out a Bible-based church that is committed to maintaining a "house of prayer." As the Apostle Paul reminds us: "For we do not wrestle against flesh and blood, but against principalities, against powers, against the rulers of the darkness of this age, against spiritual hosts of wickedness in the heavenly places" (Ephesians 6:12). While Satan's ultimate fate may be a sealed issue; there are no indications he will surrender peacefully. The Apostle Paul is referring to the methods Satan employs to thwart God's will on earth; which is a strong hierarchy designed to entrap mankind. Each believer has been provided the divine wisdom and spiritual tools for resisting such a formidable enemy.

Third, wake-up and understand the new season of conflict the Church of Jesus Christ faces. The 21st Century has emerged as a decade of extraordinary persecution against Christians. The 1980s and the 90s paved the way for this decisive hour by the dramatic repositioning of the world's familiar political and spiritual landscapes. The conflict actually started in the year of 1979, with the birth of the modern-day Islamic Jihad Movement, which was like "Pandora's Box" being unlocked upon the world. Iran became the catalyst for Islamic Jihad groups surfacing in Arab countries after the Ayatollah Ruhollah Khomeini returned and became the supreme religious leader of the Islamic Republic of Iran in 1979. Israel considers Iran to be their number-one enemy, and the United States should be making the same consensus since Iran's Ayatollah's call Israel the Little Satan, and the United States, the Great Satan!

Christ Leads the Church through the Holy Spirit

> Then Jesus answered and said to them, "Most assuredly, I say to you, the Son can do nothing of Himself, but what He sees the Father do; for whatever He does, the Son also does in like manner" (John 5:19).

Jesus testified that He and the Father are One, and He did only what the Father showed Him. Even the miracles that Christ performed were not done independently of the Father. John 1:1 reveals how Jesus was with God, and they were of one common purpose. He affirmed that the Son can do nothing of Himself. Since such a holy and perfect Lord refused to use His own ability, then how about His disciples? The Lord's life was so flawless, yet; His whole life was one which depended completely on the Holy Spirit. He did not serve His own agenda; He served only the Father's Will. Likewise, as disciples, our commitment must be the same.

How can we apply Christ's faith to ourselves? We know we do not have the mind of God as Jesus did; even so, we know that as we pray and grow in God's Word, we develop the mind of Christ. If we desire to act like Christ, then we must think like Him: "Let this mind be in you which was also in Christ Jesus….." (Philippians 2:5). As Christ willingly laid aside His heavenly glory to come to Earth and die, we should desire to look beyond our own interests for the sake of others (v. 6). As Jesus' disciples, we have the opportunity to lay down our personal rights and reputations; to give our lives in service to others for the sake of the gospel and the glory of God. This is only achieved by surrendering to the Holy Spirit.

Discernment vs. Judgmental-Critical Spirit

In life, humans tend to take God's place as judge. We are arrogant to complain and gripe about everybody and everything that does not please us. The Holy Spirit will give us unbiased discernment when we walk in obedience to the Word and develop the love of Christ. How do we know if we have a problem with judging and criticizing others? There are two kinds of judgment. First, righteous judgment comes from God to work his plans and purposes in the earth. Discernment enables us to judge situations; however, it does not give us license to carry out the judgment. Second, judgment can foster a critical spirit which is not pleasing to Christ. Pronouncing judgment on others is intentional: it criticizes, condemns, and punishes. We need to develop a balance of discernment with Christ's love, and refrain from judging others with a critical spirit. Jesus does not forbid criticism, opinions, or condemnation of wrongdoing. He does forbid faultfinding that overlooks one's personal shortcomings while assuming the role of supreme judge when regarding the sins of others. This is the spiritual principle: Refrain from judging others, be diligent to examine your own heart, and respond to the Holy Spirit's conviction. Jesus warned:

> Judge not, that you be not judged. For with what judgment you judge, you will be judged; and with the measure you use, it will be measured back to you. And why do you look at the speck in your brother's eye, but do not consider the plank in your own eye? (Matthew 7:1-3).

Seven ways to determine the difference between judgment and discernment:

Webster describes discernment: "To perceive something hidden or obscure; to comprehend mentally, showing insight and judgment."

1. Discernment is the good kind of judgment. Joseph's brothers were blinded by their jealousy, but Joseph had discernment: "And the patriarchs, becoming envious, sold Joseph into Egypt. But God was with him and delivered him out of all his troubles, and gave him favor and wisdom in the presence of Pharaoh, king of Egypt; and he made him governor over Egypt and all his house. Now a famine and great trouble came over all the land of Egypt and Canaan, and our fathers found no sustenance. But when Jacob heard that there was grain in Egypt, he sent out our fathers first" (Acts 7:9-12).

Judgment seeks to revenge for a hurt or condemns others for their visible problems. Could it be that what we hate in others is something we are struggling with ourselves? Being created in the image of God, all human beings have an equal value and should possess a loving relationship to one another and to God. Respect and honor every person, regardless of status or race. "For judgment is without mercy to the one who has shown no mercy. Mercy triumphs over judgment" (James 2:13). (Also read Romans 2:1-3; 14:10)

2. Discernment examines self before presuming to evaluate the actions of others. Only when we have our own spiritual house in order can we act out of humility, as one fellow sinner speaking to another sinner saved by grace (Galatians 6:4; 1 Corinthians 11:28; 2 Corinthians 13:5).

Judgment will form opinions on first impressions or hearsay, then looks for evidence to confirm those opinions, even though the evidence is one of a surface appearance (John 7:24; Romans 14:13; James 4:11).

3. Discernment refrains from forming an opinion until it has verified or clarified the story directly from the source (1 Thessalonians 5:21; 1 John 4:1).

Judgment deals with matters publicly (James 4:11). It gossips and maligns in order to get others to judge an individual, as well. This sort of gossip is often phrased as a prayer request.

4. Discernment deals with a matter privately. It goes to the person directly with love and involves no one else (Matthew 5:24; 18:15).

Judgment condemns the person involved. If we cannot approach the person in the same way, Jesus handled the woman caught in adultery, it is better to wait until we can (John 8:3-11). Our sin of judging could be greater than the sin found in the person we are condemning.

5. Discernment will condemn a wrong action, but truly loves the individual enough to pray for him or her. It looks beyond the fault and sees the need. Brotherly love will intercede for the person.

Judgment without mercy is intrusive. It becomes a busybody, meddling where it has no business being (1 Timothy 5:13; 1 Peter 4:15; 1 Corinthians 4:5).

6. Discernment is respectful of others correcting only when necessary. It earns the right to be heard, partly because it doesn't feel driven to confront. Prayer is usually the posture taken by the discerning Christian (1 Thessalonians 5:21; Philippians 2:5).

Judgment seeks destruction. When people tear down, they tend to point fingers, glare, use emotional words, and speak with a raised voice (James 2:13; Proverbs 24:2).

7. Discernment seeks restoration. When we build up, we should speak softly and have a tender heart (Galatians 6:1; James 1:19; Proverbs 25:11).

Judgment seeks division. Its root is a religious spirit; the same spirit that killed the prophets and the Messiah. (Proverbs 6:16-19).

Discernment is Essential for Walking in the Spirit

There is one simple solution for developing a supernatural walk: Instead of trying to live for Christ, we need to allow Him to live through us, love through us, and forgive through us. Being Christ-like is more than hard, it is impossible without the help of the Holy Spirit. Satan, the enemy of our soul, works to keep us from attaining this high goal in our lives. He has designed many traps for believers to fall into; the major one is his working through the flesh (the carnal man) which causes many to stumble. Exercise caution by avoiding to judge others, which sows discord among the brethren. Division is the mission of Satan, and a Christian is being used as his instrument when the fruit of their actions brings offenses and division. Humans tend to take God's place as judge, and those that do are arrogant to complain and gripe about everybody and everything that does not please them. King Solomon spoke of the seven things which stem from a judgmental spirit:

> There are six things which the Lord hates, seven which are an abomination to him: haughty eyes, a lying tongue, and hands that shed innocent blood, a heart that devises wicked plans, feet that make haste to run to evil, a false witness who breathes out lies, and a man who sows discord among brothers (Proverbs 6:16-19).

The Apostle Paul had to deal with severe divisions within the Corinth church, which were threatening to tear the church apart. When he had heard the news of these divisions, he sent this message from Ephesus: "Now I plead with you, brethren, by the name of our Lord Jesus Christ, that you all speak the same thing, and that there be no divisions among you, but that you be perfectly joined together in the same mind and in the same judgment" (1 Corinthians 1:10). Unity within the body of Christ is pursued by avoiding individualism and competitiveness. Honor others, and recognize Jesus as the common ground for unity, and be spiritually prepared to face perilous times ahead. Christians who serve the world system will continually be used by Satan as the enemies of the Bride.

Offenses Destroy Faith

Whoever causes one of these little ones who believe in Me to sin, it would be better for him if a millstone were hung around his neck, and he were drowned in the depth of the sea. Woe to the world because of offenses! For offenses must come, but woe to that man by whom the offense comes! –Matthew 18:6-7

Jesus warns of the severe consequences in causing another to sin. We are not even to usurp over or dominate other believers, which causes the weaker members of the body to be offended. Satan, the enemy of our soul, is subtle and delights in deception. He is shrewd in his operations to set traps for God's children. The Word of God tells us, "Therefore submit to God. Resist the devil and he will flee from you" (James 4:7). Once we allow ourselves to become offended and feed on it, then we are in danger of developing a root of bitterness. The devil knows that offenses will cause division, separation, and broken relationships. The troubles of life weigh us down and become a burden that we cannot bear. Jesus invites his children to bring their trials and cares to the "throne of grace" where they can find help in a time of need:

> Come to me, all you who labor and are overburdened, and I will give you rest. Shoulder my yoke and learn from me, for I am gentle and humble in heart, and you will find rest for your souls. Yes, my yoke is easy and my burden light (Matthew 11:28-30).

During His lifetime, Jesus saw firsthand how the burden of the Law and the Pharisaic observances were weighing down God's people. He offered his followers a yoke that was easy and light. His Covenant was based on love rather than laws they could not keep. In Romans, chapter eight, we learn that the Spirit of life, the Holy Spirit, breaks the dominion of the old law of sin and death – but too often God's children move out of grace and place themselves back under the yoke of the law which is burdensome. This is done through sin or trials that we cannot bear. The old legalistic religious system was a severe burden, but under Christ's covenant, God's love flows from the "throne of grace," and we can be assured of finding the outpouring of the Holy Spirit to help comfort and guide us. God's love has always offered mercy and forgiveness.

Offenses are Another Sign of the End of the Age

> And then many will be offended, will betray one another, and will hate one another. Then many false prophets will rise up and deceive many. And because lawlessness will abound, the love of many will grow cold. But he who endures to the end shall be saved" (Matthew 24:10-13).

Jesus spoke of offenses as being one of the signs of the end times, saying that many Christians will fall into the trap of offenses because of trials and tribulations. Jesus said in Matthew 24:12, "And because lawlessness will abound, the love of many will grow cold." The Apostle Paul observed that many became disheartened and forsook their love for the brethren when they grew weary in doing well (Galatians 6:8-9). Offenses develop into unforgiveness and hatred. There is a strong warning given in 1 John 3:15 regarding a hateful heart, "Whoever hates his brother is a murderer, and you know that no murderer has eternal life abiding in him." Hatred grows into a root of bitterness, which seeks revenge, and is capable of murder. Love for fellow Christians is just as much characteristic of the new nature as righteous living. Offended people produce evil fruit such as hatred, bitterness, resentment, strife, jealousy and envy. When an individual takes an offense, they walk into Satan's trap, which leaves them vulnerable to a root of bitterness.

The best way to guard against a victim mentality is to choose not to become offended, because our response determines our future. Jesus taught His disciples to react with forgiveness when treated unjustly (Matthew 18:21-22). Once you dwell on the thought that you were mistreated and misjudged, subsequently your unforgiveness appears to be justified. Even though we are treated unjustly, the Word of God forbids us to hold on to an offense. Pride produces a victim mentality. It hardens the heart and veils the eyes of our understanding, which keeps us from choosing forgiveness.

Self-Pity Steals Spiritual Freedom

Self-pity is a stumbling block: The attitude of many offended Christians is inward and introspective. They love themselves more than they love God. Hurt people become paranoid about their relationships and safeguard against future injuries from occurring. The truth is the breastplate of righteousness guards our heart, so we will not be hurt. This divine protection allows us to be free to give unconditional love because we are hidden in Christ. Hurt people become more and more self-seeking and self-contained. Those who become offended do not recognize they are entrapped, because they are concentrating on the wrong that was done to them. The enemy will blind them because they are focused on themselves. The Apostle Paul describes this in 2 Timothy 3:2-5:

> For men will be lovers of themselves, lovers of money, boasters, proud, blasphemers, disobedient to parents, unthankful, unholy, unloving, unforgiving, slanderers, without self-control, brutal, despisers of good, traitors, headstrong, haughty, lovers of pleasure rather than lovers of God, having a form of godliness but denying its power. And from such people turn away!

Realize that the Father Permits us to be Tested

Offenses are part of God's refining process. In Hebrews 3:13, we find that hearts are "hardened through the deceitfulness of sin." If we choose to let an offense fester, it will harden the heart just as alloys (copper, iron, and nickel) harden gold when added. This means the heart is no longer tender, creating a loss of sensitivity, which hinders us from hearing God's voice. When our accuracy to see is darkened, then this becomes the perfect setting for deception. God wants His people to have a pure heart, and Scripture tells us He will refine us with afflictions, trials and tribulations. Only the refiner's fire separates impurities such as unforgiveness, strife, bitterness, anger, and envy so the character of God can shine through our lives. Repentance will then cleanse the heart:

> Therefore, brethren, we are debtors—not to the flesh, to live according to the flesh. For if you live according to the flesh you will die; but if by the Spirit you put to death the deeds of the body, you will live. For as many as are led by the Spirit of God, these are sons of God (Romans 8:12-14).

While it is true Christ has given us a covenant of love and grace, this does not mean believers are free to sin. The Apostle Peter repented after denying Jesus three times when He was arrested. Repentance brought him back under grace. The sinful nature, which works through the flesh, is a constant enemy to holy living. Victory over sin is only possible with the faithful help of the Holy Spirit Who resides within the believer. When we repent of our sins, seek forgiveness and cleansing, then, the evil deeds of the flesh are being put to death. Under the New Covenant, the cleansing of sin is promised through the shed blood of Jesus Christ:

> Christ also loved the church, and gave himself for it; that he might sanctify and cleanse it with the washing of water by the word (Ephesians 5:25-26).

> This is the message which we have heard from Him and declare to you, that God is light and in Him is no darkness at all. If we say that we have fellowship with Him, and walk in darkness, we lie and do not practice the truth. But if we walk in the light as He is in the light, we have fellowship with one another, and the blood of Jesus Christ His Son cleanses us from all sin (1 John 1:7).

Sanctification within the believer is a continual work, along with cleansing through the blood of Jesus Christ. While sin in our lives causes God to remain distant from our prayers, sanctification allows the believer to have intimate fellowship with Him. The Father does not want to condemn and destroy His people; so He offers full forgiveness if they only repent, put aside evil, strive to do good, and obey God's Word. Scripture gives clear instruction:

> Wash yourselves, make yourselves clean; put away the evil of your doings from before My eyes. Cease to do evil, learn to do good; seek justice, rebuke the oppressor; defend the fatherless, plead for the widow (Isaiah 1:16-17).

> If we confess our sins, He is faithful and just to forgive us our sins and to cleanse us from all unrighteousness. If we say that we have not sinned, we make Him a liar, and His word is not in us. (1 John 1:9-10).

Those who refuse God's mercy and choose instead to cling rebelliously to their own ways will be destroyed (Isaiah 1:20). The Prophet Jeremiah experienced God's agony for Judah and expressed the pain and sorrow that the LORD felt at the coming desolation: "O Jerusalem, wash your heart from wickedness, that you may be saved. How long shall your evil thoughts lodge within you?" (Jeremiah 4:14). Judah's corruption had reached such a degree that few could be found who loved God's truth and righteousness. The nation was guilty; therefore, God determined to bring judgment upon His faithless people.

Likewise, believers should feel sorrow at the thought of men and women being taken captive and destroyed by sin and Satan. The terrible future of the lost should cause us to lament as Jesus did when He expressed intense grief over the lost spiritual condition of Jerusalem. It is sobering to be outside of God's grace, and not know it! Paul gives insight regarding God's mercy in 1 Timothy 5:24-25:

> Some men's sins are clearly evident, preceding *them* to judgment, but those of some *men* follow later. Likewise, the good works *of some* are clearly evident, and those that are otherwise cannot be hidden.

> The Apostle James instructed: "Draw near to God and He will draw near to you. Cleanse your hands, you sinners; and purify your hearts, you double-minded" (James 4:8).

God's presence draws near to those who turn from sin and call upon Him in true repentance. His presence brings His grace, blessings, and love. Faithful believers who are grounded and rooted in the Word will separate themselves from evil and choose to live according to Biblical revelation. Then there are the vessels of dishonor, who are carnal believers who stray from the truth. The Holy Spirit's discernment will keep us from all religions and false teachers who advocate doctrines contrary to Scripture.

Living by the Law of Love

> But I say unto you, Love your enemies, bless them that curse you, do good to them that hate you, and pray for them which despitefully use you, and persecute you (Matthew 5:44).

When you have a heart after God, you will not seek to retaliate over a hurt. Revenge manifests itself through criticism and condemnation, which have caused churches to split; families divide, and marriages shatter. We cannot take aim with words sharpened by bitterness and anger. Even though your offense may be justified, motives for revenge are impure:

> Let nothing be done through strife or vainglory; but in lowliness of mind let each esteem other better than themselves (Philippians 2:3).

Maturity is the goal! We will never overcome until we mature. What are the keys?

First: Die to Self

- Death to self is relinquishing our own determination.
- Death to pride and trying to impress others.
- Death to trusting in our own capability.

- Death to our own plans, desires and will.
- Death to all works that will impress God.
- Death to the old life: past flesh.

This type of death moves us into the New Covenant, where there is no more striving to believe. If we are to have the faith of Christ, then, He will help us. We just need to get out of the way. "He must increase, but I must decrease" (John 3:30).

Second: Deny Yourself

Denying yourself means exchanging your own decisions in daily life for the most productive and satisfying adventure of being guided by the Holy Spirit. Regrettably, many claim the Lord as their Shepherd, but they do not give up their own way of controlling situations in life. We cannot have it both ways. Either Christ is Lord of all, or He is not? Jesus warned that some will say, we "have performed many wonders in Your name....." but, He will retort, "I never knew you; depart from Me, you who practice lawlessness!" (Matthew 7:21-23). This is a sobering thought which should cause us to search our hearts, motives and personal relationship to Christ. Many teachers approach sin from a psychological understanding, which waters down the Gospel message and reduces sin to human weakness, which is excusable. Today, great emphasis is being placed on improving your self-image; while believers must follow the Bible with the Holy Spirit's interpretation, and by examining their personal motives. This quiz will help you with some self-examination:

- Do I truly belong to Christ?
- Do I truly accept His ownership of my life?
- Do I surrender to His authority?
- Do I find freedom and complete fulfillment in His Lordship?
- Do I sense a divine purpose and contentment in following His Will?
- Do I follow the Holy Spirit's direction?
- Do I trust the Lord with every decision in my life?

Third: Be Willing to Pay the Price

Christ sent the Holy Spirit to dwell inside all believers, enabling them with the same power He possessed! Answering the call of God is relying on the Holy Spirit's anointing. For example, the Holy Ghost delivered and anointed Paul for his apostolic call to the nations. "So the Lord said to him, 'Arise and go to the street called Straight, and inquire at the house of Judas for one called Saul of Tarsus, for behold, he is praying. And in a vision, he has seen a man named Ananias coming in and putting his hand on him so that he might receive his sight'" (Acts 9:11-12). Ananias was fearful because of Saul's reputation against Christians, but the Lord assured him that it was safe to approach Saul: "Go, for he is a chosen vessel of Mine to bear My name before Gentiles, kings, and the children of Israel. For I will show him how many things he must suffer for My name's sake" (vv. 15-16). "Immediately he preached the Christ in the synagogues, that He is the Son of God" (v. 20).

The key is to seek success in God's eyes, and not rely on man's approval. There is a personal cost of prayer and suffering attached to every ministry. We all understand the "prayer price," but few want to sign up for the "suffering price tag." The Apostle Paul had this to say about his suffering for the ministry in Colossians 1:24, "I now rejoice in my sufferings for you, and fill up in my flesh what is lacking in the afflictions of Christ, for the sake of His body, which is the church....."

The instinct toward self-preservation wants to divert us from jumping onto a "cross." Mel Gibson's movie, "The Passion of the Christ," gives a clear picture of the price that Christ paid, and what a small cost it is for His disciples to pick up their cross and follow Him. Many reject the idea that Christians must take up their cross; saying that Jesus paid it all eliminating the need for further suffer. Yes, Jesus did pay the full price for our sins, but he also said in Luke 9:23, "If anyone desires to come after Me, let him deny himself, and take up his cross daily, and follow Me." While salvation is a gift from God (Ephesians 2:8-9), we do not become superhuman beings after our conversion. The cost of discipleship is a walk that requires overcoming the flesh every day. Peter was sold out and fully committed to the Messiah, yet he imploded under fear when Jesus was arrested. Paul learned that God's grace is sufficient in all situations, and we are called to "glory" in the Cross (Galatians 6:14). The Cross is not a painful yoke we are under. It is much deeper than this. The Cross is coming to the end of yourself, down into a place of total helplessness: It is abandoning the struggle for freedom in your own strength.

Throughout his epistles, the Apostle Paul warns of the cost of suffering for Christ. He struggled against adversity, spiritual attacks, wild beasts, false apostles, and persecution from his own brethren. When we enlist to advance the Kingdom of God, we must expect opposition from evil forces. "For unto you it is given in the behalf of Christ, not only to believe on him, but also to suffer for his sake" (Philippians 1:29). Paul was not speaking about those who are buffeted for their own sinful ways; but also those who are consecrated and set apart for the Gospel. When you win converts, plant churches, or mentor disciples, you can expect Satan's opposition. Of course, the most severe persecution is taking place in countries that are hostile toward Christianity. The accounts of the Church in the New Testament are full of adversity. The ten churches the Apostle Paul planted were established in the face of danger.

The great and the small will always suffer for the sake of the gospel. There are some secret greats serving in dangerous areas, whose identity is humbly hidden and unknown to the mainstream body of believers. Being hidden protects them from Satan's destruction. The faithful who live for Christ in their daily routine should expect to suffer for Christ's sake. Their suffering may come through personal persecution from family members or co-workers on the job. However, through it all, our comfort is in Christ, and the joy of the Lord is our strength:

> Blessed be God, even the Father of our Lord Jesus Christ, the Father of mercies and the God of all comfort, Who comforts us in all our trouble, by the very comfort with which we ourselves are comforted by God. For as the sufferings of Christ abound in us, so our consolation also abounds in Christ. Even though we are oppressed, it is for the sake of your consolation and for the sake of your salvation that we are oppressed; and if we are comforted, it is so that you might be comforted also, to be strength in you that you may be able to bear these sufferings, the same which we also suffer. And our hope concerning you is steadfast, for we know that if you are partakers of the sufferings, you are also partakers of the consolation (2 Corinthians 1:3-7).

The highest glory and privilege of any believer are to suffer for Christ and the gospel. Christians must be willing to suffer, to share in the sufferings of Christ, and expect suffering to be a part of their walk. Peter taught, "For this is commendable, if because of conscience toward God one endures grief, suffering wrongfully. For what credit is it if, when you are beaten for your faults, you take it patiently? But when you do good deeds and suffer, if you take it patiently, this is commendable before God" (1 Peter 2:19-20). Listen to Paul's ministry report to the Corinthians:

> To the present hour we both hunger and thirst, and we are poorly clothed, and beaten, and homeless. And we labor, working with our own hands. Being reviled, we bless; being persecuted, we endure; being defamed, we entreat. We have been made as the filth of the world, the offscouring of all things until now. I do not write these things to shame you, but as my beloved children I warn you (1 Corinthians 4:11-14).

There is Authority in God's Holy Fire

Whether it is just witnessing to your neighbor or preaching a crusade, God's Holy work can never be performed without God's Holy fire. Scripture tells us that Jeremiah's lips were touched with fire from the Holy Altar in heaven. The fire from God's Holy Altar lit the incense the priest carried into the Holy of Holies. The priest placed coals from the Brazen Altar into the Golden Censor and burned the incense:

And he shall take a censer full of burning coals of fire from off the altar before the LORD, and his hands full of sweet incense beaten small, and bring it within the veil….. (Leviticus 16:12).

In the Old Testament, the presence of God's fire was manifested through the prophets, and in the time of the temple, the priests had the duty of keeping the eternal flame burning. The mandate came through Moses that the people would never let the holy fire in their temple go out. And so, it is with the Church of Jesus Christ; the believers in Christ have an obligation to keep the flame of the Holy Spirit alive in their lives. Those who are baptized with fire have become the temple of the living God (1 Corinthians 3:16; 6:19). The Old Testament prophets were God's voice in the midst of Israel's terrible apostasy to call the Hebrew nation and her leaders back to His covenant. The prophets were anointed with the Holy Spirit; however, Elijah is known as the prophet who was baptized with God's fire. Elijah and his protégé' Elisha were God's messengers during the times when Israel had an unbroken succession of kings who "wrought evil in the sight of the Lord" (560-550 B.C.).

The Prophet Elijah demonstrated the fire of God. In 1 Kings, chapter eighteen, you can read the act of Elijah's defeating the prophets of Baal when he called down God's fire to consume his sacrifice. His courage and faith have virtually no parallel in the entire history of redemption. He challenged kings, rebuked all of Israel, and confronted 450 priests of Baal with only the weapons of prayer and faith in God. Elijah's action to slay all of the priests of Baal was just because it was done under the Law of Moses (Deuteronomy 13:6-9; 17:2-5), and the people of Israel were being spiritually destroyed by their false religion. In 2 Kings, chapter one, Elijah prophesies King Ahaziah's death sentence, and the angered king with two companies of his soldiers sought to arrest him. When the captain of the king's army called Elijah to come down, fire came down from heaven; directly, by God's hand (verse 12) as a judgment against Ahaziah, who stubbornly persisted in opposing God and the prophet.

With the challenges the Church faces in these perilous times, we need the Baptism of Fire because the fire of God destroys the plans of God's enemies. In the New Testament Church, the fire of God is demonstrated through the individual believer who has received the baptism of the Holy Spirit. God's fire is mentioned when John describes in Revelation, chapter eleven, that Gods "Two Witnesses" will preach the gospel and prophesy the future to the nation of Israel. They will perform great supernatural signs and wonders as Moses and Elijah: "And if anyone wants to harm them, fire proceeds from their mouth and devours their enemies. And if anyone wants to harm them, he must be killed in this manner" (Revelation 11:5).

Baptism of Fire Empowers the Church

1. We need the fire in our belly to travail and give birth in the Spirit.
2. We need the fire in our feet to possess the ground wherever we tread.
3. We need the fire on our lips, for the anointing to break the yoke and set the captives free.
4. We need the fire to purge our minds and purify our hearts.

John the Baptizer, whom Jesus said was the spirit of Elijah returned to earth, prophesied these words in Matthew 3:11: "I indeed baptize you with water unto repentance, but He who is coming after me is mightier than I, whose sandals I am not worthy to carry. He will baptize you with the Holy Spirit and fire." Those who live without this baptism are spiritually blind; they walk in unbelief and fear. For instance, of the twelve spies, Moses sent out to survey the Promised Land, only Joshua and Caleb had discernment; they were seeing through the eyes of the Spirit. The other eight men spread a message of unbelief that affected the entire Jewish nation, who lost their inheritance and spent 40 years in the wilderness. What made Joshua and Caleb different? They had a heart after *Yahweh*, and they had the fire of God in their spirit.

In Matthew, chapter twenty-five, Jesus spoke a parable about five wise virgins who had discernment, and they lived a life of readiness. In this parable, there were also five foolish virgins who neglected the ministry of readiness and were locked out of entering into His Presence. Jesus warned, "Watch therefore, for you know neither the day nor the hour in which the Son of Man is coming" (v. 13). Abiding in the Son involves being hidden in the secret place of the "Most High" (Psalm 91). If you were in the military working close to the Commander-in-Chief, you would have access to all the hidden military secrets. Dwelling in the secret place of the "Most High" will give us access to His wisdom and direction, but you must first develop a level of trust with the LORD: "To whom much is given, much is required" (Luke 12:48). A low-ranking soldier does not enter the general's door and gain access to secret material. He would have to earn his way up by passing rigid military trainings to get into the upper ranks of leadership to be trustworthy of higher responsibility. For the Christian, this means developing "spiritual ears" to hear the Holy Spirit correctly. Spiritual hearing is not developed by those who lead a casual Christian life, jumping back and forth between the world and the Church. The diligent seeker develops spiritual insight through the Word of God (Hebrews 11:6). It requires choosing to give up self-centeredness, giving up becoming offended, and resisting the temptation of judging others:

> Most assuredly, I say to you, unless a grain of wheat falls into the ground and dies, it remains alone; but if it dies, it produces much grain. He who loves his life will lose it, and he who hates his life in this world will keep it for eternal life (John 12:24-25).

Jesus is knocking at the door of your heart to bring the kingdom into your life. He said that He came to earth to reveal His Father's Kingdom to mankind. Jesus, the Redeemer of Mankind, did not set Himself up higher than the Father, but He deferred to the Father and honored Him with obedience. In John 14:9, Jesus said, "He who has seen Me has seen the Father....." He is our example!

Jordan Represents the Baptism of the Holy Spirit

The Holy Spirit visibly anointed Jesus when He was baptized in the Jordan River to equip Him with power for His work of redemption. Later, Jesus filled His disciples with this same Holy Spirit (John 20:22). Before His ascension to the Father, Christ instructed His disciples, "Behold, I send the Promise of My Father upon you; but tarry in the city of Jerusalem until you are endued with power from on high" (Luke 24:49). After Christ's ascension to heaven, the Holy Spirit baptized His followers with fire so they would have the power for ministry:

> And when the day of Pentecost was fully come, they were all with one accord in one place. And suddenly there came a sound from heaven as of a rushing mighty wind, and it filled all the house where they were sitting. And there appeared unto them cloven tongues like as of fire, and it sat upon each of them. And they were all filled with the Holy Ghost, and began to speak with other tongues as the Spirit gave them utterance" (Acts 2:1-4).

This was promised in Joel 2:28 and reaffirmed on the Day of Pentecost when Peter preached that this promise was for all future generations (Acts 2:39). I mentioned earlier that this fiery relationship with the Spirit must be renewed and maintained. This is how believers fulfill their role to become keepers of the flame (Acts 4:31; Ephesians 5:18). It is a work of the Holy Spirit dwelling in mankind:

> Not by might, nor by power, but by my spirit, saith the Lord of hosts (Zechariah 4:6).
>
> The Church Age is the fulfillment of Joel 2:28-29: "And it shall come to pass afterward that I will pour out My Spirit on all flesh; your sons and your daughters shall prophesy, your old men shall dream dreams, your young men shall see visions. and also on *My* menservants and on *My* maidservants I will pour out My Spirit in those days."

We can only accomplish a supernatural work for His Kingdom when enabled by the Holy Spirit. Jesus achieved His ministry with the power of the Spirit, and when the Holy Spirit's fire was poured out at Pentecost, the Church was empowered for ministry (Acts 1:8; 2:4). We need to seek Him for a fresh baptism in the Spirit to keep the fire alive, if we are to overcome the enemy's opposition. With the Baptism of Fire, the Holy Spirit calls us to maintain a humble heart, and a contrite spirit, fearing the Lord, who will take care of our enemies. As long as you "fan the flame" with prayer, the Holy Spirit will assure that the fire will not go out day or night until "...Suddenly, the Lord you are seeking will come to his temple, the messenger of the covenant whom you desire" (Malachi 3:1). If we want to live in a manner worthy of the Lord, then we must be strengthened by His power. New infillings of the power of the Holy Spirit are an ongoing experience; so we can receive from God, His very own life to strengthen our inner man (Colossians 1:9-13).

The Baptism of the Holy Spirit Bears Evidence with Speaking in Tongues:

1. And these signs shall follow them that believe; in my name shall they cast out devils; they shall speak with new tongues (Mark 16:17).
2. And there appeared unto them cloven tongues like as of fire, and it sat upon each of them. And they were all filled with the Holy Ghost, and began to speak with other tongues, as the Spirit gave them utterance (Acts 2:3).
3. And when Paul had laid hands on them, the Holy Spirit came upon them, and they spoke with tongues and prophesied (Acts 19:6).
4. And.....To another the working of miracles; to another prophecy; to another discerning of spirits; to another divers kinds of tongues; to another the interpretation of tongues (1 Corinthians 12:10).

Jesus has made His Baptism of Fire available to all those who have received salvation. Simply invite the Holy Spirit to anoint you with His baptism. Do not be discouraged if you do not receive at first; He rewards those who diligently seek Him: "But without faith it is impossible to please Him, for he who comes to God must believe that He is, and that He is a rewarder of those who diligently seek Him" (Hebrews 11:6). You can seek prayer to receive this powerful gift. Ask your pastor or Bible study leader to lay hands on you, and have faith you will be anointed. When you pray, open your mouth and speak in a heavenly language that only comes from the Holy Spirit. As you live the Spirit-filled life, one question needs to be answered: Does the Holy Spirit control you and how much of you does He control?

Six basic requirements for the Spirit-led life:

1. **Salvation**
   Oftentimes, people become bound by Satan's power, either through spiritual blindness, greed, lust, drugs, gambling, alcohol, or pornography. Only the power of the Holy Spirit can deliver people out of darkness and transform a person's spirit. The Holy Spirit works internally by convicting a soul so the new birth can occur. The Spirit of Christ enters a person when they repent and make a profession of faith; receiving Jesus Christ as Lord and Savior. The Holy Spirit and the Spirit of Christ now take up residence in the believer; however, the Baptism of Fire will empower the believer in resisting Satan and becoming a firm witness for Christ. This indwelling allows the inner spirit to become strong in obeying the will of God.

2. **Healing and Deliverance**
Jesus is alive, and His miracles have only increased in the Earth; therefore, all churches should expect signs and wonders to be part of their ministry, and give emphasis to a miracle-working Jesus. From the Old Testament to the New Testament, the Bible is full of preaching and teaching on the supernatural. The Apostle James teaches one of the keys for healing: "Is anyone among you sick? Let him call for the elders of the church, and let them pray over him, anointing him with oil in the name of the Lord. And the prayer of faith will save the sick, and the Lord will raise him up....." (James 5:14-15). When the Church does what the Word says, then Jesus will confirm the Word with signs following (Mark 16:20). We glorify Him by remembering the source of this power. No one has the power to heal, but Jesus heals through us. All spirit-filled believers are anointed to heal the sick.

3. **Righteous Living**
Without the righteous fruit of the Spirit developing in one's life; the manifestation of spiritual gifts becomes polluted. The Apostle Paul says: "Walk in the Spirit, and you shall not fulfill the lust of the flesh" (Galatians 5:16). The baptism of the Spirit means walking in the Spirit, because the Spirit resides within your spirit. A believer's experience with the Holy Spirit is supposed to be a continuing experience; because receiving the fullness of the Holy Spirit is a lifetime process. The Holy Spirit is given to refine us, enable us, and empower us. The fiery tongues that manifested on the Day of Pentecost are to be associated with the holy fire of God, now living within men and women. Spirit baptism does not produce instant sanctification, but it gives one an added drive to cultivate a life pleasing to God.

4. **Gifts and Ministries**
The Baptism of Fire empowers every believer to exercise the supernatural gifts and ministries of Jesus. Luke records that Jesus was "full of the Holy Ghost" and was "led by the Spirit into the wilderness" to confront the devil (Luke 4:12). His triumph over Satan was accomplished by the Holy Spirit. The Spirit of the Lord was upon Him, ".....To preach the gospel to the poor; He has sent Me to heal the brokenhearted, to proclaim liberty to the captives and recovery of sight to the blind, to set at liberty those who are oppressed; to proclaim the acceptable year of the Lord" (Luke 4:18). When we are baptized with fire, we also have the power to conduct His heavenly ministry through the Holy Spirit (Acts 2:33). Joel prophesied: "I will pour out My Spirit on all flesh.....And also on My menservants and on My maidservants I will pour out My Spirit in those days" (Joel 2:28-29). The prophetic anointing is no longer limited to a chosen few:

Repent, and let every one of you be baptized in the name of Jesus Christ for the remission of sins; and you shall receive the gift of the Holy Spirit. For the promise is to you and to your children, and to all who are afar off, as many as the Lord our God will call (Acts 2:38-39).

5. **Communication with God**

The gift of tongues is Spirit-filled communication with God; it is a heavenly language. This divine gift should be practiced every day. The Spirit promises to lead us into all truth, and give direction in all circumstances. The genuine gift of speaking in tongues cannot be self-generated; just permit the Holy Spirit to manifest the gift. Luke writes that they spoke in tongues, "as the Spirit was giving them utterance" (Acts 2:4).

Praying in tongues, which is a heavenly language, is the immediate sign that the infilling has been received. Paul teaches that the "one who speaks in a tongue does not speak to men but to God" and the "one who speaks in tongues edifies himself" (1 Corinthians 14:2, 4). Praying in your own heavenly language strengthens the inner spirit. Paul explains, "Likewise the Spirit also helps in our weaknesses. Since we do not know what we should pray for as we ought, but the Spirit Himself makes intercession for us with groanings which cannot be uttered. Now He who searches the hearts knows what the mind of the Spirit is, because He makes intercession for the saints according to the will of God" (Romans 8:26-27; 1 Corinthians 14:5).

6. **Transforming the Culture**

The Holy Spirit's influence led First Century believers into evangelizing the world around them. Enabled by the Holy Spirit, they spread the gospel amid their hostile environment of persecution, idolatry, and political oppression. History repeats itself today, with Christians violently persecuted in theocratic countries of the world. These modern-day saints follow the early fathers; being bold in their faith, and refusing to deny Christ in the face of torture and persecution. The New Testament apostles successfully transformed pagan cultures with the gospel; regardless of public disgrace and rejection (Acts 13:6-12). They overcame demons, mobs, and villains; trusting the power of the Holy Spirit to deliver them (Acts 16:16-34). The early church, not only survived; it miraculously prospered in its worldwide outreach to spread the gospel (Acts 2-6). The gospel flourished along the *Ancient Silk Road*, where church plantings once stood as a memorial to the personal sacrifice of these brave First-century missionaries.

For centuries, Christian missionaries were involved in business or trade as they traveled to the East from Jerusalem. The Apostle Paul adopted the vocation of tent making, or leatherwork (Acts 18:1-11). Today, missionaries engaged in business and the marketplace are key to getting the gospel to unreached people groups around the globe. U. S. humanitarian and medical teams visit third- world countries to assist the poor and also offer the message of hope in the gospel. Filipino missionaries have migrated to Saudi Arabia as domestics, so they can spread the gospel into Muslim hearts. We have heard testimonies of Muslim children converted to Christianity by their Filipino nannies. I know English translators who have gone abroad to China as underground missionaries, to instruct in their colleges.

The Word of God is Truth and so is the Holy Spirit

> But when the Spirit of truth is come, he will guide you into all the truth; for he will not speak from himself, but when he hears he will speak; and he will make known to you things which are to come in the future. He will glorify me, because he will take of my own and show it to you. Everything that my Father has is mine; this is the reason why I told you that he will take of my own and show it to you (John 16:13-15).

Like Scripture, the Holy Spirit becomes our authority for everything. As we study the scriptures, we should ask the Holy Spirit to guide us into deeper truth and understanding. The Spirit works to draw our hearts closer to Christ and deepen our faith, love, obedience, communion, worship, and praise. Since the Holy Spirit, the Truth, lives within believers; we should ask Him to guide us as we seek revelation. Our minds become conformed to God's way of thinking by studying and meditating on the Word of God through the eyes of the Holy Spirit:

> If you abide in My word, you are My disciples indeed. And you shall know the truth, and the truth shall make you free (John 8:31-32).

No matter what we face, the first thing we should ask is: "What does God's Word say?" Our plans, goals, and ambitions must be measured by the Word of God; not the standards of this corrupt world. Scripture gives us a biblical worldview to base our beliefs and actions on. A methodical study of the Bible gives us a Word consciousness. I have been an avid student of the Word for over forty years, and I seek the Holy Spirit's guidance about which Bible teachers to learn from. Following popular teachers is not wise, unless they teach a well-balanced doctrine. Too many teach their own interpretation of Scripture. Beware of those who believe it is unnecessary to go to seminary and study the Word. Even when the Holy Spirit is our teacher, there is wisdom in a multitude of counselors. I have completed Bible studies at Assemblies of God colleges to qualify for ordination, which has given me a firm foundation and accountability.

Ever since the Charismatic Movement, a smorgasbord of teachers and prophets have surfaced. Some ideas are sound and some are not. One guideline to follow is: Avoid movements that are teaching an exclusive message to the Body of Christ. In addition, avoid the single crusaders who criticize the doctrines they do not agree with. Does their message judge the majority consensus of the overall Church? Our foundation must be established in Christ and the biblical example of the early Church. When we are led by the Spirit of Truth then we will be equipped to live for God. We will worship Him, obey Him, take His side against sin, stand for righteousness, resist and hate evil, perform works of kindness, imitate Him, pursue Him, serve Him, and be filled with the Spirit. The Apostle Paul describes what it takes to walk by faith:

> For what the Law could not do, weak as it was through the flesh, God did: sending His own Son in the likeness of sinful flesh and [as an offering] for sin, He condemned sin in the flesh, so that the requirement of the Law might be fulfilled in us, who do not walk according to the flesh but according to the Spirit (Romans 8:3-4).

It is the work of the Holy Spirit that helps us become Christ-like. We are quickened, made alive, by His indwelling presence. The Holy Spirit gives us the power to lay hands on the sick and see them recover. The Lord Jesus has already broken the chains of bondage that have kept God's people bound, unproductive, immature, weak and faithless.

Synopsis for ChapterFour
BURNING FAITH THAT OVERCOMES

Without a burning faith, it is impossible to please the Lord. Walking by faith changes our perspective on life and eternity. It calls for being single-minded and placing our complete trust in the Lord Jesus Christ. Without this confidence, we will shrink back in fear (Hebrews 10:38). Faith is merely trusting the LORD. Believing Christ to become our strength is not an accomplishment, but rather a willingness to allow Christ's power to keep us in difficult challenges. Leaning on the Lord gives us the power to rise above suffering and trials. With His strength, we can run the spiritual race without tiring. We will soar above every difficulty as the eagle that soars into the sky, high above the storm. God's Word promises that if we faithfully trust in Him, He will provide whatever we need to sustain us. As Truth, the Spirit becomes our authority for everything. As we study the scriptures, we should ask the Holy Spirit to guide us into deeper truth and understanding. Faith and obedience are inseparable, just as unbelief and disobedience are related. The Apostle James taught, "Faith without works is dead" (James 2:20).

Question?

Is your faith alive? Are you walking in obedience to the Lord's commands? Do you rely on the Holy Spirit, and Christ's intercession to work in your life to enable you to respond to God by faith? If we ever stop relying in God's grace and the leading of the Holy Spirit, then our faith will die.

Visit the Prayer Guide in Part Two, Chapter Three which Includes a list of scriptures to pray for numerous needs.

Part Two

Empowering Prayer with Scripture

Chapter One

The Call to Pray

Therefore He is also able to save to the uttermost those who come to God through Him, since He always lives to make intercession for them.
–Hebrews 7:25

The average Christian considers prayer to be a time when they cry out to God in a crisis for a desperate need. God will often respond to a distress S.O.S. prayer; however, reaching God's ear is certain when we have built a daily relationship with the Father. We read in Psalm, chapter 34, God hears the righteous: "The righteous cry out, and the Lord hears them; he delivers them from all their troubles. The Lord is close to the brokenhearted and saves those who are crushed in spirit" (Psalm 34:17-18). Who are the righteous? They are born-again believers cleansed by the blood of the Lamb. They have a heart after the LORD, and spend time developing their prayer relationship with the Father.

Scripture shows prayer is not seasonal; it is a daily discipline and a blessing to God. Believers should be asking this question: "What is my personal call to pray?" What does the Bible say about all of God's people praying? The answer is found in the Book of Acts, where we see the entire Church engaged in daily prayer. The early Church lived in a hostile society, and everyone spent each day with fervent persevering prayer; which made them powerful against the evil Roman Empire. Although they experienced persecution, they were victorious to expand and grow in numbers. The Gospel spread beyond Jerusalem into all of Asia Minor and even Rome itself. The gospel continues to be spread today in regions where the Body of Christ suffers under life-threatening persecution.

The *Power of the King's Scepter* is a study that enlightens the believer with a richer understanding of communicating with the Godhead in prayer. The principles of prayer always work, even if we pray silently or verbally, whether we pray at home, or in the market place. Personal prayer should be consistent in the secret prayer closet, so it will work wherever or whenever. Some Christians marvel at committed Muslims who stop to pray five times a day; however, Christians maintain a prayerful life, 24/7. This is practicing the presence of the LORD; which far surpasses the religious act of stopping to pray repetitiously five times a day. To quote E. M. Bounds: "When we say that prayer puts God to work, it is simply to say that man has it in his power by prayer to move God to work in His own way among men, in which way He would not work if prayer was not made. Thus while prayer moves God to work, at the same time God puts prayer to work."[1]

Prayer becomes a shield blocking all the fiery darts of Satan, who is the accuser of God's children. As Mediator, Jesus intercedes at the Throne reconciling us with the Father: "For there is one God and one Mediator between God and men, the Man Christ Jesus….." (1 Timothy 2:5). We rejoice that we have Jesus Christ as our Mediator; noting how Job could not identify with one during his trial, "Nor is there any mediator between us, Who may lay his hand on us both" (Job 9:33). When we are unaware of the believer's position in Jesus as Mediator, the easier it is for Satan to keep us under condemnation. Such revelations open up our understanding when we belong to a sound Bible study group. Scripture explains that Jesus Christ is the way to the Throne of Grace, "But now He has obtained a more excellent ministry, inasmuch as He is also Mediator of a better covenant, which was established on better promises" (Hebrews 8:6). Confidence to enter God's presence is only possible by the Blood of Jesus and His priestly ministry:

> And having a high priest over the House of God; let us draw near with a true heart in full assurance of faith, having our hearts sprinkled from an evil conscience, and our bodies washed with pure water (Hebrews 10:21-22).

Prayer is the Christian's Lifeline to God

Prayer is an invisible cord connecting souls with the eternal Father. In John, chapter fifteen, Jesus used the parable of the "true vine" giving life to the branches in describing a life-union with His disciples. The branch only exists to bear fruit, and Jesus is the "true vine" Who is the lifeline to God. Prayer is the lifeline which keeps the branch connected to Jesus and the Father. This is why the foundation of the Church must be built on prayer; otherwise, it is the work of man. In observing the life of Christ on earth, He stayed connected to the Father and the Holy Spirit through prayer. He set a model of prayer for His disciples and spent hours praying during the night. If we choose to model the life of Christ, then we should be determined to become people of prayer.

Paul outlines the top prayer priorities for the Church in 1 Timothy 2:1-2:

1. The nation, our President, members of the cabinet, members of Congress and the judicial system.
2. The peace of Jerusalem and Israel; the leaders of Israel's government.
3. Pastors, priests, bishops and leaders over the Church of Jesus Christ.
4. Pray for spiritual awakening and renewal in the nation and society.
5. Pray for public officials to be redeemed, delivered, healed, and baptized in the Holy Spirit.
6. Pray for the well-being of your own family members, parents, children, and loved ones.

Jesus is our Model for Prayer

The Lord Jesus performed many ministries on earth; prayer, healing, preaching, and teaching. We now see the extensions of these ministries in the Church. The high priestly ministry of Christ at the right hand of the Father is one of the revelations given to the Apostle Paul. The apostle teaches in Romans 8:34, "Who is he who condemns? It is Christ who died, and furthermore is also risen, who is even at the right hand of God, who also makes intercession for us." This is what Jesus is doing for us now in His present-day ministry at the right hand of God:

> Therefore He is also able to save to the uttermost those who come to God through Him, since He always lives to make intercession for them (Hebrews 7:25).

The Lord wants to release His heart of intercession into His body of believers; for prayers become effective when they agree with the Creator. Inclining our ear to the Lord, obeying His Voice and agreeing with Him, produces divine faith (John 14:8-16). Anything that comes into fruition happens through prayer and faith: "Now faith is the substance of things hoped for, the evidence of things not seen" (Hebrews 11:1). Sometimes, we have not, because, we ask not (James 4:2). Intercession is just as essential in the Church as pulpit preaching; some are called as full-time ministers to intercede and worship. The anointing Jesus had for ministry during the day; He received during His night of prayer. He interceded and called on the Father, then he would perform the tasks the Father showed him.

What is the foundation of our faith?

The Word of God is the foundation of our faith. When you love and fear the LORD, and have a hunger for the Word; you will be sensitive to the Holy Spirit's conviction. Then when you pray the likeness of Christ will increase within your life, and you will grow and mature in obedience and love. When we choose to obey the Word of God, we have the favor to abide in Christ. A disobedient heart cannot expect to abide in Christ. Jesus taught this kingdom principle to His disciples in John, chapter 15:

> I am the true vine, and My Father is the vinedresser. Every branch in Me that does not bear fruit He takes away; and every branch that bears fruit He prunes, that it may bear more fruit. You are already clean because of the word which I have spoken to you. Abide in Me, and I in you. As the branch cannot bear fruit of itself, unless it abides in the vine, neither can you, unless you abide in Me (John 15:1-4).

We will become dead branches if we ignore or neglect to obey the Word of God. We do not have life if we do not obey His commands, and will be pruned from the vine. There is a terrible plague of apathy sweeping over the Church today, which frustrates many sincere shepherds. Dry, dead branches are springing up all over the Lord's vineyard, bearing the evil fruit of adultery, fornication, drinking, drugs, and apostasy. These dead branches are pruned by the Vinedresser's knife, which is a two-edged sword, the Word of God. In John 15:9-10, Jesus states that He faithfully obeyed every commandment of His Father, and He calls that abiding:

> As the Father loved Me, I also have loved you; abide in My love. If you keep My commandments, you will abide in My love, just as I have kept My Father's commandments and abide in His love.

Most Christians today, do not know the Word of God because they do not take the time to read it. A CBS News poll revealed there are nearly 40 million people reading the Bible daily in the U. S. and Canada, compared with 143 million people checking Facebook every day. Here is a spiritual key or kingdom principle: It is impossible to bear the fruit of righteousness without His Word abiding in you. Neglect of the Word causes apathy within the Church and a spiritual barrenness within believers. The Epistles call the Bride of Christ a remnant who will one-day wear a robe of righteousness. Another parallel is the Bride's wedding garment, ".....Not having spot or wrinkle or any such thing, but that she should be holy and without blemish" (Ephesians 5:25). The Bride of Christ is compared to the wise virgins who trimmed their wicks and had enough oil for their lamps. The Bride is walking in the abiding presence of the Lord Jesus Christ, and will surely be ready to meet the Bridegroom. (Read the parable of the Ten Virgins in Matthew 25:1-13.)

Faith Overcomes Condemnation

We cannot expect to have our prayers answered with hidden fear, or unbelief and insecurity. These cause us to condemn our own heart, and our prayers do not reach the Father. The enemy is always at work to hammer the child of God with condemnation. We must be free of condemnation to have our prayers answered. The love of Christ gives us God's grace, and our confidence is in Christ:

> Beloved, if our heart does not condemn us, we have confidence toward God. And whatever we ask we receive from Him, because we keep His commandments and do those things that are pleasing in His sight (1 John 3:21-22).

The assurance of our standing with God gives boldness in prayer. Answered prayer is not a reward for obedience, but answered prayer is evidence that we are in harmony with God's will. Every created person has the opportunity to cry out to God; especially those who cry out during a devastating time in their lives. The loving heart of God responds to the prodigals who cry out for deliverance and salvation, or the carnal Christian, who is caught up with the world's ways. God's mercy always extends to those who call upon the Name of Jesus. The Law of God does not have the power to make one righteous, or to deliver one who is struggling against sin: "For we know that the law is spiritual: but I am carnal, sold under sin" (Romans 7:14). 1 Corinthians, chapter two, states it this way:

> But the natural man does not receive the things of the Spirit of God, for they are foolishness to him; nor can he know them, because they are spiritually discerned. But he who is spiritual judges all things, yet he himself is rightly judged by no one, (vv. 14, 15).

While the law can enlighten one's conscience, it is powerless to produce holiness in your life. You can keep your heart free from condemnation by being quick to confess sin. In that way, your heart will not condemn you. Christians must have clean hands and a pure heart before entering into prayer: ".....For everyone to whom much is given, from him much will be required; and to whom much has been committed, of him they will ask the more" (Luke 12:48). Be confident in prayer, knowing the Holy Spirit lives in you. Prayer brings us to the place where we depend on the Father, Son and Holy Spirit. Here are several keys to help you arrive at the proper mind-set when approaching the Throne of Grace:

- **Christ-centered disciples hear the heart of God; even so, they are not puffed up with spiritual pride.** They live by the Spirit of God, bear good fruit, and seek to have more power in their prayer life. They have surrendered all fleshly desires to the control of the Holy Spirit, Who completes the work of purification within their soul. The Holy Spirit gives us that hunger for solid spiritual food and a thirst to understand the deeper mysteries of God. This is the only way Christ's disciples can move toward intimacy with the Lord Jesus Christ. (Read Hebrews 5:12-14)

- **According to the Word of God, all the powers of Heaven are behind you when you pray.** Christ dwells within believers by the Holy Spirit making them to be, ".....More than conquerors through Him who loved us" (Romans 8:37). Throughout his epistles, the Apostle Paul teaches about having victory over the flesh and the devil's temptations.
- **When you pray the Word of God, the heavenly hosts are dispatched to perform it.** Angels are ministering spirits commissioned to minister to God's servants. Elisha could see the invisible army of God, which had more firepower than the horses and chariots of Syria's formidable army. In 2 Kings 6:14-17, Elisha told his servant, "'Do not fear, for those who are with us are more than those who are with them.' And Elisha prayed, and said, 'Lord, I pray, open his eyes that he may see.' Then the Lord opened the eyes of the young man, and he saw. And behold, the mountain was full of horses and chariots of fire all around Elisha."

What is Prophetic Prayer?

Scripture is powerful when proclaimed verbally. Jewish Rabbis read the Torah out loud, like Ezra read the Pentateuch out loud to the Jewish exiles after their deliverance from Babylon. It was a prophetic act when Ezekiel followed *Yahweh's* instructions to speak His Word. In Ezekiel 37:9-10, God told Ezekiel to prophesy to the wind, the Holy Ghost: "Thus says the Lord.....Bring life." When Ezekiel spoke, he was commanding the Holy Ghost to fulfill God's Word, His Covenant. It is the Holy Spirit's mission to fulfill the Word of the Sovereign God. Ezekiel's vision of Israel's restoration was fulfilled during the time of Cyrus, but it was considered truly prophetic when God gathered the Israelites to their land in 1948, following World War II. The Word of God prophesied of Israel not only experiencing a political revival, but also a spiritual rebirth.

Bible prophecies deal with future events that lie just over the horizon — they will come to pass in *Yahweh's* time frame. In this latter time of prophecy, it is easy to interpret Bible prophecy with the daily news reports. Since today's media spin masters distort the truth; then Christians must guard against listening to the opinions of the media spin masters. The average person becomes influenced by the perspectives of the news media; they become deceived and believe the lie. 2 Thessalonians 2:11 says, ".....God will send them strong delusion, that they should believe the lie."

Only the Bible has the Correct Interpretation

Knowledge of what the future holds is the best way to be prepared as we see Scripture being fulfilled. Prophecy is what God desires to reveal to us through the Spirit. I have heard evangelical preachers dissuade their congregations from focusing on end time prophecies and events. There is always great wisdom in maintaining a balanced perspective; which comes by hearing the truth and discerning by the Holy Spirit. Some pastors do not trust their congregant's ability to discern the times, which raises the question, who is encouraging the sons of Issachar today? The Tribe of Issachar, "…..had understanding of the times, to know what Israel ought to do…." (1 Chronicles 12:32).

Approximately one-third of the Bible contains prophecy, including the last book, John's Revelation of Christ which is entirely devoted to future events.[2] "Fulfilled prophecy is one of the most powerful proofs that the Bible truly is the Word of God. Since all of the prophecies that should have been fulfilled in the first coming of Christ were fulfilled to the finest detail, we can be sure that the Bible itself is God's revelation to man since no human writer could be 100% accurate. 2 Peter 1:21 says, 'For prophecy never came by the will of man, but holy men of God spoke as they were moved by the Holy Spirit.'"[3]

God's Prophetic Word Lights the Path Ahead

The Bible is not only historical; it is alive with prophecy, which is *Yahweh's* way of lighting the path ahead for His Church. Theologians estimate that close to ninety-nine percent of all Bible prophecy has previously been fulfilled. This has been proven by comparing Bible prophecies to world history. Prophecy is still being carried out today; while the stage is being set for others to occur. For example, we see Ezekiel's prophecy in chapters 38 and 39, taking shape as Russia aligns with Israel's Arab enemies: Jerusalem has become a burdensome stone for all nations (Zechariah 12:2-3); the sacrificial system of worship in the temple is ready to be resumed (Daniel 9:27, Matthew 24:15, and Revelation 11:1). Then, there are the futuristic end time prophecies: The mark of the Beast in the right hand or forehead needed to buy or sell (Revelation 13:16-18), and tribulation so severe that no flesh would survive (Matthew 24:22). We now have the technology to place a chip under the skin, or place an identification in the retina of the eye.

God's prophetic Word gives us signs to watch for that mark the end of the age. The "end times" or "last days" began at the Cross 2,000 years ago. Watching prophecy being fulfilled today is a sign that these are the last days. It is also an indicator that we need to use the remaining time to commit ourselves to holiness and evangelism. David declared, "Your word is a lamp to my feet and a light to my path" (Psalm 119:105). The Word of God is the true light in this darkened world. With today's economic woes, wars and rumors of wars, people need to know where to find, ".....The peace of God, which surpasses all understanding, will guard your hearts and minds through Christ Jesus" (Philippians 4:7). The light in the Church of Jesus Christ is the one force that can conquer and dispel the darkness. Isaiah declared, "The people that walked in darkness have seen a great light" (Isaiah 9:2). Light represents understanding. Billy Graham said: "No informed person today will deny that the human race walks in darkness. We face dilemmas and problems that seemingly have no answer. Many observers despair of solving the problems of the world; they suspect that we are people who not only walk in darkness but who walk in darkness to our doom."[4]

> All things were made through Him, and without Him nothing was made that was made. In Him was life, and the life was the light of men (John 1:3-4).

Answering God's Call to Pray and Intercede

> So I sought for a man among them who would make a wall, and stand in the gap before Me on behalf of the land, that I should not destroy it; but I found no one (Ezekiel 22:30).

Prayer comes from the inner heart and is the only way humanity can communicate with the Creator. If Jesus, the perfect Son of God, spent his nights praying to the Father; how much more do we imperfect mortals need to spend nights in prayer and in close communion with our heavenly Father. Prayer also unites the believer with the Body of Christ around the globe. Throughout the Bible, there are examples of great men and women who were willing to pay the prayer price of intercession, and develop their dependence upon God. The ability to practice continual prayer can be seen operating in the life of Abraham, Jacob, Moses, Daniel, Nehemiah, Hannah, David, Elijah, and the New Testament apostles. The great power and authority they walked in is a product of their consistent communication with the Elohim God. Most people do not pursue prayer only because they do not know how to communicate with the Godhead. They do not take time to pray because they give more priority to the cares of life. I recommend reading the life story of Rees Howell: Intercessor.

Prayer is learned by following the example of Jesus. Repeatedly, Jesus sought to be alone with His Father in prayer: "And it came to pass in those days, that he went out into a mountain to pray, and continued all night in prayer to God" (Luke 6:12). We learn to pray by observing humanity as Christ does; seeing through the eyes of God with unconditional love. Ask Jesus to help you see through His eyes of compassion, instead of looking through your own heart of selfishness. I have found the most effective way to pray is to seek the Father's heartbeat by asking: "Father, what is on your heart today?" Prayer comes naturally when we look for opportunities to help, rather than seeking what we can get. (Read John 13:13-17) Christ often worked His miracles because He had compassion for the person in need: "And when Jesus went out He saw a great multitude; and He was moved with compassion for them, and healed their sick" (Matthew 14:14).

When we pray, we must believe in Christ's identity as the Son of God, and seek His Baptism of Fire. This baptism enables believers to move in the same demonstration of power that Christ did. The 120 believers who waited in the upper room after Christ's ascension to the Father, became the first recipients of the Baptism of Fire. Peter preached that this gift is readily available to all generations (Acts 2:38-39). You will want to read another book in this series, Power of the King's Fire, which unveils the mystery of how the Holy Spirit empowers the Church. It must have fire to fulfill Christ's mission throughout the earth. The Baptism of Fire brings the power of the resurrected Christ to live within our own spirit. In John 11:25-26 Jesus said to Martha: "I am the resurrection and the life. He who believes in Me, though he may die, he shall live. And whoever lives and believes in Me shall never die. Do you believe that Jesus is the Resurrection of the dead, which John recorded in Revelation 1:18?

> I am He who lives, and was dead, and behold, I am alive forevermore. Amen. And I have the keys of Hades and of Death.

Where did the Practice of Prayer Begin?

Communication with the divine Creator began in Genesis with the creation of man, when the Creator walked and talked with Adam in the Garden of Eden. Scripture reveals that later, *Elohim* communicated with Enoch, Noah, Abraham, Isaac, Jacob. In the days of Moses, the first commandment of prayer originates with the greatest of all Hebrew commandments, the Shema. During His years on earth, Jesus followed the Judaic custom of prayer. For instance, He prayed the Shema in Mark 12:29-30: "Hear, O Israel, the Lord our God, the Lord is one. And you shall love the Lord your God with all your heart, with all your soul, with all your mind, and with all your strength.' This is the first commandment." The concept of praying and declaring the Word of God began when *Yahweh* gave specific instructions to His people about obeying His Word in Deuteronomy 6:4-9:

> And these words which I command you today shall be in your heart. You shall teach them diligently to your children, and shall talk of them when you sit in your house, when you walk by the way, when you lie down, and when you rise up. You shall bind them as a sign on your hand, and they shall be as frontlets between your eyes. You shall write them on the doorposts of your house and on your gates.

This is the most important prayer in the Hebrew Bible. Jamieson, Fausset and Brown (1871) explain in their commentary on Deuteronomy 6:4-9: The purpose of *Yahweh's* instruction here is this: "The grand design of all the institutions prescribed to Israel was to form a religious people, whose national character should be distinguished by that fear of the Lord their God which would ensure their divine observance of His worship and their steadfast obedience to His will."[5] Similarly, it was God's divine plan to establish America as a God-fearing nation. John Adams, signer of the Declaration of Independence and Second President of the United States commented: "[W]e have no government armed with power capable of contending with human passions unbridled by morality and religion. . . . Our constitution was made only for a moral and religious people. It is wholly inadequate to the government of any other."[6]

In Israel's early history, the Temple Jews also had a group of prayers everyone prayed, which have been passed along through the generations as their religious tradition. These prayers are based on the Law of God, and were specifically instructed to Joshua when *Yahweh* instructed: "This Book of the Law shall not depart from your mouth, but you shall meditate in it day and night, that you may observe to do according to all that is written in it. For then you will make your way prosperous, and then you will have good success" (Joshua 1:8). We can see that David prayed these prayers from his writings in the Psalms: "But his delight is in the law of the Lord, and in His law he meditates day and night" (Psalm 1:2). The prophets prayed them, as can be seen in their prophetic books. The Prophet Jonah recited portions of many of the Psalms (Jonah 2). Jesus proclaimed, "These are the words which I spoke to you while I was still with you, that all things must be fulfilled which were written in the Law of Moses and the Prophets and the Psalms concerning Me," (Luke 24:44).

Bible history documents how prayer has always been essential for Jews and Christians. Jesus taught His disciples to pray and then commissioned them to go out and make new disciples. The most effective method of prayer is to pray the Scriptures, and pray through the Holy Spirit Who imparts wisdom. I mentioned earlier what Paul said to Timothy, "For there is one God and one Mediator between God and men, the Man Christ Jesus….." (1 Timothy 2:5). Without a Mediator, the way to the Father is blocked by our sin. Christians are to pray to the Father through the Son Jesus Christ, Who said: "I am the way, the truth, and the life. No one comes to the Father except through Me" (John 14:6). The First Commandment of Moses' Law states: "You shall have no other gods before Me" (Exodus 20:3); which includes saints or Jesus' mother Mary.

According to the Dictionary of Biblical Imagery: Superstitious rites are not interrelated with prayer to the Creator God. Sorcery, Astrology, Tarot Cards, and Spiritualists are all connected to the occult; the demonic underworld of Satan. Scripture tells how Israel's King Saul decided to visit a medium (spiritualist), for advice (1 Samuel, chapter 28). The Spirit of the LORD has now departed Saul, and an evil spirit from the LORD troubled him (1 Samuel 16:14-23). The Prophet

Samuel is dead, and Saul is cut off from communicating with *Yahweh*; so he sought a medium, which is apostasy. How much different this was from the anointing upon David, who had open communication with *Yahweh* all of his days. Saul was self-centered; he was man's king. David was a man after God's own heart; God's king. Scripture cautions us to rely on the Holy Spirit so we can discern the apostasy present in the world today.

Apostasy is a Sign of the End-Times

"Apostasy is also pictured as the heart turning away from God (Jeremiah 17:5–6) and righteousness (Ezekiel 3:20). In the OT it centers on Israel's breaking covenant relationship with God through disobedience to the law (Jeremiah 2:19), especially following other gods (Judges 2:19) and practicing their immorality (Daniel 9:9–11). . . . Following the Lord or journeying with him is one of the chief images of faithfulness in the Scriptures. . . . The . . . Hebrew root (swr) is used to picture those who have turned away and ceased to follow God ('I am grieved that I have made Saul king, because he has turned away from me,' 1 Samuel 15:11). . . . The image of turning away from the Lord, who is the rightful leader, and following behind false gods is the dominant image for apostasy in the Old Testament."[7]

The Bible records the words prayed in ancient times, and through the Holy Spirit's instruction, they are given to us to pray. Paul said it this way, "These things we also speak, not in words which man's wisdom teaches but which the Holy Spirit teaches, comparing spiritual things with spiritual" (1 Corinthians 2:13). The *Bible Study Tools Commentary* explains: "Which things also we speak–Namely, the things which have not been seen by the eye, heard by the ear, or understood by the heart of man; the things God has prepared for his people; the deep things of God; the things of God which are only known to the Spirit; the things that are freely given to them of God, and made known to them by the Spirit of God: these things are spoken out, preached, and declared to the sons of men....."[8]

Prayer Means Commitment

The Apostle Paul told his spiritual son Timothy, "Be diligent to present yourself approved to God, a worker who does not need to be ashamed, rightly dividing the word of truth" (2 Timothy 2:15). We should be conscientious to learn all we can from the teachings of those forerunners who had a wealth of experience. Above all, allow the Holy Spirit to teach you and guide you. This study about prayer, gives insight into the depths of prophetic and apostolic intercession; the prayers of Jesus and your own personal communion with God. We need to rekindle the embers, fan the flame, and keep the gift of prayer burning. The gift of prayer which is latent within each believer needs to be stirred up as Paul taught Timothy, who is representative of all disciples who serve Jesus Christ:

> Therefore I remind you to stir up the gift of God which is in you through the laying on of my hands. For God has not given us a spirit of fear, but of power and of love and of a sound mind (2 Timothy 1:6).

Every church needs the entire congregation involved in prayer; which means the emphasis on prayer needs to be birthed into the hearts of the congregation from the pulpit. Some will pray more than others, but everyone needs to be committed to prayer. Those who are committed to serious intercession will heed the call as watchmen on the wall. Prayer takes the believer into deeper levels of intimacy with the Lord Jesus and gives a revelation of His Kingly authority. Ephesians 2:6 tells us that we are seated in heavenly places with Him; and Revelation 8:3-4 tells how our prayers become incense before the Throne of God.

The Lord Jesus is calling His Bride to stand in the presence of His throne through prayer and worship. The Bride of Christ is a parallel of Queen Esther in the Old Testament going before the king, and received favor when she touched the king's scepter. In the New Testament, the Lord will impart favor and authority to His Bride when She comes before the throne in prayer. Jesus explained this in Matthew 28:18-20:

> And Jesus came and spoke to them, saying, "All authority has been given to Me in heaven and on earth. Go therefore and make disciples of all the nations, baptizing them in the name of the Father and of the Son and of the Holy Spirit, teaching them to observe all things that I have commanded you; and lo, I am with you always, even to the end of the age." Amen.

Why Some Prayers go Unanswered

The Bride of Christ is to go into all the earth on behalf of her King, advancing His kingdom and authority. This is how the nations are to be touched by the glory of the Lord. We need the anointing of the Holy Spirit to fulfill Christ's mission. This means seeking the impartation of Christ, rather than the impartation of men or women. When the believer enters His presence, King Jesus extends His righteous scepter of favor and authority. This is how to receive an impartation of His authority, which will grow deeper when we walk in the anointing of the Holy Ghost.

Perhaps you have been discouraged or have even given up over unanswered prayers? There are a number of reasons why prayer goes unanswered. First, ask if you are praying according to Gods will, or are you seeking to satisfy your own desire? The Apostle James writes, "You ask and do not receive, because you ask amiss, that you may spend it on your pleasures" (James 4:3). Search your motives by asking, "Am I ready to submit to whatever the LORD wants, or am I dictating to Him those things that will satisfy my own heart?" Second, remember that God's timelines are another factor for His answering prayer. His timeliness involves your faith being tested, and the development of patience. Intercessors need to be encouraged since there is always a period of waiting for prayers to be fulfilled. We will be tempted by unbelief, which grieves the heart of God and cancels out His favor. Jesus explains in Matthew 21:22, "And whatever things you ask in prayer, believing, you will receive." He also taught that faith needs only to be the size of a mustard seed:

> Then the disciples came to Jesus privately and said, "Why could we not cast it out?" So Jesus said to them, "Because of your unbelief; for assuredly, I say to you, if you have faith as a mustard seed, you will say to this mountain, Move from here to there, and it will move; and nothing will be impossible for you" (Matthew 17:19-20).
>
> We do not have to develop giant faith, because while we wait upon the Lord, our strength (faith) is renewed: "But those who wait on the Lord shall renew their strength; they shall mount up with wings like eagles, they shall run and not be weary, they shall walk and not faint" (Isaiah 40:31).

The Power in Proclaiming God's Word

Every generation has a mandate to carry the torch and proclaim the Word of God; calling for His will to be carried out on earth as it is declared in Heaven! Daniel brought the nation of Israel out of captivity by proclaiming the words of the Prophet Jeremiah, who had declared the captivity in Babylon was to last seventy years. Seventy years later, Daniel called God's divine plan into fulfillment. We read his prayer in Daniel 9:19:

> O Lord, hear! O Lord, forgive! O Lord, listen and act! Do not delay for Your own sake, my God, for Your city and Your people are called by Your name.

By proclaiming the Word in prayer, we affirm it officially and publicly as a declaration over the land and the airways. Praying and proclaiming Scripture is much different from the "positive confession" or "name it and claim it" teachings, which use Scripture to control and manipulate situations. Powerful results occur when the Word of God is declared over the airwaves via the Internet, radio and television. I have influenced a number of radio and television station owners to play the Word of God during their dead (empty) air time. They have experienced many miracles in doing this. I initiated this during the seven years we occupied one of Iran's former embassy buildings in Washington, D. C. During our dead hours; we played the Bible and scripture worship 24/7. We saw mighty miracles in our government and within the countries we were interceding for around the globe. We conducted many live worship services and Bible teaching meetings each week, but we filled those dead hours with CDs. Our Embassy also operated a "war room" where we prayed over maps and proclaimed Scripture for persecuted people in hot spot countries. For instance, we prayed Scripture for the people of Afghanistan to be set free from the evil rule of the Taliban. This was answered when the United States took its "War against Terrorism" into the Middle East after the September 11, 2001 attack on the United States.

When the written Word is verbally declared with believing faith, nothing else can compare to its authority and power. This engages the Messiah's Scepter, His Sword, and even His Rod of Iron, which represents His authority to rule the nations. For instance, I just shared how our Embassy prayer teams make declarations into the government in Washington, and into countries around the globe by proclaiming God's prophetic Word. This type of prayer is spiritual mapping. There is also a personal benefit when proclaiming the Word of God. It releases God's prophetic power and authority into your spiritual life and into your circumstances, as well as world situations. As we study the Word of God every day it generates a reservoir within our spirit that enables us to speak the Word with prophetic authority into the atmosphere. This method of prayer transforms circumstances and fulfills God's plans and purposes. When you are praying according to God's Will, then you can prophesy His Word to fulfill it. For example, this generation can pray Joel 2:25-27, which speaks of God's plan to restore His people during the end times. Some believe prophetic scriptures for Israel are only spoken to the Jewish nation, but this is a legalistic viewpoint. God's prophetic Word speaks to all generations, including Gentiles; like Peter preached to all nations on the portico of the Upper Room in Acts, chapter two:

> But this is what was spoken by the prophet Joel: "And it shall come to pass in the last days, says God, that I will pour out of My Spirit on all flesh; your sons and your daughters shall prophesy, your young men shall see visions, your old men shall dream dreams" (vv. 16-17).

In Matthew 6:8-15, Jesus Christ, the Son of God, taught His disciples keys for bringing the Kingdom of God to earth by praying His model prayer to the Father. When we follow the leadership of Jesus in prayer, we are engaging in the highest form of discipleship. Jesus set the example of prayerfulness to His disciples. He would go to solitary places to pray. He prayed with great intensity, "with loud cries and tears" (Hebrews 5:7). I encourage all of Christ's disciples to "pray the Word," instead of just praying from your own thoughts! As your prayer life matures, you will learn to trust when the Holy Spirit gives words of wisdom to pray. The act of praying His covenant promises in Scripture, puts the LORD in remembrance of His Word, and keeps prayer pure. We also become engaged in spiritual warfare when we pray the Word. Remember: "The word of God is living and powerful, and sharper than any two-edged sword, piercing even to the division of soul and spirit, and of joints and marrow, and is a discerner of the thoughts and intents of the heart" (Hebrews 4:12). While we are proclaiming the Word; angelic hosts of the LORD become engaged in our battle.

In this decisive hour, we are experiencing the end time outpouring of the Holy Spirit being fulfilled (Joel 2:28, 29). The great harvest for this final season in the Church Age must be saturated with prayer and intercession. We should not withhold our travail and our tears; which comes out of our mouths, like revival raining down upon the earth (Isaiah 45:8). Be encouraged and agree with the Holy Spirit, Who is the discerner of the heart:

> Now He who searches the hearts knows what the mind of the Spirit is, because He makes intercession for the saints according to the will of God (Romans 8:27).

What does your Bible mean to you?

What place do you give the Word of God in your daily life? If you truly love the LORD, then you will fall in love with His Word. The biggest challenge is finding the time to study the Word. Bible study calendars help people read through the Bible in one year; reading a few chapters each day. This usually takes about fifteen minutes daily. I have also conducted word searches in a concordance. For example, search the word love and read all the scriptures that come up. This type of study is powerful and transforms your viewpoint. The Bible is God-breathed and becomes alive in your spirit when you study it and meditate on it. Without a foundation of the Word in their lives, people become overwhelmed with fear in these perilous times. Today, conflicts between nations are more prevalent and violent fulfilling the words Jesus prophesied in Matthew, chapter 24:

> And you will hear of wars and rumors of wars. See that you are not troubled; for all these things must come to pass, but the end is not yet. For nation will rise against nation, and kingdom against kingdom. And there will be famines, pestilences, and earthquakes in various places. All these are the beginning of sorrows.

World leaders are frustrated searching for ways to establish peace amid wars and rumors of war. World food supplies are endangered by catastrophic floods and droughts. Millions of refugees are misplaced because of rogue governments; ethnic and religious genocide deals a deathblow through physical violence and persecution in over 120 countries of the world. God's Word is the only hope of comfort during these perilous times. The Holy Spirit converts the intellectual knowledge of God's Word into Rhema; which is the key to living and moving in the power of the Holy

Ghost. It is not a work of the flesh but of the Spirit: "not by might, nor by power" (Zechariah 4:6).

How do we Meditate on God's Word?

> He who believes in Me, as the Scripture has said, out of his heart will flow rivers of living water (John 7:38).

In the King James Bible, the translation for the heart is belly. How can rivers of living water flow out of our belly? While the Almighty is in His Throne Room, at the same time, He is present within us because His Holy Spirit lives within our spirit:

> For in Him we live and move and have our being, as also some of your own poets have said, "For we are also His offspring" (Acts 17:28).

Jesus sent His Holy Spirit to help us with prayer. While praying in the heavenly language the Holy Spirit has given us, we are experiencing an active dialogue with the Father. After praying in the Spirit; wait and remain quiet and listen. Be patient, if you do not hear anything. I will often receive a word momentarily, but sometimes it could be days. Our faith is always being tested while we are practicing the presence of the Lord. When we meditate in the Word, we tarry in the Lord's presence. While you are communing with Jesus, take time to linger and absorb His Presence. Declare your love and praise of the Father. We should always reverence the LORD when praying. Addressing the Father or Jesus merely as God is very impersonal and makes them equal to the multitude of Gods in the world. Jesus is our personal Savior and Lord, and His father is our Father God. In private prayer, I always address Jesus as "Lord Jesus" and the Father as "Father God." During corporate prayer, I address them as: "Our Lord and Savior Jesus Christ," and the Almighty Father God."

Journal Those Prophetic Prayers and Revelation

A large portion of this book has been compiled from our Embassy's upper prayer room journal. Our watchmen encouraged me to compile a book from the prayers they journaled during their times praying on the wall. When we faithfully pray God's Word, we are engaging with the Holy Spirit Who releases revelation into our spirit. So be sure to record or journal the revelations the Holy Spirit enlightens within your spirit. This helps capture the truths and strategies the Spirit is speaking to you. The anointing of the Spirit within you is God's revelator. It is not just enough to study God's Word; we must surrender our heart to Him to receive His fullness. Our heart is more open to receive this fullness when we adopt the combination of prayer and fasting. Meditating on the Word and obedience go hand-in-hand. By praying the Word of God, we enter His mind and spirit, His passion. His burdens become our burdens, and His words become our words. He promises to show His power to "those whose heart is loyal to Him" (2 Chronicles 16:9). When praying the Word of God, you are joining with Jesus Christ in His heavenly intercession:

> But He, because He continues forever, has an unchangeable priesthood. Therefore He is also able to save to the uttermost those who come to God through Him, since He always lives to make intercession for them (Hebrews 7:24-25).

The Apostle John reveals in the first chapter of his gospel that Jesus is the Word! The Word came to earth and put on flesh to reveal the character of the Godhead; they are One. Scripture tells us that Christ has a divine nature; He is eternal, and He has always been in loving fellowship with the Father and the Holy Spirit. Christ's truth and power are available to all people through Him, for He is the light of the world (John 8:12). There is no other foundation for our faith. All else is sinking sand. Otherwise, we spiritualize Him through our own imaginations; developing only an ideological image of whom we think He is, ultimately missing His fullness in our lives.

> In the beginning was the Word, and the Word was with God, and the Word was God. He was in the beginning with God. All things were made through Him, and without Him nothing was made that was made. In Him was life and the life was the light of men. And the light shines in the darkness, and the darkness did not comprehend it (John 1:1-5).

After many years of ministry, it has always amazed me of the vast number of people who are unwilling to invest the time to soak in the Scriptures. When trials come along, their lives prove that their spiritual tree has shallow roots that cannot withstand the storms and trials. Jeremiah 17:8 describes a strong believer: "For he shall be like a tree planted by the waters, Which spreads out its roots by the river, And will not fear when heat comes; But its leaf will be green, And will not be anxious in the year of drought, Nor will cease from yielding fruit." I encourage those who are reading this book to believe the Holy Spirit will expand your prayer life beyond the borders of these pages. I have included a prayer guide in Part 2, Chapter Three, which includes key scriptures covering many subjects of prayer.

What are Apostolic Prayers?

The Greek word *apostolos* means to send one out as a delegate; an ambassador of the Gospel commissioned by Christ. These sent out ones are anointed with supernatural gifts that manifest miracles to save lost souls and edify the Body of Christ. An apostle is a messenger of Christ with special assignments to the Church. For instance, when I preach and teach in churches, the Holy Spirit gives me insight to what that particular body needs. Apostolic prayers send the Word of God forth to be performed according to His will. Unfortunately, today there are many praying out of their human intellect. Apostolic prayers were prayed by the apostles in the New Testament. Prophetic prayer declares scriptural prophecy in the Bible; or it receives new prophecy for future times ahead. The proof of prophecy is whether it comes to pass; it should also be discerned by church leaders.

There are many examples in the New Testament, regarding the prayers of the apostles for the Church. In Scripture, we find the apostles, the early fathers of the Church, praying for their spiritual children who belonged to the church body. While we are to love and pray for the unsaved world, we should not neglect the Church family. The Apostle Paul wrote most of the apostolic prayers in the Bible. They bring before God the concerns of the saved, whether individuals, churches or regions. Apostolic prayers should not be so general that they only ask God to bless humankind around the globe. While we pray for the needs of others, we might become part of the solution. We also may become one of the Lord's sent apostles! I always encourage believers to pray the Word and to guard against praying from their own understanding. In Matthew, chapter six, Jesus gave apostolic instruction on how to be humble in charitable deeds and to pray with piety, not like the proud Pharisees. The Lord's Prayer is included in this chapter, and is another illustration of an apostolic prayer:

> Then He said to His disciples, "The harvest truly is plentiful, but the laborers are few. Therefore pray the Lord of the harvest to send out laborers into His harvest" (Matthew 9:37-38).

New Testament Prayers are Called Apostolic

> Peter and John prayed in Acts 4:29-30: ".....Grant to Your servants that with all boldness they may speak Your word, by stretching out Your hand to heal, and that signs and wonders may be done through the name of Your holy Servant Jesus."

The Apostle Paul's prayers focused on the believer learning to know more about Christ and His power in their lives. His epistle to the Ephesians unveils the mystery of the Church as no other letter. It reveals God's secret design to form a body to express Christ's fullness on Earth. Paul faced the responsibility of uniting one people—both Jew and Gentile, among whom Christ dwells. His teachings emphasize the maturing, equipping and empowering such a body of believers. Unlike today when many give themselves the title of "apostle," the New Testament apostles never held themselves up as models for others to follow. One good example is the humility of Peter after healing the crippled man in Acts, chapter three: As the crowd began to pay homage to Peter and John because of this miracle, Peter directed them to Jesus. A true apostle is recognized by their desire to take attention away from themselves and direct people to Christ. The vessel's role is to give God the glory!

The early Pentecostal movement which began over 100 years ago was called "apostolic" because they believed it was a move of the Holy Spirit restoring the Church back to the Book of Acts. This has certainly proven to be true. Many who ministered were anointed to perform acts like the original apostles, and this continues to be active today in the Body of Christ. Later, a mighty outpouring called the Charismatic Movement spread a fire across every denomination within the Church of Jesus Christ. Some Church leaders have worked to discount the Charismatic outpouring because of the "Positive Confession" teaching that evolved out of the original movement. A genuine outpouring of the Holy Spirit should never be discounted because some redefine its intented purpose. While today's Apostolic and Prophetic Movements have received validity, believers must discern whether some of the teachings of these modern-day apostles and prophets is scriptural. I mentioned earlier that the gift of prophecy comes from the Holy Spirit, and every believer is a candidate to hear God's voice and prophesy. Some teachers claim you have to be trained for this ministry, but indeed, it is the Holy Spirit Who is doing the anointing and the teaching. Being mentored under a well-equipped teacher is always valuable, but some training centers are producing those who merely mimic others. Those who look to Jesus, and His Holy Spirit will be anointed for the five-fold offices by the Holy Spirit: "And He Himself gave some to be apostles, some prophets, some evangelists, and some pastors and teachers....." (Ephesians 4:11). Church leaders are anointed to recognize the calling of these offices.

The original apostles were anointed to minister great miracles which they used to transform their society with great faith. The early apostles remain heroes and examples of unquestionable commitment to Jesus; but the words of Paul give this testimony in 1 Corinthians 11:1, "Imitate me, just as I also imitate Christ." Jesus Christ, has passed the scepter of His power onto the Church to do even greater works today (John 14:12). Still, Scripture does not encourage believers to model themselves after the original apostles, but "to be conformed to the image of His Son" (Romans 8:29).

Apostolic Prayers of the Early Church Leaders

Apostolic ministry began in the New Testament when the founders of the Church were setting up their global mission. As I mentioned earlier, the prayers of the apostles were biblical prayers that yielded good fruit as they focused on Gods will, and the Holy Spirit directed they were to be included in the Bible. The Church grew as they directed their petitions to the Father, in the Name of Jesus Christ, and answers were received by the Holy Spirit. Apostolic prayers are foundational because they seek positive results according to God's plans and purposes. They also conduct spiritual warfare to deal with any obstacles that might be standing in the way of their mission. Apostolic prayers do not address Satan, neither do they rebuke him nor bind him in spiritual warfare (Jude 1:9). Zechariah had a vision of the High Priest in Heaven:

> Then he showed me Joshua the high priest standing before the Angel of the Lord, and Satan standing at his right hand to oppose him. And the Lord said to Satan, "The Lord rebuke you, Satan! The Lord who has chosen Jerusalem rebuke you! Is this not a brand plucked from the fire?" (Zechariah 3:1-2).

Christ did not rebuke Satan when tempted by him in the wilderness, but rather, He spoke the Word of God to the tempter. Neither did Christ address Satan while bearing the reproaches of sin and suffering on the cross. Of course, Jesus and the apostles delivered bound people by taking authority over demons. We do not read in Scripture where Jesus dealt with terrestrial principalities. He delivered people from demonic possession, but Scripture does not indicate the Son of God conducted warfare in the second heavenly. When the Apostle Paul dealt with a demon of witchcraft that controlled a woman who was harassing the meetings, the Holy Spirit did not lead Paul to deal with terrestrial principalities over the region. The Word of God is the plumbline for how spiritual warfare is performed through the believer:

> They overcame him (Satan) by the blood of the Lamb and by the word of their testimony, and they did not love their lives to the death (Revelation 12:11, Emphasis added).

The believer has been given these spiritual weapons: the Word of God, the Name of Jesus, and the blood of the Lamb. The season will soon come when Christ defeats the kingdoms of darkness once and for all: "The kingdoms of this world have become the kingdoms of our Lord and of His Christ, and He shall reign forever and ever!" (Revelation 11:15). As the Millennial reign of Christ approaches, the Holy Spirit is presently teaching His Bride to rule and reign with Him. This also means we must learn to target our prayers according to the times and seasons, like the sons of Issachar, and continue to advance the Kingdom of God until Christ's return.

Apostolic Prayers Always Bear Good Fruit

> For the fruit of the Spirit is all goodness and righteousness and truth (Ephesians 5:9).

Most Christians pray for spiritual gifts first, and overlook the need for developing spiritual fruit within their character. Spiritual gifts are extraordinary, but spiritual fruit is the product of heavenly wisdom: "But the wisdom that is from above is first pure, then peaceable, gentle, willing to yield, full of mercy and good fruits, without partiality and without hypocrisy" (James 3:17). There are nine fruits of the Spirit: "The fruit of the Spirit is love, joy, peace, longsuffering, gentleness, goodness, faith, meekness, and temperance" (Galatians 5:22-23). Scripture directs the believer to be filled with the knowledge of Gods will and includes "bearing fruit in every good work" (Colossians 1:10). Prayer in the early church was much simpler than modern religion; their only desire was to advance the Kingdom of God. Many people pray to seek God's will for their personal lives: whether they should take this job or that job, whether they should go here or go there. I have noted that getting positioned into Gods will usually happen through forced circumstances, and sometimes rather pressing ones. We bear good fruit when we are in His Will, which leads us into good works and discipleship. This begins with "being filled with the fruits of righteousness, which are by Jesus Christ, unto the glory and praise of God" (Philippians 1:11). The conditions for acquiring righteousness demand death to the old life, chastening, pruning, and abiding in Christ.

The will of God in your life comes to fruition by praying the Lord's Prayer; the model prayer Jesus taught His disciples. One portion of this prayer says, "Your Kingdom come. Your will be done on earth as it is in heaven" (Matthew 5:10). In praying this prophetic prayer, we are bringing the government of God's kingdom into our life. It is a profession of faith and shows we are submitted to the Father's will. His desire becomes our desire. Pray it daily for you and your children, and teach them to pray it every day. I have enjoyed teaching my grandchildren the Lord's Prayer.

Apostolic Prayers Reach the Nations

It takes an expanded vision to move into the realm of praying apostolic prayers for the nations. This harvest field is a promised inheritance to the Church (Psalm 2:8). Jesus Christ has passed His scepter onto the Church for the harvesting of the nations, and praying the Word gives the believer the authority of Christ's rod of iron to rule and reign. This level of prayer is only effective when anointed by the Holy Spirit's fire. In Psalm, chapter two, we read how this authority is needed to pursue the Church's inheritance of the nations with the Son of God:

> I will declare the decree: The Lord has said to Me, "You are My Son, today I have begotten You. Ask of Me, and I will give You the nations for Your inheritance, and the ends of the earth for Your possession. You shall break them with a rod of iron; You shall dash them to pieces like a potter's vessel" (Psalm 2:7-9).

Psalm 2:8 is prophetic of Christ's command for the Church to go and preach the gospel into all the nations. The Holy Spirit has given this revelation to the Bride of Christ: "He who has an ear, let him hear what the Spirit says to the churches" (Revelation 3:22). This inheritance belongs to the Church, and the nations are waiting to be conquered for the Kingdom of God. Christ did not anoint believers to stay within the Church walls:

> And Jesus came and spoke to them, saying, "All authority has been given to Me in heaven and on earth. Go therefore and make disciples of all the nations, baptizing them in the name of the Father and of the Son and of the Holy Spirit….." (Matthew 28:18-19).

The New Testament Church understood the Kingdom of God could not be established in its full power with only a few minutes of prayer a day. They were fully devoted to a life of prayer. (Read Acts 1:14; 2:42; 3:1; 6:4) Throughout modern Church history, revival and great spiritual awakening have always been birthed with fervent prayer. We can bring heaven to earth by using kingdom keys. The Scripture urges believers to:

- Continue steadfastly in prayer (Romans 12:12).
- Pray always and do not lose heart (Luke 18:1).
- Pray without ceasing (1 Thessalonians 5:17).
- Pray everywhere (1 Timothy 2:8).
- Pray with supplication in the Spirit (Ephesians 6:18).
- Persevere in prayer (Colossians 4:2).
- Pray fervently (James 5:16).

Nothing happens for the Kingdom of God without prayer. These exhortations in Scripture affirm there is no substitute for consistent daily prayer. Following them will help you gain the victory in the battle against sin, Satan, and the world. They will also enable you to succeed in your mission to win the lost. The Holy Spirit will place a nation on your heart; consider adopting it with prayer and receive your inheritance of the nations.

Synopsis for Chapter One
New Testament Prayer Focus

Jesus sent the Holy Spirit to help us with prayer. While praying in the heavenly language the Holy Spirit has given us, we are experiencing an active dialogue with the Father. Proclaiming the Word of God in prayer affirms it officially and publicly as a declaration over the land and the airways. Powerful results occur when the Word is declared over the airwaves via the Internet, radio and television. Throughout Church history, revival and great spiritual awakening have always been birthed with fervent prayer. This type of prayer is only effective with the Baptism of Fire, which enables us to move in the same demonstration of power as Christ did. Scripture indicates that prayer is not seasonal; it is a daily discipline and a blessing to God. While we are called to love and pray for the unsaved world, we should remember the true needs of the Church by developing a heart for the poor and suffering saints. We learn to pray with compassion by seeing humanity through the eyes of Christ's love (Matthew 25:35-40). While the first mission of the Church is to reach out to lost humanity with the gospel, we must never forget those in the Body of Christ, who are suffering for the sake of the cross.

Question?

Have you committed to seek the Kingdom of God and its full power with fervent prayer? Have you sought the Baptism of Fire? Are you remembering the suffering Church around the world?

Visit the Prayer Guide in Chapter Three which Includes a list of scriptures to pray for numerous needs.

Chapter Two

UNIQUE ROLE OF THE INTERCESSOR

And the smoke of the incense, with the prayers of the saints, ascended before God from the angel's hand. –Revelation 8:4

Prayer is communication with the Father, Son and Holy Ghost. Every believer is called to pray, but intercession is a ministry gift. An intercessor is one who stands in the gap. One does not choose to be an intercessor; it is an internal working of the Holy Ghost within one's spirit. Intercession is travail; a closet ministry praying behind the veil before God in prophetic intercession. *Yahweh* spoke to the Prophet Isaiah of His need for an intercessor. He was astonished there are too few conscientious to intercede:

> So truth fails, and he who departs from evil makes himself a prey. Then the LORD saw it, and it displeased Him that there was no justice. And he saw that there was no man, and wondered that there was no intercessor; Therefore His own arm brought salvation for Him; and His own righteousness, it sustained Him (Isaiah 59:15-16).

Intercession is a vital part of the Church, just like the Word being preached from the pulpit. Intercessors are called before the Throne of God on behalf of the House of God. Heaven takes notice of God's intercessors. Angels lift their ears when their voices come up to heaven. The calling is to be taken seriously and requires Holy Ghost training.

INTERCESSION IS WHEN WE BECOME DESPERATE FOR GOD!

God responds when we pray as Rachel weeping for her children: "A voice was heard in Ramah, lamentation, weeping, and great mourning, Rachel weeping for her children, refusing to be comforted, because they are no more" (Matthew 2:18). The Prophet Joel called the priests to intercede during a desperate time for the nation:

> Now, therefore, says the Lord, "Turn to Me with all your heart, with fasting, with weeping, and with mourning." So rend your heart, and not your garments; return to the Lord your God, for He is gracious and merciful, slow to anger, and of great kindness; and He relents from doing harm (Joel 2:12-13).

> Verse 17, God's priests are told: Let the priests, who minister to the Lord, weep between the porch and the altar; let them say, "Spare Your people, O Lord, and do not give Your heritage to reproach, that the nations should rule over them. Why should they say among the peoples, 'Where is their God?"

Intercessors stand in the gap against the wrath of God. Men and women who are willing to prevail with God, will surely receive the answer to their prayers. Those who are called to intercede are standing as a minister at God's altar. Intercession is a harp and bowl ministry: praise, worship, and prayer. Intercessors stand between Heaven and earth, asking God to grant mercy to unsaved people and grace to His Church. They intercede for situations the Holy Spirit has revealed for the nations and the government.

Standing in the Gap

The Church can only prosper and succeed with intensive prayer. Organized prayer is beneficial, timely and necessary. Home prayer groups are powerful to protect and shield the nation; they spare families from the onslaught of Satan against their lives. For forty years, I have personally been connected with local prayer groups, which have experienced many miraculous answers to prayer. The key to their success is the power of united prayer.

You could be instrumental in organizing the following in your home or church:

- Intercessory prayer gatherings
- Prayer watches and vigils
- Prayer conference calls
- All-night prayer watches
- 24-hour prayer chains
- Prayer before and during church services

"Be diligent to present yourself approved to God, a worker who does not need to be ashamed, rightly dividing the word of truth" (2 Timothy 2:15). We gain vision by studying the great intercessors in the scriptures and biographies of the forerunners. Take time to follow the greats who knelt before the Throne of Grace, like Moses, Daniel, Job, Nehemiah, and the many prophets of God. They interceded for God's people and confessed their national sins. We can follow their example by being faithful to stand in the gap and pray for our leaders. The Apostle Paul taught this in 1 Timothy 2:1-3:

> Therefore I exhort first of all that supplications, prayers, intercessions, and giving of thanks be made for all men, for kings and all who are in authority, that we may lead a quiet and peaceable life in all godliness and reverence. For this is good and acceptable in the sight of God our Savior.

Intercession is God's Heartbeat

> So I sought for a man among them who would make a wall, and stand in the gap before Me on behalf of the land, that I should not destroy it; but I found no one (Ezekiel 22:30).

The heart of God is always searching for those who will stand in the gap on his behalf. While we all recognize prayer is beneficial, why do so many neglect it? We can spend time reading books that will give us a fuller understanding on prayer; however, prayer matures when we invest time to develop a prayer life with the Holy Spirit. God's perfect will is often thwarted when there is a lack of intercessors to stand in the gap. Without intercession, souls are in jeopardy of destruction; darkness invades regions, and people come under demonic influence.

Currently, America is experiencing a great spiritual void. The nation is stunned at the increase in mass shootings occurring in our schools, malls, movie theatres, and on a well-protected military base. In 2012, violence and lawlessness erupted in communities across America: a shooting in an elementary school in Newtown, Connecticut; a movie theatre in Aurora, Colorado; and a Sikh Temple in Oak Creek, Wisconsin. Several years earlier it was the Ft. Hood Military Base in Texas; the Virginia Tech. Campus; and the Columbine High School in Littleton, CO. Why has violent crime surged in America by more than 460 percent since 1960? Many ask what is happening to our culture. Some call it a cultural implosion. We are not only dealing with a decline in morality; we are experiencing a spiritual void. The prayer shield is missing over America's local communities. This spiritual void is being replaced by sports, entertainment, and self-indulgence.

Today, it is rare to see a church that will stand out as a "house of prayer" protecting and shielding local communities. When praying people are willing to stand in the gap they bring healing to the polluted land which has become corrupted by sin. Their intercession convicts people to repent of their sin; otherwise, sin causes a breach in the hedge of protection surrounding a community and allows evil to pour in upon the people. When God's judgment is imminent, there is a gap between God and man, and only intercession can repair the breach. Repentance is the only way back:

> If My people who are called by My name will humble themselves, and pray and seek My face, and turn from their wicked ways, then I will hear from heaven, and will forgive their sin and heal their land (2 Chronicles 7:14).

Abraham Interceded for Sodom and Gomorrah

Elohim shared with Abraham His plan to destroy Sodom and Gomorrah: "Because the outcry against Sodom and Gomorrah is great and because their sin is very grave...." (Read Genesis 18:16-33; 19:1-27). Biblical history reveals that these cities were given over to sodomy, homosexuality and selfish lust. God revealed His plan to Abraham because he was a friend of *Elohim*; he feared the LORD. History would prove that Abraham was to become a great nation, and even the Messiah would come from his loins:

> .....Abraham shall surely become a great and mighty nation, and all the nations of the earth shall be blessed in him (Genesis 18:18).

> The secret of the Lord is with those who fear Him, and He will show them His covenant (Psalm 25:14).

> .....His secret counsel is with the upright (Proverbs 3:32).

In Genesis 18:22-23, Abraham pleaded with *Elohim* to spare Sodom, because his nephew Lot and his family lived there. He interceded for Sodom and Gomorrah to be spared for the sake of the righteous; however, they could not be spared because not even ten righteous were found in the twin cities. God answered Abraham's prayer for Lot and his family to be spared from the destruction of Sodom and Gomorrah. They were rescued by the same angels who were sent to execute the fiery judgment of the Almighty, which destroyed the cities forever.

Standing in the Gap for your Nation

> Therefore I exhort first of all that supplications, prayers, intercessions, and giving of thanks be made for all men, for kings and all who are in authority, that we may lead a quiet and peaceable life in

all godliness and reverence. For this is good and acceptable in the sight of God our Savior..... (1 Timothy 2:1-3).

The sovereign Lord commands us in Scripture to pray for our leaders, whether we agree with them or not. Pray they will be led by the sevenfold spirit of the LORD, following His wisdom and discernment (Isaiah 11:1-4). Pray they will govern with the fear of the Lord and uphold the provisions of the nation's Constitution. Faith trusts the sovereign Lord, even if the country is heading in the wrong direction; prayer reaches the Throne of God who holds the nations in His hand:

- I am God Almighty; walk before Me, and be blameless (Genesis 17:1).
- Nothing will be impossible for God (Luke 1:37).
- I know that You can do all things, and that no purpose of Yours can be thwarted (Job 42:2).

Our leaders face heavy decisions, and they need our prayers. The fate of the nation hangs in the balance when it comes to 55 million abortions, a $17 trillion debt, high unemployment, and challenges with so many rogue nations. We must all pray for the president, his cabinet and foreign policy team. Pray for the leaders in the Congress, the Supreme Court justices and military leaders. If you are among those who criticize rather than pray, then repent of an ungodly attitude. We all need to humble ourselves before Almighty God:

> If we confess our sins, He is faithful and just to forgive us our sins and to cleanse us from all unrighteousness (I John 1:9).

The fear of the LORD is what caused the ancient city of Nineveh to repent and be spared of God's judgment. Start praying daily for your leaders, according to the Scriptures:

- **Pray** for divine intervention to spare America from God's judgment.
- **Pray** for the Lord's mercy to grant us a Third Great Awakening.
- **Pray** for the Lord to end abortion and forgive us of this terrible sin.
- **Pray** for traditional marriage to be restored state by state.
- **Pray** according to His will not your own.
- **Stand** with Israel and "Pray for the peace of Jerusalem" (Psalm 122:6).

Believe the Lord will answer your prayers:

- The prayer of a righteous man is powerful and effective (James 5:16).
- This is the confidence we have in approaching God: that if we ask anything according to his will, he hears us. And if we know that He hears us, whatever

we ask, we know that we have the petitions that we have asked of Him (1 John 5:14-15).

- And pray in the Spirit on all occasions with all kinds of prayers and requests. With this in mind, be alert and always keep on praying for all the saints (Ephesians 6:18).
- In the same way, the Spirit helps us in our weakness. We do not know what we ought to pray for, but the Spirit himself intercedes for us with groans that words cannot express (Romans 8:26).
- When you ask, you do not receive, because you ask with wrong motives, that you may spend what you get on your pleasures (James 4:3).
- And I will do whatever you ask in my name, so that the Son may bring glory to the Father. You may ask me for anything in my name, and I will do it (John 14:13-14).

Man's impatient nature hates to wait for God. The self-sufficient person prefers to act on the impulse of a good idea, but sometimes good ideas get in the way of God's plans. Some ideas seem creative, but to God, they are self-made ideas. The Word says, "There are many plans in a man's heart, nevertheless the Lord's counsel—that will stand" (Proverbs 19:21). We must surrender our thoughts to the LORD, "Trust in the Lord with all your heart, and lean not on your own understanding..." (Proverbs 3:5). Learn to test every idea, asking if it comes from the Holy Spirit, or your own thinking. Some choose to be busy with activity rather than wait on God. Christ commands that we choose to give up our natural tendencies to design our own plan or activity. Wait for the genuine leading of the Lord:

> Unless the Lord builds the house, they labor in vain who build it;
> unless the Lord guards the city, the watchman stays awake in vain
> (Psalm 127:1).

How do we Qualify as an Intercessor?

In my early years of ministry as an evangelist, I had been asking the Father to show me what was on His heart because I wanted to pray for His needs. God's heartbeat is for souls to be saved, so my prayers were already directed toward the salvation of souls. It was my desire to press further and know what His intimate needs are, so I could address them in prayer. One day, I began to experience a thumping inside my being. I was not hearing this with my natural ears; the thumping came from within my spirit. The Holy Spirit gave me the understanding that this was the Father's heartbeat. I began to receive direction to pray, in particular, for areas that had never been of special interest to me before: Africa, India, and America. At times, there were more specific instructions, but my prayer focus was beginning to expand.

This can be compared to Isaiah's experience who had developed an intimacy with Elohim and could hear the LORD's heart:

> In the year that King Uzziah died, I saw the Lord sitting on a throne, high and lifted up, and the train of His robe filled the temple. Above it stood seraphim; each one had si4x wings: with two he covered his face, with two he covered his feet, and with two he flew. And one cried to another and said: "Holy, holy, holy is the Lord of hosts; the whole earth is full of His glory!" (Isaiah 6:1-3).

Intercessory prayer is conducted by a faithful heart that is willing to communicate with the Father, Son and Holy Ghost. Intercession is a ministry gift which is an internal working of the Holy Ghost within you. Intercession is travail, when the Holy Spirit wakes you up in the early hours before dawn with burdens that are on God's heart. Intercessors are willing to be God's instruments to avert judgment intended for cities and countries. They stand in the gap to intercede for government leaders who are in authority, and they pray for spiritual revival in the Church and the nation.

Prayer Acknowledges Dependence upon the LORD

We must call upon the Lord, who enables us to resist the spiritual battles and win. Prayer is our intimate connection with the Lord and our reliance upon Him. 1 John 5:14-15, assures us of success in prayer:

> Now this is the confidence that we have in Him, that if we ask anything according to His will, He hears us. And if we know that He hears us, whatever we ask, we know that we have the petitions that we have asked of Him.

We can be confident in prayer when we know our hearts are right with God. The key is to believe He will answer, and when we pray, ask in Jesus' name (John 14:13, 14). When we pray according to His will, He will hear our prayers, and answer what we ask for. The Lord is committed to our success, but our responsibility for success lies in having God's plan match our desires. We gain dependence on the LORD when we develop a routine of prayer.

Prayer Depends on Right Motives!

Christ has called His people to live out their faith in the midst of a hostile world. He has equipped them to meet this challenge with the spiritual authority and power given through the Holy Spirit. They are instructed to become salt and light within every corner of society, so He can extend mercy on humanity. Being willing is not enough; right motives are essential! We are unworthy of being God's instrument if our heart is contaminated with selfish motives. Right motives reflect a healthy fear of the LORD:

> Then those who feared the Lord spoke to one another, and the Lord listened and heard them; so a book of remembrance was written before Him for those who fear the Lord and who meditate on His name (Malachi 3:16).

Each one of the New Testament apostles had a very special and unique commitment to Christ and the mission of His Church. The Apostle Paul shines out as one of the most zealous of all the apostles. Remember, Paul was Saul of Tarsus, a hard-line religious Sadducee who murdered Christians in his quest to eliminate them. He was a true enemy of the Cross. It is believed that his strong commitment was due to his dynamic conversion on the Damascus Road. We read about his spiritual encounter in Acts 9:3-6:

> As he journeyed he came near Damascus, and suddenly a light shone around him from heaven. Then he fell to the ground, and heard a voice saying to him, "Saul, Saul, why are you persecuting Me?" And he said, "Who are You, Lord?" Then the Lord said, "I am Jesus, whom you are persecuting. It is hard for you to kick against the goads." So he, trembling and astonished, said, "Lord, what do You want me to do?"

Jesus was warning this proud Sadducee that he was hurting himself in resisting the truth and the teaching of His Church, and he would truly suffer if he persisted. This visitation was a true conversion for Saul, and his hate for Christians was transformed into a deep love for Jesus as Savior and Lord. His name was changed afterward to Paul. What kept Paul fired up for Christ? Paul's writings often express his love for Jesus; his reverence and fear of the judgment day. This is not the great white throne judgment of the unsaved. However, it is the hour when all believers stand before the righteous judge Jesus Christ, who will judge every believer's works. This is when crowns are rewarded to those who will see their works withstand the fire of His judgment (1 Corinthians 3:12-13).

Paul is saying the power that saves us is the same power that keeps us, and when we walk out our salvation in fear and trembling then our motives will be right. Believers never need to face the great white throne judgment when the wicked and ungodly are judged. This judgment does not affect believers who are redeemed with the blood of the Lamb, for their past sin is covered with the blood. However, their deeds will be judged at the judgment seat of Christ:

> Therefore we make it our aim, whether present or absent, to be well pleasing to Him. For we must all appear before the judgment seat of Christ, that each one may receive the things done in the body, according to what he has done, whether good or bad (2 Corinthians 5:9-10).

Paul's single desire was to please the Lord Jesus in all that he did. He was commissioned as the apostle to the Gentiles, and suffered much persecution in that calling; nevertheless, his joy was based on the blessed hope of eternal life:

> For the grace of God that brings salvation has appeared to all men, teaching us that, denying ungodliness and worldly lusts, we should live soberly, righteously, and godly in the present age, looking for the blessed hope and glorious appearing of our great God and Savior Jesus Christ, who gave Himself for us, that He might redeem us from every lawless deed and purify for Himself His own special people, zealous for good works. Speak these things, exhort, and rebuke with all authority. Let no one despise you (Titus 2:11-15).

Consecration Gives us the Right Motives

Prayer is only successful with clean hands and a pure heart. If our hearts and minds are contaminated with the pollution of the world, we are unqualified to stand in the gap and be instruments of salvation and deliverance. If we desire to be God's instruments, we must submit to the Holy Spirit as David prayed in Psalm 139:23-24: "Search me, O God, and know my heart; try me, and know my anxieties; and see if there is any wicked way in me, and lead me in the way everlasting." This is the heart the Bible heroes prayed with: Moses, David, Daniel, Nehemiah and Esther.

We are Responsible to Guide our Heart in the Way it Should Go

> Do not let your heart envy sinners, but be zealous for the fear of the Lord all the day; for surely there is a hereafter, and your hope will not be cut off. Hear, my son, and be wise; and <u>guide</u> your heart in the way (Proverbs 23:17-19, Emphasis added).

Why is following our heart not enough? I have heard Christians confess, "But, God knows my heart." The scriptures communicate a much stronger message because our hearts are subject to change and completely untrustworthy: "He who trusts in his own heart is a fool, but whoever walks wisely will be delivered" (Proverbs 28:26).

How do we Lead our own Heart?

We just read the Proverb that says we cannot trust our own heart, which means we have to take some responsibility. Man's free will gives us the power to take our hearts off one intent and direct it to something else. It merely comes down to making the right or wrong choices. For instance, Jesus pointed out that our heart determines where we invest our time, money and energy: "For where your treasure is, there your heart will be also" (Matthew 6:21). Christ warns that treasures are a stumbling block: "Do not lay up for yourselves treasures on earth, where moth and rust destroy and where thieves break in and steal; but lay up for yourselves treasures in heaven, where neither moth nor rust destroys and where thieves do not break in and steal" (Matthew 6:19-20) Scripture gives advice for keeping the heart pure, which will help us make the right choices in life:

- 1 Kings 8:61, Let your heart therefore be loyal to the Lord our God to walk in His statutes, and keep His commandments, as at this day.
- John 14:27, Peace I leave with you, My peace I give to you; not as the world gives do I give to you. Let not your heart be troubled, neither let it be afraid.
- James 4:7-8, Therefore submit to God. Resist the devil and he will flee from you. Draw near to God and He will draw near to you. Cleanse your hands, you sinners; and purify your hearts, you double-minded.
- James 5:8, You also be patient. Establish your hearts, for the coming of the Lord is at hand.

Prayer that Reaches the Throne

> The LORD promises, I will give you a new heart and put a new spirit within you; I will take the heart of stone out of your flesh and give you a heart of flesh (Ezekiel 36:26).

We receive a new heart when we invite Jesus Christ to become our Lord and Savior: "Therefore, if anyone is in Christ, he is a new creation; old things have passed away; behold, all things have become new" (2 Corinthians 5:17). This is a supernatural miracle which instantly changes the heart. Jesus stands in perfect holiness at the Throne of the Father, and He will come to live in any heart that accepts Him to abide there (Revelation 3:20). Jesus is the way to the Father, and everyone who desires to stand before the heavenly Father with their petitions must be in Christ. I mentioned earlier, that Jesus would respond with mercy to the unsaved or prodigals that call out to Him. Since God hears our heart before He hears our prayers, therefore, it is necessary to avoid praying and confessing with any selfish motives. Invite the Holy Spirit to see if there is any darkness in your heart that would block the effectiveness of your prayers (Psalm 139:22-24). There are veils over the heart, which are like the many layers of an onion that need to be peeled off one by one. There is the "veil" of the world which we are delivered from at the time of salvation; but then there are thin veils that have been built up by our carnal nature, which some refer to as our "flesh."

As we surrender ourselves to the Holy Spirit, these veils begin to peel away from our heart. Here is just one example: When we surrender pride and ask the Holy Spirit to help us become humble and resist Satan's temptation, then that veil will eventually be peeled away. We also need the axe of the Word to cut that root of pride, which will destroy the whole tree. Allow the fear of the LORD to help you heed His Word, as the Psalmist writes: "Pride goes before destruction, and a haughty spirit before a fall" (Proverbs 16:18).

The Powerful Call of the Watchman

I have set watchmen on your walls, O Jerusalem; they shall never hold their peace day or night. You who make mention of the Lord, do not keep silent, and give Him no rest till He establishes and till He makes Jerusalem a praise in the earth.
–Isaiah 62:6-7

The watchman guards by protecting and preserving the walls of the nation. What are the walls? They are the standards of Judeo-Christian principles in society. When the standards are broken down, then anything can go in and out. Our Embassy's mission is to stand as watchmen on the walls of the nation's capital while influencing lawmakers on behalf of the Church: A true Nehemiah mission! We have maintained a *threshing floor* in Washington, D.C. for 30 years. There are hundreds of Christian ministries operating as watchmen at the nation's capital. There are hundreds of Christian ministries operating as watchmen at the nation's capital, with a large support-army standing with them. They stay on top of what the nation's leaders are doing for the good or for the bad on behalf of the people. They give oversight to check and balance the actions of the government. Many hold public offices within the branches of the government. They need your prayers and support.

In the Old Testament, we see how God appointed watchmen on the walls of Zion to be faithful spiritual guardians for the glory of Jerusalem. The watchmen are intercessors, which have the anointed gift of prophecy. Watchmen are entrusted with the spiritual well-being of their nation. They make moral demands on the rulers and the people; often calling them to repentance as Daniel did to Nebuchadnezzar. The Prophet Samuel had to strip King Saul of his anointing. The Prophet Nathan was the spiritual adviser to King David, who had to reveal his sin with Bathsheba, and pronounce God's judgment for David's murdering her husband.

Jerusalem is *Elohim's* Holy City. At the LORD's appointed time, the Messiah will return and rule the world from Jerusalem. During Isaiah's time, God's people lived in Babylonian captivity, and their Holy City Jerusalem lay in ruins. Even so, prophecy promised that Jerusalem would become a glory, and praise in the earth! Isaiah describes the watchmen as those who cry to Him on behalf of Jerusalem. They were to cry out until God establishes Jerusalem as a praise of the earth.

The re-gathered Hebrew people in Jerusalem were hindered to rebuild because of enemies from the North. King Artaxerxes commissioned Nehemiah to return to Jerusalem and rebuild the city's wall and the temple (Nehemiah, chapter 2). Rebuilding the city's wall and gates took only 52 days, and Jerusalem was restored as a sovereign self-governing city-state. Their enemies perceived the work was done by their God (Nehemiah 6:16). As Isaiah had prophesied, Jerusalem was made "a praise in the earth!"

Nehemiah is called the "watchman who would not come down off the wall." We read in Nehemiah 4:6: "So we built the wall, and the entire wall was joined together up to half its height, for the people had a mind to work." They rebuilt the walls around Jerusalem with a weapon in one hand, and a tool in the other. While the Temple was being restored, Ezra the scribe worked to regenerate spiritual faith within the people. After returning from 70 years of captivity in Babylon, the people needed their hearts renewed by God's Word. They had forgotten the Law of Moses, and they wept while they were being taught the Word:

> And Nehemiah, who was the governor, Ezra the priest and scribe, and the Levites who taught the people said to all the people, "this day is holy to the Lord your God; do not mourn nor weep." For all the people wept, when they heard the words of the Law (Nehemiah 8:9).

We labor in prayer to see and experience a similar revival for our generation. The Church has spiritual walls around it, built by prayer and the preaching of God's Word. This has produced good fruit within the Church, like prayer, love and inspiration, which build up the Body of Christ and attract lost souls. When the mission of the Church is genuinely undertaken in faith and humility, we can be assured that no matter how great the difficulties, God will defeat its enemies:

> And I also say to you that you are Peter, and on this rock I will build My church, and the gates of Hades shall not prevail against it (Matthew 16:18).

In the New Testament, believers have the same calling to stand as watchmen and intercede unceasingly for the establishment of God's Kingdom and Christ's righteous rule over the earth. (Read Mark 16:15; Luke 24:47; Acts 2:38, 39, 42) A growing number of Zionists are responding to the scriptural call to serve as watchmen for Jerusalem and the Jewish people. As believers lay hold of God's heart for Israel, many are beginning to follow *Yahweh's* charge in Psalm, chapter 122, to pray for the peace of Jerusalem. This has been proven by the extraordinary growth of the *Day of Prayer for the Peace of Jerusalem*, which now mobilizes hundreds of thousands of believers the first Sunday of every October.

In looking beyond the place of personal prayer and intercession, we learn five important *kingdom keys* for serving as watchmen:

1. **The Watchman Stands on the Walls of the City and the Country**
   We just discussed how *Yahweh* appointed watchmen on the walls of Zion. Some stood guard on top of the city walls to warn of any threat from an invading army, and others served as spiritual watchmen who interceded to establish God's kingdom on earth and for the glory of Jerusalem. Habakkuk, the prophet, said, "I will stand my watch and set myself on the rampart, and watch to see what He will say to me, and what I will answer when I am corrected" (Habakkuk 2:1). Today, New Testament believers have the same calling to stand as watchmen, and intercede unceasingly for the establishment of God's kingdom, and for Christ's righteousness to rule over the earth. These are the ones who pray for prophecy to be fulfilled on behalf of the nations. The Great Commission has been given to the Church, and Christ's disciples must expand and guard over the harvest until it is fulfilled: "And He said to them, 'Go into all the world and preach the gospel to every creature'" (Mark 16:15). Believers have the personal responsibility to watch and be prepared for the Lord's Return (Luke 21:36). They must guard against negligence or complacency that would cause them to be overcome by sin. They are to watch and be alerted of religious deception and warn others:
   But of that day and hour no one knows, not even the angels in heaven, nor the Son, but only the Father. Take heed, watch and pray; for you do not know when the time is (Mark 13:32-33).

2. **The Watchman Guards the Moral Condition of the People**
   The LORD will also call His watchmen to do something in the natural realm in response to the spiritual burden they carry. The first and primary responsibility of a watchman is to be alert. The Greek word *gregoreo*, translated as *watch*, means to keep awake and watch. Today, modern-day watchmen can sound the alarm instantly and warn of threats to the community by the Internet, social media, television and radio. Watchmen have a duty to be Zionists and intercede for Israel. Perhaps the Lord has given you a revelation of His burden for Israel. To pray effectively for Israel, we should be mindful of their enemies. This means knowing the difference between Hamas and Hezbollah. Are you aware of the consequences and implications of disengagement? Be knowledgeable of the threats that Iran's leaders have made against Israel, and the progress they have achieved toward developing a

nuclear arsenal? Do you know that anti-Semitism is taking place at record-high levels on American and European university campuses?

3. The Watchman is to Warn

When we prayerfully respond to God's call as a watchman, we will discern in the spirit what others would see as irrelevant. Like the Prophet Ezekiel was told, we will be held accountable for what we do in response to what we see. If the watchman does not issue a warning, he will be held responsible for the ensui3g calamity. This is very sobering:

So you, son of man: I have made you a watchman for the house of Israel; therefore you shall hear a word from My mouth and warn them for Me. When I say to the wicked, "O wicked man, you shall surely die!" and you do not speak to warn the wicked from his way, that wicked man shall die in his iniquity; but his blood I will require at your hand. Nevertheless if you warn the wicked to turn from his way, and he does not turn from his way, he shall die in his iniquity; but you have delivered your soul (Ezekiel 33:7-9).

Our Embassy's mission in the nation's capital is to watch, warn, and intercede. For years, the Holy Spirit has given me many warnings for the country. In turn, I have blown the shofar to the Church to stir up prayer across the nation. For instance, a few years ago the Holy Spirit showed me an angel of death hovering over Washington, D.C. This angel was hovering above the Arlington National Cemetery looking toward the government buildings along the National Mall. It reminded me of the angel of death that hovered over Jerusalem when King David sinned by numbering the people:

Then David spoke to the Lord when he saw the angel who was striking the people, and said, "Surely I have sinned, and I have done wickedly; but these sheep, what have they done? Let Your hand, I pray, be against me and against my father's house" (2 Samuel 24:17).

The purpose of this revelation was to blow the shofar and call God's Church to stand in the gap and repent according to 2 Chronicles 7:14. We blow the shofar through our Embassy's *Operation Prayer Shield,* inviting you to join with praying people across the country by committing to pray at least five-minutes each day asking the LORD to heal our land. We must stand together in rebuilding the spiritual foundation of our country. Visit our website for more information: www.embassyforworldpeace.org

4. God is Merciful, and Responds to Repentance

Like David's intercession stayed the hand of God's judgment, our intercession intervenes to restrain the judgment this nation deserves. The Holy Spirit told me twenty-five years ago that the LORD wanted to send a Nineveh-type revival to America; instead of the judgment, we have earned. If you ask the Lord, He will show you practical ways to keep watch and issue warnings.This is a time to stand boldly for the truth and refuse to compromise our convictions. It is a time when we need to display the same courage as watchmen in times past. For instance, the nation of Israel is in great need of watchmen on its walls. The Church has the call of Esther to stand in the gap for God's chosen people. Psalm, chapter 83, is a prayer to confound a conspiracy against Israel. Many experts and political leaders in Israel are convinced the situation is just as grave for the Jewish people today as in pre-World War II Germany, and with good reason. The question and challenge for us are whether we will follow through with the heart God has given us for Israel by *blowing a trumpet* and warning others.

5. *Yahweh's* warning to the unfaithful Watchman

Again the word of the Lord came to me, saying, When I bring the sword upon a land, and the people of the land take a man from their territory and make him their watchman, when he sees the sword coming upon the land if he blows the trumpet and warns the people, then whoever hears the sound of the trumpet and does not take warning, if the sword comes and takes him away, his blood shall be on his own head. He heard the sound of the trumpet, but did not take warning; his blood shall be upon himself. But he who takes warning will save his life. But if the watchman sees the sword coming and does not blow the trumpet, and the people are not warned, and the sword comes and takes any person from among them, he is taken away in his iniquity; but his blood I will require at the watchman's hand (Ezekiel 33:1-6).

Importance of Fasting with Prayer

Yet they seek Me daily, and delight to know My ways, as a nation that did righteousness, and did not forsake the ordinance of their God. They ask of Me the ordinances of justice; they take delight in approaching God. "Why have we fasted," they say, "and You have not seen? Why have we afflicted our souls, and You take no notice?"–Isaiah 58:2-3

God's people fasted, but persisted in their sins. They afflicted their souls, but still gratified their lusts. They continued to be covetous and unmerciful. They mocked God and deceived themselves. These children of Israel were only offering external services to God and then were angry with Him when He did not accept their offering. They were acting like Cain who was furious with *YHWH* because his offering was unacceptable.

Fasting is to be Done unto the LORD

Isaiah is charging the House of Israel with being hypocritical towards *Yahweh*. They worshiped and sacrificed regularly, but their works were dead because they ignored the real needs of the poor. Israel's leaders had oppressed the people with social injustice, which made them poor. They were spoiling God's vineyard and offering superficial fasts before their Holy God. Isaiah warns that they must stop oppressing the poor and observe the Sabbath with pure and joyful worship. Then the LORD will give light, healing, and full restoration:.

> Is this not the fast that I have chosen: to loose the bonds of wickedness, to undo the heavy burdens, to let the oppressed go free, and that you break every yoke? Is it not to share your bread with the hungry, and that you bring to your house the poor who are cast out; when you see the naked, that you cover him, and not hide yourself from your own flesh? (vv. 6-7)
>
> Then your light shall break forth like the morning, your healing shall spring forth speedily, and your righteousness shall go before you; the glory of the Lord shall be your rear guard. Then you shall call, and the Lord will answer; you shall cry, and He will say, "Here I am'" (vv. 8-9).

Christ Expects His Disciples to Fast

> And Jesus said to them, "Can the friends of the bridegroom mourn as long as the bridegroom is with them? But the days will come when the bridegroom will be taken away from them, and then they will fast" (Matthew 9:14-15).

Fasting suggests mourning, but Jesus' disciples were celebrating the coming of the Kingdom of Heaven in the presence of their Messiah. Jesus never commanded the disciples to fast, but He said, "when you fast." He already knew that fasting would become a part of the spiritual life of His Church after His ascension to the Father. He placed emphasis on the motive for fasting and warned against religious displays for the sake of impressing men. Fasting with prayer adds boldness to our faith. Even though the natural man diminishes when we deny the body; the spirit man is strengthened and bolstered in the Lord. Have today's Christians become a pampered generation enjoying the comforts of this world? Many are overlooking the necessity to fast! With the decline of our great nation, the Church should be standing in the gap for the land with mourning and fasting:

> Consecrate a fast, call a sacred assembly; gather the elders and all the inhabitants of the land into the house of the Lord your God, and cry out to the Lord (Joel 1:14).

> Matthew quotes Jesus as saying: Moreover, when you fast, do not be like the hypocrites, with a sad countenance. For they disfigure their faces that they may appear to men to be fasting. Assuredly, I say to you, they have their reward. But you, when you fast, anoint your head and wash your face, so that you do not appear to men to be fasting, but to your Father who is in the secret place; and your Father who sees in secret will reward you openly (Matthew 1:16-18).

Fasting Intensifies Prayer

The Church is called to minister like Jesus. Scripture confirms how He expects His disciples to follow the same pattern of His own ministry. Christ displayed to His disciples how fasting and prayer are a necessary step in ministry. After failing to deliver a young boy, the disciples asked Him privately, "Why could we not cast it out?' So Jesus said to them, "Because of your unbelief; for assuredly, I say to you, if you have faith as a mustard seed, you will say to this mountain, 'Move from here to there,' and it will move; and nothing will be impossible for you. However, this kind does not go out except by prayer and fasting" (Matthew 17:20-21). They had already been healing the sick and casting out devils; however, they were completely powerless for this situation. Ministry can become mechanical, and this was a perplexing situation of unbelief on the part of the disciples. This kind of stubborn devil will be defeated with fasting–you starve him out by starving yourself for the sinner's sake. This is especially true for an alcoholic or drug addict. Fasting is to deny yourself of anything you consider a denial of your flesh.

Fasting and prayer played a vital role in the growth of the New Testament Church. The early Christians received direction and power from the Holy Spirit concerning the divine development of the Church. For instance, they fasted and prayed when they appointed apostles to go forth as missionaries. The same was done for the appointment of elders and the establishment of local churches. In Acts 13:1-3, we read how the Holy Spirit gave direction when the leading ministers in Antioch prayed and fasted together. Ministering to the Lord is a first fruit offering, which precedes ministering to the Body of Christ. When we practice ministering to the Lord, then the Holy Spirit releases the power and direction for effective ministry to the Body of Christ.

Fasting is Prayer without Words

Earnest times of prayer should be accompanied with fasting. The Bible repeatedly demonstrates how God honors all who will seek Him with sincere hearts through prayer and fasting:

- God's people have fasted in order to obtain humility and to seek God's will to be done.
- Fasting is a form of self-denial, and submission to God; to seek His grace, help, protection, and favor.
- Fasting is effective along with repentance when seeking God for revival and restoration, and during national emergencies.

In the Old Testament, they worshiped God on the Day of Atonement with fasting, prayer and repentance. Daniel fasted 21 days to see God's Word fulfilled for the restoration of Jerusalem: ".....I, Daniel, understood by the books the number of the years specified by the word of the Lord through Jeremiah the prophet, that He would accomplish seventy years in the desolations of Jerusalem. 'Then I set my face toward the Lord God to make request by prayer and supplications, with fasting, sackcloth, and ashes" (Daniel 9:2-3). We can also note Nehemiah fasting for the restoration of Jerusalem (Nehemiah 1:4). And, Christ Himself practiced this discipline during His 40 days in the wilderness. Scripture records that the New Testament Church practiced fasting. (Study Acts 13:2-3; 14:23; 27:33.) I mentioned earlier, that Christ stated that His disciples would also fast while He would be absent from their presence. The period of the Bridegroom's absence is the age from the time of His ascension until His return. Fasting in the Church Age is a sign of the believer's return to his first love for the Lord.

When the Church loses its love for this world and sets its heart on fire with love for the Bridegroom, there will be a longing for His soon return. When we see believers developing a sorrow for sin and evil in this world, this will be a sign that the Church is preparing for Christ's coming. Guard against developing an attitude of indifference, which overlooks sinful lifestyles overtaking society. You cannot waver between two opinions and serve the LORD in your life. Do you love the LORD your God with all your heart, or do you love the world? According to the Word, you cannot have both. If the LORD is your God, then follow him! We must choose whom we will serve; as Joshua told God's people who were wavering, "..... As for me and my house, we will serve the LORD" (Joshua 24:15).

There are many purposes for fasting:

1. Fasting honors the one true eternal God as we seek Him and draw near to Him. (Study Psalm 73:28; James 4:8; Acts 13:2)

2. Fasting humbles the soul before God; bringing surrender to God's revelation, wisdom, and understanding concerning the will of God. (Study Ezra 8:21; Psalm 69:10; Isaiah 11:2-5; 58:3-6,11; Daniel 9:3,21-11; Acts 13:2,3)
3. Fasting mourns over personal sin and failures; the sins of the church, nation and the world (1 Samuel 7:6; Nehemiah 9:1-2).
4. Fasting prepares us for trials and reaffirms our consecration to God (Matthew 4:2).
5. Fasting and prayer are the foremost effective weapons against the forces of evil. (Study Judges 20:26; Ezra 8:21,23, 31; Jeremiah 29:12-14; Joel 2:12; Luke 18:3; Acts 9:10-19)
6. Fasting reinforces repentance and allows God to reverse His intended judgment. (Study 2 Samuel 12:16, 22; 1 Kings 21:27-29; Jeremiah 18:7; Joel 2:12-14; Jonah 3:5-10)
7. Fasting helps to save souls from the bondage of evil. (Study Isaiah 58:6; Matthew 17:14-21; Luke 4:18)
8. Fasting opens the way for the outpouring of the Holy Spirit and Christ's return for His Bride (Matthew 9:15).
9. Fasting must be done with right motives and without formalism. The heart must hunger and thirst for God and His righteousness (Psalm 42:1-5; Matthew 5:6).

There are certain ways to fast:

1. Fasting refers to the discipline of abstaining from food for spiritual purposes. Fasting is also achieved by abstaining from comforts in life and entertainment like television, entertainment, social functions, sports, shopping, pleasurable things that pamper our flesh.
2. Daniel's fast was a partial fast. It was a restriction of diet rather than complete abstention. It was an extended fast for 21 days. Daniel 10:3: "I ate no pleasant food, no meat or wine came into my mouth, nor did I anoint myself at all, till three whole weeks were fulfilled."
3. Some people in ministry practice a "fasted life." Their fasting is not seasonal, but a way of life for the sake of fulfilling ministry. Partial fasting involves giving up partic-ular foods, or giving up one of the mealtimes of the day. It could also include sacrificing specific activities (Luke 14:26).

Types of fasting:

1. Forty days is the maximum fast abstaining from all food, solid or liquid, but not from water. Matthew comments on Christ's time of fasting in the wilderness, "And when He had fasted forty days and forty nights, afterward He was hungry (4.2). It does not say he was thirsty. Forty days without water would

have required supernatural ability, and Christ lived as a man according to physical law.

2. The absolute fast is abstaining from both food and water, which should only be done for three days. This is known as an Esther fast. (Esther 4:16) Saul of Tarsus was "three days without sight, and neither did eat nor drink" (Acts 9:9).
3. Daniel fasted for 21 days without eating any delicacies, meat or wine. He ate a vegan diet of fruit, vegetables and legumes (Daniel 10:1-22). Prophecy indicates that we live toward the end of the Church Age when Scripture points to the rapture of the saints. This calls all believers to be self-controlled and sober-minded; keeping an attitude of fasting with prayer (Luke 21:36; 1 Peter 1:13; 5:8, 9). Believers look for the return of Christ in the clouds of heaven (Mark 14:62; Acts 1:11; 1 Thes. 4:16, 17).

Powerful results from fasting:

1. ***Fasting intensifies prayer*****.....**Fasting with prayer has been established as a routine discipline throughout the Bible. Examples of fasting are recorded, signifying how the power of the Holy Spirit moved the Hand of God to fulfill His plans and purposes on behalf of mankind. Prayer and fasting were involved in the growth and development of the New Testament Church, when they sought to receive direction from the Holy Spirit for decisions concerning the Church's mission. For instance, in Acts 3:2: "As they ministered to the Lord and fasted, the Holy Spirit said, 'Now separate to Me Barnabas and Saul for the work to which I have called them.'"
2. ***Fasting is a form of mourning*****.....**Mourning is found in the beatitudes. Jesus spoke in Matthew 5:4, "Blessed are they that mourn: for they shall be comforted." In Isaiah 61:3, the LORD offers special blessings to those who mourn in Zion: "To give them beauty for ashes, the oil of joy for mourning, the garment of praise for the spirit of heaviness; that they may be called trees of righteousness, the planting of the Lord, that He may be glorified." This type of mourning is when the believer shares the burden of the LORD with His own grief over the sin of humanity. In the Old Testament, God's prophets spoke "the burden of the Lord" to the people, so they would repent of their sins. Today, we mourn for the perilous times the world is facing. Nations need to turn back to God when there is no apparent human solution for their present calamity. (We list a few examples under number five.)
3. ***Fasting disciplines the flesh*****.....**In Galatians 5:17, Paul describes the opposition that exists between the Holy Spirit of God and the carnal nature of man: "For the flesh lusts against the Spirit and the Spirit against the flesh; and these are contrary to one another, so that you do not do the things that you wish." Fasting brings the soul and body into subjection to the Holy

Spirit. David testifies in Psalm 35:13, "I humbled my soul with fasting." Christ placed emphasis upon the motive for fasting and warned against any religious display for the sake of impressing men (Matthew 6:1-18).

4. ***Fasting Brings Personal Deliverance.....*** In Matthew, chapter 17, when the Lord's disciples were unable to cast demons out of a man's lunatic son, He gave them the *key of prayer and fasting* for performing difficult deliverances. "Then Jesus answered and said, 'O faithless and perverse generation, how long shall I be with you? How long shall I bear with you? Bring him here to Me. And Jesus rebuked the demon, and it came out of him; and the child was cured from that very hour'" (vv. 17-18). "Then the disciples came to Jesus privately and said, 'Why could we not cast it out?' So Jesus said to them, 'Because of your unbelief; for assuredly, I say to you, if you have faith as a mustard seed, you will say to this mountain, 'Move from here to there,' and it will move; and nothing will be impossible for you. However, this kind does not go out except by prayer and fasting.'" (vv. 19-21).
5. ***Fasting for a national crisis.....***Scripture gives numerous examples of God's deliverance for His nation of Israel. In the face of enemy invasion, God's people joined forces to protect their national heritage. For instance, in 2 Chronicles chapter 20, we see how Jehoshaphat called God's people to unite in public, collective fasting and prayer for deliverance from their enemies. Jehoshaphat led them in prayer proclaiming *Yahweh's* covenant with Abraham, appealing to God's promised mercy based on that covenant. This brought an immediate, supernatural intervention from God. The enemies of Jehoshaphat relied on carnal weapons; while Jehoshaphat and his people had only one choice, their deliverance had to come from their God, *Yahweh*. The weapons they used to defeat the enemy were spiritual: *fasting and united prayer.*

Since the First World War, the free nations of the world have collectively faced a host of hostile and formidable enemies as those that threatened Judah in the days of Jehoshaphat. After the Second World War, author Norman Grubb wrote the biography of a Welsh man named Rees Howells, who led a small battalion of praying Christians against Hitler, Mussolini and Stalin. These prayer warriors fasted and prayed to defeat these demonic agents who were vying to become world dictators over Europe. Today, we have the same threats from rogue nations, which are brewing destruction against Israel and the United States. While the Holy Spirit has raised up millions of intercessors, most Christians refuse to seek God's intervention against these ominous threats. For instance, after the first terrorist attack on U. S. soil on September 11, 2001, most of the country returned to a state of apathy. Those who even returned to attending church grew lukewarm again. The devastating terrorist bombing at the *Boston Marathon Race* in 2013 sent another wake-up call for the nation to turn back to God Almighty, but did not produce a spiritual awakening across the country.

The LORD has anointed prophetic voices like the late David Wilkerson and Rabbi Jonathan Cahn, who have warned of the apparent judgment that is upon America. Rabbi Cahn believes that everything from 9/11 to the collapse of the U.S. economy is a prophetic warning that God is sending judgment to America. This message is based on his search of the Scriptures and how the events in the United States parallel with the history of Israel's earlier decline as a nation. Clearly, America needs a Nineveh-type revival. Only prayer, repentance and fasting, will remove the veils from the slumbering Church and the nation. Nevertheless, God has an army that is currently exercising the practice of fasting and repentance to restrain the enemies of the free world. Living in a hostile world should draw us back to dependence upon the *Elohim* God of Abraham, Isaac, and Jacob!

Here are examples of how fasting with repentance cancels divine judgment:

When God's people gather for fasting and repentance during a critical hour, the result is: The Heavens will respond with an outpouring of the Holy Spirit and divine deliverance. Jehoshaphat, Esther, Joel, and Jonah all lived during a time of national crisis, yet they did not surrender to despair and apathy. They knew how *YHWH* had always intervened to spare the Hebrew nation. All of these leaders knew how to turn a nation back to God:

1. In 2 Chronicles, chapter 20, Israel's king faced the greatest crisis of his life when a multitude from Moab and Ammon came up to battle against Judah. Jehoshaphat immediately sought the LORD and called all the people to fast and pray with him. Verse 3 says, "All Judah stood before the Lord, with their little ones, their wives, and their children." When they put their trust in the LORD then He responded with a divine intervention and fought against the enemies of Israel, and the nation was spared from their most formidable enemy.
2. Queen Esther and her Jewish people faced a national disaster when Haman, the prime minister of Persia, sought to destroy all the Jews in the Hashemite kingdom. Esther chose to cast herself upon the Throne of Grace: "If I perish, I perish." After she and her people fasted for three days, Queen Esther presented herself before the king's court, and *Yahweh* had the king look upon her with compassion (Esther 4). Under the providence and direction of God, Esther and her uncle Mordecai overturned this evil plot. The downfall of Haman and his wicked plan to wipe out all Jewish people were thwarted. (Read the entire book of Esther.)
3. The Prophet Joel delivered *Yahweh's* message calling Israel to pray for God's intervention. In Joel 2:15-18, we see the people of all generations being called to fast together. When sin reaches a certain fullness, judgment is unavoidable. Because of the plagues on the land and decadence among

the people, the prophet Joel called the people to intercede with fasting and prayer night and day, and to repent for all sin. God answered their repentance and humble prayers, and Israel was restored.

4. The Prophet Jonah eventually obeyed *Yahweh* and warned ancient Nineveh of the impending judgment God intended to send upon them. Jonah was full of unbelief, but the Ninevites responded by conducting a true fast with repentance, which brought God's divine mercy. They believed that God was justly angry with them because of their wretched sin, and if He carried out this judgment, then everyone would perish. Fasting for sin is not enough, but we must fast in order to abandon wickedness in our hearts.

Synopsis for Chapter Two
Prayer Takes Commitment

Every generation has the responsibility to carry the torch and proclaim God's Word, so the Lord's will can be declared in the earth as it is declared in Heaven! God's Word is prophetic and releases power and revelation into our spirit man. By praying the Word of God, we enter His mind and spirit—His passion. Praying and proclaiming Scripture is powerful, but much different than the "positive confession," or the name it and claim it teachings, which use scriptures to control and manipulate circumstances. Man's free will gives us the power to take our heart off one thing and set it on something else; while the heart of God is always searching for those who will stand in the gap on His behalf. It merely comes down to making the right or wrong choices. For instance, Jesus pointed out that our heart determines where we invest our time, money and energy. "For where your treasure is, there your heart will be also" (Matthew 6:21).

Question?

Have you been willing to invest the time and sacrifice to soak in the Scriptures? Are you seeking the gifts of the Spirit while bypassing the first need for spiritual fruit in your character? Have you discovered there is no substitute for consistent daily prayer and the support of like-minded prayer partners?

Visit the Prayer Guide in Chapter Three which Includes a list of scriptures to pray for numerous needs.

Chapter Three

Keys for Effectual Prayer

Key One

Preparing Your Heart for Prayer

Before beginning your prayer time, reflect upon your own personal consecration to overcome the self-life and enter the heart of Christ. This can be achieved by taking the following steps:

1. Pray the *Model Prayer of Personal Consecration and Preparation* found several paragraphs ahead in this chapter. Put on the full armor of God in Ephesians 6:10-18, and proclaim yourself and your family covered by the Blood of the Lord Jesus Christ.
2. Pray Psalm, chapter 91, for yourself and your family members. This will only take a few minutes. Read it aloud and proclaim these verses for protection. In doing this, you and your family members will not come under retaliation for your service to the Lord. This Psalm keeps you covered under His shadow; hidden and invisible from the evil forces in this world. This is *stealth* warfare.
3. Worship the LORD. All of Heaven worships the King of kings, day and night. The Word tells us we can get into this Holy atmosphere by entering "His gates with thanksgiving and His courts with praise" (Psalm 100:4). Worship prepares the heart to be sensitive to His righteousness. "Seven times a day I praise You, because of Your righteous judgments" (Psalm 119:164).

As you follow this outline for prayer, the Holy Spirit (the only true guide) will reveal other scriptures to expand your prayer life. I encourage the biblical practice of apostolic prayer by proclaiming Scripture in prayer. Prayer is a declaration to the Godhead, and it also speaks life into the earth and the heavenly realm. The power of heaven is behind us when we make the Word our prayer. Silent prayer and meditation are intended for private communion with the LORD, and when we need to be still to hear His Voice.

Prayer for Overcoming Inwardly

For God has not given us the spirit of fear; but of power, and of love,
and of a sound mind.
–2 Timothy 1:7

Once again, I address the necessity of maintaining a clear mind, since the greatest battle, we all face is right between our ears–our mind! We are not qualified to go onto the battlefield until we first overcome this *inward struggle*. We must defeat the Goliaths within our own lives before we can enter the arena to gain victory in prayer, and possess the kingdoms of this world for our Lord Jesus Christ (Revelation 11:15). The battle for the mind involves mindsets, habits, lusts, selfishness, lack of discipline, and unbelief. Only when we conquer these strongholds can we even begin to engage in spiritual warfare for the Kingdom of God.

The mind is what the devil seeks to control. Jesus encountered and exorcised the Gadarene demoniac who was possessed by a horde of demons called Legion (Mark 5:1-20). His deliverance was beyond miraculous, which terrified a lot of local people. On a modern-day level, this type of demonic possession is found in the minds of terrorists and serial killers. Psychiatrists have diagnosed that serial murderers, and terrorists have a "darkened" mind. Their brain is black, void of any light; an empty dark hole. The trademark of the psychopathic murderer is the inability to recognize others as worthy of respect. Their victims are dehumanized and flattened into worthless objects in the murderer's mind. Ephesians 4:17-18 explains what causes a darkened mind:

> So I tell you this, and insist on it in the Lord, that you must no longer live as the Gentiles do, in the futility of their thinking. They are darkened in their understanding and separated from the life of God because of the ignorance that is in them due to the hardening of their hearts.

What is a hardened heart? It is a heart that is ignorant of divine truth and divine laws. A dark understanding comes from a darkened mind. These are the pagans, and the godless the Apostle Paul spoke of in his epistles, and such are those of a hardened heart. The Holy Spirit will renew our mind when we are willing to change our thinking, because our past mindsets become grave clothes. Some theologians call the transition from the old to the new, a paradigm shift. A paradigm is a "mental grid," or a set way of thinking. Only the Holy Spirit can break down a "grid," which requires that we yield. If we want to hear from the Holy Spirit, and fulfill God's Will; then we must be willing to be transformed in the way we think. The Apostle Paul teaches in Romans 12:2:

> Do not be conformed to this world, but be transformed by the renewing of your mind, that you may prove what is that good and acceptable and perfect will of God.

The real battle is within, not without. If we do not succeed to overcome inwardly we are unable to move forward into service for Christ's Kingdom. All it takes is a decision to embrace discipline, meditation, intercession, action, and fasting. However, we cannot do this within our own ability–the only way to avoid sin is through Jesus! Enjoy intimate fellowship with Jesus, your Lord and Savior, and allow His Spirit to do a transforming work in your spirit. Make the right choices, meditate on the Word of God, and His righteousness will spring up within your life. The Apostle Paul gives this instruction to therefore.....

> Come out from among them and be separate, says the Lord. Do not touch what is unclean, and I will receive you (2 Corinthians 6:17).

This is an invitation to forsake idolatry and worldly carnal ways. How many modern-day churches have allowed idolatry to enter the temple? We are to keep our own temple clean, washed by the Word of God. Why would we sit in polluted temples that worship the agendas of carnal men, which is simply idolatry? "For you are the temple of the living God. As God has said: "I will dwell in them and walk among them. I will be their God, and they shall be My people" (2 Corinthians 6:16; Leviticus 26:12; Jeremiah 32:38; Ezekiel 37:27).

Model Prayer for Personal Consecration
An Invitation for God's Kingdom to be Made Manifest in Your Life Today

In proclaiming this short prayer, you give the Holy Spirit permission to complete the vital work of consecration in your life:

1. **Surrender of Body**
   Father, in the Name of Jesus, I surrender my life to the Holy Spirit as a living sacrifice (Romans 12:1).
   a. I commit the members of my body (especially my tongue) to be used as an instrument of Your righteousness, peace, joy and love today (Romans 6:13, 19).

   b. I commit my way this day to You Lord Jesus so that You can cause me to walk in Your way (Psalm 37:5).
   c. I commit my works to You Lord Jesus so that Your will can establish my thoughts (Proverbs 16:3).
2. **Surrender of Soul**
   a. I commit my will to the Holy Spirit so the Lord can bring His will to pass in my life today.
   b. I commit my mind to You Lord Jesus so that it will be stayed upon You all day long. When my mind is stayed upon You, I will not have to be worried or anxious. Your peace will keep me all day long. Your peace is perfect (Isaiah 26:3).
   c. I commit my emotions to You Lord Jesus. I invite the garment of praise into my soul so that I will not be depressed, despondent, or in despair today (Isaiah 62:3).
   d. I anchor my emotions in Christ's hope today, for You are my hope and the bishop of my emotions and the shepherd of my emotions. You make my emotions lie down and be at peace. You restore my soul (Hebrews 6:19; I Peter 2:25; Psalm 23).
3. **Surrender of Spirit**
   I commit my spirit to the Holy Spirit today. Help me to walk in the Spirit of Grace and not the flesh, and give me a double portion of Your anointing (Psalms 31:5).
4. **Surrender the Intent of Heart**
   Let the words of my mouth and the meditations of my heart be acceptable in your sight, O Lord, and let the things that I do glorify You this day. (Psalms 19:14)
5. **Ask for a Sound Mind**
   Father, in the Name of Jesus, I ask you to stir up the gift of God that is in me through the Holy Spirit. "For God has not given us a spirit of fear, but of power and of love and of a sound mind" (2 Timothy 1:6-7).
6. **Pray for Veils to be Removed**
   "But even if our gospel is veiled, it is veiled to those who are perishing" (2 Corinthians 4:3). Lord Jesus, please remove any veils over my mind, eyes, and ears. Anoint me with the sevenfold spirit to walk in your "wisdom and understanding, the Spirit of counsel and might, the Spirit of knowledge and of the fear of the Lord. His delight is in the fear of the Lord, and He shall not judge by the sight of His eyes, nor decide by the hearing of His ears....." (Isaiah 11:2-3).

The Powerful Act of Worship

Intercession is very effective when conducted in a harp and bowl style which employs musical prayer along with proclamations of Scripture. We see an example, in Revelation 5:8, which describes heavenly creatures ".....Each holding a harp and golden bowls full of incense, which are the prayers of the saints." Revelation 8:2-4 continues to describe what happens with these prayers:

> And I saw the seven angels who stand before God, and to them were given seven trumpets. Then another angel, having a golden censer, came and stood at the altar. He was given much incense, that he should offer it with the prayers of all the saints upon the golden altar which was before the throne. And the smoke of the incense, with the prayers of the saints, ascended before God from the angel's hand (Revelation 8:2-4).

We personally benefit by offering worship to the Throne of God, because it becomes a spiritual garment and weapon. More importantly, we need to understand that the *Elohim* God created humankind for fellowship and to offer worship. Scripture describes how the Throne Room of God has angelic beings continuously offering worship to the Almighty God. This is described in Revelation, chapter four:

> The four living creatures, each having six wings, were full of eyes around and within. And they do not rest day or night, saying: "Holy, holy, holy, Lord God Almighty, Who was and is and is to come!" (v. 8).

> Whenever the living creatures give glory and honor and thanks to Him who sits on the throne, who lives forever and ever, The twenty-four elders fall down before Him who sits on the throne and worship Him who lives forever and ever, and cast their crowns before the throne, saying: "You are worthy, O Lord, to receive glory and honor and power; for You created all things, and by Your will they exist and were created" (vv. 9-11).

Worship is Surrender

The Apostle Paul admonished New Testament Christians: ".....Present your bodies a living sacrifice, holy, acceptable unto God, which is your reasonable service" (Romans 12:1). Paul understood that a surrendered life is the highest act of worship. As we consecrate our life to God, we become a living sacrifice placed on the altar of surrender. Surrendering areas of our lives to the lordship of Christ helps us to experience worship–in spirit and in truth.

The Old Testament patriarch Abraham is one of the most dynamic examples of the surrendered heart of a true worshiper. Look at Abraham's response when *Yahweh* asked him to sacrifice Isaac, the promised son whom he and Sarah had waited for so many years: He rose up early and took his precious son with him for the three-day journey. When he arrived at the place of sacrifice, he told those who were with him, ".....The lad and I will go yonder and worship, and we will come back to you" (Genesis 22:5). When Abraham was ready to thrust a dagger into Isaac, he heard a ram caught in the thicket. This was a ram that *Yahweh* had sent to be the sacrifice instead of his son, and he called the place Jehovah-Jireh, "the LORD will provide."

Only a trusting heart worships God when it is filled with pain to the point of breaking. When we feel overwhelmed and do not know why God has allowed a painful situation to test our lives, we must reaffirm our faith in Him with our surrender to His lordship. Job did this when he proclaimed, "Though He slay me, yet will I trust in Him" (Job 13:15). Though Job's friends falsely accused him and judged him, he was vindicated before God. He received a new revelation of God as a result of the tragedies he suffered and could declare: "I have heard of You by the hearing of the ear, but now my eye sees You. Therefore I abhor myself, and repent in dust and ashes" (Job 42:5-6). Job rejoiced and worshiped the LORD for His faithfulness.

Worship is a Spiritual Weapon that Defeats Satan

A sincere worshiper is one who truly loves the LORD. He does not only worship in demonstration, but worship is his way of life. Worship gives us peace within our inner man, which passes all understanding. Worship defeats fear so our trust in God's faithfulness is unshakable. Regardless of whatever negative circumstances, emotional pain or personal loss we may be facing, we can be lifted up when we bow our hearts with worship to the living God: "Blessed be the name of the Lord from this time forth and forevermore!" (Psalm 113:2).

The one we worship is the one who reigns over the heavenly realm. Satan and his demonic kingdom will always resist and strike aggressively against God's Kingdom on earth. The Church has a mandate to overcome the kingdoms of darkness and advance the Kingdom of God. The Lord of Hosts has given us spiritual weapons, so we are not vulnerable to any vicious attacks. When we become presumptuous about our Scriptural authority on earth, and engage in warfare within the "second heavenly," we choose to enter a deadly realm where we have no protection or authority. This is where the Lord's angels battle against the demonic army of Satan:

> And you He made alive, who were dead in trespasses and sins, in which you once walked according to the course of this world, according to the prince of the power of the air, the spirit who now works in the sons of disobedience..... (Ephesians 2:1-2).

The "third heavenly" is where God the Father and Jesus dwell. Stepping into the "second heavenly" (Ephesians 6:12), to battle against Satan's principalities could open both, yourself and your family members to major attacks from these higher-ranking demons. Scripture does not give instruction for rebuking Baal, the Queen of Heaven, or Python, etc. I am unaware of one verse in the Bible where Jesus or His disciples battled against any demons who were operating in the "second heavenly." They cast out demons who were tormenting people living on the terrestrial level on earth, the "first heavenly" realm. Spiritual authority must line up with the Word of God. God is a God of perfect order. To help understand spiritual authority better, we have an example in Acts, chapter 19, of Jewish exorcists who were presumptuous in trying to cast out demons without receiving the Holy Spirit's authority. They came under attack, and the demons even wounded these men, who had to run for their lives:

> Then some of the itinerant Jewish exorcists took it upon themselves to call the name of the Lord Jesus over those who had evil spirits, saying, "We exorcise you by the Jesus whom Paul preaches." Also there were seven sons of Sceva, a Jewish chief priest, who did so. "And the evil spirit answered and said, 'Jesus I know, and Paul I know; but who are you?" Then the man in whom the evil spirit was leaped on them, overpowered them, and prevailed against them, so that they fled out of that house naked and wounded. This became known both to all Jews and Greeks dwelling in Ephesus; and fear fell on them all, and the name of the Lord Jesus was magnified (Acts 19:13-17).

> For we do not wrestle against flesh and blood, but against principalities, against powers, against the rulers of the darkness of this age, against spiritual hosts of wickedness in the heavenly places (Ephesians 6:12).

In all we do, we must glorify Christ. Our worship brings glory and honor to God and Christ. When we do this, the battle against powers and principalities in the "second heavenly" belongs to the Heavenly hosts, the angelic army of the Lord, who are engaged to win the battle. When the armies of the Church worship Jesus as Lord and Savior, then He is lifted up:

> Therefore God also has highly exalted Him and given Him the name which is above every name, that at the name of Jesus every knee should bow, of those in heaven, and of those on earth, and of those under the earth, and that every tongue should confess that Jesus Christ is Lord, to the glory of God the Father (Philippians 2:9-11).

Praise Leads to the Throne Room of God

Enter into his gates with thanksgiving, and into his courts with praise: be thankful unto him, and bless his name. –Psalm 100:4

King David knew how to worship the Lord. He also knew that he only entered the Throne Room by joining the heavenly chorus of worship. Praising the "triumph" of Christ brings us into His presence. It brings His presence into our midst, and we experience Heaven coming to earth. The secret key for entering into the presence of the One who sits on the Throne begins at the gate of thanksgiving. Begin by thanking the Father for everything you can be grateful for: His Son, Jesus Christ, our Lord and Savior, and the presence of the Holy Spirit.

Pray for the full restoration of Biblical worship! John 4:23 declares, "But the hour is coming, and now is, when the true worshipers will worship the Father in spirit and truth; for the Father is seeking such to worship Him." With praise, we are seeking the Kingdom of God and His righteousness first; humbling ourselves before our Creator. Embracing a posture of humility and repentance will alter the atmosphere around us because God dwells with those who are contrite and humble. (Study Isaiah 57:15; 66:2; Psalm 34:18.)

Praise is a Spiritual Garment

Heaviness comes through disappointments in life, but praise is a spiritual garment that every believer can wear at all times. High praises to God move us into tremendous victory. Isaiah 61:3 speaks of salvation giving us the "garment of praise for the spirit of heaviness." We should triumph in praises to God, thanking Him for the gift of salvation. "Save us, O Lord our God, and gather us from among the Gentiles, to give thanks to Your holy name, to triumph in Your praise" (Psalm 106:47). Praise literally sanctifies the atmosphere which helps us to focus on the positive thoughts of God. The polluted negatives within our minds and the strongholds that move in supernatural areas around us are transformed by the act of praise. Satan and his demons actually flee our presence when we create an atmosphere of praise to the Lord. Lucifer was the archangel of worship before he was cast out of Heaven, and worship from the *redeemed* further indicts his fallen status.

When we praise the LORD, we are invited to sit in His presence. The opposite is true if we don't praise, we are outside of His Presence. Where are we entering when we praise God? Isaiah 60:18 speaks of the city of God, ".....But you shall call your walls Salvation, and your gates Praise." The Throne of God is surrounded in a city, with a wall that is called salvation. The way to get into the city is through the gates of praise–that is, praise to Jesus Christ the Son of God, the King of kings, and Lord of lords. We don't get access to the Throne by beginning first with petitions or supplications. We begin with praise. When we give praise to God in our times of adversity, it becomes a sacrifice to Him. An offering of sacrificial praise pleases the Lord, and we will see the miraculous as Paul and Silas did when they were thrown into prison and shackled. "At midnight Paul and Silas prayed, and sang praises unto God" (Acts 16:25). Even though they were beaten badly, Scripture says, they were singing praises to God–loud enough for the other prisoners to hear them. "And suddenly there was a great earthquake, so that the foundations of the prison were shaken: and immediately all the doors were opened, and everyone's bands were loosed" (v. 26). This is a perfect illustration of how God responds to sacrificial praise.

Praise is celebrating Christ's triumph over our enemies

> Save us, O Lord our God, and gather us from among the heathen, to give thanks unto thy holy name, and to triumph in thy praise (Psalm 106:47).

A *triumph* is a celebration of the victory already won! Our praise makes us a part of the celebration. Christ has gathered the Gentiles to take their place with Him in victory, and to triumph with praises to His Name for the blessed gift of salvation.

> Enter into His gates with thanksgiving, and into His courts with praise: be thankful unto him, and bless His Name (Psalm 100:4).

When we take our place with praises to Christ for the victory, we are stepping into the "chariot of triumph" with Him. The Apostle Paul writes of Christ's victory at the Cross, "Having disarmed principalities and powers, He made a public spectacle of them, triumphing over them in it" (Colossians 2:15). Based on this description of Christ's triumphant victory, we can see ourselves standing in the same place with Christ Jesus when we praise Him.

Some years ago, during one of my prayer times, I had an open vision where Jesus drew me up into the Third Heavenly with Him. The saints of the Church were also drawn up, which I understood to be the rapture. Once there, I stood before the Lord Jesus who was in a chariot with two white horses. He was ready to descend to the earth, but He had paused to watch and wait until certain events happened. Jesus invited me to stand in the chariot with Him and wait until it was time for Him to descend. I told the Lord, I was not worthy to step into the chariot with Him, but He insisted. As I stood with Him for a while, it seemed to be a very long time we were waiting, and I asked Him three times, how long Lord? He told me to wait patiently as He continued to watch the earth. The view of the earth looked like a photograph the astronauts had taken on one of their space missions. While we waited, I saw all the believers of the Church who had been raptured were now gathered on a large cloud nearby. A gigantic glass cathedral was placed over them as they waited patiently for the fulfillment of events on earth. Suddenly, I saw the entire earth ignited by a great fire, and immediately; the Lord charged toward the earth, followed by all the overcoming saints who were on white horses. I was now among the saints when we descended toward the earth to conquer Christ's enemies. What did this vision mean?

The Lord Jesus was giving me a symbolic vision of Revelation 19:11-16, which describes how the overcoming believers will return to the earth in victory with Christ. Why did I see Jesus in a chariot instead of sitting on his white horse? This was a personal message telling me that I had qualified as an overcomer to stand with Christ in His "chariot of triumph." Roman generals were given a parade after their victory, and rode in a special triumphal chariot pulled by two horses. Jesus was in a triumphal chariot and all of his overcomers are qualified to stand beside Him. The glass cathedral over the believers was a symbol identifying Christ's raptured Church. The three times the Lord Jesus told me to be patient could possibly be the three and one-half years when the anti-Christ causes havoc in the earth:

> Now I saw heaven opened, and behold, a white horse. And He who sat on him was called Faithful and True, and in righteousness He judges and makes war. His eyes were like a flame of fire, and on His head were many crowns. He had a name written that no one knew except Himself. He was clothed with a robe dipped in blood, and His name is called The Word of God. And the armies in heaven, clothed in fine linen, white and clean, followed Him on white horses. Now out of His mouth goes a sharp sword, that with it He should strike the nations. And He Himself will rule them with a rod of iron. He Himself treads the winepress of the fierceness and wrath of Almighty God. And He has on His robe and on His thigh a name written: KING OF KINGS AND LORD OF LORDS (Revelation 19:11-16).

During these perilous times, the prophetic scriptures give us much to rejoice about, since the overcoming believer stands in the "chariot of triumph." Let us rejoice and praise the Lord now! David rejoiced in Psalms, chapter 47:

V. 1–Oh, clap your hands, all you peoples! Shout to God with the voice of triumph!
V. 5–God has gone up with a shout, the Lord with the sound of a trumpet.
V. 6–Sing praises to God, sing praises! Sing praises to our King, sing praises!
V. 7–For God is the King of all the earth; sing praises with understanding.
V. 8–God reigns over the nations; God sits on His holy throne.
V. 9–The princes of the people have gathered together, the people of the God of Abraham. For the shields of the earth belong to God; He is greatly exalted.

Another powerful message we can rejoice about is found in Revelation 1:18 where Christ declares, "I am he that lives, and was dead; and, behold, I am alive for evermore, Amen; and have the keys of hell and of death."

Praise Triumphs over Satan

Praise will only have power over the devil when it is coupled with the Word, the Name of Jesus and the Blood. These are the weapons we use to resist the devil, so he will flee from us. Corporate praise will attack spiritual strongholds. We can get a better understanding about triumphing in Jesus Christ by looking back into a tradition that was prevalent in ancient civilizations. As I mentioned earlier, during the ancient Roman Empire, a March of Triumph was the highest honor that was bestowed upon any famous Roman general. When he was successful in his battle exploits for the Roman Empire, the Senate would vote him a triumph when he returned to Rome. A triumph was a celebration of victory where the general would parade in a special triumphal chariot pulled by two horses. This triumph was declared a holiday in the city, and the people would line the streets to applaud for the honored general when his entourage would pass by.

Behind the general's chariot, the rulers of the conquered nations were lined up as prisoners of war and led in chains behind the chariot. Rank after rank, the defeated army generals, captains, majors, and lieutenants were pulled along. The spoils of war from that nation were also displayed in the parade. This is the background for what the Apostle Paul was talking about in 2 Corinthians 2:14: "Now thanks be to God who always leads us in triumph in Christ....." We are to join the pageant of triumph with Christ. In order to do this, we must have the mindset that our "praises offered up to the Lord" makes us a part of the victory celebration. We triumph in our praise, for the battle is already won, past tense. Our praise moves us into a position of triumph. I will mention Colossians 2:15 again because it fits perfectly: "Having disarmed principalities and powers, He made a public spectacle of them, triumphing over them in it."

Through our praise, we are joining in the "triumphal celebration" for the victory Christ previously won for us on the cross. We can celebrate that disease is already defeated, and that demonic oppression is defeated. We have been set free, and we will continue to walk in that freedom as long as we triumph in Christ. We celebrate victory over financial problems, because He has delivered us from the curse. Throughout the Psalms, we see David entering into spiritual warfare with worship and praise to God. "O Lord our Lord, how excellent is Your name in all the earth! Who have set Your glory above the heavens....." (Psalm 8:1). The weapon David is using in his worship is the Name of the LORD. His enemies are evil spirits, the vessels Satan uses to come against believers. They can manifest in human beings, and if we understand that all spiritual weapons are launched through the mouth, we can silence the devil with a mouth full of praise to God. John the Revelator saw how the devil's weapons are launched through the mouth of unclean spirits:

> And I saw three unclean spirits like frogs come out of the mouth of the dragon, and out of the mouth of the beast, and out of the mouth of the false prophets (Revelation 16:13).

Observing the Sabbath is a Sanctuary in Time

> Jesus said, "The Sabbath was made for man, and not man for the Sabbath" (Mark 2:27).

In the New Testament, the matter of the Sabbath comes up when Jesus, and the disciples were walking through the grain fields on the Sabbath. They were hungry, and began to pluck heads of grain and to eat. When the Pharisees saw it, they said to Him, "Look, Your disciples are doing what is not lawful to do on the Sabbath!" (Matthew 12:2). Jesus clarified that the true Sabbath was meant to bless man. His authority to say this was explained in His answer to the Pharisees, "For the Son of Man is Lord even of the Sabbath" (v. 8). His titles, "Son of Man" and "Lord" refer to His sovereign power. As man's Lord and representative He is stating His equality with God, since the Sabbath is the Lord's Day. The Pharisaic interpretation of the Sabbath placed mankind under narrow man-made rules which God never originally intended. Christ was explaining that the true meaning of the Sabbath was intended for the spiritual and physical benefit of God's people. Jesus was not abolishing the Sabbath law, but was clarifying that there is a level of grace provided in the Sabbath. From the cornfields, Jesus entered the synagogue and healed a man with a withered hand on the Sabbath, which further agitated the Pharisees:

> Now when He had departed from there, He went into their synagogue. And behold, there was a man who had a withered hand. And they asked Him, saying, "Is it lawful to heal on the Sabbath?"—that they might accuse Him. Then He said to them, "What man is there among you who has one sheep, and if it falls into a pit on the Sabbath, will not lay hold of it and lift it out? Of how much more value then is a man than a sheep? Therefore it is lawful to do good on the Sabbath." Then He said to the man, "Stretch out your hand." And he stretched it out, and it was restored as whole as the other. Then the Pharisees went out and plotted against Him, how they might destroy Him (Matthew 12:9-13).

The Sabbath Law originated in the fourth of the Ten Commandments given to Moses for the Jewish people, (Exodus 20:8-11). The first four of the Ten

Commandments address man's duty to God, and the Sabbath is the seventh day which is to be kept holy for God. In Genesis, we learn that God Himself worked six days during the Creation and then rested on the seventh day, being well-pleased with His work. God did not rest because He was tired, but this was a spiritual rest. The Sabbath was the beginning of God's kingdom of grace, which was consummated by the Son of God, man's redeemer. As mentioned above, the Pharisee's interpretation of the Sabbath placed mankind under narrow man-made rules which God never originally intended. We learn from the Son of God, the Christian Sabbath we observe is the seventh day commemoration celebrating the rest of God the Son, Who finished the work of redemption–Just as God the Father had entered into resting on the seventh day of His Creation.

Shabbat is the Jewish Sabbath. It has always been the most observed holy day in the ancient world. "Then God blessed the seventh day and sanctified it, because in it He rested from all His work which God had created and made" (Genesis 2:3). The Sabbath is a command which is emphasized as one of the *Ten Commandments*: "Remember the Sabbath day, to keep it holy. Six days you shall labor and do all your work, but the seventh day is the Sabbath of the Lord your God" (Exodus 20:8-10). The aspect of *Shabbat* is beautifully described by Rabbi Abraham Joshua Heschel, who states, "Jewish ritual may be characterized as the art of significant forms in time, as architecture of time. Most of its observances—the Sabbath, the New Moon, the festivals, the Sabbatical and the Jubilee year—depend on a certain hour of the day or season of the year. It is, for example, the evening, morning, or afternoon that brings with it the call to prayer. The main themes of faith lie in the realm of time. We remember the day of the exodus from Egypt, the day when Israel stood at Sinai; and our Messianic hope is the expectation of a day, of the end of days."[1] Isaiah records the LORDs word regarding the *Shabbat*:

> If you turn away your foot from the Sabbath, from doing your pleasure on My holy day, and call the Sabbath a delight, the holy day of the Lord honorable, and shall honor Him, not doing your own ways, nor finding your own pleasure, nor speaking your own words, then you shall delight yourself in the Lord; and I will cause you to ride on the high hills of the earth, and feed you with the heritage of Jacob your father. The mouth of the Lord has spoken (Isaiah 58:13-14).

Hebrews, chapter four, helps us to understand that the seventh day of the Creation parallels the spiritual rest found in Christ the Redeemer. The redeemed in Christ enter this rest. Through David, God promised another rest, which Israel failed to enjoy, the rest that is found in Christ. Through David, God promised another rest, which Israel failed to enjoy, the rest that is found in Christ:

> Since therefore it remains that some must enter it (rest), and those to whom it was first preached did not enter because of disobedience, again He designates a certain day, saying in David, "Today," after such a long time, as it has been said: "Today, if you will hear His voice, do not harden your hearts." For if Joshua had given them rest, then He would not afterward have spoken of another day. There remains therefore a rest for the people of God. For he who has entered His rest has himself also ceased from his works as God did from His (Hebrews 4:5-9. Emphasis Added).

Those who trust in Christ can rest in His work of redemption. They can cease striving for salvation through their own good works, and can depend upon the Holy Spirit's help for daily life. The Word of God reveals whether a person is living a carnal or spiritual life. We rest in Christ as our great High Priest, who can bring us into immediate fellowship with God the Father:

> Seeing then that we have a great High Priest who has passed through the heavens, Jesus the Son of God, let us hold fast our confession. For we do not have a High Priest who cannot sympathize with our weaknesses, but was in all points tempted as we are, ye t without sin. Let us therefore come boldly to the throne of grace, that we may obtain mercy and find grace to help in time of need (Hebrews 4:14-16).

Jesus observed firsthand how Jewish-legalism had become a heavy burden on God's people. Jesus called for an open, free, and loyal relationship (His yoke), which enables obedience to the Law's righteousness (My burden):

> Come to Me, all you who labor and are heavy laden, and I will give you rest. Take My yoke upon you and learn from Me, for I am gentle and lowly in heart, and you will find rest for your souls. For My yoke is easy and My burden is light (Matthew 11:28-30).

Key Two

Prayer for America

America needs a Third Great Awakening, and God is prompting His people to pray for such a revival within the Church and for the nation. Natural disasters and social and economic problems are warnings that God's "judgment is coming." The solution will not be found through our political or military might. The answer is to fall on our face before God and cry out to Him in humble repentance of sin. We need more than a fix for the economy, or new politicians. God is sovereign, not the state. The country needs a sweeping, weeping, reaping move of God! God is judging the heinous sins of America and the nations of the world. The Lord God will answer the prayers of His faithful who cry out to Him over the nation and the church falling deeper into sin. Still, many are too busy to pray. It will take millions more! America needs an increase of prayer to reach the Throne of Grace!

We need men like Daniel and Nehemiah, who were willing to pray during their captivity. During Israel's captivity in Babylon, Daniel had been promoted by King Darius to the highest office in the land, "Then this Daniel distinguished himself above the governors and satraps, because an excellent spirit was in him; and the king gave thought to setting him over the whole realm" (Daniel 6:3). The demand for all these high level responsibilities did not distract Daniel from praying three times a day to his Hebrew God. Daniel's faithfulness gained him favor with His Hebrew God, Who gave him wisdom and prophecies for dealing with the Babylonian kingdom. Jealous competition enraged his counterparts when the king gave thought to setting Daniel over the whole kingdom:

> So the governors and satraps sought to find some charge against Daniel concerning the kingdom; but they could find no charge or fault, because he was faithful; nor was there any error or fault found in him. Then these men said, "We shall not find any charge against this Daniel unless we find it against him concerning the law of his God" (Daniel 6:4-5). They had the king order a decree, ".....That whoever petitions any god or man for thirty days, except you, O king, shall be cast into the den of lions" (v. 7).

Even so, Daniel continued to pray: "Now when Daniel knew that the decree was signed, he went to his upper room, with his windows open toward Jerusalem, he knelt down on his knees three times that day, and prayed and gave thanks before his God, as was his custom since early days" (Daniel 6:10). His jealous colleagues reported Daniel's prayer time to the king, and because of the law decreed, he was thrown into the lion's den. However, Daniel was miraculously protected from the lions by the Hebrew God of Israel. After a night of prayer and torment, King Darius checked to see if Daniel was alive:

> Then Daniel said to the king, "O king, live forever! My God sent His angel and shut the lions' mouths, so that they have not hurt me, because I was found innocent before Him; and also, O king, I have done no wrong before you." Now the king was exceedingly glad for him, and commanded that they should take Daniel up out of the den. So Daniel was taken up out of the den, and no injury whatever was found on him, because he believed in his God (Daniel 6:21-23).

Are you willing to die for what you believe in? Not too long ago, I presented this question to a group of church leaders, who were speechless to respond. The Church of Jesus Christ is presently facing challenging times from the government, and in the natural, we have very little ability to stop the current course of events in America. So we must pray like Daniel prayed. As a nation of people, we must cry out to God for His mercy, His grace, and His favor for our nation and leaders. We must seek the Lord in prayer, and fasting to receive His wisdom for the Church and its spiritual leaders.

Author Joel C. Rosenberg believes, "The Lord is shaking our country and purifying His Church. He is requiring all of us to reconsider what we value, where our treasure is, where our hearts are. He is preparing us to see Him face-to-face. And when we see Him, there will be a day of accounting. He will ask us what we did with the resources He entrusted to us. What, then, shall we say?"

What is the present condition of the Church in America? The good news is that souls are being saved; churches are being planted, and communities are being transformed. Even so, while many areas are experiencing a spiritual awakening, other regions are sliding away from the Lord. As the nation hangs on a potential economic implosion, many believe that such a crisis could lead to a reassessment of values; a revived love for the Lord and a fresh harvest of souls. Pray that, across America, multitudes will experience revival and a reawakening within the Church.

Again, history is repeated, as we see in the 1865 era of General William Booth, the founder of the Salvation Army. His analysis of the chief dangers of the 19th century could also apply for today's 21st century. Booth itemized six dangers at that time, which are like reading a list from today's America:

1. Religion without the Holy Spirit
2. Christianity without Christ
3. Forgiveness without repentance
4. Salvation without regeneration
5. Politics without God
6. Heaven without Hell

These describe a "lukewarm" attitude toward God, which demands that we pray for repentance. Repentance is the only answer to the societal ills of today. This means a change of mind and lifestyle in how we respond to these social ills. God would like to see His character represented in all the nations. The objective of our action to these social ills is to help bring about a biblical world view in most aspects of society. For instance, the pro-life movement has made significant progress in re-educating the hearts and minds regarding the sanctity of life and creating a culture of life in America.

How has America become captive to its anti-God, anti-Constitutional government? Scripture instructs that we should especially pray for our leaders, but first of all, we must elect God-fearing leaders—who will influence our education, economy and commerce, our livelihood and the nation's security. We should pray that God will guide them to make the right decisions, and in the fear of God, they would promote what is righteous and punish the wrong.

The Church has a biblical responsibility and constitutional right to offer counsel and spiritual guidance to the state in order to remain in line with the principles of God's Word and the nation's fathers of faith. As we pray, we should also become a prophetic voice in the land. We should speak against the evils in our nation and commend the good, asking God to revive the Church so that it will be salt and light, which are powerful enough to transform society.

Scriptures to Pray for America

Matthew 5:14, 16 and Ephesians 5:6-11, 15
Proclaim that America Remain the Light of the World

America has not only been the natural bread basket of the world; it has also been a spiritual bread basket to the world. Rev. Billy Graham once said, "If the light goes out in America, the light will go out around the world."

> **Prayer:** America, you are called to be God's light in this world, so let your light shine before men of every nation that they may see your good works and glorify your Father Who is in heaven. Let no one deceive you, America, with vain words, nor be a partaker of those who deceive. Although you were once in darkness, now you are walking in the light of the Lord, so live as children of the light. The fruit of the Holy Spirit is goodness, righteousness and truth: "And have no fellowship with the unfruitful works of darkness, but rather expose them" (Ephesians 5:11). "Have no fellowship with the unfruitful works of darkness, America, but rather reprove them" (v. 11). "See then that you walk circumspectly, not as fools but as wise, redeeming the time, because the days are evil" (vv. 15-16).

2 Chronicles 7:14
Humility and Repentance

If My people who are called by My name will humble themselves, and pray and seek My face, and turn from their wicked ways, then I will hear from heaven, and will forgive their sin and heal their land.

Isaiah 60:1, 2
Let Your Light Shine to the Uttermost Parts of the Earth

Arise and shine (America), for your light has come and the glory of the Lord is risen upon you. Although darkness shall cover the earth and gross darkness the people, the Lord shall arise upon you, and His glory will be seen upon you.

1 Timothy 2:1-3
Pray for Leaders

Pray in this way for kings and all others who are in authority over us, or are in places of high responibility, so that we can live in peace and quietness, spending our time in Godly living and thinking much about the Lord. This is good and pleases God our Savior.

- **Pray** much for others; plead for God's mercy upon them; give thanks for all He is going to do for them.
- **Pray** for God's Will to be done on earth as it is declared in Heaven for the nation.
- **Pray** for the President and all those in his administration. No matter what party we support, our President needs our help with prayer. This country belongs to: "We the people"…..and "In God We Trust."

Psalm 119
Pray for Leaders to Live by Biblical Principles

V. 10–For them to see You with their whole heart.
V. 18–For their eyes to be opened to Your Word.
V. 22–For You to deliver them from reproach and contempt.
V. 27–For them not to wander from Your commandments.
V. 29–For you to redeem them from lying ways.
V. 34–For them to observe Your law with their whole heart.
V. 35–For You to make them go in the path of Your Word.
V. 37–For them to turn from vanity and be quickened in Your way.
V. 46–For them to speak Your testimonies and not be ashamed.
V. 58–For them to entreat You Lord for Your favor.
V. 76–For them to be comforted by Your merciful kindness.
V. 87–For them to be quickened by Your loving kindness.
V. 97–For the Word of God to be their meditation day and night.

V. 101- For them to refrain from evil ways and keep the Word of God.
V. 117- For the Lord to hold them up and keep them safe.
V. 125- For them to have understanding of the Word of God.
V. 134- For deliverance from the oppression of men.

Nehemiah 2:17
Standing in the Gap

Lord, you see the distress we are in—come let us build the walls that we may no longer be a reproach.

Intercessors are those who are willing to be numbered among the transgressors. As a Church, we need to be mindful that the Word of God instructs us to be humble before the Holy God and confess our national and religious pride. There seems to be an abundance of pride inhabiting the prayer camps, especially on a national level. Father, forgive us for falling from our first love. Forgive us for loving this evil world and all it offers our appetites. Forgive us for the sins of worldliness and prayerlessness. As a nation, we have gathered against the life of the righteous and condemned innocent blood, through abortion. We have also redefined traditional marriage, openly endorsing same-sex marriages in society and the military.

Psalm 94:20-23
The Holocaust of Abortion

They gather together against the life of the righteous, and condemn innocent blood. But the Lord has been my defense, and my God the rock of my refuge. He has brought on them their own iniquity, and shall cut them off in their own wickedness; the Lord our God shall cut them off. Shall the throne of iniquity, which devises evil by law, have fellowship with You?

Deuteronomy 30:19
Pray for America to Choose Life

I call heaven and earth to witness today against you, that I have set before you life and death, blessing and cursing; therefore choose life that you and your descendants may live!

Abortion is America's holocaust. Abortion is plainly child sacrifice. As a nation, we cannot expect to have the favor of a Holy God when we have aborted more than 55 million children since 1973. We must fear for our future, unless we wake up and reverse course. Judgment is already at the door!

- **Pray** for the pro-life ministries that are standing by faith to overturn the many facets of the abortion industry. We ask You O Lord to raise up intercessors who will pray day and night that our nation will once again create a culture of life and help end the evil scourge of abortion and infanticide.

- **Pray** for God-fearing legislators on the state and national level that can pass legislation to overturn abortion and defund Planned Parenthood dispensaries that assist teens and young women to have access to abortion, contraception and the morning-after pills.
- **Pray** for those who are refusing to bow down and accept the HHS Mandate which dictates against religious freedom.

1 Corinthians 4:5
Cleanse the Motives of our National Heart

We ask that the Lord will, ".....Bring to light the hidden things of darkness, and reveal the counsels of the hearts: Then each one's praise will come from God."

Prayer: It is God who will bring to light the hidden things of darkness and reveal the counsels of the hearts in America. Cleanse the motive of your heart, America, through repentance and submission to Almighty God so that He will be glorified in Jesus' Name. Be not overwhelmed with evil, America, but overcome evil with good.

Psalm 22:28

For the Kingdom is the Lord's; and He is the governor among nations.

Psalm 33:12

Blessed is the nation whose God is the Lord.

Daniel 2:21

And God changes the times and the seasons; He removes kings, and sets up kings; He gives wisdom unto the wise, and knowledge to them that know understanding.

Psalm 9:17

The wicked shall be turned into hell, and all the nations that forget God.

Proverbs 19:23

The fear of the Lord leads to life; and he who has it will abide in satisfaction; He will not be visited with evil.

Proverbs 21:1

The king's heart is in the hand of the Lord, as the rivers of water: he turns it wherever he wishes.

Psalm 33:10, 11
God Judges the Nations

The Lord brings the counsel of the nations to nothing; He makes the plans of the peoples of no effect. The counsel of the Lord stands forever, the plans of His heart to all generations. Blessed is the nation whose God is the LORD, The people He has chosen as His own inheritance.

- **Pray** that God will grant the President, as Commander-in-Chief, continued revelation, wisdom and understanding in the fear of the LORD to know the mission he is to accomplish in the remainder of his presidency.
- **Pray** the LORD will grant him grace, protection and wisdom for his Cabinet members, and to all working in his administration; and all involved in U.S. foreign policy. Intercede for inspiration, wisdom, and tactics for dismantling and overcoming the terrorist networks and tactics of the Islamic Jihad movement (Ezekiel 32:22-25; Acts 9:1-6).
- **Pray** the Holy Spirit will restrain Iran's evil agenda against Israel and the United States–and that the U.S. will unequivocally stand to help protect Israel against her numerous enemies in the Middle East.

1 Kings 18:30
Restoring the Altar in America

Then Elijah said to all the people, "Come near to me." So all the people came near to him. And he repaired the altar of the Lord that was broken down.

During these end times when the Church of Jesus Christ presses to bring in the final harvest of souls (Joel 3:13-14), America is fighting for its survival to remain a "light to the world." Restoring a prayer shield over the nation is part of restoring the true altar of the Lord, like Elijah did prophetically on Mount Carmel so that fire could fall from heaven. When the fire of the LORD fell and consumed Elijah's sacrifice, it also burned up the rocks on his altar. This revived the faith and worship of their Hebrew God, and reduced them to their first love and their first works. When Jesus spoke of John the Baptist He said, "To be sure, Elijah comes and will restore all things" (Matthew 17:11). John the Baptist came with the same fiery spirit as Elijah to restore God's people, to revive dead religion, and to turn the hearts of the fathers to the children. Elijah restored Israel; and John preached repentance, which prepared the way for the Messiah. God has also promised Israel that He would send the prophet Elijah before the great and dreadful day of the Lord (Malachi 4:5-6).

- **Pray** for spiritual renewal and revival fire to fall from heaven so the Church in America will fulfill Christ's mission to spread the gospel. Churches need a supernatural fire like Elijah received that will not only burn up our sacrifice, but the old altars we have built for ourselves.

- **Pray** for the Bride of Christ, the "wise virgins," to trim their lamps and be ready for the Bridegrooms appearing.

Isaiah 59:19

The Fear of the Lord

So shall they fear the name of the Lord from the west, and his glory from the rising of the sun. When the enemy shall come in like a flood, the Spirit of the Lord shall lift up a standard against him.

When America has God's favor, then the Lord will battle against its enemies. Pray for a great Christ-awakening to bring the fear of the LORD back to America.

Psalms 64:2, 3

Prayer: Father, we pray You would hide America from the secret plots of the wicked "from the rebellion of the workers of iniquity, who sharpen their tongue like a sword.....Lord, close the mouths of those who would shoot out bitter words and cause them to stumble over their own tongue."

Psalms 31:20

Prayer: Lord, hide us in the secret place of Your presence from the plots of men, and shelter us from the strife of tongues.

Psalms 124:6, 7

Prayer: Blessed be the Lord, who has not given us as prey to their teeth, but has enabled us to escape as a bird from the fowler's snare.

Psalms 5:12; 32:10

Prayer: Bless us, Lord, and surround us with Your shield of favor and mercy.

Psalms141:9, 10

Prayer: Keep us from the snares the enemy has laid for us, and from the traps of the workers of iniquity. Let the wicked fall into their own nets, while we escape safely.

Key Three

Prayer for the Nation of Israel

He who keeps Israel shall neither slumber nor sleep. –Psalm 121:4

Jerusalem is ground zero for spiritual warfare in the world today. During this crucial and critical time in Israel's history, Scripture calls us to pray for the peace of Jerusalem: "May they prosper who love you. Peace be within your walls, prosperity within your palaces" (Psalm 122:5-7). Every Christian is to cry out, intercede, and seek *Yahweh* to intervene for the peace of Jerusalem. We cannot be silent; our cry must come up before the Throne of God, on behalf of the Land. World leaders will never produce a lasting peace, until the Day of the Lord when the Messiah returns. The promise is clear:

Jeremiah 33:3

Call to Me, and I will answer you, and show you great and mighty things, which you do not know.

Genesis 12:3

This is the Covenant God made with Abraham and his seed: "I will bless those who bless you, and I will curse him who curses you; and in you all the families of the earth shall be blessed."

Psalm 137:5, 6

We discover how serious the Lord is about His call to pray for Jerusalem. "If I forget you, O Jerusalem, let my right hand forget its skill! If I do not remember you, let my tongue cling to the roof of my mouth—if I do not exalt Jerusalem above my chief joy." It is imperative to continue in prayer, during this pivotal time in history when the Palestinians have declared Jerusalem a Muslim capital for Islam.

Isaiah 62:6, 7

The Prophet Isaiah gives us the correct response to the request for our prayers for the Middle East: "I have set watchmen on your walls, O Jerusalem; they shall never hold their peace day or night. You who make mention of the Lord, do not keep silent, and give Him no rest till He establishes and till He makes Jerusalem a praise in the earth." *Yahweh* promises to bless all who bless Israel.

Right and Wrong thinking about modern Israel.....
God's covenant with Israel is everlasting!

Christian anti-Semitism has been voiced through the false Replacement Theology which claims the Church has replaced Israel in the purposes of God. Liberal theologians believe that Israel has lost its special covenant relationship with the Hebrew God based on their rejection of Jesus and that Jews are subject to the curses found in the Bible. According to Scripture, this viewpoint is wrong. Replacement Theology was introduced to the Church when the Gentile leadership took over from Jewish leadership. They interpreted the destruction of the Temple and Jerusalem as a sign that God had abandoned Judaism. This led to the thinking that the Gentiles were now set free from Jerusalem's influence and could develop their own Christian theology. The Church of Rome perceived Christianity to be an extension of Judaism and produced Gentile anti-Semites.

Scripture is the final word for right thinking toward Israel. We are forbidden from being arrogant about God's covenant people the Jews. Israel's rejection of Christ is momentary, until the door for the Gentile harvest is closed, and all those who will be saved and receive Christ. Salvation will then come to a large number of Jews through the 144,000 witnesses from the twelve tribes of Judah, who will preach the gospel of Christ (Revelation 7 and 14). In Romans, chapter 11, the Apostle Paul warns against boastfulness, pride, and presumption, since the Gentile Church is but a wild olive tree grafted in because of Israel's unbelief (Romans 11:17-18). The New Testament clearly states that the Church is to love and honor the Jewish people and the patriarchs–God will fulfill the covenant promises made to these Judaic fathers of faith (Romans 11:28, 31; 9:4). In Romans 11:26-27, *Yahweh* affirms that His covenant with His chosen nation is everlasting–and so all Israel will be saved, as it is written: "The Deliverer will come out of Zion, and He will turn away ungodliness from Jacob; for this is My covenant with them, when I take away their sins." *Yahweh's* covenant with His chosen nation is everlasting, and no failure on Israel's part can nullify it:

> Yet for all that, when they are in the land of their enemies, I will not cast them away, nor shall I abhor them, to utterly destroy them and break My covenant with them; for I am the Lord their God (Leviticus 26:44).

> .....Yet I will not forget you. See, I have inscribed you on the palms of My hands; your walls are continually before Me (Isaiah 49:16).

> But this is the covenant that I will make with the house of Israel after those days, says the Lord: I will put My law in their minds, and write it on their hearts; and I will be their God, and they shall be My people (Jeremiah 31:31).

The Bible describes two significant occasions, during modern times, when the Jews would return to the LORD. The first return was physical in nature, which occurred in 1947 after World War II when the Jews were gathered together as a nation after the Diaspora. Both Isaiah and Ezekiel were given prophecies about the Jewish people being returned to their own *Homeland*. (Read Isaiah 49:22; 60:10-11) Ezekiel was given a detailed vision of this gathering where He saw the people united, but they were a valley of dead, dry bones. Ezekiel commanded them to arise, and as they did they were given muscles and flesh, then the Holy Spirit breathed new life into them. The Jewish people were united back into a national spirit by the Spirit of the Living God. The gathering of the Israeli people to their *Homeland* was certainly an event for the entire world to see. Ezekiel's prophetic vision is found in chapter 37:

> So I prophesied as He commanded me, and breath came into them, and they lived, and stood upon their feet, an exceedingly great army. Then He said to me, "Son of man, these bones are the whole house of Israel." They indeed say, "Our bones are dry, our hope is lost, and we ourselves are cut off!" Therefore prophesy and say to them, "Thus says the Lord God: 'Behold, O My people, I will open your graves and cause you to come up from your graves, and bring you into the land of Israel. Then you shall know that I am the Lord, when I have opened your graves, O My people, and brought you up from your graves. I will put My Spirit in you, and you shall live, and I will place you in your own land. Then you shall know that I, the Lord, have spoken it and performed it,' says the Lord." (vv. 10-14).

Israel's second return to the Lord will be spiritual. Zechariah prophesies that the nation is already in their *Land* before She looks upon Him whom She has pierced. This has not happened yet, but many theologians agree this is after the Third Temple Mount has been built, and the Jews are betrayed by the Anti-Christ:

> And I will pour on the house of David and on the inhabitants of Jerusalem the Spirit of grace and supplication; then they will look on Me whom they pierced. Yes, they will mourn for Him as one mourns for his only son, and grieve for Him as one grieves for a firstborn (Zechariah 12:10).

Before the great Day of the Lord, a significant remnant in Israel will believe in Jesus as *Messiah*. In Revelation, chapter seven, this harvest of Jewish souls will be reached by the 144,000 witnesses raised up from the twelve tribes of Israel. Their witness will have worldwide effect:

> After these things I saw four angels standing at the four corners of the earth, holding the four winds of the earth, that the wind should not blow on the earth, on the sea, or on any tree. Then I saw another angel ascending from the east, having the seal of the living God. And he cried with a loud voice to the four angels to whom it was granted to harm the earth and the sea, saying, "Do not harm the earth, the sea, or the trees till we have sealed the servants of our God on their foreheads." And I heard the number of those who were sealed. One hundred and forty-four thousand of all the tribes of the children of Israel were sealed….." (vv. 1-4).

The Jewish people need to accept *Yeshua* as Lord and savior to be saved. The Abrahamic Covenant is recorded in the Old Testament and is repeated in the Siddur, the Jewish prayer book. Many religious Jews are not conscious of any personal and redemptive relationship with the Father, but have found *Yeshua* in their search for deeper love. The pressures on Israel's political situation should not be our primary focus. Christian Zionists should be supporting the Israeli people in their struggle against their enemies. Love for Israel should be expressed in support for Israel's survival in her own land, and Zionists should be pressing their home nation to stand with Israel. Zechariah, chapter 14 makes it clear that when all the nations turn against Israel just before the end of this age, which is described as the *Day of the Lord,* their Messiah will intervene and battle on their behalf:

> Behold, the day of the Lord is coming, and your spoil will be divided in your midst. For I will gather all the nations to battle against Jerusalem; the city shall be taken, the houses rifled, and the women ravished. Half of the city shall go into captivity, but the remnant of the people shall not be cut off from the city (vv. 1-2).

> Then the Lord will go forth and fight against those nations, as He fights in the day of battle. And in that day His feet will stand on the Mount of Olives, which faces Jerusalem on the east….. (vv. 3-4)

True peace will finally come to Israel when the *Prince of Peace* dwells among His people. Only then will God's Word be fulfilled: "My people will dwell in a peaceful habitation, in secure dwellings, and in quiet resting places" (Isaiah 32:18). You can help the Jewish people preserve their Promised Land by becoming a Zionist, and praying for Israel. You can help refute the harmful teaching of Replacement Theology, that the Church has replaced Israel as God's chosen people. Jesus always directed the message of the Kingdom to the Jew first, and so did the apostles:

> For I am not ashamed of the gospel of Jesus Christ, for it is power of God unto Salvation to everyone that believes for the Jew first, and also for the Greek (Romans 1:16).

After years of reconciliation, the Jewish people who have suffered such horrible persecutions at the hands of Christians, have now come to trust them as their most reliable friend during these perilous times when they stand alone against their enemies. Those who threaten Israel in any destructive way "touch the apple of His eye" (Zechariah 2:8). Those who bless Israel touch the heart of God.

Watchmen on the Walls of Jerusalem

Psalm 121 is known as the *Watchmen's Psalm*:

He who watches over you will not slumber, indeed He who watches over Israel will neither slumber nor sleep (v. 3).

Yahweh is the Chief Watchman:

- He watches the righteous and the wicked (Psalm 1:6; Proverbs 15:3).
- His eyes watch the nations (Psalm 66:7).
- He watches the earth (2 Chronicles 16:9).
- He watches over His Word (Jeremiah 1:12).
- He watches over Israel (Psalm 121:4).

Jerusalem is the Center of the Earth:

- Jerusalem is called the Throne of the LORD (Jeremiah 3:17).
- Jerusalem is the city of righteousness, and faithful city (Isaiah 1:26).
- Jerusalem is Zion, the City of David (2 Samuel 5:7).
- God's fire is in Zion and His furnace in Jerusalem (Isaiah 31:9).
- Jerusalem is called the Holy city (Isaiah 52:1).
- Jerusalem is a cup of trembling, a burdensome stone (Zechariah 12:2).

Yahweh watches over His Word for Israel:

> Scripture will be fulfilled because *Yahweh* is faithful and true: "So shall My word be that goes forth from My mouth; it shall not return to Me void, but it shall accomplish what I please, and it shall prosper in the thing for which I sent it" (Isaiah 55:11).

Yeshua said in Matthew 5:18, "For assuredly, I say to you, till heaven and earth pass away, one jot or one tittle will by no means pass from the law till all is fulfilled."

Special significance of the Name of *Yahweh*:

Yahweh is the name of the supreme and only true God Almighty. The Concordant explains: ".....Yahweh, He is the only Elohim. Elohim means 'the Mighty One.' Deuteronomy 4:35 states, "There is no one else aside from Him." Verse 39 clarifies: "So you know today, and you recall it to your heart that Yahweh, He is the only Elohim in the heavens above and on the earth beneath; there is no one else."[1]

Special significance of the Shofar:

The rabbis say the shofar (ram's horn) was used to "confuse the devil" and for healing. It was also used as an expression of thankfulness (at the feasts) and in bringing people out of bondage. In Revelation 1:10-11, it is noted as the actual voice of *Yahweh*. The shofar itself should only be blown under the anointing of the Holy Spirit. When blown without the proper anointing, it brings confusion on God's people. We have come under spiritual attack at our prayer embassy when saints have picked up the shofar and blown it without direction from the Holy Spirit. Some intercessors that are freely yielded to the Holy Spirit have had their voices used as shofars.

Special significance of the Biblical watches:

- A one-hour watch (Matthew 26:40).
- 12-hour night watch (6:00 PM–6:00 AM) (Psalm 63:6).
- 4-hour watch (day/night divided into 3 watches) (Judges 7:19).
- 24-hour Biblical watch (Isaiah 62:6-7; Revelation 4).
- Other watches (Luke 12:38; Matthew 24:43; Revelation 16:15).
- Why Christians should watch? (Luke 21:36).

Scriptures to Pray for Israel's Covenant Land

Isaiah 31:4, 5
God will deliver Jerusalem

For thus the Lord has spoken to me: "As a lion roars, and a young lion over his prey (When a multitude of shepherds is summoned against him, He will not be afraid of their voice nor be disturbed by their noise), so the Lord of hosts will come down to fight for Mount Zion and for its hill. Like birds flying about, so will the Lord of hosts defend Jerusalem. Defending, He will also deliver it; passing over, He will preserve it."

Genesis 15:18-21
The Promised Land

On that day the Lord made a covenant with Abram and said, "To your descendants I give this land, from the river of Egypt to the great river, the Euphrates—the land of the Kenites, Kenizzites, Kadomites, Hittites, Perizzites, Rephaites, Amorites, Cananites, Girgashites and Jebusites."

Genesis 17:7, 8
Canaan

The whole land of Canaan, where you are now an alien, I will give as an everlasting possession to you and your descendants after you; and I will be their God.

Exodus 23:31
Israel's Borders

I will establish your borders from the Red Sea to the Sea of the Philistines, and from the desert to the River. I will hand over to you the people who live in the land and you will drive them out before you.

Deuteronomy 11:24
Biblical Inheritance

Every place where you set your foot will be yours; your territory will extend from the desert to Lebanon, and from the Euphrates River to the western sea.

Jeremiah 16:16
Pray for the Jews to return to their Homeland

But now I will send for many fishermen, declares the Lord, and they will catch them. After that I will send for many hunters.....

There is an ongoing mission within the Body of Christ to help the Jewish people escape persecution in anti-Semitic regions of the world. One example is Ebenezer's Operation Exodus, which reports that inside Siberian cities, Jews fear for their lives. With offices in every major city in Russia and members in key places such as the police, the military and civil administrations, the nationalists aim to control the country by AD 2000. There is strong evidence that city administrators all over Russia maintain lists of all Jews in the country. These are signs that the hunters have started as anti-Semitism increases. Ebenezer fishing teams are throughout the former Soviet Union helping Jews making Aliyah. "See.....The Gentiles.....Will bring your sons in their arms and carry your daughters on their shoulders," Isaiah

49:22. They help transport Jews back to Israel by plane to Tel Aviv and through sea passages from Odessa to Haifa.

Charitable ministries like Rabbi Yechiel Eckstein's *International Fellowship of Christians and Jews* have played a major role in assisting Jewish immigrants from the former Soviet Union. Presently, they are helping new immigrants from western Russia get to Finland, where they are taken to Christian safe houses who host them for a few days before they fly home to Israel. There are many other ministries, acting as angels of mercy throughout the former Soviet Union. Pray for those who are working to fulfill prophetic Scripture in these last days. Jesus said, "I must work the works of Him who sent Me while it is day; the night is coming when no one can work. As long as I am in the world, I am the light of the world" (John 9:4). As long as the Church is in this world, we must complete the mission of the Lord Jesus Christ.

Psalm 37:22; Leviticus 25:23, 24
For those blessed by Him shall inherit the earth, but those cursed by Him shall be cut off.

Pray for the Jewish people to return to the commands and roots of their forefathers, Abraham, Isaac and Jacob. Like America, Israel has gross national sins and needs to return to its foundational faith. Many Jews are receiving Christ as Savior and are highly persecuted for it. Israel's land will only be secured and peaceful when the hearts of the Jewish people return to their God: "Wait for the Lord and keep his way. He will exalt you to inherit the land; when the wicked are cut off, you will see it" (Psalm 37:34).

Ezekiel 34:13
Aliyah

And I will bring them out from the peoples and gather them from the countries, and will bring them to their own land; I will feed them on the mountains of Israel, in the valleys and in all the inhabited places of the country.

When you pray, call the Jews home from the lands where they are scattered. The "Third Exodus" of Jewish peoples is already underway as Jews' flood to the government offices to immigrate to Israel. **Pray** for the many ministries who are helping to return the Jews home to Israel.

Isaiah 49:22
American Jews

Thus says the Lord God: "Behold, I will lift My hand in an oath to the nations, and set up My standard for the peoples; they shall bring your sons in their arms, and your daughters shall be carried on their shoulders….."

Pray for American Jews to be prepared to make Aliyah to Israel when it is time.

Jeremiah 31:8
See, I will bring them from the land of the north.

Pray for the large numbers of Jews continuing to return to the land, especially from the former USSR, or Soviet Union. Since the modern state of Israel was founded in May 1948, 2.6 million Jews have made Aliyah—900,000 from the former Soviet Union. Nearly a million have entered Israel in this decade alone. The Jewish Agency believes that over a million, Jews remain in Russia.

PRAYER FOR ISRAEL AND THE PEOPLE

Proverbs 21:1
Pray for divine wisdom for the leaders of Israel!
The king's heart is in the hand of the Lord, like the rivers of water; He turns it wherever He wishes.

Psalm 125:3
Pray for Israel's leaders to have the wisdom of God.
For the scepter of wickedness shall not rest on the land allotted to the righteous, lest the righteous reach out their hands to iniquity.

Prayer: Father, we ask you to break the strongholds of false religion, pride and wickedness that seek to bewitch (cast a spell on and gain control over) the people of Israel (Galatians 3:1-5).

PSALM 55:9
Pray for Anti-Semitism
Destroy, O Lord, and divide their tongues, for I have seen violence and strife in the city.

Pray against the avalanche of anti-Semitism in Europe, Great Britain and other parts of the world. Lord, deal justly and swiftly with Your enemies. Lord, confuse the wicked and confound the words of those who would incite violence against Israel.

Genesis 12:1-3

As a nation, pray for Israel, bless Israel and comfort her.

I will make you into a great nation and I will bless you; I will make your name great, and you will be a blessing. I will bless those who bless you, and whoever curses you I will curse; and all peoples on earth will be blessed through you.

Prayer: Israel has been and is the vehicle of world redemption. *Yahweh's* great acts of redemption have come to the Gentile nations through Israel. Jesus is a Jew; salvation is of the Jews, and the Bible has a Jewish background. Truly, as the Apostle Paul taught, we are indebted to them. America has stood with Israel and much of the blessing that is ours as a nation is because of this. This is the promise of God's eternal word. We must pray that the special relationship between Israel, and the United States of America will not be broken or corrupted by any of our national leaders.

Psalm 102:13, 14

Pray and remind the Lord of his promise to show mercy to Zion!

You will arise and have mercy on Zion; for the time to favor her, yes, the set time, has come. For Your servants take pleasure in her stones, and show favor to her dust.

Psalm 81:13-15

Israel must have *Yahweh's* favor if they are to see their enemies defeated.

Oh, that My people would listen to Me, that Israel would walk in My ways! I would soon subdue their enemies, and turn My hand against their adversaries. The haters of the Lord would pretend submission to Him, but their fate would endure forever.

Zechariah 12:10, 11

Pray for the outpouring of the Spirit of grace and supplication upon the Jewish people!

And I will pour on the house of David and on the inhabitants of Jerusalem the Spirit of grace and supplication; then they will look on Me whom they pierced. Yes, they will mourn for Him as one mourns for his only son, and grieve for Him as one grieves for a firstborn. In that day there shall be a great mourning in Jerusalem, like the mourning at Hadad Rimmon in the plain of Megiddo.

Psalm 124

Praise be to the Lord, who has not let us be torn by their teeth. We have escaped like a bird out of the fowler's snare; the snare has been broken, and we have escaped. Our help is in the name of the Lord, the Maker of heaven and earth.

Zechariah 8:14, 15

For thus says the Lord of hosts: "Just as I determined to punish you when your fathers provoked Me to wrath," says the Lord of hosts, "And I would not relent, so again in these days I am determined to do good to Jerusalem and to the house of Judah. Do not fear."

Pray for a Harvest of Jewish Souls

Zechariah 10:1, 2

Pray for the restoration of Judah and Israel

Ask the Lord for rain in the time of the latter rain. The Lord will make flashing clouds; He will give them showers of rain, grass in the field for everyone. For the idols speak delusion; the diviners envision lies, and tell false dreams; they comfort in vain. Therefore the people wend their way like sheep; they are in trouble because there is no shepherd.

Zechariah 8:20-23

Pray for the promised return back to Zion and the ancient paths!

And many peoples and powerful nations will come to Jerusalem to seek the Lord Almighty and to entreat him. This is what the Lord Almighty says: "In those days ten men from all languages and nations will take firm hold of one Jew by the hem of his robe and say, 'Let us go with you, because we have heard that God is with you.'"

Romans 11:15, 16

Pray for the outpouring of the spirit of grace and supplication upon Jerusalem!

For if their being cast away is the reconciling of the world, what will their acceptance be but life from the dead? For if the firstfruit is holy, the lump is also holy; and if the root is holy, so are the branches.

Prayer for Israel's Enemies

Obadiah 1:15

God's Word Declares Judgment against Israel's Enemies

For the day of the Lord upon all the nations is near; as you have done, it shall be done to you; your reprisal shall return upon your own head.

The people of Israel have experienced the Day of the Lord numerous times in their history through invasions by foreign enemies. Obadiah explains what will happen to any nation which comes against Israel—or attempts to divide her land. America must repent of pressuring Israel to divide her land—and the Holy City Jerusalem, the capital city of David. The First Coming of Christ and the Church Age began a new phase of the Day of the Lord. The Second Coming of Christ will usher in the third aspect of the Day of the Lord, during which Christ's righteous universal rule will restore God's order in the Earth (Isaiah 11:6-9; Amos 9:13).

Prayer Declarations Against Israel's Enemies

All of Israel's enemies, except for Russia, are Muslim. Iran and Syria have been conducting a proxy war against Israel using their militant groups' Hamas (Palestinian Sunni Islamic) and Hezbollah (Lebanon Shiite) to destroy Israel.

Isaiah 62:6, 7

I have set watchmen on your walls, O Jerusalem; they shall never hold their peace day or night. You who make mention of the Lord, do not keep silent, and give Him no rest till He establishes and till He makes Jerusalem a praise in the earth.

Psalm 129:5, 6

Let them all be confounded and turned back that hate Zion. Let them be as grass upon the housetops, which withers before it grows up.

Psalm 83:2-4; 16, 18

Pray for a mighty revival in the Muslim world!

See how your enemies are astir, how your foes rear their heads. With cunning they conspire against your people; they plot against those you cherish. "Come," they say, "let us destroy them as a nation, that the name of Israel be remembered no more."

- **Pray** the Lord will "Cover their faces with shame so that men will seek your name, O Lord.....Let them know that you, whose name is the Lord—that you alone are the Most High over all the earth."
- **Pray** for multitudes of Muslims to have their eyes unveiled from Islam, so they will come to know Jesus as their true Savior. Pray for an end to terrorist warfare. Pray the Holy Spirit will be at work in the hearts of many Muslim terrorists–bringing them into a saving knowledge of Christ–as He did with Saul of Tarsus.
- **Pray** for those workers who are trying to reach Muslims with the liberating Gospel of Jesus Christ. Pray for their safety and for their success.

Psalm 122:6-9

Pray for Peace (Shalom)

Pray for the Peace of Jerusalem: May they prosper who love you. Peace be within your walls, prosperity within your palaces. For the sake of my brethren and companions, I will now say, "Peace be within you." Because of the house of the Lord our God I will seek your good.

Revelation 11:15

Peace will come when Yeshua HaMashiach rules the nations from Jerusalem!

The kingdoms of this world are become the kingdoms of our Lord, and of his Christ; and he shall reign for ever and ever.

1 John 5:14-15

The Lord answers prayers that are petitioned according to His Will

Now this is the confidence that we have in Him, that if we ask anything according to His will, He hears us. And if we know that He hears us, whatever we ask, we know that we have the petitions that we have asked of Him.

Key Four

Prayer for the Church

So continuing daily with one accord in the temple, and breaking bread from house to house, they ate their food with gladness and simplicity of heart, praising God and having favor with all the people –Acts 2:46,47

What produces a prevailing Church? The Church of Jesus Christ is vital and powerful when it is united, in one accord. The 120 disciples who were waiting for the outpouring of the Holy Spirit were all in one accord when they were filled with "fire" from Heaven (Acts 2:1). Their unity brought forth a worshiping Church–we read in verse 43, that fear came upon every soul, and wonders, and signs were done through the apostles. The first key to the power of the Church is the Baptism of the Holy Spirit. The second key is the unity of the Body. The early Church had authority to "bind" and "loose." Thirdly, Scripture specifically discloses that there is power in the agreement of two or three. There must be at least two or three witnesses to stand up and testify what they have seen or heard from the Holy Spirit. If these testimonies agree and they are confirmed by the Word of God, then there is the authority to "bind" and to "loose."

The principle of two or three witnesses was established in the Old Testament Law and is also instituted in the New Testament Church. It appears; there is more justice found in two or three key witnesses than "mob" rule! It is wisdom for shepherds and church overseers, to come into agreement for the overall Body, then trying to have the whole assembly come into agreement. Most denominations hold an annual business conference where delegate pastors and laymen vote on behalf of the full assembly.

Here are some Scriptures that mention the principle of two or three witnesses:

- One witness shall not rise against a man concerning any iniquity or any sin that he commits; by the mouth of two or three witnesses the matter shall be established (Deuteronomy 19:15).
- But if he will not hear, take with you one or two more, that "by the mouth of two or three witnesses every word may be established" (Matthew 18:16).
- Assuredly, I say to you, whatever you bind on earth will be bound in heaven, and whatever you loose on earth will be loosed in heaven. Again I say to you that if two of you agree on earth concerning anything that they ask, it will be done for them by My Father in heaven (Matthew 18:18-19).
- Jesus said, "For where two or three are gathered together in My name, I am there in the midst of them" (Matthew 18:20).

- Do not receive an accusation against an elder except from two or three witnesses (1 Timothy 5:19).
- Anyone who has rejected Moses' law dies without mercy on the testimony of two or three witnesses (Hebrews 10:28).

Pray for Church Leaders

Pray for the fullness and all that the Lord intends for His ministering servants: Pastors, elders, prophets, apostles, evangelists, teachers and intercessors. Pray they will be sensitive to the leading of the Holy Spirit and the sevenfold anointing from God's Word. Ask the Father to pour out upon each of His church leaders the sevenfold anointing:

Isaiah 11:2, 3
Sevenfold Spirit of the Lord

The Spirit of wisdom and understanding, the Spirit of counsel and might, the Spirit of knowledge and the fear of the Lord. By the power of the Spirit of the Lord, make them quick in their understanding of the fear of the Lord so that they will judge righteously, not by the hearing of their own ears nor by the sight of their own eyes but with Your righteous judgment.

Prayer: Father, we ask the Holy Spirit to open their ears so that they may hear Your voice and be sensitive to the cry of the people. Allow the precious blood of Jesus to give them clean hands. We commit their works to You and ask You to establish their thoughts. Let the Word of God guide their feet so that you can direct their path, and they will walk in Your ways.

Thank you Father for hearing this prayer of consecration for your ministering servants. Thank you for Your Word, which says You are able to keep that which we have committed to You from falling against that day (2 Timothy 1:12). Just as Jesus Your Son prayed for You to keep the disciples from evil, we pray You will deliver them from wicked men and evil counsel.

Father, in the Name of Jesus, we place the full armor of God upon each leader. "Stand therefore, having girded your waist with truth, having put on the breastplate of righteousness, and having shod your feet with the preparation of the gospel of peace; above all, taking the shield of faith with which you will be able to quench all the fiery darts of the wicked one. And take the helmet of salvation, and the sword of the Spirit, which is the word of God; praying always with all prayer and supplication in the Spirit, being watchful to this end with all perseverance and supplication for all the saints….." (Ephesians 6:13-17).

Prayer for the Body of Christ (the Bride)

1 Peter 2:5

Christ is the foundation of the Third Spiritual Temple

You also, as living stones, are being built up a spiritual house, a holy priesthood, to offer up spiritual sacrifices acceptable to God through Jesus Christ.

For generations, we have heard how a remnant church will be raised up to set the captives free, bringing forth a final harvest that will affect all nations (Revelation 12:17). This is the offspring of Israel (the engrafted Gentile Church) who is actively ministering as witnesses of Jesus Christ. They will prepare the way for the redeemed of the Lord to return to Zion. They must come through fiery trials which very few will be able to stand. These overcomers are willing to suffer the Baptism of Fire, which qualifies them for their priestly and kingly role; which gives them governing authority with the Bridegroom. The sons and daughters of such a kingdom will have their faith tested and purified like gold:

….That the genuineness of your faith, being much more precious than gold that perishes, though it is tested by fire, may be found to praise, honor, and glory at the revelation of Jesus Christ….. (1 Peter 1:7).

The Bride of Christ is this Holy Priesthood!

1 Peter 2:9, 10

But you are a chosen generation, a royal priesthood, a holy nation, His own special people, that you may proclaim the praises of Him who called you out of darkness into His marvelous light; who once were not a people but are now the people of God, who had not obtained mercy but now have obtained mercy.

Psalm 94:14, 15

Judgment Begins at the House of God

The Lord will not cast off His people, nor will He forsake His inheritance. But judgment will return to righteousness, and all the upright in heart will follow it. **Prayer:** O Lord, purge your Body of Believers. Send your Baptism of Fire upon the righteous, so they will be refined as pure gold. Let Your Bride glorify Your Name in the earth. Prepare Your Bride without spot or wrinkle—deliver her of filthiness and religious tradition.

Ephesians 5:8-10
Walk in Purity and Holiness

For you were once darkness, but now you are light in the Lord. Walk as children of light (for the fruit of the Spirit is in all goodness, righteousness, and truth), finding out what is acceptable to the Lord.

- **Pray** for the Body of Christ to walk in love with humbled hearts (2 John 1:6).
- **Pray** that the Body of Christ will keep themselves from idols (1 John 5:21).
- **Pray** for the peace of God to rule in their hearts and the Word of Christ to dwell in them richly with all wisdom (Colossians 3:15, 16).
- **Pray** for them to cleanse themselves from all filthiness in the flesh and in spirit perfecting holiness in the fear of God (2 Corinthians 7:1).
- **Pray** for them to be vessels of honor sanctified and worthy for the Master's use and prepared for every good work (2 Timothy 2:21).

Philippians 1:20
Courage and Inner Strength

.....According to my earnest expectation and hope that in nothing I shall be ashamed, but with all boldness, as always, so now also Christ will be magnified in my body, whether by life or by death.

Pray for the Body of Christ to have the inner strength to persevere and withstand hardship and have the presence of mind against odds—courage to glorify Your Name.

1 Corinthians 15:58
Do not Grow Weary

Therefore, my beloved brethren, be steadfast, immovable, always abounding in the work of the Lord, knowing that your labor is not in vain in the Lord.

Revelation 3:7, 8
Let us be the Faithful Church

And to the angel of the church in Philadelphia write, "These things says He who is holy, He who is true, "He who has the key of David, He who opens and no one shuts, and shuts and no one opens":

"I know your works. See, I have set before you an open door, and no one can shut it; for you have a little strength, have kept My word, and have not denied My name.

The key of David symbolizes authority. The Church at Philadelphia represents the "true church" throughout Church history, and is a parallel to the lukewarm Church at Laodicea, a church largely in a state of apostasy (vv. 14-22).

Pray for the Church to experience a revival of fire, which is only produced when we separate ourselves from the cares of life and the secular conduct of society.

Jeremiah 20:11
Our Enemies Shall Be Confounded

But the Lord is with me as a mighty, awesome One. Therefore my persecutors will stumble, and will not prevail. They will be greatly ashamed, for they will not prosper. Their everlasting confusion will never be forgotten.

1 Corinthians 15:58
His Presence Gives Victory

The Lord is with us as a mighty terrible one; therefore, our persecutors shall stumble, and they shall not prevail; they shall be greatly ashamed, for they shall not prosper. Their everlasting confusion shall never be forgotten.

Matthew 16:18, 19
The Kingdom of God is at Hand

And I also say to you that you are Peter, and on this rock I will build My church, and the gates of Hades shall not prevail against it. And I will give you the keys of the kingdom of heaven, and whatever you bind on earth will be bound in heaven, and whatever you loose on earth will be loosed in heaven.

The keys of the Kingdom of Heaven are received by believing in the revelation of Christ as the Resurrection. This is the principle the Church is built upon, the foundation of Christ the Rock. Jesus gave the Church the keys to the Kingdom of God, and the gates of hell will not prevail against it (Matthew 16:18-19). Pray for Church leaders and lay ministers to walk in the revelation of how to administer this authority while fulfilling the mission of the Church. Certainly, the fire of the Holy Spirit is necessary for advancing this great mission to advance the Kingdom of God.

Revelation 11:15
Possessing the Kingdoms of this World

The kingdoms of this world have become the kingdoms of our Lord and of His Christ, and He shall reign forever and ever!

Rejoice: The seventh trumpet represents the consummation of God's reign. Christ has fulfilled God's purpose in the Earth. The timeframe is the end of the last three and one-half years of the Tribulation. This verse praises the glory of the coming reign of Christ on Earth, and His Kingdom is proclaimed. This is the concluding victory described in Revelation 12:10 when God's power and authority are established by the final overthrow of Satan.

2 Chronicles 7:14, 15
God's People Need to Forsake Their Own Sin

If My people who are called by My name will humble themselves, and pray and seek My face, and turn from their wicked ways, then I will hear from heaven, and will forgive their sin and heal their land. Now My eyes will be open and My ears attentive to prayer made in this place.

Woe to us because we have not kept the Word of God. In Jeremiah, chapters three to five, the prophet spoke to Israel that the nation had a whore's forehead, because it refused to be ashamed. America is in the same condition. Even the Church has only displayed partial repentance. We have not fully forsaken our idols and turned to the LORD. We worship leaders rather than God Himself. When Jeremiah spoke these words, Israel was in the midst of one of the greatest reformations in its history under King Josiah–yet it had not touched the people's hearts. Outward holiness was not taking place within their hearts. Their repentance was still on the surface, and all was in vain. Self-sufficiency and apathy pulls Christ's bride away from "first love."

> **Prayer:** Father, the Church of Jesus Christ has called for political and social reformation. We want our leaders to call America back to God, but if there is not an awakening in our own hearts, then we will reap judgment. We are hardhearted when we cannot consider the poor and the persecuted (Matthew 25:40). Christians are too busy to minister to the LORD Himself.

- Pray that the Bride of Christ will choose to strive for purity and holiness rather than greatness! (Matthew 22:12).
- Pray that the Bride will keep God's laws and commandments in Scripture. (Matthew 5:17-20)
- Pray that discipleship will be restored in the Church! (Matthew 28:19)

Prayer for Persecuted Christians

Matthew 25:40

Assuredly, I say to you, inasmuch as you did it to one of the least of these My brethren, you did it to Me.

Who are the poor and needy in the world today? We should always have a heart to share our food with the hungry and provide clothing for those who lack the basic necessities in life; however, our brothers and sisters who are persecuted for the sake of the Gospel must come first. Christians who are suffering and being martyred are the true, poor and needy in the world today. At this moment, thousands of Christians around the world are suffering for their faith. Without your prayers, their pain goes on. In many totalitarian countries, accusing Christians of wrong-doing is an effective means to get them out of the way. They are punished for merely practicing their faith. Many find themselves locked up in a prison cell, where routine physical and psychological abuse can wreck a person's health for life.

For example, since a mass revival of Christianity has broken out all over India, this has presented a challenge to the Hindu leadership. As the number of new converts continues to grow Christian leaders have been marked for assassination. The Hindu leadership has developed a plan to reconvert the youth who have become Christians. This is being done by force, combing through villages to drive a massive re-conversion program. Many Christian communities have already been burned. In Sudan, the slavery of Christians has increased and missionary groups are helping to relocate thousands of Sudanese slaves. The number of people still enslaved is estimated to be between 30,000 and 90,000. Nearly five million people have been displaced from their lands; many of these are now dying from starvation and disease.

Who is doing this and why? The National Islamic Front has been establishing Islam as the dominant religious, political and military power in the northeast African Continent. For instance, the fundamentalist government in Khartoum, Sudan continues to commit genocide on Christians. It has legitimized the slaughter and slavery of Christians because they are viewed as "infidels" according to the Koran. Southern Sudan is still under fire even though it won full independence with religious freedom entirely separate from political interference.

In Sudan, leading relief and development organizations state that 2.5 million persons face death by starvation as the radical Islamic government of Khartoum continues their barbaric campaign of death and slaughter against the larger Christian South Sudan. Christians in Sudan have been expelled from their homes and exiled into tent cities in the wilderness. If they deny Christ, they can return to their homes. If they do not deny Christ, then they will starve to death. For years, extremist Muslims in Indonesia have been conducting "jihad" or "holy war" attacks on Christians. Their violence is also vented on the ethnic Chinese and the Ambonese. Circumstances have reached an acutely dangerous stage for Christians and racial minorities, and a global prayer effort is being called to save them.

- **Pray** that believers throughout Indonesia and the Northern Horn of Africa will be protected by God from undue harm and that Christians will have the strength and fortitude to endure the onslaughts which test their faith.
- **Pray** also that this will result in many souls being saved as they call upon the Name of Jesus.
- **Pray** that a great revival will take place in Indonesia, the Middle East, and the Northern Horn of Africa.
- **Pray** for the mercy of God upon the Muslims as they gather in their mosques and hear the many fiery talks that cause them to be militant against Christians.

- **Pray** the Lord will roll back the Islamic Veil from their eyes to see His everlasting Glory. Many miraculous conversions have been reported when Jesus has appeared to Muslims.

Ethnic cleansing (genocide) is being performed on a grand scale in civil wars around the world. Whole communities of Christians face assault, bloodshed and possible annihilation, with any attempt at reconciliation ignored or punished by governments hostile to peace. Coptic Christians in Egypt are being rounded up and brutally tortured, if they do not deny Christ. In Islamic countries, becoming a Christian is made an offence punishable by imprisonment or death. Thousands of Christians are being rounded up by police and interrogated with torture sessions in order to extract false confessions. Churches have been closed around Laos and Vietnam, and Christians have been sent to prison for re-education. In Pakistan, the nation's civil legal system is being replaced with Islamic law, while blasphemy laws make it virtually impossible for Christians and other non-Muslims to defend themselves against charges of blasphemy, which require the death penalty. These are but a few of the reports published regularly detailing what Christians face in over 50 nations worldwide. If you rightly understand these persons to be your brothers and sisters, you would not easily distance yourself.

Pray for the many Christian human rights organizations, which work to defend the rights of Christians everywhere, through prayer, campaigning and practical action. Our *Embassy for World Peace* has given this issue public awareness with our media coverage. For one example, we gave coverage on my *Washington Report* for the *International Religious Persecution Act* introduced by Congressman Frank Wolf and Senator Don Nickels. This established the *International Religious Freedom Commission* which operates through the U. S. State Department.

Remember Your Persecuted Brothers and Sisters

Hebrews 13:3

Remember the prisoners as if chained with them—those who are mistreated—since you yourselves are in the body also.

The War on Christians has become global, with persecution being reported in 151 countries. In 2014, the Pew Research Group found that official "restriction on religion" was at the highest level for six years, and the number of Christian martyrs had doubled since 2012. We are presently praying for the release of Pastors Irani Benham, Saaed Abedini, and Robert Asserian who are undergoing severe torture in Iran's prison system. The ayatollahs fear that Islam and their privileges as rulers would likely disappear if Christians were free to share Christ with Muslims. Syria is experiencing a whole new level of persecution and violence of Christians, moving from the 36th on the list to the third worst persecutor of Christians. Syria and North Korea are considered the most dangerous countries in the world for Christians. Syria has moved to third position for Christian persecution, and the communist North Korean regime has been at the top of the list for twelve years. On March 2014, thirty three Baptist missionaries were sentenced to death on the personal orders of Kim Jong-un.

Heaven is not deaf! Those who persevere, and stand firm through trials and suffering will be rewarded by God for their faithfulness with a crown of life (James 1:2). The Church should be ever present to uplift the persecuted in prayer. When Peter was kept in prison, the Church fervently prayed to God on his behalf (Acts 12:5). And it was Paul, who asked the Church in Colossians to "remember my chains" (Colossians 4:18). Let us "rejoice with those who rejoice, weep with those who weep" (Romans 12:15). Remember those we cannot name who are in chains today, and pray that their chains would indeed advance the gospel with courage and fearlessness. In addition, may our actions of prayer and support continue to advance the Gospel?

> **Pray** that the leaders of liberal democracies will use their influence to find ways to reduce, if not end, persecution in countries where it occurs. Just as the Apostle Paul appealed to Caesar to seek justice, so we can appeal to secular governments. Amen.

Pray for Physical Protection and Deliverance of the Persecuted

Matthew 26:39

My Father, if it be possible, let this cup pass from me; nevertheless, not as I will, but as you will.

Philippians 1:19

For I know that through your prayers and the help of the Spirit of Jesus Christ this will turn out for my deliverance.

Philemon 1:22

I am hoping that through your prayers I will be graciously given to you.

Romans 15:30, 31

I appeal to you, brothers, by our Lord Jesus Christ and by the love of the Spirit, to strive together with me in your prayers to God on my behalf, that I may be delivered from the unbelievers in Judea, and that my service for Jerusalem may be acceptable to the saints.

Pray They Would Fearlessly be a Witness for Christ

Ephesians 6:19, 20

[Pray] also for me, that words may be given to me in opening my mouth boldly to proclaim the mystery of the gospel, for which I am an ambassador in chains, that I may declare it boldly, as I ought to speak.

Colossians 4:2-4

Continue steadfastly in prayer, being watchful in it with thanksgiving. At the same time, pray also for us, that God may open to us a door for the word, to declare the mystery of Christ, on account of which I am in prison—that I may make it clear, which is how I ought to speak.

Pray God's Grace is Sufficient and His Power is Perfected in Their Weakness

2 Corinthians 12:9, 10

But he said to me, "My grace is sufficient for you, for my power is made perfect in weakness." Therefore I will boast all the more gladly of my weaknesses, so that the power of Christ may rest upon me. For the sake of Christ, then, I am content with weaknesses, insults, hardships, persecutions, and calamities. For when I am weak, then I am strong.

Pray They Rejoice in Sharing the Sufferings of Jesus

Hebrews 10:34

For you had compassion on those in prison, and you joyfully accepted the plundering of your property, since you knew that you yourselves had a better possession and an abiding one.

Matthew 5:12

Rejoice and be glad, for your reward is great in heaven, for so they persecuted the prophets who were before you.

I Peter 4:13

But rejoice insofar as you share Christ's sufferings, that you may also rejoice and be glad when his glory is revealed.

Pray They Will Endure

Hebrews 10:36

For you have need of endurance, so that when you have done the will of God you may receive what is promised.

Psalm 10:17, 18

O Lord, you hear the desire of the afflicted; you will strengthen their heart; you will incline your ear to do justice to the fatherless and the oppressed, so that man who is of the earth may strike terror no more.

Pray They Remember that Suffering Eradicates Sin

1 Peter 4:1

Since therefore Christ suffered in the flesh, arm yourselves with the same way of thinking, for whoever has suffered in the flesh has ceased from sin.

Hebrews 5:8

Although he was a son, he learned obedience through what he suffered.

Pray They Will Love Christ Far More Than Life Itself

Philippians 1:21

For to me, to live is Christ, and to die is gain.

Acts 20:24

But I do not account my life of any value nor as precious to myself, if only I may finish my course and the ministry that I received from the Lord Jesus, to testify to the gospel of the grace of God.

Pray They Have Christ's Love for Their Enemies

Luke 6:27-31

But I say to you who hear, Love your enemies, do good to those who hate you, bless those who curse you, pray for those who abuse you. To one who strikes you on the cheek, offer the other also, and from one who takes away your cloak do not withhold your tunic either. Give to everyone who begs from you, and from one who takes away your goods do not demand them back. And as you wish that others would do to you, do so to them.

Pray They Know Christ Also Suffered Such Persecution

Philippians 1:29
For it has been granted to you that for the sake of Christ you should not only believe in him but also suffer for his sake.

Pray They Experience the Joy of the Lord Before Their Persecutors

Acts 16:25
About midnight Paul and Silas were praying and singing hymns to God, and the prisoners were listening to them.

Philippians 1:27-28
Only let your manner of life be worthy of the gospel of Christ, so that.....I may hear of you that you are standing firm in one spirit, with one mind striving side by side for the faith of the gospel, and not frightened in anything by your opponents. This is a clear sign to them of their destruction, but of your salvation, and that from God.

Pray They Remember Their Unbelievable Future Glory

Romans 8:18
For I consider that the sufferings of this present time are not worth comparing with the glory that is to be revealed to us.

Pray They Rejoice to Bear the Marks of Christ in Their Bodies

Galatians 6:17
From now on let no one cause me trouble, for I bear on my body the marks of Jesus.

Pray Rejoice in Filling up That Which is Lacking in Christ's Sufferings

Colossians 1:24
Now I rejoice in my sufferings for your sake, and in my flesh I am filling up what is lacking in Christ's afflictions for the sake of his body, that is, the church.

Key Five

Racial Healing

We deceive ourselves if we say racial prejudice is no longer rampant in our nation. There are two people groups which our nation still needs to heal from the sin against them. Even though progress has been achieved in publicly acknowledging the ill treatment that our ancestors committed against Black African-Americans and the First Nation Indians; racial hatred and bigotry need to be purged from American society. A biblical perspective teaches there is no partiality:

- Acts 10:34, Then Peter said to the Roman centurion Cornelius, "In truth I perceive that God shows no partiality."
- Romans 2:11, "For there is no respect of persons with God," Paul declared.
- James 1:25, "All men are under the same law. Men today, regardless of race, education, or location, are under the "perfect law of liberty."

Below is a brief history for each race in revealing the truth as recorded in history:

And you shall know the truth, and the truth shall make you free. –John 8:32

The American Indian

When our forefathers and mothers first came to America, they were greeted by their hosts, the people of the First Nations who had inhabited this great land for untold millennia. These European newcomers ate with their hosts, gave thanks with them and were on many occasions rescued from death by them. Even so, as the settlements became established, and America grew stronger, cooperation gave way to oppression; gratefulness gave way to greed, and respect degenerated into genocide.

Our First Nations' population was reduced from 66 million when the European first arrived to 250,000 at the start of this century. We must admit that the government of the United States, with the President often leading the way, embarked on a policy of relocation and, in many cases, extermination that was, over time, greater in magnitude than the atrocities committed by the Nazis during World War II.

Some ask, "Why apologize to the Native Americans?" They were the first nations to occupy this land, and they were our hosts, yet we engaged in the longest and most devastating genocidal action by one race against another according to history at that time. Two-thirds of the original tribes were exterminated, and 371 ratified treaties were broken. Today, Native Americans comprise the poorest, shortest-lived, (40.9 years for men), and saddest (teen suicide rate 3-5 times the national average) threads in our American tapestry.

Pray that the light of the Gospel will heal the wounds and scars of our First Nations. Kelsey Begaye the president of the Navaho Nation is a professing Christian. Pray for the election of other tribal chiefs and the head of the sovereign Indian Nations. "Lighthouses of Prayer" are being raised up on all 576 Native American reservations.

Others ask, "Why should we take responsibility for something someone else did in the past?" It is because of the lingering effects of bitterness, and the need for forgiveness. Forgiveness is the starting place for our journey in the twenty-first century. Obviously, we cannot bring back those who died at the hands of the slave masters, and we cannot replace those First Nations that we exterminated. Nevertheless, each of us can, in whatever way we can, demonstrate a tangible respect and love for our neighbor, whatever race, color, creed, or religion he or she happens to be.

The deeds that have hurt these individuals may have been done to others long ago, but that does not diminish the lingering effects these deeds have had on them personally. The roots of bitterness run deep in our First Nations' people, and it is not hard to understand why. Apology and forgiveness are often difficult because of the gravity of the deeds that were done, the magnitude of the guilt, and the depth of the bitterness. God is going to give them back in the Spirit what they lost in the natural. We have received a new vision for the nation, and I believe that it is imperative that we step into that which God is doing today. The vision is yet for an appointed time (hour), and the First Nations People of America are ready to accept what God has for them.

U. S. Congress Apologizes to American Indians

On May 19, 2010, with the leaders of five tribes in attendance, Senator Sam Brownback of Kansas read a congressional resolution apologizing for badly planned policies and acts of violence against American Indians by the U. S. government. Senator Brownback, a Republican, had pushed for the resolution since 2004. Both houses of Congress approved it, and President Barack Obama signed it in December 2009. The resolution does not authorize or support any claim against the U. S. government or serve as a settlement of any claim. In the text, the resolution "acknowledges years of official depredations, ill-conceived policies and the breaking of covenants" by the U.S. government toward tribes and "apologizes on behalf of the people of the United States to all Native Peoples for many instances of violence, maltreatment and neglect inflicted on" American Indians by U.S. citizens. Creek Nation Second Chief Alfred Berryhill called the apology a historic step in the relationship between the U. S. government and the tribes, which still maintain themselves as sovereign nations.[1]

Black African-Americans: Descendants of Slavery

The legacy of slavery still affects us all. Blacks were the victims of this sin that caused oppression, violence, cultural and ethnic division, strife, and murder to stain our communities and remains alive in these modern times. If we say that prejudice is no longer rampant in our country, we deceive ourselves. President William J. Clinton appointed a special commission to work on behalf of healing the racial issue in America. The White House and the U.S. Congress recognize the public need for reconciliation and healing in our land. When the government has to legislate laws against hate crimes in our nation, there is a great need for revival. All the laws on the books across the land will not change the behavior of the people of that land. Only a spiritual reawakening in the conscience of the people will change their hearts from the sin of racial hatred.

There has been gross distortion in our history concerning African-Americans and their history. Early roots of distortion began when white men were enslaving blacks across the ocean on the other continents. The slave trade was only one issue. Money was the other. In America, as early as the 1600s, some people were beginning to admit that slavery was morally wrong. In 1641, Massachusetts enacted a law called "Body of Liberties." The law stated that only prisoners of war, or strangers willingly sold, could be slaves.

In 1772, the first noteworthy American in the war against slavery was Anthony Benezet, a Quaker. Despite the growing conviction that slavery was evil, it was still legal when the Declaration of Independence was signed. Thomas Paine considered it hypocrisy to fight for freedom while maintaining slavery. Patrick Henry lamented that he could not justify slavery. George Washington told Jefferson that it was among his first wishes to see some law adopted to abolish slavery. In 1807, British Parliament member John Wilberforce was finally successful in having the Parliament pass a law, which completelyl abolished the trading of slaves. Whites in America held onto slavery until 1864. Whites justified their domination over blacks by making the African man the inferior race. History shows that the black race originally taught and civilized Europe.

Even now with slavery being abolished since 1865, African-American parents deal with how to prepare his or her child for the inevitability of racism. Washington Redskins Darrell Green says, "Racism is a reality. Satan is real. Satan wants to separate people from God. To do this, he must separate them from each other. Sunday morning at 11 a.m. is the most racially divided hour on the planet. It is a reality from both sides of the fence. Signing an anti-racism pledge does not solve the problem. Nothing like this can be taught logically. There must be an individual revelation from God for a change in one's heart. The subtle, subjective legacy of slavery and racism cannot change until we recognize our own darkness of heart and mind and be willing to expose it to the glorious light and love of Jesus Christ. Ask God to give you love for others outside your racial comfort zone. Ask the Holy Spirit to reveal the racism in your heart, even in its most subtle forms. Teach your children that racism is a sin.

Apology for Slavery Goes on the Record in 2009

On June 18, 2009, the U. S. Senate passed a resolution apologizing for slavery and for the segregationist Jim Crow laws, 144 years after the Civil War and 45 years after passing the Civil Rights Act. The resolution was written with the intention that it could not be used to support claims for monetary reparations.[2] The spectrum of emotions evoked in this debate is a result of two hundred plus years of frustration in the relationship between whites and blacks on American soil. Of course, everyone would grant that an earlier apology without the hard work that has been done to end discrimination and racial injustice would have been a particularly empty gesture. One of the reasons for the delay was the complicated and complicating idea of reparations for slavery. Some have worried that the existence of an official apology would only strengthen the case for reparations; time, it seems, has just diminished those concerns. Shockingly late timing aside, there are passages of inescapable truth in the resolution that make it worth reading. It says, for example, that "an apology for centuries of brutal dehumanization and injustices cannot erase the past, but confession of the wrongs committed and a formal apology to African-Americans will help bind the wounds of the Nation that are rooted in slavery."[3]

Why does the Black race need to repent? Church of God in Christ's evangelist Earl Carter Sr. states it this way in his book "No Apology Necessary, Just Respect": "We were in Egypt, in power for 3,000 years. We are indeed the descendants of Egyptians. We were scientists and inventors, educators and writers. But, that also means we were the first slave masters. We enslaved Israel for 400 years. We were on top, but now we're not because we picked a fight with God. So, our real problem is with God, not the white man."[4]

> Isaiah, chapter nineteen, speaks about *Yahweh's* judgment upon Egypt because of its idolatry, witchcraft and sorcery:
>
> And the Egyptians I will give into the hand of a cruel master, and a fierce king will rule over them," Says the Lord, the Lord of hosts, (v. 4).
>
> Ezekiel 30:9 reads, "On that day messengers shall go forth from Me in ships to make the careless Ethiopians afraid, and great anguish shall come upon them, as on the day of Egypt; for indeed it is coming!"

Prayer for Racial Healing in America

Isaiah 18:1, 2

God's Promised Future to Black People

Woe to the land shadowed with buzzing wings, which is beyond the rivers of Ethiopia, which sends ambassadors by sea, even in vessels of reed on the waters, saying, "Go, swift messengers, to a nation tall and smooth of skin, to a people terrible from their beginning onward, a nation powerful and treading down, whose land the rivers divide."

Psalm 68:30, 31
Ethiopia brings the LORD spiritual gifts.

Ethiopia shall soon stretch out her hands unto God rebuke the beasts of the reeds, the herd of bulls with the calves of the peoples, till everyone submits himself with pieces of silver. Scatter the peoples who delight in war. Envoys will come out of Egypt; Ethiopia will quickly stretch out her hands to God.

Note: Verse 30 states that Egypt brings material gifts; however, in verse 31, Ethiopia brings spiritual gifts to the Lord in adoration.

Zephaniah 3:10

This speaks of the daughter of God's dispersed ones, from beyond the river of Ethiopia, "shall bring My offering." They have been dispersed even to the shores of America.

Genesis 9:18, 19
All of humanity had its origins in the three sons of Noah

Acts 17:26-28

And He has made from one blood every nation of men to dwell on all the face of the earth, and has determined their preappointed times and the boundaries of their dwellings, so that they should seek the Lord, in the hope that they might grope for Him and find Him, though He is not far from each one of us; for in Him we live and move and have our being, as also some of your own poets have said, "For we are also His offspring."

Pray for Racial Harmony and Unity in our Land

Acts 10:34

Then Peter opened his mouth and said: "In truth I perceive that God shows no partiality."

The fact that the Creator God does not show partiality means, how much more we should accept everyone, regardless of nationality or ethnic orientation. There are no restrictions for race in the Kingdom of God. As a nation, we need to respect all the races' God has brought to our land, for they all need to be evangelized. The Apostle James warns against showing personal favoritism or partiality, "My brethren, do not hold the faith of our Lord Jesus Christ, the Lord of glory, with partiality" (James 2:1). What is James talking about here? We should never give special attention to a person because of his social standing, position, wealth, celebrity status, appearance, or influence.

- **Pray** for harmony among the races of the people in our land: Father, we pray in the name of our Lord Jesus, that the Body of Christ will be united in perfect harmony, and full agreement in our hearts. That there would be no dissensions or factions or divisions among us regardless of race, and that we would respect one another in our opinions and judgments.
- **Pray** for the Holy Spirit to help us to agree together as Christ prayed for His disciples in John 17:21, so that we will be united to the Godhead. In this way, we can be confident of having our prayers answered according to 1 John 5:14-15, "Now this is the confidence that we have in Him, that if we ask anything according to His will, He hears us. And if we know that He hears us, whatever we ask, we know that we have the petitions that we have asked of Him."
- **Pray** that believers within the Body of Christ will live with complete lowliness of mind in humility, and meekness (unselfishness) towards others who are not of like race. That we will be patient, bearing one another and making allowances in the Spirit of Christ. We ask the Holy Spirit to help give us the love of Christ for the varied races in our own neighborhoods and churches.

Key Six

Inheriting the Nations for Christ Jesus

Ask of Me, and I will give you the nations for your inheritance, and the ends of the earth for your possession. You shall break them with a rod of iron; you shall dash them to pieces like a potter's vessel. –Psalm 2:8-9

As Christ's representatives in the earth, we are to advance the Kingdom of God, which involves harvesting souls to possess the nations (Revelation 11:15). Jesus told His disciples to pray this: "Our Father in heaven, Hallowed be Your name. Your kingdom come. Your will be done on earth as it is in heaven" (Matthew 6:9-10). It is the mission of the Church to intercede unceasingly for the Father's will to be done on earth. We must continually cry out and "give him no rest" until He brings to pass all He has promised. This also means the restoration of Jerusalem, the seat of Christ's future Kingdom government described in Isaiah 62:1-3:

> For Zion's sake I will not hold My peace, and for Jerusalem's sake I will not rest, until her righteousness goes forth as brightness, and her salvation as a lamp that burns. The Gentiles shall see your righteousness, and all kings your glory. You shall be called by a new name, which the mouth of the Lord will name. You shall also be a crown of glory in the hand of the Lord, and a royal diadem in the hand of your God.

Verse 4 signifies how *Yahweh* renewed His Covenant with Jerusalem:

> You shall no longer be termed Forsaken, nor shall your land any more be termed Desolate; but you shall be called Hephzibah, and your land Beulah; for the Lord delights in you, and your land shall be married.

Isaiah also speaks of a day when Jerusalem is filled with the glory and righteousness of the Lord; God's people will dwell within its walls in peace and joy, and all the world will benefit from its exaltation. This day will take place after the Savior comes — at the end of the Church age — to establish righteousness upon the earth and bring praise to Jerusalem for His name's sake. Indeed, the Lord has proclaimed to the end of the world:

> Say to the daughter of Zion, "Surely your salvation is coming; behold, His reward is with Him, and His work before Him" (Isaiah 62:11).

BE FAITHFUL: THE LORD ANSWERS PRAYER IN WAYS WE CANNOT IMAGINE

Let me encourage you to be faithful in your prayer life. Be consistent and steadfast, and the LORD will reward you. After many years of petitioning for certain regions of Africa, the Holy Spirit allowed me to see how some of my prayers were being answered. I had made numerous mission trips throughout East Africa, but there were two particularly needy regions that had caught my heart, prayerfully, for fifteen years. I burdened in prayer for the destitute children in one area of Nairobi known as, Mathare Valley, where an estimated 60,000 homeless children struggle to survive in this valley of despair. Shanties made of tin, mud and wood line this slum located on a garbage dump. Children and goats comb the trash heaps for food, and they lap water from an open sewer. These are the families of people who left their primitive villages to come to the big city of Nairobi looking for an upgraded lifestyle. Most lack education and there are not enough jobs for them.

After several visits, it remained my fervent prayer to establish a school for these children and upgrade their lives from poverty; like the one, I visited in Calcutta at Mother Teresa's Mission of Mercy. There the children who came to school received a bath, clean uniform, and a meal—then they were taught academics, and they also learned about Jesus Christ. Often, I had asked the Lord, why it seemed impossible for me, or others to pioneer such a school. One Sunday at church, I picked up the current week's edition of the Pentecostal Evangel (Nov.1, 1998) which contained two articles about Africa. There on the cover I saw my prayers were being answered. There was the picture of an African boy, wearing a face of hunger from the slums of Nairobi. Many children like this boy were on my heart and mind for fifteen years. I didn't have to get out the photographs I took there on my visits; they were embedded in my mind forever.

A feature article in the Pentecostal Evangel Magazine told of an Assembly of God church in this very slum, Malango Kubwa. It was run by Pastor Harun Ndungu, whose church feeds about 210 children twice a week and has a school with about 100 students. It is a small beginning, but I was overly joyful to see the LORD had watered the seed of prayer which I had planted. Now, I pray for many others to take up the burden and give to the Africa's Children Fund so this work can grow. Each day, countless children are on the outside, peering through the gates looking in at the privileged few. I have just learned of another orphanage, which has been opened by missionaries in this same area.[1]

It was my heart's desire to take the gospel to some of the unreached people groups like the Maasai tribe in Kenya and Tanzania. They are a group of clans that migrated from the Upper Nile in the 17th and 18th centuries. For decades, many missionaries considered the Maasai unreachable. Less than 1 percent of the Maasai and Sonji tribes of Tanzania are believers. A Kenyan pastor had broken through with revival on a number of visits to the Maasai, and he invited me to go preach open air evangelistic crusades among them. We also held Bible training sessions for his new native pastors that would never get to Bible School. While with the Maasai at Oloitokitok near Mount Kilimanjaro, the LORD used me and the team of pastors to deliver this region from a spiritual stronghold. Often, regions like this are spiritually dark because the people worship false gods and idols.

On the first evening we arrived, I had a spiritual encounter with a python principality over that region. This king snake appeared to me in an open vision and challenged me with these words: "This is my territory, not yours." I spoke Scripture to it, proclaiming the Blood of Jesus Christ to be LORD over this territory. Jesus only spoke the Word to Satan in the wilderness, and He did not engage in conversation with him. I had mentioned earlier that we do not go out looking for demonic principalities to do a "clean-sweep" over regions; however, when they affront us, then we take authority to restrain their power. This struggle persisted for about twenty minutes, and finally; the demonic viper disappeared. During the planning for this mission, the Holy Spirit had instructed me to teach the Blood Covenant to the village pastors, which would set them free from their history of idolatry. When entering the age of manhood, the Maasai males have a tradition of drinking cow's blood and milk, both mixed together. There were other idolatrous practices they were also involved in, and this demonic principality wanted to prevent these people from being delivered from its power. As a result of this spiritual victory, many souls were saved to Christ; many were delivered of demon possession and healed of life-threatening diseases.

My prayers over many years have been that churches would be established among the Maasai. They would drift from meeting to meeting, and the few congregations were small and weak. This prayer has now been answered. Today more than 100 Maasai Assembly of God churches have been established in Kenya and Tanzania. The pastor of the mother church in Narok was given a vision to build a Bible school. Praise be to God!

We must be faithful, even if we do not see the result. How wonderful it is that the LORD would let me see how these years of prayers are bearing fruit. Perseverance brings a spiritual harvest! "Let us not be weary in well doing: for in due season we shall reap, if we faint not" (Galatians 6:9). God has called us to serve wherever He plants us. Above all that we will ever do for the Kingdom of God, let us be faithful first in prayer. We must lift up His standard in every area of our walk. When we learn this basic truth and depend upon the Word of God, then, He will send us to gather the "heathen for our inheritance, and the uttermost parts of the earth for our possession" (Psalm 2:8).

Healing for the Nations

One day, during an early-morning prayer time on an overnight train trip across Kenya, the Holy Spirit commissioned me to the nations. Our team was traveling from Nairobi to Mombasa for a regional pastor's seminar and crusade, and I was scheduled as the keynote speaker and evangelist. During my morning prayer on the train, I was giving thanks to the Father for the African people, when the Holy Spirit spoke these words into my spirit: "Your ministry focus will change from the healing of the individual to the healing of the nations." I immediately pondered: Just how does one go about the ministry of healing the nations? I was not given any clue as to how this would be achieved, but as you read my *Power of the King Series*, you will see how God's plans unfold when we follow the footsteps of Jesus Christ! I had already spent years interceding for numerous countries as the Holy Spirit would lead me, particularly in many regions of Africa and the Middle East. Since that time, I have had the privilege of preaching the Word of God on satellite radio across the 20/70 Window nations, leading many souls to Christ, including Muslims.

Let me be clear; this ministry did not develop within my own ability. The first key to success is to recognize opportunities that will cross your path as a result of prayer; then respond when they are made visible. "Whatever your hand finds to do, do it with your might...." (Ecclesiastes 9:10). Jesus is our example of obedience and flexibility to the Holy Spirits leading for ministry opportunities. Jesus spent much time in prayer and when he walked among the people, miracles happened. Many were healed as they just crossed His path and cried out to Him. Multitudes gathered to hear Jesus teach of the Kingdom of God. Sometimes they would remain for days without any thought of provision for food or lodging (Matthew 14:14-21).

Today, a ministry of faith should not rely on the flesh to design and provide for ministry. Too many have been tempted to rely on fundraising and marketing techniques to develop their ministry. I will make a distinction here–there is nothing wrong with publicizing and inviting people to partner with your ministry. On the other hand, many are using hard-sales methods to promote and raise funds. We must exercise faith to trust the Lord Jesus to build a ministry. We observe the power of Jesus in Isaiah 22:22: "The key of the house of David I will lay on his shoulder; so he shall open, and no one shall shut; and he shall shut, and no one shall open." When you understand whom it is you serve, that takes the pressure off! We are reminded of the Almighty's power in Zechariah 4:6: "Not by might, nor by power, but by my spirit," saith the Lord of hosts. Military might; political power, or human strength cannot accomplish the work of God. We can only do God's work when we are enabled by the Holy Spirit. *Yahweh's* stamp must be upon all ministries.

The fear of not pleasing the Lord has helped keep me from entering into good works. I am humbled by the meager personal sacrifice that I offer with my service to God's Kingdom work. I never feel like I am doing anything notable for the Father, Who is the God the Universe. There have been times when I have admired another ministry that appears to be doing a great work, and the Holy Spirit has quickly interjected a response: "And that is all it is, a good work." There are times when we must not be afraid to fail in trying, and we need to repent of the sin of comparing ourselves to others.

A major key for success in ministry is to understand and submit to spiritual authority. Here is an example: Whenever I have visited other countries to conduct ministry, I would only go by invitation from the lead pastor or bishop. I was always accompanied by a team of elders from the host church when we visited their village churches and held regional crusades. This resulted in protection and anointed ministry. By submitting to their spiritual leaders, entire cities and regions experienced transformation, and the local churches experienced revival. We glorified the Lord Jesus Christ and His Church!

Interceding for the Harvest Among the Nations

Pray for those countries which the Holy Spirit has given you a burden for—Africa was a continent the Lord placed upon my heart as a young youth. During my early school years, I studied as much as possible about this great continent of people. Years later, the doors for ministry opened up for me to go, teach and preach in East Africa. Other regions in Africa also opened up. Then the Lord Jesus sent me on missions to India and Israel. There are numerous nations where I also have an inheritance of souls through my radio messages that have been transmitted around the globe via satellite. It all begins with prayer, and it all ends with prayer. Nothing is done in the Name of the Lord Jesus Christ without first praying. You do not even have to travel by foot via the airwaves.

Prayer is where your inheritance of the nations is fulfilled. I directed our international prayer team in Washington, D.C. to intercede for Indonesia. We prayed for the Christians who were being slaughtered by Muslim Jihadists. They were going from island to island burning up villages and committing genocide on every Christian community in their path. Twenty years later, the Lord has intervened on their behalf, and a new revival has swept across Indonesia's 17,000 islands, 250 million people, and 200 unreached people groups. Assembly of God missionaries are reporting spiritual breakthroughs and church planting in regions where the blood of the martyrs has been shed.

Possessing Your Inheritance of the Nations

Joel 3:13, 14
The Harvest is Overripe

Put in the sickle, for the harvest is ripe. Come, go down; for the winepress is full, the vats overflow—for their wickedness is great. Multitudes, multitudes in the valley of decision! For the day of the Lord is near in the valley of decision.

Revelation 19:15, 16
Christ will Rule the Nations with the Rod of Iron

And from His mouth comes a sharp sword, so that with it He may smite the nations; and He will rule them with a rod of iron.....and on His robe and on His thigh He has a name written, "King of Kings, and Lord of Lords."

Revelation 21:6, 7
Overcomers Inheritance

I am the Alpha and the Omega, the Beginning and the End. I will give of the fountain of the water of life freely to him who thirsts. He who overcomes shall inherit all things, and I will be his God and he shall be My son.

Psalm 16:5-8
The Lord is our Inheritance

You, O Lord, are the portion of my inheritance and my cup; You maintain my lot. The lines have fallen to me in pleasant places; Yes, I have a good inheritance. I will bless the Lord who has given me counsel; my heart also instructs me in the night seasons. I have set the Lord always before me; because He is at my right hand I shall not be moved.

Isaiah 58:12
Restoring the Earth

Those from among you shall build the old waste places; you shall raise up the foundations of many generations; and you shall be called the Repairer of the Breach, the Restorer of Streets to Dwell In.

Isaiah 40:15, 17

Behold, the nations are as a drop in a bucket, and are counted as the small dust on the scales; look, He lifts up the isles as a very little thing." Verse 17, All nations before Him are as nothing, and they are counted by Him less than nothing and worthless.

Verses 22, 23

It is He who sits above the circle of the earth, and its inhabitants are like grasshoppers, Who stretches out the heavens like a curtain, and spreads them out like a tent to dwell in. He brings the princes to nothing; He makes the judges of the earth useless.

Psalms 33:10, 11

The Lord brings the counsel of the nations to nothing; He makes the plans of the peoples of no effect. The counsel of the Lord stands forever, the plans of His heart to all generations.

Pray with the Rod of Iron for the Enemies of God's Harvest

Psalms 83:16-18

Fill their faces with shame, that they may seek Your name, O Lord. Let them be confounded and dismayed forever; yes, let them be put to shame and perish, that they may know that You, whose name alone is the Lord, are the Most High over all the earth.

Psalms 68:1, 21, 30

Let God arise, let His enemies be scattered; let those also who hate Him flee before Him.....But God will wound the head of His enemies, the hairy scalp of the one who still goes on in his trespasses.....and will "scatter the peoples who delight in war."

Key Seven

Taking the Spoils for the Kingdom of God..... How to Pursue and Recover Losses

I encourage all believers to possess the nations for God's Glory, and be sure to ask for the spoils of the nations. We learn about the spoils of war in 1 Chronicles 26:26-27:

> Shelomith and his brethren were over all the treasuries of the dedicated things which King David and the heads of fathers' houses, the captains over thousands and hundreds, and the captains of the army, had dedicated. Some of the spoils won in battles they dedicated to maintain the house of the Lord.

> Another example is David's conflict with the Amalekites when the LORD told him to "pursue and recover." We read in 1 Samuel, chapter thirty, that while David and his men were fighting a battle, the Amalekites came and stripped their camp, including their families: "So David inquired of the Lord, saying, 'Shall I pursue this troop? Shall I overtake them?' And He answered him, 'Pursue, for you shall surely overtake them and without fail recover all'" (v. 8). David did just that! He recovered all he lost and even divided a portion to each person that helped him win the battle, and those who had helped him during his adversity. He monetarily blessed those who helped him stand in the Lord. In the Church Age, our intercession pursues the Kingdom work for Jesus Christ:

> And from the days of John the Baptist until now the kingdom of heaven suffers violence, and the violent take it by force (Matthew 11:12).

We have entered the time frame on *Yahweh's* calendar when the nations are being shaken. They are being recognized as either sheep or goat nations. God wants a kingdom harvest out of the nations, and when we enter the battle, we also share in these spoils of war. The skill for achieving this Kingdom mission is stewardship. This means finding ways to bear fruit for the Kingdom of God wherever we are planted. For instance, in 1976 just prior to entering full time ministry, the LORD opened up a job for me in property management for two years. A mortgage company hired me to manage three apartment and condominium complexes in Orlando, Florida. One property was located at a sprawling country club in North Orlando, which had a lake, in the middle of its beautiful cypress wooded acreage and golf course. My office was located in this peaceful setting, and I prayed every day in the Spirit as I drove around the lake between the country club and the condominiums.

At that time, my prayer focus was hearing God's heartbeat for souls since I was preaching on Sundays in prisons.

Some years later, a television station was raised up by God on the edge of this property, proclaiming the Gospel message across Central Florida. When I met the station owner of Super Channel 55 through the National Religious Broadcasters, I told him how my daily prayers had saturated that area for several years, asking the LORD to glorify Himself on this land. Where one plows another will harvest; nevertheless, we all share in the spoils. My reward for this labor is stored up in heaven, and who knows how many souls have been won to Christ through this satellite television network, which reaches around the globe. The key to proclaiming the land for Christ's kingdom is to act wherever the Holy Spirit guides! Pray Scripture and proclaim the Blood of Jesus to cleanse the land, which is a prophetic work and is up to the Lord's timing for how and when it is fulfilled in the natural.

While we are looking for another Great Awakening in America, we must remember what the LORD has already done to answer prayer and thank Him with a grateful heart. In 1990, the Holy Spirit spoke a word to me that the LORD was going to take His scepter of power off the White House and place it on the Congress. In 1992, when Bill Clinton was inaugurated as President, the Religious Right went into sackcloth and mourning–not because of his political affiliation–but because of his far left socialistic leanings. There was no fear of God during the Clinton administration, and in 1994, as God's people repented and cried out to Him, changes occurred in the Congress. The LORD literally cleaned House, and the scepter was turned over to Republican control! At that time, the Democrats had become corrupt in every way, and the people transferred the power to the other party. In several years, we soon found out that the Republicans were not much better in keeping their promises.

When the turning of the tide happened in 1994, the media announced that Rep. Newt Gingrich, the new speaker of the House, had the same power as the president. The presidential prophecy the LORD had given me was being confirmed! While far from perfect, this was the old guard changing over to the new guard, with corruption being set back in a great measure. Years later, the scales tipped once more in the other direction; with the cleaning of the House and Senate in 2010. Ninety nine brand new freshmen entered office that were committed to God and not the political process.

Taking the Spoils with the Rod of Iron

Jeremiah 1:10-12
God will perform His word.

See, I have this day set you over the nations and over the kingdoms, to root out and to pull down, to destroy and to throw down, to build and to plant. Moreover the word of the Lord came to me, saying, "Jeremiah, what do you see?" And I said, "I see a branch of an almond tree." Then the Lord said to me, "You have seen well, for I am ready to perform My word."

Luke 19:12-27
Occupy till I come

Jesus told the parable of the good servants who made their spiritual investments were considered faithful in little, and would be honored with authority over cities. In verse 13, He said to "Occupy till I come."

Colossians 2:15
The Enemy is Defeated

Having disarmed principalities and powers, He made a public spectacle of them, triumphing over them in it.

Proverbs 19:21
God's Will Supersedes Man's Will

There are many plans in a man's heart,
Nevertheless the Lord's counsel—that will stand.

Psalms 83:16-18
Ask the Lord to Confound the Enemy

Fill their faces with shame, that they may seek Your name, O Lord. Let them be confounded and dismayed forever; yes, let them be put to shame and perish, that they may know that You, whose name alone is the Lord, are the Most High over all the earth.

Jeremiah 23:29
God's Word Distinguishes the True from the False

"Is not My word like a fire?" says the Lord,
"And like a hammer that breaks the rock in pieces?

Revelation 11:15
Possessing Territory

Possessing territory for the Kingdom of God is learning to rule and reign with Christ. We are in training for Christ's future kingdom: "The kingdoms of this world have become the kingdoms of our Lord and of His Christ, and He shall reign forever and ever!"

Genesis 13:14-17
Possessing our Inheritance with His Word

And the Lord said to Abram, after Lot had separated from him: "Lift your eyes now and look from the place where you are—northward, southward, eastward, and westward; for all the land which you see I give to you and your descendants forever. And I will make your descendants as the dust of the earth; so that if a man could number the dust of the earth, then your descendants also could be numbered. Arise, walk in the land through its length and its width, for I give it to you."

Joshua 1:3-5
Joshua Led Abraham's Seed into the Promised Land

Every place that the sole of your foot will tread upon I have given you, as I said to Moses. From the wilderness and this Lebanon as far as the great river, the River Euphrates, all the land of the Hittites, and to the Great Sea toward the going down of the sun, shall be your territory. No man shall be able to stand before you all the days of your life; as I was with Moses, so I will be with you.
I will not leave you nor forsake you.

The Land of Canaan was promised to the early patriarchs, and now that the fourth generation had expired, and the iniquity of the Amorites was full; the time had finally come for the children of Israel to possess what had been expected for generations. Even though their forefathers provoked *Yahweh* in the wilderness, they will inherit the Promised Land. For the sake of Abraham, Isaac, Jacob, Joseph and Moses, the promise would be fulfilled. These are the children of those who murmured that God said would enter Canaan. Joshua is assured of God's presence with him to achieve this great work to which he was called. The presence of God shall never be withdrawn from him, as long as he remains in the presence of the Lord. Joshua is promised clear success—the enemy shall not make any headway against him. This is what *Yahweh* commissioned to Joshua:

> Moses My servant is dead. Now therefore, arise, go over this Jordan, you and all this people, to the land which I am giving to them—the children of Israel. Every place that the sole of your foot will tread upon I have given you, as I said to Moses (Joshua 1:1-3).

By his own example of observing the law, Joshua maintained the honor and power of his position. Joshua's success hinged on his obedience to God's Word:

> This Book of the Law shall not depart from your mouth, but you shall meditate in it day and night, that you may observe to do according to all that is written in it. For then you will make your way prosperous, and then you will have good success. Have I not commanded you? Be strong and of good courage; do not be afraid, nor be dismayed, for the Lord your God is with you wherever you go (Joshua 1:8-9).

You might not feel as though you are called to possess the land, but your obedience to pray and proclaim the Word of God wherever you are planted may just birth a television or radio station, a church or mission, or it could bring revival to your entire community. The same promises given to Joshua are extended toward today's generations who are commissioned to advance the Kingdom of God.

Jeremiah 29:14
The Restoration of the Nations Begins with Israel
I will be found by you, says the Lord, and I will bring you back from your captivity; I will gather you from all the nations and from all the places where I have driven you, says the Lord, and I will bring you to the place from which I cause you to be carried away captive.

BREAKING THE CURSE OF POVERTY!

Poverty is not just the lack of basic necessities, but it is a fear that you will always lack. It is often inherited from curses in one's family background, and it can occur through wrong choices. Those who live with a curse of poverty become defeated with the struggle. What will break the curse of poverty? The Word of God gives instruction for prospering:

> Bring all the tithes into the storehouse, that there may be food in My house, and try Me now in this, Says the Lord of hosts, "If I will not open for you the windows of heaven and pour out for you such blessing that there will not be room enough to receive it" (Malachi 3:10).

For the windows of heaven to open up on our behalf, we need to obey *Yahweh's* command of stewardship and returning one-tenth of our income to God's house, the Church. We also need to adopt a new mindset for financial stewardship; breaking every wrong habit in our lives, so we can overcome the enemy's plan to cripple us. The Apostle Paul wrote:

> For we know that the law is spiritual, but I am carnal, sold under sin. For what I am doing, I do not understand. For what I will to do, that I do not practice; but what I hate, that I do. If, then, I do what I will not to do, I agree with the law that it is good. But now, it is no longer I who do it, but sin that dwells in me. For I know that in me (that is, in my flesh) nothing good dwells; for to will is present with me, but how to perform what is good I do not find. For the good that I will to do, I do not do; but the evil I will not to do, that I practice. Now if I do what I will not to do, it is no longer I who do it, but sin that dwells in me (Romans 7:14-20).

There are times when many of us feel the same as Paul did. Does it seem as if you are a slave to your bad habits? If so, you are not alone. Education and discipline are necessary for better financial management. Giving to God's kingdom work is a good way to pay your way out of debt. Of course, giving should be in obedience to God's command to tithe into your local church. Offerings are then contributed, according to how the Holy Spirit would lead or inspire you. Just giving away money to receive God's blessing will not work. Worldly investments also work the same way. Once you have done all to obey God's law concerning your money, then cancel Satan's assignment and proclaim God's promises to overcome the stronghold of poverty, which is a plundering spirit. The Greek translation for violent is, to force, or to press into, which takes perseverance. In my faith walk, I have concluded it this way: "If I do not quit, then the devil loses the battle." When Jesus sees you standing in obedience with perseverance, wholly trusting in His deliverance; the battle now becomes the Lords, and He will defeat the devil for you. We still take authority over the devil and restrain him with the Word of God, but the actual battle is the Lords.

How to Prevent Poverty

Our increase will decrease when we withhold the first fruits of our income from the Church and its missionaries. Our first duty belongs to the House of God, which is the storehouse in Malachi, chapter three. When we sow our seed, we can expect crops to grow; however, if we are not good stewards, then an assignment of poverty will begin to develop against us. When we are doing everything right and obeying the biblical command to tithe, and we still experience poverty; then spiritual warfare is needed to stop the hand of the enemy from stealing. Proverbs 6:30-31 states:

> People do not despise a thief if he steals to satisfy himself when he is starving. Yet when he is found, he must restore sevenfold; he may have to give up all the substance of his house.

Kindness and generosity to others also combat poverty. One example is helping those that have been devastated by a national tragedy. For instance, the persecuted Sudanese people who are experiencing genocide are good soil for sowing seed to help others. Besides, the majority of the Sudanese in Southern Sudan are Christian. The earthquake victims in Haiti are another opportunity to give a helping hand to those who have lost everything. In the first few days after the earthquake in Haiti, the practice of voodoo and the occult was renounced, and the President of Haiti dedicated the island back to God Almighty. They needed Christian guidance along with humanitarian assistance. The U. S. homeland has seen great devastation with Hurricane Sandy, which wiped out a large chunk of the New Jersey seashore. Hundreds of tornadoes have also flattened towns and cities across the nation. These are all opportunities for the gospel, since people in crisis generally turn to God.

Christian ministries are typically the first responders to these areas of devastation. Ministries like the Assemblies of God Convoy of Hope, Franklin Graham's Samaritan's Purse and CBN's Operation Blessing are there on the frontline as soon as these tragedies occur. James and Betty Robison find ways to feed the starving children in Africa and dig wells to provide safe drinking water. When we support these charities, our increase will multiply. Another act of charity is to pray for persecuted Christians around the world. Follow ministries like *Voice of the Martyrs, Open Doors* and CBN's *Christian World News* to learn how to stand in the gap on their behalf. They also offer ways for how you can get involved. The advantage in supporting Christian outreaches to the poor, is that the gospel message accompanies their humanitarian help, while they comfort people who have just had their lives devastated.

Giving is an Act of Worship!

Giving is not bringing a trivial amount to church and placing it in the offering. Biblical giving is an act of worship based upon our covenant relationship with the living God. Abraham gave Melchizedek a tenth offering out of the gratefulness of his heart for all that God had given him. Giving occurs when we release what we have received out of a heart filled with praise! Giving is being faithful to the household of God. The New Testament Church shared their possessions among the Christian community:

> Now the multitude of those who believed were of one heart and one soul; neither did anyone say that any of the things he possessed was his own, but they had all things in common (Acts 4:32).
>
> Nor was there anyone among them who lacked; for all who were possessors of lands or houses sold them, and brought the proceeds of the things that were sold, and laid them at the apostles' feet; and they distributed to each as anyone had need (vv. 34, 35).

The New Testament Church is an example for how the modern Church should glorify Christ. There was no such thing as discord or division among them. They met in small home congregations, according to where their dwellings were; their worship united them as one heart, and one soul. The presence of God's grace made the early believers willing to take care of one another. What we have in the world belongs to God. We must use it for Him since we are accountable to Him for our stewardship. The early church was liberal toward the needs of the poor among them, and they were dead to the desire for worldly possessions. They lived with anticipation of the coming return of Christ. There was a testimony of the grace of God upon them, causing others to respect this Body of believers.

Governments Often Oppress the Poor

Poverty also exists because it is common for the wealthy to oppress the poor. In this season of time, governments are oppressing the middle class and the poor with an overload of taxes. A nation becomes corrupt and falls under a curse when it exploits the poor. Communism has brought a huge curse upon countries like Russia and China. In the Old Testament, the Egyptian pharaohs had oppressed *Yahweh's* people, Israel, for generations–420 years–until the Hebrew God sent His deliverer Moses with a simple message to Pharaoh: "Let My people go!"

Israel took refuge in Egypt to be saved from a great famine that lasted seven years. Jacob's son Joseph held a position of stewardship over Egypt, "to save many people alive" (Genesis 50:20). It had been God's divine plan for Pharaoh to appoint Joseph as governor over his house and all the land of Egypt. Pharaoh declared: "..... Only in the throne will I be greater than thou" (Genesis 41:37-44). After 420 years in captivity, *Yahweh* delivered His people out of Egypt according to the tribes of Israel (Exodus 12:51). He brought them out with the Ark, the presence of God (1 Samuel 4:5-6). He used forces of nature when necessary to help them survive as a nation, and gave them supernatural provision during their wilderness journey.

In the New Testament, Jesus Christ delivered mankind from the curse when He paid the sacrificial price on the Cross. Still, there are many Christians who remain enslaved by their thinking and become depressed. They forget they are the head and not the tail. As soldiers, Christians must be willing to overcome difficulties and suffering, and wage spiritual warfare (2 Timothy 2:3-4). Such spiritual conflict requires the necessary armor described in Ephesians 6:11-17. Even so, many are afraid to do battle and take possession of what God has promised. Jesus waged a triumphant battle on the Cross against Satan, when He disarmed the evil powers and authorities of wickedness, released a host of captives, and redeemed the believer from Satan's dominion. Wow! That is powerful. It means that we will always be victorious in life and death:

> In Him you were also circumcised with the circumcision made without hands, by putting off the body of the sins of the flesh, by the circumcision of Christ, buried with Him in baptism, in which you also were raised with Him through faith in the working of God, who raised Him from the dead. And you, being dead in your trespasses and the uncircumcision of your flesh, He has made alive together with Him, having forgiven you all trespasses, having wiped out the handwriting of requirements that was against us, which was contrary to us. And He has taken it out of the way, having nailed it to the cross. Having disarmed principalities and powers, He made a public spectacle of them, triumphing over them in it (Colossians 2:11-15).

Key Eight

Praying for the Harvest

The Lord Jesus Christ has commissioned His Church to become witnesses of the Gospel throughout the world. Jesus said to them, "Go into all the world and preach the gospel to every creature" (Mark 16:15). How different the world would be if every Christian became a soul winner. Christ calls for an unselfish total life commitment that includes personal evangelism as a part of the Christian's lifestyle. The first impulse a new Christian receives from the Holy Spirit is to share the miracle that has happened in his heart with others. The greatest authority of the Gospel comes from your own personal experience of God's transforming grace through Jesus Christ. It is not what you know, but who you know. Of course, the most important question is, "Does Christ know you?" It makes no difference, whether you are a new Christian, or if you have known Christ many years. The command is the same to all: be a witness for Christ and the Holy Spirit will produce the fruit.

Jesus made it very clear, in the last words He spoke on earth that His chief purpose in leaving His disciples in the world is that they might lead others to salvation through faith in Him. In John 17:18, in His prayer for His disciples Jesus said, "As You sent Me into the world, I also have sent them into the world." His purpose in the world is demonstrated to Zacchaeus by the offer of salvation, ".....For the Son of Man has come to seek and to save that which was lost....." (Luke 19:10). After His resurrection, Jesus showed the disciples His pierced hands and side. These were the heartrending symbols of His dedication to His own sacrificial mission of reconciling sinful man to His Father. So Jesus said to them again, "Peace to you! As the Father has sent Me, I also send you," John 20:21. He explained the unspeakable rewards of bringing God to man and man to God: "If you forgive the sins of any, they are forgiven them; if you retain the sins of any, they are retained" (John 20:23).

Understanding the Harvest

Psalm, chapter two, explains the covenant between God the Father, and God the Son, that the Eternal Son will receive the nations for His inheritance and the ends of the earth for His possession. Psalm 2:7-9 reads:

> I will declare the decree: The Lord has said to Me, You are My son. Today I have begotten You. Ask of Me and I will give You the nations for Your inheritance, and the ends of the earth for Your possession. You shall break them with a rod of iron. You shall dash them to pieces like a potter's vessel.

The word for "nations" in Hebrew/Aramaic is "goya," which refers to those people (not of the nation of Israel) considered to be pagan, unfamiliar to the ways of the "True Holy God." Israelites often called the "goya" dogs. They also believed in converting the heathen people who lived among them. Proverbs 11:30 reads: "The fruit of the righteous is a tree of life and he who wins souls is wise." The Apostle Paul also prayed this for the New Testament saints (Also read Ephesians 1:17-19 and Colossians 1:9-10). God intended for all believers, that is the disciples of Jesus Christ, to share in the harvesting of the souls who are destined for the Kingdom of God. The Bride of Christ shares an inheritance in this promised harvest in Psalms, chapter two. Jesus instructed His followers how to pray for the harvest:

> Then He said to them, "The harvest truly is great, but the laborers are few; therefore pray the Lord of the harvest to send out laborers into His harvest"(Luke 10:2).

Jesus is saying that the harvest is over-ripe, waiting to be harvested. The problem is with the lack of laborers. Even, the laborers who are already toiling in the harvest fields are not fully equipped to bring in the harvest. There are also many who are called, but refuse to answer, or do not have the faith to overcome the obstacles. It is very important to understand the season in which we are living. When Jesus spoke these instructions to His disciples, it was the beginning of the harvest. Christians who live in the end days of the end times need to be aware that the harvest has entered into its fullness of time, meaning the Gospel is almost over. One of the signs is the great Muslim harvest which has been underway in Arab lands the past 20 years. The harvest behind the Islamic Veil has taken off like the speed of lightning, and is even alarming leaders of Muslim nations like Iran and Saudi Arabia. While traditional Christian populations are being driven out of Arab countries, Muslims are converting to Christianity at what missionaries and other Church leaders describe as an unprecedented rate. More Muslims are coming to faith in Jesus Christ today than at any other time in history.

The Lord Equips the Laborer

In Acts 1:5, Jesus promised the Baptism of the Holy Spirit to provide the empowerment for ministry. Since the harvest is a supernatural work of the Holy Spirit, this work can only be accomplished through the presence of the Holy Spirit:

> But you shall receive power when the Holy Spirit has come upon you; and you shall be witnesses to Me in Jerusalem, and in all Judea and Samaria, and to the end of the earth (Acts 1:8).

Paul goes further to explain the preparation that will equip those who preach and teach the Word of God. Paul said to his spiritual son Timothy:

> I charge you, therefore, before God and the Lord Jesus Christ, who will judge the living and the dead at His appearing and His kingdom: Preach the word! Be ready in season and out of season. Convince, rebuke, exhort, with all longsuffering and teaching. For the time will come when they will not endure sound doctrine" (2 Timothy 4:1-3).

Paul encourages Timothy to "give attention to reading, exhortation, and doctrine" (1 Timothy 4:13) from the Holy Scriptures that is indeed "profitable…..for reproof, correction, for instruction in righteousness (so) that the man of God may be complete, thoroughly equipped for every good work," as in 2 Timothy 3:16-17. We must pray for such an equipping to be continually transferred from one generation to another, so the harvest of souls can be a deep abiding work that remains. A consistent prayer life coupled with the regular proclaiming of the Word will give you favor with God and men. Pray daily for your loved ones and friends who need to come to salvation. Ask the Holy Spirit to remove the veils over their hearts that would hinder the work of salvation. Pray for the Holy Spirit to open up opportunities to witness to them.

Since our testimony must express the Scriptural basis for salvation, then our motivation for witnessing should be centered on all three persons of the Trinity: the Father, the Son, and the Holy Ghost. Do not use a formula in your testimony to others, but let the Holy Spirit personalize it for those you are witnessing to. Since our motivation for witnessing flows directly from the Word of God, hide the Word in your heart and ask the Holy Spirit to fill your mouth with the right words. An effective witness is one who is established in the faith, being rooted and grounded in God's Word. Peter said, "Be ready to give a defense to everyone who asks you a reason for the hope that is in you, with meekness and fear….." (1 Peter 3:15). The following scriptures will help prepare you to share your own experience with others; while trusting the power of the Holy Spirit to anoint your testimony. "So shall My word be that goes forth from My mouth; It shall not return to Me void, But it shall accomplish what I please, And it shall prosper in the thing for which I sent it" (Isaiah 55:11).

How do we Witness?

Matthew 28:18-20
Know that Christ Himself is With You as You Witness

And Jesus came and spoke to them, saying, "All authority has been given to Me in heaven and on earth. Go therefore and make disciples of all the nations, baptizing them in the name of the Father and of the Son and of the Holy Spirit, teaching them to observe all things that I have commanded you; and lo, I am with you always, even to the end of the age."

Psalm 1:1-3

Those Who Trust in God's Word Will Prosper

Blessed is the man who walks not in the counsel of the ungodly, nor stands in the path of sinners, nor sits in the seat of the scornful; but his delight is in the law of the Lord, and in His law he meditates day and night. He shall be like a tree planted by the rivers of water, that brings forth its fruit in its season, whose leaf also shall not wither; and whatever he does shall prosper.

Hebrews 4:12

The Power of the Word Exposes Sin

For the word of God is living and powerful, and sharper than any two-edged sword, piercing even to the division of soul and spirit, and of joints and marrow, and is a discerner of the thoughts and intents of the heart.

1 Peter 1:23

Word Brings About the Work of Salvation

Having been born again, not of corruptible seed but incorruptible, through the word of God which lives and abides forever.....

How to be an Effective Witness

Matthew 4:19

Jesus Has Called You

As Jesus walked by the sea of Galilee He saw two fishermen: Simon, called Peter and Andrew, his brother. "Then He said to them, "Follow Me, and I will make you fishers of men."

Acts 5:32

The Holy Spirit Empowers the Believer to Witness

Peter said, "And we are His witnesses to these things, and so also is the Holy Spirit whom God has given to those who obey Him."

1 Corinthians 6:19-20

Depend on the Spirit's Indwelling When You Witness

What? Do you not know that your body is the temple of the Holy Spirit who is in you, whom you have from God, and you are not your own? For you were bought at a price; therefore glorify God in your body and in your spirit, which are God's.

2 Corinthians 4:3, 4

The Holy Spirit Illuminates the Mind of the Unbeliever

But even if our gospel is veiled, it is veiled to those who are perishing, whose minds the god of this age has blinded, who do not believe, lest the light of the gospel of the glory of Christ, who is the image of God, should shine on them.

Acts 2:37

The Word Convicts the Heart of the Unbeliever

As Peter preached Christ, the listeners were convicted and 3,000 were converted. Now when they heard this, they were cut to the heart, and said to Peter and the rest of the apostles, "Men and brethren, what shall we do?"

Luke 15:18

The Word Moves the Will of the Unbeliever

The prodigal returned home when he came to himself and said: "I will arise and go to my father, and will say to him, "Father, I have sinned against heaven and before you….."

SALVATION IS GOD'S FREE GIFT

John 3:16, 17

It is a Fact That God Loves You

For God so loved the world, that He gave his only begotten Son, that whoever believes in him should not perish, but have everlasting life. For God did not send His Son into the world to condemn the world, but that the world through Him might be saved.

Romans 3:23

It is a Fact That You Are a Sinner

For all have sinned, and come short of the glory of God.….

Romans 6:23

It is a Fact That You Are Now Dead in Sin

For the wages of sin is death, but the gift of God is eternal life in Christ Jesus our Lord.

Romans 5:6-8

It is a Fact that Christ Died for You

For when we were still without strength, in due time Christ died for the ungodly. For scarcely for a righteous man will one die; yet perhaps for a good man someone would even dare to die. But God demonstrates His own love toward us, in that while we were still sinners, Christ died for us.

Psalm 107:10-14
Christ Died for the Sinner

There were those who dwelt in darkness and in the shadow of death, prisoners in misery and chains, because they had rebelled against the words of God....Then they cried out to the Lord in their trouble. He saved them....He brought them out of darkness and the shadow of death and broke their bands apart.

Pray for those who are locked in lifestyles that hold them in darkness. Some desperately search in vain to escape the grim misery of their lives. Some feel the chill of death already overshadowing them.

Acts 16:30, 31
Salvation Comes by Faith in the Lord Jesus Christ

And he brought them out and said, "Sirs, what must I do to be saved?" So they said, "Believe on the Lord Jesus Christ, and you will be saved, you and your household."

1 John 5:10-13
Knowing you are Saved

He who believes in the Son of God has the witness in himself; he who does not believe God has made Him a liar, because he has not believed the testimony that God has given of His Son. And this is the testimony: that God has given us eternal life, and this life is in His Son. He who has the Son has life; he who does not have the Son of God does not have life. These things I have written to you who believe in the name of the Son of God, that you may know that you have eternal life, and that you may continue to believe in the name of the Son of God.

Acts 5:29
You are now a Child of God called to Obedience

But Peter and the other apostles answered and said: "We ought to obey God rather than men."

Understanding the New Birth

2 Corinthians 5:17
New Creatures in Christ

Therefore, if anyone is in Christ, he is a new creation; old things have passed away; behold, all things have become new.

Ephesians 2:1-9
By Grace through Faith

And you He made alive, who were dead in trespasses and sins, in which you once walked according to the course of this world, according to the prince of the power of the air, the spirit who now works in the sons of disobedience, among whom also we all once conducted ourselves in the lusts of our flesh, fulfilling the desires of the flesh and of the mind, and were by nature children of wrath, just as the others. But God, who is rich in mercy, because of His great love with which He loved us, even when we were dead in trespasses, made us alive together with Christ (by grace you have been saved), and raised us up together, and made us sit together in the heavenly places in Christ Jesus, that in the ages to come He might show the exceeding riches of His grace in His kindness toward us in Christ Jesus. For by grace you have been saved through faith, and that not of yourselves; it is the gift of God, not of works, lest anyone should boast.

Titus 3:5

New Birth is Regeneration

.....Not by works of righteousness which we have done, but according to His mercy He saved us, through the washing of regeneration and renewing of the Holy Spirit....."

2 Peter 1:4

New Birth is Partaking of the Divine Nature of God

By which have been given to us exceedingly great and precious promises, that through these you may be partakers of the divine nature, having escaped the corruption that is in the world through lust.

John 1:12, 13

New Birth is Receiving Jesus Christ as Savior and Lord by Faith

But as many as received Him, to them He gave the right to become children of God, to those who believe in His name: who were born, not of blood, nor of the will of the flesh, nor of the will of man, but of God.

2 Corinthians 5:21

Becoming the Righteousness of God

For He made Him who knew no sin to be sin for us, that we might become the righteousness of God in Him.

John 3:5-8

Christ Explains the Two Births

Jesus answered, "Most assuredly, I say to you, unless one is born of water and the Spirit, he cannot enter the kingdom of God. That which is born of the flesh is flesh, and that which is born of the Spirit is spirit. Do not marvel that I said to you, 'You must be born again.' The wind blows where it wishes, and you hear the sound of it, but cannot tell where it comes from and where it goes. So is everyone who is born of the Spirit."

1 John 3:9

New Birth Issues a New Sinless Nature

Whoever has been born of God does not sin, for His seed remains in him; and he cannot sin, because he has been born of God.

I Peter 1:23

New Birth is Incorruptible

.....having been born again, not of corruptible seed but incorruptible, through the word of God which lives and abides forever.....

John 3:14-18

Conditions of Salvation

And as Moses lifted up the serpent in the wilderness, even so must the Son of Man be lifted up, that whoever believes in Him should not perish but have eternal life. For God so loved the world that He gave His only begotten Son, that whoever believes in Him should not perish but have everlasting life. For God did not send His Son into the world to condemn the world, but that the world through Him might be saved.

I John 5:1-3

Marks of the New Birth

Whoever believes that Jesus is the Christ is born of God, and everyone who loves Him who begot also loves him who is begotten of Him. By this we know that we love the children of God, when we love God and keep His commandments. For this is the love of God, that we keep His commandments. And His commandments are not burdensome.

Hebrews 9:24

We Preach Christ Resurrected

For Christ has not entered the holy places made with hands, which are copies of the true, but into heaven itself, now to appear in the presence of God for us.

Hebrews 9:26

Christ Sacrificed Himself

He then would have had to suffer often since the foundation of the world; but now, once at the end of the ages, He has appeared to put away sin by the sacrifice of Himself.

Hebrews 9:28

He is our Soon Coming King!

So Christ was offered once to bear the sins of many. To those who eagerly wait for Him He will appear a second time, apart from sin, for salvation.

1 Thessalonians 4:16, 17

For the Lord Himself will descend from heaven with a shout, with the voice of an archangel, and with the trumpet of God. And the dead in Christ will rise first. Then we who are alive and remain shall be caught up together with them in the clouds to meet the Lord in the air. And thus we shall always be with the Lord.

Revelation 22:17
The Invitation

And the Spirit and the bride say, "Come!" And let him who hears say, "Come!" And let him who thirsts come. Whoever desires, let him take the water of life freely.

Key Nine

How to Pray for the Middle East

While we recognize there are many peace-loving Muslims in the world, it is quite a different matter to say that Islam is a peaceable religion. When did the "Holy War" (Jihad) begin? Following Muhammad's death (632 A.D.), Muslim armies cleared the Christian Byzantines out of Syria, Palestine, and Egypt (636 A.D.), and Christians, and Muslims have been at war with one another since that time. The late Chuck Colson states: "Without religious freedom, efforts to spread democracy are futile, because societies that don't respect the rights of religious minorities cannot be expected to respect any other human rights. What this tragic turn of events proves is that, contrary to the politically-correct wisdom of our day, not all worldviews or religions are alike. And the differences really matter—just ask the Christians living in the Islamic world."[1] (Colson was speaking of the 2012 Danish cartoon controversy.)

Islam is a False Religion

Since the September 11th attack on America, the Muslim religion has received a lot of media attention. The general Muslim population would like it to be portrayed as a peace-loving, peace-preaching religion. While that may be true for the majority of Muslims, is it true for the ideology and doctrines of Islam itself? Islam is not a religion, even though Muslims worship a God. "The heart of Islamic teaching is that religion is not just a part of life, but life is a tiny part of religion. Thus, everything in life is dominated by this religion. As such, Islam is a system. It is a socio-political, socio-religious, socio-economical, educational, legislative, judicial, and militaristic system garbed in religious terminology."[2]

The word Islam simply means submission to God. A Muslim is a person who follows Islam's Sharia Law. In many ways, Islam is a religion of paradox; it contradicts itself. Islam is not merely a religion or a philosophy; it is a false religion. Islamic law does not recognize the fundamental freedoms of the Western world, and this is why non-Muslims, such as Christians or Baha'is living in Muslim States are denied the most basic civil rights. Islam's Sharia law mandates the seventh-century Arabian head-to-foot dress for women as the dress code for modern Muslim women in every Arab nation. While this was a practical dress for those who lived in the desert and needed to be protected from severe heat, to impose such desert garb on women everywhere is a form of cultural imperialism.

Even so, Christians should maintain a positive attitude towards Muslims. Jesus Christ taught His followers not to denigrate or criticize anyone. Jesus said, "Love your neighbor as yourself." God desires to bring multitudes of Muslims into His kingdom. This great harvest of souls has accelerated in the 1990s due to the increased prayer for the Muslim world. Our Embassy prayer teams have prayed for the Lord Jesus to appear to Muslims, even while they were worshiping Allah.

> Praying for Muslims is simply part of fulfilling Jesus' command to make disciples of all nations (Matthew 28:18-20). He also said to pray for the laborers to be sent into the harvest (Matthew 9:37-38). Our Lord desires that "all men to be saved and to come to the knowledge of the truth" (1Timothy 2:4). God has promised that all the nations would be blessed through Abraham's seed (Genesis 12:1-3). Jesus is the fullest manifestation of that seed. Are we going to participate with Him in blessing the nations and harvesting multitudes of souls for the Kingdom of God?

Islam's Penetration into Western Nations

At the nation's capital, we are discovering by the week and month about the infiltration of radical Muslims into high-level government positions, including the military. They are also embedded within the CIA. As we saw at the Ft. Hood shooting in Texas, Muslims are not patriotic when they belong to the *Muslim Brotherhood*, which has many cells within the U. S. Former Congressman Allen West of Florida says, "Indeed, there are Islamic terrorist training camps in America." It is on public record that they have training camps throughout the country. One in upper New York State is called *Islamabad*, which has been operating since the 1980s and has a network of 22 villages around the U. S. We have learned from Arizona that Hamas, Iran's terrorist army, has embedded in Mexico and are coming across the border using their "drug cartels" that are passed off as banditos. A jihadist enclave was recently discovered in Texas, which belongs to the network of *Muslims of the Americas*, a radical group linked to a Pakistani militant group called Jamaat ul-Fuqra. Its members are devoted followers of Sheikh Mubarak Ali Gilani, an extremist cleric in Pakistan."[3]

I highly recommend reading the book, "Muslim Mafia: Inside the Secret Underworld That's Conspiring to Islamize America." The book is written by counter-terrorism investigator P. David Gaubatz and "Infiltration" author Paul Sperry. They give a truthful account of the Islamization of America in Washington, D.C. and on Capitol Hill. It documents CAIR's ultimate purpose to transform the United States into an Islamic nation under the authority of the Quran. To learn more about these Muslim groups just Google their names: Muslim Brotherhood, Holy Land Foundation, ISNA, and CAIR. (The Obama's largest charitable contribution in 2009 was to CAIR.)

Let me be clear; we are not talking about being an Islamaphobic. Through the Muslim Brotherhood, the world is witnessing the Rise of the Ottoman Empire, with Europe first and America is following close behind England. Islam is a political ideology; its Sharia Law controls the life of every person with its rules for society. Islam means 'submission' which is not compatible with freedom and democracy because Sharia dictates every aspect of life. Islam is a parallel to communism or national-socialism, which are all totalitarian ideologies. It is a myth that the Islamic religion worships the same God as Jews and Christians. Those who accept this myth, also believe there are many ways to God. Muslims are taught that Allah is their god; an eternal hereafter is promised with a reward of 72 virgins for every martyr. Jesus Christ said, "I am the way, the truth, and the life. No one comes to the Father except through Me" (John 14:6).

There is good news happening behind the Islamic Veil: Muslims are reaching out beyond the veil because Islam is not meeting their spiritual needs, and many are experiencing supernatural visions and dreams of Jesus Christ and receiving Him as Lord and Savior. Missionaries cannot go into Muslim countries because they are not given entry, and would face death if they went underground. Even so, Jesus has been appearing to thousands over the past fifteen years and thousands upon thousands are coming to faith. The persecution watchdog group, Open Doors USA, reports: "Despite the Iranian government's ongoing crackdown of Christians living in the primarily Islamic country, the number of Muslims converting to become Christians is growing at an explosive rate.....There is even talk of witnessing a Christian revival, especially among young people living in the country, say Open Doors ministry workers in the Middle East."[4]

Strategic Spiritual Warfare

Isaiah 54:17
Holding Your Enemy Back!

No weapon formed against you shall prosper, and every tongue which rises against you in judgment you shall condemn. This is the heritage of the servants of the Lord, and their righteousness is from Me, Says the Lord.

Most times a consistent profession of faith will hold the enemy back. For instance, proclaiming the above Scripture every day will stop something that could be a problem for you from getting too close or from getting worse.

Isaiah 14:2-6
The fall of Islam and Terrorism

V. 2, Then people will take them and bring them to their place, and the house of Israel will possess them for servants and maids in the land of the Lord; they will take them captive whose captives they were, and rule over their oppressors.

Vv. 3-4, It shall come to pass in the day the Lord gives you rest from your sorrow, and from your fear and the hard bondage in which you were made to serve, that you will take up this proverb against the king of Babylon, and say:

Vv. 5-6, How the oppressor has ceased, the golden city ceased! The Lord has broken the staff of the wicked, the scepter of the rulers; He who struck the people in wrath with a continual stroke, He who ruled the nations in anger, is persecuted and no one hinders.

Pray for Iran and the Evil Rule of the Ayatollahs

Pray for Iran's Mullahs to be replaced with democratic leaders. In addition, pray for the Iranian nuclear program to be dismantled or neutralized. **Pray** for an increase of witnesses to the descendants of the ancient Persian Empire.

The Islamic Republic of Iran is the number-one enemy against freedom in the Middle East. The ruling ayatollahs are the perpetrators of terrorism and continually threaten to eliminate the Israeli people; essentially, by declaring a second holocaust against Israel and the United States. Their goal is to create world turmoil, which is supposed to hasten the return of their (Shiite) Islamic Mahdi, the 12th Imam, which is to be achieved by causing violence and war in the world.

Isaiah 25:7
Removing the Veil of Spiritual Darkness

And He will destroy on this mountain the surface of the covering cast over all people, and the veil that is spread over all nations.

The Prince of Persia is an ancient territorial principality that has operated in the Middle East for centuries. The Holy Spirit revealed to me that the "henchman spirit," has its roots in Islam, which incites Jihad terrorism and assassination. It is only restrained with spiritual warfare (Matthew 16:18), and winning the hearts and minds of Muslims, who have a darkened mind. When the Ottoman Empire tried to conquer all of Europe up to Austria, all the military forces of Europe could not stop them. The enemy was only defeated when the Crusaders stood up as a Godly force and took up the sword. The enemy we face today is a spiritual entity that can only be defeated with spiritual weapons. There are bad memories of the Crusaders still fresh in Muslim minds after 900 years, so we must pray for these bitter thoughts to be removed from their minds. Pope John Paul II went to Muslim countries and publicly repented for these brutal wars before the entire Muslim world. He also sought forgiveness and reconciliation toward the nation of Israel for the Christian Crusades.

Islamic governments are intolerant of Christians. Prayer can help meltdown anger, fear and violence in militant Muslims, who are martyring Christians. Islam is a violent religion that would like to conquer the world. The invisible power of prayer will send the kingdom of light to penetrate this kingdom of darkness. The late Chuck Colson made this comment on loving our Muslim neighbors: ".....Many Muslims lack inner peace, and do not experience genuine, unconditional love; they don't understand true spiritual freedom. This means we might present Christ as the peace-giver who truly loves them and brings them freedom. Finally, before we invite a Muslim to follow Christ, we must understand the cost we are asking him to pay. Conversion may mean a complete loss of family, friends, career, and culture."[5]

- **Pray** for the LORD to rend the Islamic veil over the people of the Middle East and around the world.
- **Pray** that Muslims will come to faith in Christ, turning those Saul's into Paul's.
- **Pray** that the Lord would send the laborers to bring in the appointed harvest across the Middle East.
- **Pray** for Muslims in general that they will come to know the true G-d, the Father "YHWH," His Son Jesus Christ and the person of the Holy Spirit. Allah of Islam is not a Father. Calling Allah "Father' or Jesus "Son of G-d" is a blasphemy that Allah and his servants hate and punish by capital death. Muslims call Jesus `Isa. However, His name in Arabic is "Yasu'e." `Isa is a twisted name for Jesus. It is actually "Esau." It is also said that `Isa was the name of a false god! The point being that Satan in Islam is not even willing to spell Jesus' name correctly, showing his great fear for the name of Yehshua.[6]
- **Pray** for the Gospel of Christ to be released into all the Muslim world and that the Lord will raise many witnesses among the Muslims to bring a plentiful harvest of souls.
- **Pray** that the Body of Christ in the Muslim world will gain maturity, strength, power and boldness to do His work and set many Muslims free.
- **Pray** for our Christian brothers who are suffering persecution for converting Muslims.

2 Corinthians 3:14-17
Removing the Veil

But their minds were blinded. For until this day the same veil remains unlifted in the reading of the Old Testament, because the veil is taken away in Christ. But even to this day, when Moses is read, a veil lies on their heart. Nevertheless when one turns to the Lord, the veil is taken away. Now the Lord is the Spirit; and where the Spirit of the Lord is, there is liberty.

Removing the veil of hatred is a supernatural work of the Holy Spirit. The Hadith is an Islamic oral tradition which has been canonized like the Koran. "A Quote from the Hadith, on page 103, the Islamic apocalyptic prophecy is genocidal, hideous and totally objectionable: "Islamic tradition describing the conditions for the 'Final Hour,' for the Day of Judgment and for the establishment of the ideal (Islamic) divine order. According to this tradition, attributed to the Prophet Mohammed, himself, the 'Hour' will not come before the Muslims fight a final battle with the Jews and annihilates them. In the course of the war, the Jews will hide from their Muslim pursuers behind rocks and trees. On that Day, Allah will give mouths to the rocks and to the trees, and they will call out: 'O Muslim, there is a Jew behind me, come and kill him.' The same quote also appears frequently on handbills issued by the Hamas terrorist organization in territories administered by Israel as a rally cry to kill Jews."[7]

The Judeo-Christian religions are both based on a God of love. The coming of the Messiah, whether it is the first or second, will usher in the messianic era, which will be an era of love and peace for all God's children. Jews and gentiles will serve the Lord together in Jerusalem (Isaiah 60). Judaism and Christianity have the same biblical foundation, both believe in the precepts of the Bible, the coming of the Messiah, and eternal life. The Messiah, both for Jews and Christians, is a man of love.

Ezekiel 38 and 39
An End Time Islamic Prophecy for Jerusalem

Jerusalem is the battleground of the world. The Palestinian message declares that Jerusalem must be Jew-free; it is over this issue that they desire a Palestinian State The annihilation of the Jewish race is the true objective of the Palestinian Authority and the Muslims, who are 95% of the Palestinian people. *Yahweh* describes this in Ezekiel 39:1-5:

> And you, son of man, prophesy against Gog, and say, "Thus says the Lord God: 'Behold, I am against you, O Gog, the prince of Rosh, Meshech, and Tubal; and I will turn you around and lead you on, bringing you up from the far north, and bring you against the mountains of Israel. Then I will knock the bow out of your left hand, and cause the arrows to fall out of your right hand. You shall fall upon the mountains of Israel, you and all your troops and the peoples who are with you; I will give you to birds of prey of every sort and to the beasts of the field to be devoured. You shall fall on the open field; for I have spoken,' says the Lord God."

Ezekiel is describing how the armies of many nations will rise to wage war on Israel's Jerusalem, but the Lord God Himself intervenes on their behalf. Jerusalem is never mentioned in the Koran. It is not a holy city for Islam, but it has become a goal for Islam to dispossess it from the Jews and Christians, or destroy it all together because it is the center for the Judeo-Christian religion of love. The fanatic Islamic program is to turn the Holy Land into the mass graveyard of the Jews. This is tantamount to Hitler's objective of world domination and the extermination of the Jews. God will not allow this to happen. Zechariah, prophecies in chapter 12:

V. 1, The burden of the word of the Lord against Israel. Thus says the Lord, who stretches out the heavens, lays the foundation of the earth, and forms the spirit of man within him:
V. 2, Behold, I will make Jerusalem a cup of drunkenness to all the surrounding peoples, when they lay siege against Judah and against Jerusalem.
V. 3, And it shall happen in that day that I will make Jerusalem a very heavy stone for all peoples; all who would heave it away will surely be cut in pieces, though all nations of the earth are gathered against it.
V. 4, In that day," says the Lord, "I will strike every horse with confusion, and its rider with madness; I will open My eyes on the house of Judah, and will strike every horse of the peoples with blindness.
V. 5, And the governors of Judah shall say in their heart, "The inhabitants of Jerusalem are my strength in the Lord of hosts, their God."
V. 6, In that day I will make the governors of Judah like a firepan in the woodpile, and like a fiery torch in the sheaves; they shall devour all the surrounding peoples on the right hand and on the left, but Jerusalem shall be inhabited again in her own place—Jerusalem.
V. 7, The Lord will save the tents of Judah first, so that the glory of the house of David and the glory of the inhabitants of Jerusalem shall not become greater than that of Judah.
V. 8, In that day the Lord will defend the inhabitants of Jerusalem; the one who is feeble among them in that day shall be like David, and the house of David shall be like God, like the Angel of the Lord before them.
V. 9, It shall be in that day that I will seek to destroy all the nations that come against Jerusalem.

The Prophet Zechariah prophesied of the Lord intervening on behalf of Israel and Jerusalem; and how five-sixths of the enemy that comes up against Jerusalem will be smitten directly by the Lord. Zechariah describes God's judgment against those neighboring countries who attack Israel. There will be a remnant that will be spared who will repent and accept the Lord. They will join the Gentiles and Jews, who are serving the Lord in Jerusalem. That is why it is so important for the Jews and Christians to witness to the Muslims and pray for their salvation. Every Muslim who has been converted from Islam and brought over into Christianity is a new ally and one less enemy. When one Muslim abandons the Koran, he loses his hatred of the Jews and Christians. I continue to meet former Muslim terrorists who have now been converted and have become evangelists and pastors to their Muslim brothers and sisters.

Hebrews 4:12

Sharing the Word of God is the only effective way to win over false God's

For the word of God is living and powerful, and sharper than any two-edged sword, piercing even to the division of soul and spirit, and of joints and marrow, and is a discerner of the thoughts and intents of the heart.

Islamic leaders fear the Word of God and are aggressive in preventing Muslims from having access to it. The Gospel has become readily available in every Muslim language through radio, CDs, videos, books, tracts, and the Internet. The *JESUS Film* has been one of the most powerful tools to present the Gospel to both literate and illiterate Muslims. Hundreds of thousands of Muslims have been accepting Jesus as Savior this way. There is a modern-day supernatural harvesting of a multitude of Muslim souls underway. About twelve years ago at our Embassy prayer tower, the Holy Spirit inspired us to pray asking Jesus to appear before Muslims, even while they are making their once in a lifetime pilgrimage to Mecca. We received confirmation that this is actually happening when an underground Filipino evangelist, who lives in Saudi Arabia, came and shared his ministry with us at the Embassy. I was amazed when he told us how Jesus is appearing to Muslims everywhere. They were receiving visions and dreams, even visitations from Jesus, and were accepting Him, as Lord and Savior while they were circling the Hajj.

For years, I preached the gospel on radio into the Middle East from our Washington, D. C. headquarters at Iran's former embassy complex. Many letters were received testifying of how they had accepted Jesus Christ into their hearts when I offered a prayer for salvation at the end of each program. Entire families would kneel together around their radio and repeat the sinner's prayer with each other. Glory to God!

Islam calls for the Murder of Infidels

Among the 21 Arab nations, not one is a democracy. While Turkey is more secular, it is not fully democratic. Sharia law stifles democracy and keeps the people hostage to the "dark ages" of seventh-century Arabia. Iran is a perfect example of how oppression comes upon the people when the Islamic clergy controls the government. One of the roots of current Islamic extremism lies in Saudi-Arabian Wahhabism, which is a violent and intolerant strain of Islam that is fueled by Saudi leaders and oil money. Islamic extremism has also been driven by Salafist Sunni Muslims and Iran's revolutionary-style Shi'ism. Democracy cannot survive without religious freedom because societies that do not respect religious minorities will not respect any other human rights. A half a century of relations with Arab countries has not produced the slightest concession on human rights. Minor sanctions have been placed on countries like Saudi Arabia and Pakistan, who are cited for their violations of religious freedom. So, the message from the world community is that we are not truly serious about freedom and democracy.

Today in Sudan, African Christians are viewed as 'infidels' and are the victims of an ongoing Islamic jihad, or "holy war." A brutal campaign by the Islamic fundamentalist government, based in the Sudanese capital of Khartoum, continues to enslave, murder and starve tens of thousands of believers in an attempt to erase Christianity and seize control of southern Sudan.

The Muslim-Jewish Conflict over the Temple Mount in Jerusalem

"An Islamic Waqf has managed the Temple Mount continuously since the Muslim reconquest of the Kingdom of Jerusalem in 1187. On June 7, 1967, soon after Israel had taken control of the area during the Six-Day War, Prime Minister Levi Eshkol assured that "no harm whatsoever shall come to the places sacred to all religions". Together with the extension of Israeli jurisdiction and administration over east Jerusalem, the Knesset passed the Preservation of the Holy Places Law, ensuring protection of the Holy Places against desecration, as well as freedom of access thereto. Israel agreed to leave administration of the site in the hands of the Waqf."[8]

"One of the world's leading Biblical Archaeologists Dr. Barkay explains the Jewish and Christian connections to the Temple Mount in answer to the question of why it is vital to stop the destruction of Jewish antiquities on the Temple Mount...... "The Temple Mount represents the Near Eastern conflict in a nutshell and whatever happens to the Temple Mount will happen to the rest of the country. If the Temple Mount is under Palestinian rule and there is no accessibility to Jews to the Temple Mount and no control upon the antiquities discovered there that means that the legitimacy of Jews in the entire country is questioned."[9]

Dr. Barkay writes: "The Temple Mount is the heart, soul, and spirit of the Jewish people. It is the only holy place that Jews have and it is the place that is identified with the place chosen by the almighty which is mentioned in Deuteronomy. This is the place which is believed to be the place of the binding of Isaac, this is the place where David built the altar on the threshing floor of Aravna the Jebusite to stop the plague, this is the place where the first temple was built and the second followed it built by the returnees to Zion from the Babylonian captivity. This is also the place of the third edifice built on the site by King Herod the Great–that is the building which is so frequently mentioned in the New Testament." The temple Mount occupies about 1/6th of the total area of the old city of Jerusalem and this is one of the most important cornerstones of Western Civilization. It is at the moment the focus of a political battle and it is embodies within it the crux of the Near-Eastern conflict as both parties claim to have historical linkage to the site."[10]

Prayers that Reach Beyond the Veil

Jesus Christ is revealing Himself throughout the Islamic countries. Intercessors have been praying this for the past decade, and now we are spectators watching this miraculous harvest unfold before our eyes. We have prayed from our prayer embassy that the Lord Jesus would reveal Himself before Muslims while they are on their pilgrimage to Mecca. Thousands who are searching the Koran have received direct revelations of the Son of God. They have dreams or visions, or a visitation from the Spirit of the Lord, and they are seeking to know about the Lord Jesus Christ.

We need to pray that Christians in Muslim countries will be anointed witnesses for Christ. The Apostle Paul explains the spiritual darkness in 2 Corinthians 4:3-4 that the gospel is veiled to those whose minds are blinded by the god of this age. How, then, do we "open their eyes and turn them from darkness to light, and from the power of Satan to God?" Acts 26:18. If we want to liberate veiled minds, so they can respond to the gospel we must pray for the blinding influence of demonic strongmen to be removed. Jesus spoke of this in Mark 3:27, "No one can enter a strong man's house and plunder his goods, unless he first binds the strong man. And then he will plunder his house." Ask for the Lord to "rend the veil" of Islam that covers the eyes of each Muslim. Only the power of the Gospel will break the spiritual forces and strongholds off their lives.

> Pray for God's kingdom to come into their hearts, and that His will be done on earth as it is in heaven. (Matthew 6:9-10) The kingdom of God is a redemptive process that the Apostle Paul identified as "righteousness and peace and joy in the Holy Spirit" (Romans 14:17).

This gospel message is what the Church has been commissioned to preach worldwide. It is more than a message of values and ethics. The kingdom of God brings salvation, deliverance and healing by the power of the Word and the Holy Spirit (Isaiah 61:1). Jesus is awakening the Muslim world through dreams and visions, and when you commit to pray for Muslims and penetrate the darkness of Islam, you have engaged in an aggressive mission, which is best approached with compassion for the souls behind the Islamic Veil. Ask the Lord Jesus to send the laborers in their midst to help birth their souls into the Kingdom of God. The Holy Spirit has been revealing Jesus to Muslims who are searching to go deeper with God. They are also shown a person in their dream or vision who will help explain the gospel message to them. (Recommended reading: *Dreams and Visions* by Tom Doyle)

Be wise when considering tearing down strongholds and principalities. As much as we cannot force the unsaved to be converted, we are not capable of removing demonic powers that are still objects of people's worship. We cannot tear down Islam over people who are stiff-necked and rebellious. The strongman's "enchantment" must first be lifted off their minds. When the veil of false religion is removed, it needs to be replaced by the power of God's Holy Spirit and His Word, which is the sword of the spirit. (Hebrews 4:12) Once the people's hearts and minds are unfettered, then truth has a chance to take root. This supernatural work of the Holy Spirit is achieved when people intercede.

"Therefore if the Son makes you free, you shall be free indeed" (John 8:36). The Muslim and Hindu harvest is a supernatural work of the Holy Ghost's bringing captives out of false religions. In India, it has been reported that Jesus has supernaturally visited villages prior to ministry teams arriving with the "Jesus Film." When the villagers see the gospel message come alive in the film, they recognize the One who has already visited them, and entire villages have come to salvation. The same thing is happening right now in Muslim countries. The fastest growing church in the Middle East is in Iran. Miraculously, the gospel is being preached by Iranians in the USA on satellite television, which is being beamed into Iran.

The only way revival comes is through a heart change in the people. What we are asking is for spiritual blindness to be lifted, which prevents men and women from hearing the truth at the heart level. It is a "heart change" that God is seeking. Only the power of the Holy Spirit can deliver people from their spiritual enchantment. A perfect example is found in Scripture when Israel's King Joash made a national decree which removed idols and restored the priesthood, but the people's hearts returned to worshiping idols.

Since Satanic forces are increasing in these end times, it is unrealistic to believe that we can eliminate all demonic powers prior to the Second Coming of Christ. We can help those captives to be set free who are experiencing an inner working of the Holy Spirit. When God makes his light shine in their hearts, it enables them to see, often for the very first time, "the knowledge of the glory of God in the face of Christ" (2 Corinthians 4:6). People can then repent of their sins for a permanent change to happen in their lives.

Christianity once thrived in the Arab-Persian countries, and now the blood of the martyrs cries out for redemption. Islam's war on Christians has intensified in the aftermath of the Arab Spring which originated in Tunisia in December 2010 and became a domino effect in many other Arab countries. A growing human rights crisis has exploded for Christians living in Islamic countries. The Arab Spring has become the Christian Winter. The media and the Obama administration have decided to ignore this growing epidemic of human pain and suffering. The United Nations has reported that 100,000 Christians around the world are violently killed every year for their faith, with the majority of these attacks taking place in Middle East Islamic countries.

"In Egypt, security forces recently launched an unprecedented assault on Cairo's St. Mark's Cathedral. In March in Pakistan, an angry Muslim mob forced 170 Christian families from their homes after a Christian was accused of blasphemy. Meanwhile in Iran, American house church pastor Saeed Abedini is suffering internal bleeding from the beatings and torture he's endured in Tehran's notoriously brutal

Evin Prison. And in Iraq, Islamic extremists say their goal is to drive all Christians out of the country."[11]

Prayer for the Suffering Church

1. Pray for the suffering Christians in these countries and for the international Church of Jesus Christ to thrive.
2. Pray that the Body of Christ will gain a greater understanding of God's heart toward the suffering church around the world.
3. Pray for protection, grace and encouragement for those serving in difficult and dangerous situations among the Muslim people.
4. Pray for their government leaders and officials, as well as spiritual strength and renewal for church leaders.
5. Pray that the age-old animosity between Christians, Muslims and Jews caused by the Christian Crusades would come to an end.
6. Pray for a resurrection of Christianity in the Muslim countries and that the Holy Spirit would sweep over these nations, creating a hunger in the hearts of men and women to know the Lord Jesus Christ.

Ask Jesus to give you a genuine love for the Muslim people, and the courage to reach out to them in sincere love and friendship. God loves Arabs and Jews. Remember, we are praying for the descendants of Isaac and Ishmael to walk in the way of righteousness and peace. God made a covenant with both. God has a peace plan for Jerusalem and the Middle East. It will not favor or love one people over another, but it will be true to the covenantal promises and responsibilities of His Word. The greatest harvest of all times has been occurring in the past several decades among the millions of Muslims. Pray for the restraining of the spirit of Jihad terrorism, and the security and salvation of Israel. The seed of Isaac and Ishmael share an inheritance in the Kingdom of God when they receive Jesus Christ as Savior.

When praying for the Middle East ask the Holy Spirit to lead you: "Likewise the Spirit also helps in our weaknesses. For we do not know what we should pray for as we ought, but the Spirit Himself makes intercession for us with groanings which cannot be uttered," Romans 8:26. The Holy Spirit appeals to the Father, "according to the will of God" (v. 27). Believe for an outpouring of the Holy Spirit upon Muslims worldwide. Pray and believe for the fulfillment of Revelation 7:9-10:

> After these things I looked, and behold, a great multitude which no one could number, of all nations, tribes, peoples, and tongues, standing before the throne and before the Lamb, clothed with white robes, with palm branches in their hands, and crying out with a loud voice, saying, "Salvation belongs to our God who sits on the throne, and to the Lamb!"

How to Pray for Muslims

- **Pray** that *Yeshua* will appear and bring revelations, wherever Muslims gather.
- **Pray** that *Yeshua* will confound Muslims who are motivated by hate and warring spirits; dismantle terrorist groups and Islamic front organizations.
- **Pray** for a canopy of protection over all Jews, Christians, and others, who are within the path of Muslim hate and terrorism.
- **Cry out** for *Yahweh's* mercy to touch all Muslims, wherever they are among the nations.

Testimonies of Transformation in Today's Muslim World

The chaos and uncertainty of today's world may be slowly hardening the hearts of some Christians against the world's Muslims, but the arrival of satellite TV and the Internet have dramatically changed how Muslims view Christianity. CBN News recently reported: "A Christian revival is touching the northernmost reaches of Africa. In a region once hostile to the Gospel, now tens of thousands of Muslims are following Jesus. As the sun sets over the Mediterranean Sea, Muslims across Northern Africa are converting to faith in Jesus Christ in record numbers."[12]

"From the shores of Casablanca, Morocco, to Tripoli, Libya, experts say the growth of Christianity, especially in the last 20 years, has been unprecedented. One of the largest churches in Algeria reports some 1,200 believers attending the church..... One pastor in Algeria commented, "Every new Christian in the church comes from a Muslim background. Since the church opened, they have baptized on average 150-160 believers per year."[13] Technology has made a big difference. "Today in North Africa on TV, you can hear native Arab Christians talking about their faith, who are mature Christians, answering questions, involved in debates....."Emboldened by God's power, Algerian Christians are now on a mission to take the Gospel to the four corners of the globe."[14]

Key Ten

The Battle is the Lord's

When we proclaim the Word of God as a command, it becomes our shield and buckler, and we also release the battle into the Lord's hand. Sometimes people have a difficult time accepting the full dynamics of God's Word. Scripture has authority; it is not just a history book we are reading. If we are going to overcome Satan's fiery darts, schemes and plans against our lives, families and ministry, then we must learn to be a doer of the Word. Scripture is not useful as long as it remains head knowledge. We must believe the Word and act on our faith if we want to receive the anointing of His spiritual authority.

For the Christian, conflict in this world can only be counterattacked with spiritual warfare: "For the weapons of our warfare are not carnal but mighty in God for pulling down strongholds" (2 Corinthians 10:4). (Also read 1 Timothy 1:18-19; 6:12). Jesus Christ waged a triumphant battle against Satan, disarmed the evil powers and authorities of wickedness, led captive a host of captives, and redeemed the believer from Satan's dominion (Colossians 1:13-14; 2:15; Matthew 12:29; Luke 10:18; John 12:31). Christ's followers are commissioned to do the same works that He performed and even greater works after He went to the Father (John 14:12). Spiritual warfare can only be conducted with the power of the Holy Spirit (Romans 8:13). There are those internal struggles against the corrupt desires within themselves (1 Peter 2:11). There are temptations coming from the ungodly pleasures of the world, and traps that Satan assigns against all believers (Matthew 13:22; Galatians 1:4; James 1:14-15; 1 John 2:16).

As Christian soldiers, we must not think it strange when fiery trials come our way. We can rest knowing that we have spiritual weapons, which equip us to face any spiritual conflict (2 Corinthians 10:3-5). These are orchestrated by the powers of darkness, which are organized into a highly systematic empire of evil with rank and order. Additional scriptures to study on this subject are: (Genesis 3:1-7; Daniel 10:12-13; Matthew 13:38-39; John 12:31; 14:30; 16:11; 2 Corinthians 4:4; 1 Peter 5:8; 1 John 5:19; Revelation 12:4, 7). The believer has the sword of the Spirit to use as an offensive weapon in his war against these powers of evil. For this reason, Satan will make every effort to undermine or destroy the Christian's confidence in the Word. This is why it is so very important we walk in the revelation that God's Word will deliver us from all the power that Hell tries to throw at us, because Jesus has already defeated our enemy:

> And I also say to you that you are Peter, and on this rock I will build My church, and the gates of Hades shall not prevail against it (Matthew 16:18).

Prayer is not a weapon: It is the vehicle for launching our spiritual weapons, which are the Word, the Name of Jesus, and the Blood of the Lamb. Conducting warfare against Satan's invisible forces calls for a childlike trust in prayer. The Apostle Paul comforted the believers at Philippi, "Be anxious for nothing, but in everything by prayer and supplication, with thanksgiving, let your requests be made known to God; and the peace of God, which surpasses all understanding, will guard your hearts and minds through Christ Jesus" (Philippians 4:6-7). To fail to pray diligently, is to surrender to the enemy and cease to fight. However, when we do our part to pray, then we can rest in the fact that the Holy Spirit does the warfare.

The Power of God's Spoken Word

The Holy Spirit waits to move in power whenever the Word is proclaimed by those who keep the covenant with the Father. The covenant is only effective when we are fully submitted to God's authority. Genesis 1:2-4 gives an example of the power in God's spoken word:

> In the beginning God created the heavens and the earth. The earth was without form, and void; and darkness was on the face of the deep. And the Spirit of God was hovering over the face of the waters. Then God said, "Let there be light"; and there was light. And God saw the light, that it was good; and God divided the light from the darkness.

Jesus was fully submitted to God's authority, and moved with spiritual authority when He spoke God's Word (Hebrews 1:3; Colossians 1:17). During the wilderness temptation, Christ spoke the Word with power and defeated Satan's temptation. Christ's example is our model for spiritual warfare. Satan had never been defeated by the authority of God's Word through a man. In Matthew 4:3-11, we find Jesus in the identical wilderness as the nation of Israel under Moses, and Christ overcomes the same temptations to which Israel succumbed. When the Word of God is directed against Satan, it strikes him as a sharp sword and disables him. Of course, we must be sure to be wearing our spiritual armor:

> Therefore take up the whole armor of God, that you may be able to withstand in the evil day, and having done all, to stand (Ephesians 6:13-17).

The Word will come out of our mouth impulsively when we sow the Word of God into our heart every day. As Jesus demonstrated, we will have an automatic response during a time of temptation or oppression. Praise God!

Ephesians 6:11-18

Spiritual Weapons to Destroy Satan's Strongholds

Put on the whole armor of God, that you may be able to stand against the wiles of the devil. For we do not wrestle against flesh and blood, but against principalities, against powers, against the rulers of the darkness of this age, against spiritual hosts of wickedness in the heavenly places. Therefore take up the whole armor of God, that you may be able to withstand in the evil day, and having done all, to stand. Stand therefore, having girded your waist with truth, having put on the breastplate of righteousness, and having shod your feet with the preparation of the gospel of peace; above all, taking the shield of faith with which you will be able to quench all the fiery darts of the wicked one. And take the helmet of salvation, and the sword of the Spirit, which is the word of God; praying always with all prayer and supplication in the Spirit, being watchful to this end with all perseverance and supplication for all the saints—

Jude 9

Contending with the Devil or Evil Spirits

Yet Michael the archangel, in contending with the devil, when he disputed about the body of Moses, dared not bring against him a reviling accusation, but said, "The Lord rebuke you!" If the greatest archangel Michael refused to rebuke Satan but relied on the power of God, how much more should we as humans refrain from challenging and speaking abusively against all things, including evil spirits.

2 Peter 2:11

Whereas angels, who are greater in power and might, do not bring a reviling accusation against them before the Lord.

Isaiah 54:15-16

Satan's Weapons Null and Void

Behold, they may gather together *and* stir up strife, but it is not from Me. Whoever stirs up strife against you shall fall *and* surrender to you. Behold, I have created the smith who blows on the fire of coals and who produces a weapon for its purpose; and I have created the devastator to destroy.

Verse 17

God Himself is our Defense

No weapon formed against you shall prosper, and every tongue which rises against you in judgment You shall condemn. This is the heritage of the servants of the Lord, and their righteousness is from Me, Says the Lord.

Galatians 3:13, 14
Christian Believers are Released from the Curse

Christ has redeemed us from the curse of the law, having become a curse for us (for it is written, "Cursed is everyone who hangs on a tree"), that the blessing of Abraham might come upon the Gentiles in Christ Jesus, that we might receive the promise of the Spirit through faith.

Proclaiming this Scripture is the ammunition you need to break those generational curses off your loved ones, when it is obvious that they are bound by them.

Matthew 16:18-20
Binding and Loosing
Governing with the Keys of Authority given to the Church

And I will give you the keys of the kingdom of heaven, and whatever you bind on earth will be bound in heaven, and whatever you loose on earth will be loosed in heaven.

Jesus gave the Church authority with the keys of the Kingdom of Heaven. "Heaven" is a biblical synonym for "God." The Lord speaks this to all the apostles regarding the keys: "Receive the Holy Spirit. If you forgive the sins of any, they are forgiven them; if you retain the sins of any, they are retained," (John 20.22-23). This reference to "binding and loosing" has been chiefly misunderstood as an instruction on how to bind up Satan, so I want to clarify the meaning of this term. At the time of Jesus, the rabbis used the legal terms of "bind" or "loose" which only meant "to forbid" or "to permit" something. The Sages would determine what an individual was or was not permitted to do on the Sabbath. They would decide if this or that action was permitted, or was a thing, or person ritually clean, etc. Jesus was now instituting this power to the apostles and the Church. He is saying that whatever they forbid in the Church would have divine authority; whatever they permitted, or commanded would be bound or loosed in heaven and would meet the approval of God.

"Binding" and "loosing" typically refers to rites and ceremonies in the Church. Jewish customs meant that what the apostles would forbid were to be forbidden, and those they thought suitable to permit were to be allowed. The Apostle Paul argued the case against the apostles who were considering that it was proper to return to circumcision under the Law (Acts 15). The apostles' decisions for the Church were challenged when the gospel expanded to the Gentile nations. In Acts chapter fifteen, we also see they set up guidelines for the Gentile converts to "abstain from pollutions of idols, and from fornication, and from things strangled, and from blood" (v. 20).

The act of "binding and loosing" is frequently used with intercession, and when we understand this portion of Scripture, it is easy to understand that Jesus was not giving the Church spiritual authority to bind up the devil. Believers are warned against adjuring Satan in Jude 9. Since the Lord has already disarmed these principalities and powers, then all we have to do is hold the devil's agents accountable to the Word of God. When we command the devil to flee from us, or others, it must be spoken with the Word of God, in the Name of Jesus Christ, and declaring the Blood of the Lamb. These are the spiritual weapons that give believers authority to defeat demons. I can attest to firsthand experiences that the Word absolutely works when you are moving in Christ's authority.

Jesus has already overcome Satan for us, and we can set people free from Satan's demonic assignment, but binding Satan is unscriptural and ineffective. He will be bound up for one thousand years during the millennial reign of Christ. We read in Revelation 20:1-3 that the angels will bind up Lucifer during Christ's thousand-year reign. Through spiritual warfare, we can cancel Satan's assignments and release people from demonic activity, but we must also bring the Kingdom of God to earth into the person's life replacing the void that gave Satan permission to control and possess them. When a person is delivered from Satan's assignment, then they need to be bound to God's Word. For example, when Jesus resurrected Lazarus from the tomb, He told them to "loose" him from the grave clothes; or "permit" him to go free (John 11:38-44). He was not liberated while bound up in his grave clothes. And, so it is with those who are bound up by Satan's demons. We can pray to loose whatever we have petitioned from the Father, according to Revelation 8:3-5, where the prayers of the saints are poured out upon the earth after the angel lifts them up to the Throne of God as a sweet-smelling incense:

> Then another angel, having a golden censer, came and stood at the altar. He was given much incense, that he should offer it with the prayers of all the saints upon the golden altar which was before the throne. And the smoke of the incense, with the prayers of the saints, ascended before God from the angel's hand. Then the angel took the censer, filled it with fire from the altar, and threw it to the earth. And there were noises, thunderings, lightnings, and an earthquake.

The keys for spiritual authority come from the Resurrected Christ in Revelation 1:18, "I am He who lives, and was dead, and behold, I am alive forevermore. Amen. And I have the keys of Hades and of Death." Jesus Christ conquered Satan and passed the keys of His authority over to His Church (Revelation 20:1-2).

Prayer to Negate Psychic & Soulish Prayers

I proclaim the supremacy of Jesus Christ over familiar spirits and false prophecy, and affirm the finished work of Christ according to Colossians 1:12-18 and Revelation 1:5-6. I cancel and annul all "hate speech, curses and evil intent" against myself, my family, and all those who labor with me in the ministry. I pray against the curse of poverty, plundering spirits, spirit of death and accidents assigned against myself and my family. With the Blood of Jesus Christ, I negate every curse, division, violence, negative word, psychic and soulish prayers. I negate every hex, every vex, chant, spell, white magic, black magic, voodoo, Jezebel spirit, all other forms of witchcraft, Babylon spirit; every demon assigned against me, my family, our health, jobs, finances, ministry and everything that has to do with me and my children. The curse is unable to succeed because "…..a curse without cause shall not alight" (Proverbs 26:2). In the Name of Jesus Christ, I command Lucifer, Satan to cease binding the promises of God in my life and my family.

Triumph of God's Kingdom

Worship demolishes Satan's opposition with greater impact than trying to adjure him (Jude 9). We have always worshiped in our ministry with songs that glorify our High Priest and King of kings. It is powerful to declare His Kingdom over all kingdoms in this earth and the second heavenly.

Revelation 11:15
Declare Christ's Kingdom

The kingdoms of this world have become the kingdoms of our Lord and of His Christ, and He shall reign forever and ever!

Revelation 12:11
Declare the Victory

And they overcame him by the blood of the Lamb and by the word of their testimony, and they did not love their lives to the death.

Colossians 2:15
Christ Has Disarmed All Principalities

Having disarmed principalities and powers, He made a public spectacle of them, triumphing over them in it.

Isaiah 41:10-20
Divine Strength Promised

Fear not, for I am with you; be not dismayed, for I am your God. I will strengthen you, Yes, I will help you, I will uphold you with My righteous right hand. Behold, all those who were incensed against you shall be ashamed and disgraced; they shall be as nothing, and those who strive with you shall perish.

(Their evil efforts will perish. Vv. 13-20)

We cannot stand in our own strength, but the Lord will strengthen us (Philippians 4:13).

The Apostle Paul said, "For when I am weak, then I am strong" (2 Corinthians 12:10).

Isaiah 41:15
God Promises Invincibility to His People

Behold, I will make you into a new threshing sledge with sharp teeth; you shall thresh the mountains and beat them small, and make the hills like chaff. You shall winnow them, the wind shall carry them away, and the whirlwind shall scatter them; you shall rejoice in the Lord, and glory in the Holy One of Israel.

This is a powerful proclamation to declare. In this portion of Scripture, God promises to defeat our enemies, to restore our strength; then He will build up the waste places in our land.

Psalm 68
Fate of the Wicked

Let God arise, let his enemies be scattered: let them also that hate him flee before him.

Isaiah 51:21-23
Promise to the Afflicted

Therefore please hear this, you afflicted, and drunk but not with wine. Thus says your Lord, the Lord and your God, Who pleads the cause of His people: "See, I have taken out of your hand the cup of trembling. The dregs of the cup of My fury; you shall no longer drink it. But I will put it into the hand of those who afflict you, who have said to you, "Lie down, that we may walk over you." And you have laid your body like the ground, And as the street, for those who walk over.

Isaiah 43:1-7
Victory for the Afflicted

Fear not, for I have redeemed you; I have called you by your name; You are Mine. When you pass through the waters, I will be with you; and through the rivers, they shall not overflow you. When you walk through the fire, you shall not be burned, nor shall the flame scorch you.

Key Eleven

How to Prosper and Succeed God's Way

Only be strong and very courageous, that you may observe to do according to all the law which Moses My servant commanded you; do not turn from it to the right hand or to the left, that you may prosper wherever you go. –Joshua 1:7

In the entire first chapter of the Book of Joshua, the Lord instructed Joshua how to serve Him with success. It gives the account of the Lord's instructions of preparation for leading the Hebrew people into the Promised Land. He is told not to be afraid, or be dismayed: "for the Lord your God is with you wherever you go" (v. 9). We cannot expect to live with God's blessings if we do not have confidence in His Covenant Word. When we profess God's Word into action, it accomplishes God's will on our behalf. As Christians, we must know how to be prepared for spiritual warfare against unseen but very real powers of Satan (Ephesians 6:12). Without the Holy Spirit and the proper use of God's Word, the believer cannot overcome the temptations of Satan.

Financial adversity is an assignment from Satan against believers. Sometimes we tend to think that all will go well if we are obeying God's Word and remain faithful in doing good works. To the contrary, this can be the very reason we will attract a fiery trial. Remember, God's best servant Job was tested because Satan charged that Job only served the LORD because he was blessed. Job was faithful and obedient to His God, Who increased him with abundance. Satan thought adversity would turn Job from God, so the LORD permitted him to test His righteous servant with adversity, knowing that Job would pass the test. It is true throughout the Bible, that God will allow Satan to buffet His sanctified servants in order to purify their faith and lives, just as gold is refined by the fire (1 Peter 1:6-7). As we see in Job, severe testing will result in an increased measure of spiritual integrity and humility in God's people. Finding examples in the Word encourage the believer to move into a position of overcoming; so his faith will be strengthened and increased.

Righteousness does not make us immune from trials. Believers under the New Testament covenant are not exempt from being tested by Satan, but we are in a better position than Job. We have a High Priest, Who has shown us how to overcome the fiery darts of the enemy. Jesus Christ came to earth to establish the Kingdom of God, destroy the works of Satan (1 John 3:8), and deliver mankind from Satan's dominion (Luke 4:18; Acts 26:18). Satan would like to take you away from God and bring you into his captivity. When we are experiencing a fiery trial, we must follow the example of Jesus, the Son of God, and stand in the authority of God's Word. If Satan cannot turn you away from God, he will tempt you into making wrong decisions during your adversity; like he distorted the scriptures to tempt the Son of God to sin. We must know God's Word thoroughly and beware of those who pervert the

Scriptures in order to influence the sinful, carnal nature. The Apostle Peter speaks of those who distort the Scriptures to their own destruction in 2 Peter 3:14-16:

> Therefore, beloved, looking forward to these things, be diligent to be found by Him in peace, without spot and blameless; and consider that the longsuffering of our Lord is salvation—as also our beloved brother Paul, according to the wisdom given to him, has written to you, as also in all his epistles, speaking in them of these things, in which are some things hard to understand, which untaught and unstable people twist to their own destruction, as they do also the rest of the Scriptures.

Staying focused on God's Word will bring God's plans and purposes into your life:

1. Realize that, through the Word of God, you have the power to resist any appeal Satan can make (John 15:3, 7).
2. Memorize the Word of God into your heart (James 1:21).
3. Meditate day and night on the verses you have memorized (Deuteronomy 6:6; Psalm 1:2; 119:47-48).
4. Speak the Scriptures out loud and make them a proclamation:
   (a) This is good for increasing your own faith (Romans 10:17).
   (b) It speaks directly to Satan as Jesus Christ did in the wilderness (Luke 4:12).
   (c) It reminds God of His covenant (Isaiah 43:26).
5. Surround all the above with spirit-led prayer (Ephesians 6:18).
6. Submit to the prompting of the Holy Spirit to help you obey God's Word (Romans 8:12-14; Galatians 5:18).
7. Guard your Spirit against fearing the future (2 Timothy 1:7), and worry over finances (Matthew 6:24-34; Philippians 4:6).

Guard against unbelief and establish your faith in God's Word:

1. Proverbs 3:5-6, "Trust in the Lord with all your heart, and lean not on your own understanding; in all your ways acknowledge Him, and He shall direct your paths."
2. Proverbs 28:25, "He who is of a proud heart stirs up strife, but he who trusts in the Lord will be prospered."
3. Psalm 20:7, "Some trust in chariots, and some in horses: but we will remember the name of the Lord our God."
4. Philippians 4:19, "But my God shall supply all your needs according his riches in glory by Christ Jesus." He is Jehovah Jireh: The Lord who provides for those who acknowledge their dependence on Him.

5. 1 John 3:21-22, "Beloved, if our heart does not condemn us, we have confidence toward God. And whatever we ask we receive from Him, because we keep His commandments and do those things that are pleasing in His sight."

Be Ready Spiritually for any Crisis!

When a crisis strikes, there is not enough time to build yourself up in prayer and faith. Those who build their relationship with Jesus and spend time in His Word are always ready. His grace becomes sufficient:

> God is our refuge and strength, a very present help in trouble. Therefore we will not fear, Even though the earth be removed, and though the mountains be carried into the midst of the sea; though its waters roar and be troubled, though the mountains shake with its swelling (Psalm 46:1-3).

Know When to Act—There is a time to quit praying and start acting

"Delight yourself in the Lord and he will give you the desires of your heart" (Psalm 37:4). These desires result from fervent prayer, which reveals God's will. When we delight ourselves in the Lord, fresh new desires are conceived within us, and those desires give us brand new direction. For instance, while Isaiah was delighting in the Lord with worship, He had a heavenly vision and heard God's voice saying: "Whom shall I send. And who will go for Us?" Without considering what this would involve, Isaiah replied: "Here am I. Send me" (Isaiah 6:1-8).

We need more faithful men like Nehemiah: a man of prayer and a courageous leader.....

The desire Nehemiah had to rebuild the wall of Jerusalem was conceived in his spirit through prayer when he heard the sad news of his beloved city, Jerusalem. After he fasted and prayed, Nehemiah chose to take responsibility for the burden God had put in his heart. Nehemiah prayed as if it depended on God, and later he worked as if it depended on him. Nehemiah expressed the practical, everyday faith in His God. He challenged the people to show faith by works; some fought while others labored. They carried a sword in one hand and worked with a tool in the other. Nehemiah was a courageous leader who defied the odds and encouraged others to endure until the work was finished.

God-ordained passions are an overwhelming burden to bear. Anything that causes you to weep and mourn, and fast and pray for days, weeks or months, is a good indicator that it will bear fruit and be fulfilling. We can delight in what we do for God's Kingdom. In reading about the Creation in the Book of Genesis, we see how God delighted in His own work: "And God saw that it was good" (Genesis 1:31).

Faith Produces Signs and Miracles

> And they went out and preached everywhere, the Lord working with them and confirming the word through the accompanying signs (Mark 16:20).

Whenever you take a step of faith, signs will follow. Signs also follow our decisions. For example, Nehemiah did not wait for a sign; he had the courage to put his job on the line. And when he did, God confirmed the desire in his heart with signs following. We can see this also happening in modern times. People everywhere prayed for years for the Berlin Wall to be torn down. It finally happened shortly after President Ronald Reagan made his famous speech at the Brandenburg Gate in 1987, commanding the Soviet leader: "Mr. Gorbachev, tear down this wall!" The wall separated East and West Berlin between 1961 and 1981 to separate Germany and the communist Eastern Bloc during the post-World War II period. While praying people had agonized for years around the globe, but certain leaders had to take action for the signs and miracles to happen.

A Priestly Blessing to Pray from the Torah
By Dr. Roni Wexler, Ten Commandments Commission
(ww.tencommandmentsday.com)

The Three Fold Blessing from Numbers 6:24-26

The Lord bless you and keep you;
The Lord make His face shine upon you,
And be gracious to you;
The Lord lift up His countenance upon you,
And give you peace.

This reading portion from the Torah bestows a blessing upon you. It is called the *Birkat Cohanim*, or the priestly benediction (Aaron's) recited by the priest and by parents to their children, every Friday night (Numbers 6:24-26). It is interesting how this benediction is divided into three sentences, each containing two important elements: God's blessing and a prayer to avoid possible pitfalls of the blessing.

In the first part, the priest states: "May the Lord bless you and keep you." We can understand this to refer to monetary benefits. However, money has the potential to corrupt. Therefore, a blessing for money is not complete unless accompanied by an assurance of protection from its dangers. Hence the last word of the sentence, "May the Lord Guard you." The first blessing aims at making us realize that our material wealth, physical well-being, and natural abilities come from God, and that He gave it to us for a reason.

In the second section, the priest states: "May the Lord cause His light to shine upon you." The light of the Lord is often associated with Bible knowledge (Proverbs 6:23). However, while one can know every word of the Bible, one can still lack the ability to interact and engage others in an appropriate manner. Hence, this blessing concludes with the Hebrew word, *ve-hunekah*, a derivative of grace. Thus, this last statement is telling us to remain gracious to others because knowledge often makes one insular, even arrogant. The second blessing aims at making us realize that we have a responsibility to elevate ourselves through our every thought and action.

In the final part, the priest states: "May the Lord lift His face to be near you." This blessing expresses the hope that one will always feel the presence of God, for too often; we sense that God's face is hidden from us. (The Hebrew word yeesah, to lift, is the opposite of God being lowered or hidden.) Although we hope to be absorbed in God's presence at all times, sometimes even that experience can distort one's perception of how to change the world, especially when people have done dastardly things in the name of God.

Therefore, the text concludes, with a blessing of a grounded belief in God, of shalom, coming from the word *shalem*, whole. The third blessing aims at making us realize that we have a say in the world's level of peace, and in increasing peace around the world by using the other two blessings correctly. It is no coincidence that having provision, spiritual growth, and peace all starts from within our spirit. God concludes the blessings by teaching us that if we simply notice God's name and hand in all we have and all we do; we will realize that we are already blessed!

Psalm 34:8, 9
Promise to Believers

Oh, taste and see that the Lord is good; blessed is the man who trusts in Him!
Oh, fear the Lord, you His saints! There is no want to those who fear Him.

2 Corinthians 9:8-11
Spiritual Abundance through Benevolence

And God is able to make all grace abound toward you, that you, always having all sufficiency in all things, may have abundance for every good work. As it is written: "He has dispersed abroad, He has given to the poor; His righteousness endures forever." Now may He who supplies seed to the sower, and bread for food, supply and multiply the seed you have sown and increase the fruits of your righteousness, while you are enriched in everything for all liberality, which causes thanksgiving through us to God.

Joel 2:25-27
Restoration from Poverty

So I will restore to you the years that the swarming locust has eaten, the crawling locust, the consuming locust, and the chewing locust, My great army which I sent among you. You shall eat in plenty and be satisfied, and praise the name of the Lord your God, Who has dealt wondrously with you; and My people shall never be put to shame. Then you shall know that I am in the midst of Israel: I am the Lord your God and there is no other. My people shall never be put to shame.

Isaiah 61:7; Job 42:10
Double Portion

Instead of your shame you shall have double honor, and instead of confusion they shall rejoice in their portion. Therefore in their land they shall possess double; everlasting joy shall be theirs.

And the Lord restored Job's losses when he prayed for his friends. Indeed the Lord gave Job twice as much as he had before.

Isaiah 45:2, 3
Supernatural Way Provided

I will go before you and make the crooked places straight; I will break in pieces the gates of bronze and cut the bars of iron. I will give you the treasures of darkness and hidden riches of secret places, that you may know that I, the Lord, Who call you by your name, Am the God of Israel.

Malachi 3:10-12
Protection from the Devourer

V. 10, Bring all the tithes into the storehouse, that there may be food in My house, and try Me now in this," Says the Lord of hosts, "If I will not open for you the windows of heaven and pour out for you such blessing that there will not be room enough to receive it."

V. 11, And I will rebuke the devourer for your sakes, so that he will not destroy the fruit of your ground, nor shall the vine fail to bear fruit for you in the field, Says the Lord of hosts.

We cannot be self-righteous and withhold our tithes and offerings that belong to the Lord, and expect to have God's blessings and spiritual fullness. The Old Testament law required the first fruits be offered up to the priests. Ten percent is an Old Testament requirement. In the New Testament, we come under Grace, when everything we have belongs to the Lord. We see how gross sin over the people in the earth has caused famines, pestilence, earthquakes, and all sorts of weather disorders destroying the crops, water supplies and leveling cities. In times ahead, God's people will have to trust God for miraculous provision beyond the world system. It will be evident who are the "wise virgins," and who are the "foolish."

Deuteronomy 28:1-14
God's Covenant to the Obedient
Abraham Worshiped God with his Obedience

V. 1, Obedience: "Now it shall come to pass, if you diligently obey the voice of the Lord your God, to observe carefully all His commandments which I command you today, that the Lord your God will set you high above all nations of the earth."

V. 2-3, Blessings: "And all these blessings shall come upon you and overtake you, because you obey the voice of the Lord your God: 'Blessed shall you be in the city, and blessed shall you be in the country.'"

V. 4, Increase: "Blessed shall be the fruit of your body, the produce of your ground and the increase of your herds, the increase of your cattle and the offspring of your flocks."

V. 5-6, Plenty Promised: "Blessed shall be your basket and your kneading bowl." "Blessed shall you be when you come in, and blessed shall you be when you go out."

V. 7, Invincibility: "The Lord will cause your enemies who rise against you to be defeated before your face; they shall come out against you one way and flee before you seven ways."

V. 8, Divine Supplies and Promised Land: "The Lord will command the blessing on you in your storehouses and in all to which you set your hand, and He will bless you in the land which the Lord your God is giving you."

V. 9, Established as God's People: "The Lord will establish you as a holy people to Himself, just as He has sworn to you, if you keep the commandments of the Lord your God and walk in His ways."

V. 10, Enemies Fear You: "Then all peoples of the earth shall see that you are called by the name of the Lord, and they shall be afraid of you."

V. 11, Posterity Promised: "And the Lord will grant you plenty of goods, in the fruit of your body, in the increase of your livestock, and in the produce of your ground, in the land of which the Lord swore to your fathers to give you."

V. 12, Work Blessed with Prosperity: "The Lord will open to you His good treasure, the heavens, to give the rain to your land in its season, and to bless all the work of your hand. You shall lend to many nations, but you shall not borrow."

V. 13, God's People Exalted: "And the Lord will make you the head and not the tail; you shall be above only, and not be beneath, if you heed the commandments of the Lord your God, which I command you today, and are careful to observe them."

V. 14, Forsake Idolatry: "So you shall not turn aside from any of the words which I command you this day, to the right or the left, to go after other gods to serve them."

Proverbs 6:30, 31
Sevenfold Restitution from Losses

People do not despise a thief if he steals to satisfy himself when he is starving. Yet when he is found, he must restore sevenfold; He may have to give up all the substance of his house.

Pray and command the North, South, East and West to release every dollar that has been stolen from you. Ask the Father to dispatch angels to return the money with an increase, every dollar that the enemy has stolen, as interest for your suffering and shame.

Isaiah 54:2-5
Restoration to a Place of Favor and Expansion of the Land

Enlarge the place of your tent, and let them stretch out the curtains of your dwellings; do not spare; lengthen your cords, and strengthen your stakes. For you shall expand to the right and to the left, and your descendants will inherit the nations, and make the desolate cities inhabited. "Do not fear, for you will not be ashamed; neither be disgraced, for you will not be put to shame; for you will forget the shame of your youth, and will not remember the reproach of your widowhood anymore. For your Maker is your husband, the Lord of hosts is His name; and your Redeemer is the Holy One of Israel; He is called the God of the whole earth."

Note: Proclamations are declarations of praise unto God. We praise His Name with the Word of God. Here are additional scriptures to proclaim, which speak comfort, restoration and increase into your life:

Job 28:11, hidden things brought to light.
Jeremiah 23:29, the word is a consuming fire and hammer.
Micah 2:13, the breaker anointing goes before you.
Hebrews 4:12, the Word is powerful.
Matthew 6:33-34; 7:7-8, seek God, ask and it shall be given.
Matthew 10:26, Satan's schemes exposed.
Mark 6: 35-43, multiplication.

Praying For Financial Breakthroughs

Isaiah 59:19

When the enemy comes in like a flood, the Spirit of the Lord will lift up a standard against him.
The Lord will intervene and put the enemy to flight when we lift up the standard of the Word.

Matthew 6:9-13

Call the Father's Will from heaven to earth and continue until it happens.
Daily proclaim the Lord's Prayer which Jesus taught His disciples.

Habakkuk 2:3, 4

The vision has an appointed time and the righteous wait on God's timing.

Hebrews 10:38

The righteous do not shrink back in fear.
Now the just shall live by faith; but if anyone draws back, My soul has no pleasure in him.

Hebrews 11:1

Believe it and possess it by faith.
When the title deed is possessed in the Spirit, then we need it to be made manifest in the natural. Now faith is the substance of things hoped for, the evidence of things not seen.

1 Timothy 5:17-18; 1 Corinthians 9:9-14

Let the elders who rule well be counted worthy of double honor, especially those who labor in the word and doctrine. For the Scripture says, "You shall not muzzle an ox while it treads out the grain," and, "The laborer *is* worthy of his wages."

If God cares about oxen, then certainly those who preach the gospel should receive their substance from the gospel.

Isaiah 1:8, 9; Romans 9:28; Matthew 9:37, 38
God needs you to prosper for His kingdom work

God will spare a remnant of His people so the work of the Gospel will go forward. Jesus said to His disciples, "The harvest truly is plentiful, but the laborers are few. Therefore pray the Lord of the harvest to send out laborers into His harvest."

Psalm 107:3; Luke 13:29; Matthew 8:11
Call God's provision forth from the East, the West, the North and South.

Lord, send forth your angels who harvest the provision for God's servants. We bind ourselves to the open windows of heaven, and Jehovah-Jireh. Lord Jesus, gather those who will bring your provision and supplies.

Isaiah 45:2, 3; Isaiah 61:7; 2 Corinthians 9:8-11
Pray for God's abundance to come into your bosom.

> And God is able to make all grace abound toward you, that you, always having all sufficiency in all things, may have an abundance for every good work. As it is written: "He has dispersed abroad, He has given to the poor; His righteousness endures forever." Now may He who supplies seed to the sower, and bread for food, supply and multiply the seed you have sown and increase the fruits of your righteousness, you are enriched in everything for all liberality, which causes thanksgiving through us to God (2 Corinthians 9:8-11).

Key Twelve

Seeking God's Direction

We should always seek God first, through the Holy Spirit and the Word of God. There are three ways to hear from the LORD: The Holy Spirit directs our path; we hear the still small voice of the LORD, and we receive confirmation in a portion of Scripture. When we receive a confirmation in the Word of God, then we should proclaim it aloud. In doing this, we are prophesying that God's Word will be fulfilled. In Jeremiah 23:29, we read that God's Word is like a hammer and a consuming fire: "Is not My word like a fire?" says the Lord, "And like a hammer that breaks the rock in pieces?" When we profess the Word of God, it becomes a hammer against the enemy until we gain the victory. It protects and preserves the will of God in our lives. The fire of God's word will consume our enemies, protect our future, and the situations we are praying for according to His perfect will.

Proverbs 19:21
Seeking God's Counsel
There are many plans in a man's heart, nevertheless the Lord's counsel—that will stand.

Psalm 34
Looking Heavenward
I sought the Lord, and He heard me, and delivered me from all my fears. They looked unto Him, and were lightened: and their faces were not ashamed.

Psalm 37:23, 24
God Orders Our Steps
The steps of a good man are ordered by the Lord, and He delights in his way. Though he fall, he shall not be utterly cast down; for the Lord upholds him with His hand.

Proverbs 3:5, 6
Trust God with Whole Heart
Trust in the Lord with all your heart, and lean not on your own understanding; in all your ways acknowledge Him, and He shall direct your paths.

Proverbs 15:22
Counsel
Without counsel, plans go awry, but in the multitude of counselors they are established.

Proverbs 16:7, 9
Pleasing God

When a man's ways please the Lord, He makes even his enemies to be at peace with him. Better is a little with righteousness, than vast revenues without justice. A man's heart plans his way, but the Lord directs his steps.

Isaiah 40:31
Wait Upon God

But they that wait upon the Lord shall renew their strength; they shall mount up with wings as eagles; they shall run, and not be weary; and they shall walk and not faint.

Jeremiah 29:11-14
Promise to Those Who Seek God

For I know the thoughts that I think toward you, says the Lord, thoughts of peace and not of evil, to give you a future and a hope. Then you will call upon Me and go and pray to Me, and I will listen to you. And you will seek Me and find Me, when you search for Me with all your heart. I will be found by you, says the Lord, and I will bring you back from your captivity; I will gather you from all the nations and from all the places where I have driven you, says the Lord, and I will bring you to the place from which I cause you to be carried away captive. (Captivity could be debt, falling out of God's will, a divided marriage, or rebellious children.)

Luke 1:45-50
Blessing for Believing God's Word

Blessed is she who believed, for there will be a fulfillment of those things which were told her from the Lord.....For He who is mighty has done great things for me, and holy is His name. And His mercy is on those who fear Him from generation to generation.

Isaiah 14:24-26
Declaring God's Will for Your Life
Deliverance from Oppression

The Lord of hosts hath sworn, saying, surely as I have thought, so it shall come to pass; and as I have purposed, so it shall stand.....then his yoke shall be removed from them, and his burden removed from their shoulders.....

Verse 27
God's Will Stands

For the Lord of hosts has purposed, and who will annul it? His hand is stretched out, and who will turn it back?

Isaiah 40:1-8
Obstacles Removed

"Comfort, yes, comfort My people!" Says your God. Speak comfort to Jerusalem, and cry out to her, that her warfare is ended, that her iniquity is pardoned; for she has received from the Lord's hand double for all her sins. The voice of one crying in the wilderness: "Prepare the way of the Lord; make straight in the desert a highway for our God. Every valley shall be exalted and every mountain and hill brought low; the crooked places shall be made straight and the rough places smooth; the glory of the Lord shall be revealed, and all flesh shall see it together; for the mouth of the Lord has spoken." The voice said, "Cry out!" And he said, "What shall I cry?" "All flesh is grass and all its loveliness is like the flower of the field. The grass withers, the flower fades, because the breath of the Lord blows upon it; surely the people are grass. The grass withers, the flower fades, but the word of our God stands forever."

Key Thirteen

Forgiveness, Restoration and Reconciliation

Those from among you shall build the old waste places; you shall raise up the foundations of many generations; and you shall be called the Repairer of the Breach, the Restorer of Streets to Dwell In.–Isaiah 58:12.

Humankind always has need to be reconciled to the Almighty. The ministry of reconciliation deals with our sins, our faults and the alignment of our will with the will of God. Reconciliation begins first in our own lives; then it spreads out into our families, our local church, our workplace, and into our community. Being reconciled to God in a perfect way requires a realignment of our will with God's will, which requires a daily reconciling of our heart to God's Word. God wants to reach the deep-rooted things in the affections of our heart. We need the Holy Spirit's help to search our heart, so we can deal with those unclean areas in our life. If our heart is after truth and righteousness, then we will seek God for whatever help we need. Our first choice should be to respond privately to the conviction of the Holy Spirit. If this is beyond our ability, then we need to seek the help of a trusted pastor or a prayer partner.

In Galatians, chapter six, Paul tells us to help one another. This chapter speaks about helping to restore the weak. The ministry of reconciliation breathes life, strength and power into our lives, and it should always be free of condemnation. As repairers of the breach, the mercy that we have received from God gives us the meekness that we need to touch the heart of other's lives because we too are touched with the feeling of their infirmities. Because the issues of another person's life are a deep well, we are called to stand in the gap and apply the Word to their lives. The Word is their lifeline to get up out of the deep darkness of life. Prayer will help enlist the wisdom of God into their hearts.

Counselors should refrain from using logic in helping resolve the problems in another person's life. Too much counseling makes others co-dependent on man rather than God. The purpose of prayer is to reconcile their will back to the Fathers. Anything else is to pray out of ignorance and use manipulation. When we pray according to Gods will and His heart, He responds to work powerfully on our behalf. There is a line in prayer we cannot cross, and it revolves around the issue of controlling circumstances. We cannot change circumstances or people. To try to do so is to play with witchcraft. Circumstances will change when there is a change of heart within the people, and their thinking is transformed. God wants the door to their heart open, and we need to minister the Word of God into the center of their lives. They need to be encouraged to stand in their own faith, in the Lord and His Word. All trials are not the result of sin, so we must minister without condemnation. It is vital to discern the difference between sin and Satan's attacks. We must pray for the Lord to touch the heart of a person to have the right response to their calamity.

Our battle in the priestly ministry of reconciliation is not with flesh and blood it is a spiritual battle with the kingdom of darkness. In order to help deliver a weaker one out of the mouth of the wolf (Satan), the person's will needs to be bound to the Father's will. The door to rebellion in their heart needs to be shut by severing relationships with the kingdom of darkness—they must be loosed. Jesus has given us the authority to deal with demonic forces, but we must help guide a person to shut the door on Satan's influence and open the door for the works of God. This fully describes the ministry of binding and loosing. We loose them by cancelling Satan's assignment, and we bind them to the Word of God.

When you help restore a victim from condemnation, Satan will try to convince them that they are the problem. Satan needs to be restrained for their sake. Sometimes people are victims of the sins of their forefathers, which cause generational curses that need to be broken in the spiritual realm with the Word of God. Cities and nations can be set free by repenting the sins of the forefathers as Nehemiah did for the sins of Israel. A revival through the preaching of the Word of God will transform the hearts of the people in that region. Jesus commands us to love one another, as He has loved us. True love does not hold bitterness or unforgiveness against any person.

John 15:12

Unforgiveness Shows we do not Know the Love of Jesus

This is My commandment, that you love one another as I have loved you.

John 14:24

He who does not love Me does not keep My words; and the word which you hear is not Mine but the Father's who sent Me.

Matthew 6:15

Unforgiveness Prevents God from Forgiving our Sins

But if you do not forgive men their trespasses, neither will your Father forgive your trespasses.

Matthew 18:21

The Parable of the Unforgiving Servant

Then Peter came to Him and said, "Lord, how often shall my brother sin against me, and I forgive him? Up to seven times?"

Mark 11:24, 25

Unforgiveness can Block God from Answering our Prayers

Therefore I say to you, whatever things you ask when you pray, believe that you receive them, and you will have them. And whenever you stand praying, if you have anything against anyone, forgive him, that your Father in heaven may also forgive you your trespasses.

1 Peter 3:8, 9
Have Compassion

Finally, all of you be of one mind, having compassion for one another; love as brothers, be tenderhearted, be courteous; not returning evil for evil or reviling for reviling, but on the contrary blessing.

Pray for those who have offended you. Mend little rips and tears in your relationships. Take the initiative and be the one to make the first call, send the first e-mail, schedule a visit, or arrange a lunch.

Romans 12:12-15
Serve and support those who are weaker

.... rejoicing in hope, patient in tribulation, continuing steadfastly in prayer; distributing to the needs of the saints, given to hospitality. Bless those who persecute you; bless and do not curse. Rejoice with those who rejoice, and weep with those who weep.

Pray for and comfort those who are suffering. Show compassion and love to those who are grieving or hospitalized, or wounded by life.

Key Fourteen

Fortified in God's Word

Isaiah 41:15, 16
Invincibility over Enemies

Behold, I will make you into a new threshing sledge with sharp teeth; you shall thresh the mountains and beat them small, and make the hills like chaff. You shall winnow them, the wind shall carry them away, and the whirlwind shall scatter them; you shall rejoice in the Lord, and glory in the Holy One of Israel.

Over the years, some of our intercessors have encountered accidents after leaving a prayer session. There was a season with a series of broken limbs, which we attributed to be more than coincidence. We now pray for personal protection and observe communion after every prayer session at the nation's capital. We make it a practice to pray for safe travel when intercessors come and go. The Eucharist is the best way to seal yourself in the Blood of Jesus. It is also an act of rear guarding and placing the blood over the doorposts of our house and family members. We do not need to become paranoid about the enemy's plots against the redeemed, but it certainly helps to understand that we become more vulnerable when we go about conducting the business of advancing the Kingdom of God.

A spiritual victory is not a signal to celebrate. Rear-guarding is the act of arming yourself after a prayer battle. Satan showed up to tempt Christ when he completed his forty day fast in the wilderness. Even though Satan initially resists the work of God going forward, he will also show up to retaliate when you have completed your assignment for the Kingdom. Being on guard and ready will lessen or even cancel his attack. Do not lay down your sword after the battle, but sharpen it for the rear-guard. Guard against fear or unbelief, for this, will invite Satan even more. The confession of your mouth must be the Word of God that builds a hedge about you and your family. Always include your family members in your protection effort. Proclaim the Blood of Jesus when you come and go into different spiritual environments, i.e.: Shopping malls and grocery stores, business settings and public transportation. "Re-entry" is when you come out of your protected environment and enter another atmosphere where you become vulnerable. On the other hand, it can be the reverse, such as, when I go on a mission trip and fly back into Washington, D.C. my prayer partners pray for a smooth spiritual re-entry. There have been occasions when I hear Satan's threats the moment the airplane lands on the tarmac.

Our heart must be right when we pray.....

1. **Pray with a clean heart.** David declared, "If I had cherished sin in my heart, the Lord would not have listened; but God has surely listened and heard

my voice in prayer. Praise be to God, who has not rejected my prayer….." (Psalm 66:18-20). Christ Jesus seeks out those who are pure hearted. Pray for the Holy Spirit to help you become more like Jesus and walk holy before Him, all the days of your life.

2. **Pray with humility.** James said, "God resists the proud, but gives grace to the humble" (James 4:6). A submissive and obedient spirit is another precondition to successful prayer. When we approach the Creator God be humble to acknowledge His sovereignty and splendor. Our primary focus should be on pleasing the Lord.
3. **Pray with passion and fervor.** James said, "The effective, fervent prayer of a righteous man avails much" (James 5:16). We do not want to pray with vain repetition or mindless words. Be acquainted with the object of prayer, the person, the situation, or country. Only then can we see things from God's perspective.
4. **Pray with persistence.** Paul said, "Pray without ceasing" (1 Thessalonians 5:17). Persistent faith will overcome. Find out the will of God first and pray accordingly. Prayer is not getting your request answered in heaven; it is bringing God's will in your life to earth.
5. **Praying with importunity is a recurring theme in Scripture.** Importunity does not grow weary. Romans 8:26 describes how the Holy Spirit pleads and prays for the believer. It is the Holy Spirit that gives us the desire to pray consistently with urgency and boldness.
6. **Pray with faith not presumption.** Jesus told the parable of the proud Pharisee and the humble tax collector praying in the temple (Luke 18:9-14). Our authority in prayer comes from the cleanness of our hearts, the purposes and timing of God, and a pure commitment to those for whom we are praying.

Scriptures to Proclaim

When praying Scripture, personalize it to yourself or others you are praying for.

Isaiah 55:11; Jeremiah 1:12; 33:3
God's Word is sure when we declare it

So shall My word be that goes forth from My mouth; it shall not return to Me void, but it shall accomplish what I please, and it shall prosper in the thing for which I sent it."

"I am ready to perform My word.

Call to Me, and I will answer you, and show you great and mighty things, which you do not know.

Isaiah 54:17

God's Invincibility upon Your Life

No weapon formed against you shall prosper, and every tongue which rises against you in judgment You shall condemn. This is the heritage of the servants of the Lord, and their righteousness is from Me, Says the Lord.

(Also see: Zechariah 3:2; Romans 8:33-34; 2 Samuel 24:16)

Acts 20:24

Steadfastness to fulfill the call of God

But none of these things move me; nor do I count my life dear to myself, so that I may finish my race with joy, and the ministry which I received from the Lord Jesus, to testify to the gospel of the grace of God.

Romans 10:4

Christ our Righteousness

For Christ is the end of the law for righteousness to everyone who believes.

I Corinthians 15:58

Steadfastness in the Work of the Lord

Therefore, my beloved brethren, be steadfast, immovable, always abounding in the work of the Lord, knowing that your labor is not in vain in the Lord.

Philippians 4:13

Divine Strength

I can do all things through Christ who strengthens me.

Revelation 12:11

Overcomers

And they overcame him by the blood of the Lamb and by the word of their testimony, and they did not love their lives to the death.

The Psalms are powerful when read in their entirety. They are the war songs of the Prince of Peace. They give comfort and build our faith in God. By proclaiming them aloud you are prophesying the fulfillment of God's Word.

Psalm 20:6-8

God is our Strength

Now I know that the Lord saves His anointed; He will answer him from His holy heaven with the saving strength of His right hand. Some trust in chariots, and some in horses; but we will remember the name of the Lord our God. They have bowed down and fallen; but we have risen and stand upright.

Psalm 23:1, 6
God's Grace

The Lord is my shepherd; I shall not want.....Surely goodness and mercy shall follow me all the days of my life: and I will dwell in the house of the Lord for ever.

Psalm 25:14
Confidence in Prayer

The secret of the Lord is with those who fear Him, and He will show them His covenant.

Psalm 27:1
Faith Sustained by the Power of God

The Lord is my light and my salvation; whom shall I fear? The Lord is the strength of my life; of whom shall I be afraid?

Psalm 29:1
The Power of God's Voice

Give unto the Lord the glory due unto his name; worship the Lord in the beauty of holiness.

Psalm 30:1
An Exhortation to Praise God for Deliverance

I will extol You, O Lord, for You have lifted me up, and have not let my foes rejoice over me.

Psalm 31:1
Asking God for His Help

In You, O Lord, I put my trust; Let me never be ashamed; deliver me in Your righteousness.

Psalm 34:1, 22
Bless God and Trust Him

I will bless the Lord at all times: his praise shall continually be in my mouth..... The Lord redeems the soul of His servants, and none of those who trust in Him shall be condemned.

Psalm 41:11
Charitable Men Have Enemies

By this I know that You are well pleased with me, because my enemy does not triumph over me.

Psalm 91

Divine Protection

This psalm is a powerful covering of protection for you and family members when you pray it every day. The righteous are hidden in the secret place of the Most High with this Psalm. Proclaim this Psalm by reading it aloud. Read yourself and others into it by using the first-person reference. This Scripture declares that we have authority to deal with any spiritual enemies, because of Christ's victory over all demonic opposition.

Psalm 92:12

Exhortation to Praise God

The righteous shall flourish like a palm tree, he shall grow like a cedar in Lebanon.

Psalm 103:1, 2

Bless God for His Mercy

Bless the Lord, O my soul: and all that is within me, bless his holy name. Bless the Lord, O my soul and forget not all his benefits.....

Psalm 121:8

Putting Trust in God's Protection

The Lord shall preserve your going out and your coming in from this time forth, and even forevermore.

Psalm 126:6

Restoration and Spiritual Harvest

He who continually goes forth weeping, bearing seed for sowing, shall doubtless come again with rejoicing, bringing his sheaves with him.

Psalm 141:2

Clear Conscience

Let my prayer be set before You as incense, the lifting up of my hands as the evening sacrifice.

1 Timothy 6:5-10

Spiritual Destitution

.....Who suppose that godliness is a means of gain. From such withdraw yourself.....Now godliness with contentment is great gain. For we brought nothing into this world, and it is certain we can carry nothing out.

1 John 2:15, 16
Do Not Love the World

Do not love the world or the things in the world. If anyone loves the world, the love of the Father is not in him. For all that is in the world—the lust of the flesh, the lust of the eyes, and the pride of life—is not of the Father but is of the world. And the world is passing away, and the lust of it; but he who does the will of God abides forever.

1 Peter 4:1, 2
Do Not Faint or Grow Weary

Therefore, since Christ suffered for us in the flesh, arm yourselves also with the same mind, for he who has suffered in the flesh has ceased from sin, that he no longer should live the rest of his time in the flesh for the lusts of men, but for the will of God.

Arm yourself to suffer: Spiritual growth comes from suffering like Christ, who learned obedience through suffering. Spiritual growth comes when you still obey God while you are under the fire of the enemy. React in the Holy Ghost. Spiritual maturity causes you to have the mind of Christ.

Genesis 37:5-7
The Refiner's Fire is God's Will

Now Joseph had a dream, and he told it to his brothers; and they hated him even more. So he said to them, "Please hear this dream which I have dreamed: There we were, binding sheaves in the field. Then behold, my sheaf arose and also stood upright; and indeed your sheaves stood all around and bowed down to my sheaf."

Verse 28, Then Midianite traders passed by; so the brothers pulled Joseph up and lifted him out of the pit, and sold him to the Ishmaelites for twenty shekels of silver. And they took Joseph to Egypt.

God gave Joseph a dream of leadership. His Word from God took him into slavery. He had to go through the furnace, so he could be prepared to handle the power that God would place within him. Joseph was a slave for ten years without a promise. God was forging leadership into Joseph's life. Right before the promise came forth; Joseph was put into the dungeon.

Psalm 105:16-22
God's Divine Providence

Moreover He called for a famine in the land; He destroyed all the provision of bread. He sent a man before them—Joseph—who was sold as a slave. They hurt his feet with fetters, He was laid in irons. Until the time that his word came to pass, the word of the Lord tested him. The king sent and released him, the ruler of the people let him go free. He made him lord of his house, and ruler of all his possessions, to bind his princes at his pleasure, and teach his elders wisdom.

Esther 4:14-16
Understand Your Calling

And Mordecai told them to answer Esther: "Do not think in your heart that you will escape in the king's palace any more than all the other Jews. For if you remain completely silent at this time, relief and deliverance will arise for the Jews from another place, but you and your father's house will perish. Yet who knows whether you have come to the kingdom for such a time as this?

Then Esther told them to reply to Mordecai: "Go, gather all the Jews who are present in Shushan, and fast for me; neither eat nor drink for three days, night or day. My maids and I will fast likewise. And so I will go to the king, which is against the law; and if I perish, I perish!

Note: Do not forsake wherever God has planted you, or you will lose your reward. You will reap if you do not faint. The pressure before the victory is always the most intense.

1 Samuel 1:3-5
God's Vessel

So it was, year by year, when she went up to the house of the Lord, that she provoked her; therefore she wept and did not eat.

It was the LORD, who closed Hannah's womb. God was forging into Hannah's life the character to handle what God wanted to birth through her a new priesthood. Her son, Samuel, satisfied her heart's desire and brought revival to the entire nation of Israel. The harder it is, the closer you are to your victory. Obey even when it seems impossible. No one can abort God's plan for you. Only you can abort it, by losing faith. Hannah prayed with importunity until she received her answer. She gave her promised son back to the Lord.

Drawing Strength from the Names of God

He is Jehovah Roi (Raah): The Lord My Shepherd to those who hear Him.
He is Jehovah Jireh: The Lord who provides for those who acknowledge their dependence on Him.
He is Jehovah M'Kaddesh: The Lord who sanctifies those who want to live pleasing to Him.
He is Jehovah Nissi: The Lord our banner for those who choose to faithfully follow Him.
He is Jehovah Shammah: The Lord who is there for those who long to behold Him at the end of days.
He is Jehovah Sabaoth: The Lord of Hosts for those wise enough to have their battles fought by Him.

Conclusion

The Authority of the Believer

It is my sincere prayer that the teachings within these pages have offered some encouragement and depth as you pursue your visions and dreams through the power of the Holy Ghost. Hopefully, you will be stirred to serve the kingdom purposes of Christ with effectiveness and excellence by first laying a firm foundation in the Word of God. Without this foundation, we are standing on sand, which only sinks with each incoming tide. The Word of God is Logos; the thoughts of God, and Rhema is the spoken word. "Logos" and "Rhema," are two Greek words that are translated "word." God's thoughts (Logos) are put into a written form (Rhema) in the Bible. We need the foundation of the Logos in order to walk in the revelation of the Rhema Word, which provides guidance for our future and our daily living. Logos and Rhema are both equally associated with the "word" and "saying." The Holy Spirit gives revelation of what the Word means; bringing it to life within our understanding. The Bible was never meant to be a history book; it is a book of revelation when seen through the eyes of the Holy Spirit. The resurrected Christ said, "He that hath an ear, let him hear what the Spirit saith" (Revelation 2:7). Many in the Church need to be restored back to the Word of God. A recent Barna Group study reveals that we have a crisis of biblical illiteracy in the Church.

With simplicity, the *Power of the King's Scepter* unveils biblical keys for spiritual authority, which enable the believer to live with overcoming faith every day. God has chosen to make His authority visible to the world through the Church of Jesus Christ, which is manifested through the members of the Body of Christ. The key to receiving God's scepter of authority, is we must first learn how to submit to His authority.

The Bible reveals that the whole universe is under the dominion of God; therefore, we must choose to submit ourselves to His authority: "I am the Lord, that is My name; and My glory I will not give to another, nor My praise to carved images" (Isaiah 42:8). At the time of the creation, we learn that God's throne is established on His authority. His word is authority. John 1:1-3, testifies to the preexistence of Jesus Christ in the creation:

> In the beginning was the Word, and the Word was with God, and the Word was God. He was in the beginning with God. All things were made through Him, and without Him nothing was made that was made.

All things are created by the sovereign God, and His authority sustains all natural laws of the universe. All mankind will either choose to yield to God's authority or rebel against it. To obey God's authority, we must be submitted to Him with all our heart, even to recognize that God's authority works through man. Satan is not afraid of our witnessing or preaching Scripture; his greatest fear is when the believer is totally surrendered to the authority of Christ. The message of obedience to God's Will resonates throughout the Bible. God does not demand that His children deny themselves or make offerings; God's greatest desire is for his people to sacrifice their will and obey His Word. The wrong motive of self-will or desire will pollute our sacrifice. Obedience honors God, for then His Will becomes the center of our life. Obedience is how we gain God's authority. The self-life needs to die: "He must increase, but I must decrease" (John 3:30). The Apostle Paul instructed the Gentile churches about submitting to those who are in authority:

> Let every soul be subject to the governing authorities. For there is no authority except from God, and the authorities that exist are appointed by God. Therefore whoever resists the authority resists the ordinance of God, and those who resist will bring judgment on themselves (Romans 13:1-2).

God's divine will signifies His authority. No one can be submitted to God's authority if he does not pray or have a heart to know His will. Those who know His will and obey Him are walking in His authority. Those who ignore that God has a divine purpose for their lives lack the fear of the Lord: "There is no fear of God before his eyes" (Psalm 36:1). To deny divine authority is a rebellion far more serious than that of sinning against God's holiness. Sinning is more easily forgiven than rebellion:

> For rebellion is as the sin of witchcraft, and stubbornness is as iniquity and idolatry. Because you have rejected the word of the Lord, He also has rejected you from being king (1 Samuel 15:23).

The Church is here in the Earth to fulfill God's purposes for His Kingdom. As God's servants, the first commitment we make, is to come under Christ's authority.

The greats in the Bible did not choose their own role. Once they heard the call of God, they submitted to His authority and obeyed. Noah obeyed God's command to build an ark so a remnant would be spared from the judgment of mankind. It is recorded that Noah pleased God. Abram followed Noah, and was called out by God to begin the Hebrew nation. He heard the voice of a God he had never known. His obedience made him righteous before the Elohim God. His name was changed to Abraham, and he became the first member of the Hebrew nation. The secret to Abraham's success was that he had spiritual authority with God.

In the New Testament, salvation and authority go hand in hand. We are not to find work to do for God; we are sent to work by God. A servant's greatest testimony is when he can say he has been sent by God. That servant walks with all of Heaven's authority behind his mission. Our entire relationship with God is totally dependent, upon whether or not we have submitted to His authority. God's work is genuinely anointed when it comes from His authority. In Matthew chapter seven, we find our Lord admonishing those who prophesy and cast out demons and doing many mighty things in His name. Why? They went out in His name, but they went under their own authority. They had a verbal profession of lordship without obedience to the will of God:

> Not everyone who says to Me, "Lord, Lord," shall enter the kingdom of heaven, but he who does the will of My Father in heaven. Many will say to Me in that day, 'Lord, Lord, have we not prophesied in Your name, cast out demons in Your name, and done many wonders in Your name?' And then I will declare to them, "I never knew you; depart from Me, you who practice lawlessness!" (Matthew 7:21-23).

Lawlessness is sin because it is disobeying God's authority. Jesus made this clear in His assessment about false workers who produce spectacular ministry without walking in genuine, obedient discipleship. Their wrong motives led them into apostasy, even though they produced miracles using the authority of the Scriptures and the name of Jesus. Christians should be on guard and only follow those who preach a biblical gospel. Such discernment becomes clear when we are studying the Word of God, which opens our spiritual eyes. Some of today's prominent preachers insist they are evangelical even though they have abandoned the biblical gospel for a social gospel. Some even teach the mission of the Church is primarily to assist the poor and oppressed which will usher in the Kingdom of God on earth. Poverty will never be eradicated from the earth until the Millennial Reign of the King of kings. While we should help the poor and needy, the true mission of the Church is to increase the Kingdom of God by converting souls. The act of loving our neighbor, especially our poor neighbor, is an act of compassion that should never be overlooked, but, on the other hand, it should not just be a social outreach. Providing humanitarian needs and sharing the gospel go hand-in-hand. In Luke 4:4 Jesus said,

"It is written, 'Man shall not live by bread alone, but by every word of God.'" Lost people are starving for the living bread from Heaven that alone can satisfy their spiritual hunger. This present age is characterized by lawlessness. Authority in the world is progressively declining until; at the end, the son of lawlessness shall appear:

> For the mystery of lawlessness is already at work; only He who now restrains will do so until He is taken out of the way. And then the lawless one will be revealed, whom the Lord will consume with the breath of His mouth and destroy with the brightness of His coming (2 Thessalonians 2:7).

The lesson of obedience appears to be a hard message and turns many away. God's love draws us to the Cross, but remaining there for a "love feast" is parallel to the mentality of the flower children of the 1960s. Jesus spoke a hard word when He told the rich young man: "One thing you lack: Go your way, sell whatever you have and give to the poor, and you will have treasure in heaven; and come, take up the cross, and follow Me" (Mark 10:21). Living the daily walk of faith with victory is only possible when we endure with spiritual authority in our trials:

> Now the just shall live by faith; but if anyone draws back, My soul has no pleasure in him. (Hebrews 10:38).

We face authority everywhere—in the workplace, in our community, at home, and in the Church. While on the earth, the Lord Jesus submitted to His Father's authority, and also to those in authority over society. How many Christians today accept being submitted to those in authority? Obedience to authority is the first lesson a disciple must learn to avoid confusion and disorder. Since all authorities come from God, we must learn to obey them all. The true test of conversion to Christ is whether the person is willing to come under the authority of Christ's lordship. For example, Saul of Tarsus was a Pharisee, who had a great zeal to exterminate all believers of the Way; the Church of Jesus Christ. He was confronted by Christ on his way to Damascus who revealed he was not just persecuting Christians; he was going against Christ's authority. The Lord Jesus blinded Saul and knocked him off his horse, and he immediately fell to the ground and acknowledged Jesus as Lord saying, ".....Lord, what do You want me to do?" (Acts 9:6). Undoubtedly, this is considered the mightiest conversion in the New Testament, and Paul was given his new name as proof of his new identity.

Even though spiritual authority is God-ordained through the Holy Spirit, there is still a strong independent spirit within the Church, which is rebellion. Spiritual authority is only present with those who are obedient to His Word. God Himself looks upon the heart when anointing His vessels with authority. In Genesis 17:16, we see that Sarah, the wife of Abraham, was chosen as much as Abraham. Sarah's

Egyptian handmaiden Hagar ceased to submit to her authority once she was carrying Abraham's seed. Even though God made it clear that Sarah is the one anointed to be Abraham's wife, Hagar entered into rebellion because she assumed that bearing Abraham's seed automatically gave her superior spiritual authority. Likewise, salvation for the believer is deliverance from the old life and receiving the gift of eternal life, but spiritual authority comes by subjection to God's authority, which comes by obeying Scripture. Righteous actions should proceed from the heart of a new life reborn in Christ; the proof of true conversion. When we fear the Lord, we want to please Him. While obedience is a choice, those who choose to obey need the Holy Spirit's help and God's grace to walk it out. There is a difference between one calling himself a Christian, and being a true Christian living under spiritual authority. God has given us the free will to choose the wide path or the narrow gate:

> Enter by the narrow gate; for wide is the gate and broad is the way that leads to destruction, and there are many who go in by it. Because narrow is the gate and difficult is the way which leads to life, and there are few who find it (Matthew 7:13-14).

Eternity is the Great Reward for the Obedient

The Bride of Christ consists of an obedient remnant which has separated herself from the apostate Church. Jesus spoke to the disciples in Matthew, chapter twenty-four, about what it would be like in the end times. He described it as a time when man will become lukewarm towards God, and only a few will fear the LORD, and then the Son of Man will suddenly appear to snatch His Bride from the Earth. Christ explained that the condition of mankind would be like the days of Noah:

> But of that day and hour no one knows, not even the angels of heaven, but My Father only. But as the days of Noah were, so also will the coming of the Son of Man be. For as in the days before the flood, they were eating and drinking, marrying and giving in marriage, until the day that Noah entered the ark..... (Matthew 24:36-38).

In Matthew, chapter twenty-five, Jesus taught preparedness for His return. The parable of the wise and foolish virgin's compares Christ's return for His bride to a wedding procession in which those who are unprepared cannot participate:

> Then the kingdom of heaven shall be likened to ten virgins who took their lamps and went out to meet the bridegroom. Now five of them were wise, and five were foolish. Those who were foolish took their lamps and took no oil with them.....(Matthew 25:1-3).

The rapture of the Church (1 Thessalonians 4:16-13-18) is not to be confused with Christ's Second Coming; when He returns with His army to defeat Satan at the Battle of Armageddon (Revelation 19:14). At the rapture, only His own elect will see Him. At the Second Coming, every eye will see Him (Revelation 1:7). The Bride of Christ is saved from this wrath:

> Watch therefore, and pray always that you may be counted worthy to escape all these things that will come to pass, and to stand before the Son of Man (Luke 21:36).

This message is for the obedient wise virgins who are preparing their hearts for the coming of the Lord. Commit yourself to grow in your relationship with the Lord Jesus, which includes prayer, worship, and studying to understand the Bible. Keep the presence of the Holy Spirit anew in your life. This is the lifestyle of the children of light, who have salvation in Jesus. Eternity is the reward. Even so, come quickly Lord Jesus:

> But concerning the times and the seasons, brethren, you have no need that I should write to you. For you yourselves know perfectly that the day of the Lord so comes as a thief in the night. For when they say, "Peace and safety!" then sudden destruction comes upon them, as labor pains upon a pregnant woman. And they shall not escape. But you, brethren, are not in darkness, so that this Day should overtake you as a thief. You are all sons of light and sons of the day. We are not of the night nor of darkness. Therefore let us not sleep, as others do, but let us watch and be sober. For those who sleep, sleep at night, and those who get drunk are drunk at night. But let us who are of the day be sober, putting on the breastplate of faith and love, and as a helmet the hope of salvation. For God did not appoint us to wrath, but to obtain salvation through our Lord Jesus Christ, who died for us, that whether we wake or sleep, we should live together with Him (1 Thessalonians 5:1-10).

Watch Out for Apostasy!

Grace and acceptance do not mean approval–Christians should demonstrate the grace of God to accept everyone as a human being, but this does not mean they should approve their wrong actions. Love the sinner, but hate the sin! There is a severe danger in turning a blind eye to sinful social issues that are deceiving people from living according to the truth of God's Word. While Jesus commanded His disciples to love one another, God's love does not eliminate justice. The righteousness of God is His way of justifying sinners; turning them back to His righteousness.

There is a trend among millennial Christians to avoid today's culture differences; by accepting everyone has the free will to make their own choice for their lives. Jesus calls His followers to a counter-cultural faith, in which they gain the favor of heaven, but earn the hatred of the world. It seems some of today's younger generation would rather overlook a gay worship leader on the platform than stand up for what the Word of God says about immorality:

For the wrath of God is revealed from heaven against all ungodliness and unrighteousness of men, who suppress the truth in unrighteousness, because what may be known of God is manifest in them, for God has shown it to them (Romans 1:18-19).

Persevering faith stands up for the truth of the Gospel and does not compromise, and Evangelical church leaders are concerned about the emergence of what they call the false "gospel of nice," which is leading many into apostasy. Daniel Darling, vice-president of Communications for the Southern Baptist Convention's Ethics and Religious Liberty Commission comments: "Younger Christians are weary of pitched cultural battles and are longing for the 'real Jesus'–a Jesus who talks more about washing feet and feeding the poor than flashpoint issues like same-sex marriage and the sanctity of life."[1] Our perception of God will shape our entire life. The Word of God speaks positive words into our divine destiny, but we often block them with the constant negative words we think and say. We open our spirit to God's Spirit when we pray and study His Word. God has placed His glory within us, and the Holy Spirit will do everything possible to help us succeed. We must ask: "When the Son of Man comes, will He really find faith on the earth?" (Luke 18:8). Jesus also shared a parable about advancing His kingdom until He returns: "So he called ten of his servants, delivered to them ten minas, and said to them, 'Do business till I come'" (Luke 19:13). We are guardians over the Kingdom harvest, which includes being the defenders of religious liberty—the Judeo-Christian faith.

Resources & Endnotes

Book Resources:

Rees Howells Intercessor–By Norman Grubb
This book gives the testimony of a man who endeavored to hear from the Lord, and then walked out God's instructions with obedience. A beautiful guide on learning how to discern through the Holy Spirit; and a personal example of the benefits of walking in obedience.

The Coming Revival (Dr. Bill Bright)
This book explains how the power of fasting is a discipline lost in the 20th Century Church in America. This book helps equip our churches, our nation, and us for the greatest spiritual awakening since the first century!

7 Basic Steps to Successful Fasting and Prayer (Dr. Bill Bright)
Practical information on: "How to Begin Your Fast," "What to do While You Fast," and "How to End Your Fast Properly"

The Brotherhood: America's Next Great Enemy (Erick Stakelbeck)
Erick sounds the alarm against the Muslim Brotherhood, who are openly dedicated to the destruction of America. The Brotherhood and its members are now inside the U. S. Government. Erick gives names, places, and proof of the Muslim Brotherhood's penetration of the uppermost levels of our government. Many of these Muslim advisors are honored guests in the White House giving out their Muslim extremist advice. It is called "stealth Jihad."

ENDNOTES:

Part One. Keys to the Kingdom
Chapter One. The King's Scepter

1. Research: Matthew Henry's Commentary, sec. Num. 17:8-9, para. 3, Verses 8-13, http://www.biblestudytools.com/commentaries/matthew-henry-complete/numbers/17.html
2. Source: Haaretz Article: Peres suggests holy sites in J'lem be declared 'world capital', paras. 1, 2, http://www.haaretz.com/news/peres-suggests-holy-sites-in-j-lem-be-declared-world-capital-1.94963
3. Prophecy by Don Franklin, Roundtable Ministries, Lakeland, FL. http://www.propheticroundtable.org
4. Source: Vine's Complete Expository Dictionary of Old and New Testament Words, "Kingdom", http://studybible.info/vines/Kingdom
5. Source: Bible Scripture, Ruth, sec. 1, paras. 1, 3, http://biblescripture.net/Ruth.html

Chapter Two: The Sword

1. Source: Gods Word, Research, sec. Word Wealth, or para. 5, Strong's Concordance #1756 https://sermons.logos.com/submissions/63441-Gods-Word_Research#content=/submissions/63441
2. Source: sec. 2, out of His mouth went a sharp two-edged sword, para. 2; http://www.biblestudytools.com/commentaries/revelation/revelation-1/revelation-1-16.html
3. Research: Blueletter Bible, Matthew Henry's Commentary, Matthew 25:31-46. sec. I, para. 5

Chapter Three: Keys to Spiritual Authority

1. Source: The National Day of Prayer, sec. What Makes Prayer Work?, para. 2 http://www.syvcbmc.org/ourmission.html
2. Source: Pray for KC, sec. It's All About Your Relationship With Source, para. 4, Prayer=Love, Posted on January 19, 2013 by L Buchner, http://prayforkc.org/
3. Source: The Trinity Review, The Biblical Covenant of Grace by John W. Robbins and Sean Gerety, para. 6. http://www.trinityfoundation.org/journal.php?id=98#sthash.4WS3sIgI.dpuf

Part Two. Empowering Prayer with Scripture
Chapter One: The Call to Pray

1. Source: CBN.com, The Weapon of Prayer: Putting God to Work, by E. M. Bounds Intercessors Network, para. 3, http://www.cbn.com/spirituallife/prayerandcounseling/intercession/weapon_prayer_0303b.aspx
2. Book: Revelation Explained at Last! by David C. Pack, sec. Mystery Book, para. 4, http://rcg.org/books/real.html
3. Source: Excerpts from: The Prophecy Puzzle, para. 3, http://www.bibleprophecy.com/fulfilled.htm
4. Source: Decision Magazine, Light for a Darkened World, by Billy Graham, para. 1 http://ww1.billygraham.org/articlepage.asp?articleid=381
5. Source: Bible Study Tools, sec. Deuteronomy 6:1-25. Moses Exhorts Israel to Hear God and to Keep His Commandments, para. 1, http://www.biblestudytools.com/commentaries/jamieson-fausset-brown/deuteronomy/deuteronomy-6.html
6. Source: Wallbuilders, Importance of Morality and Religion in Government, sec. John Adams, para. 3, http://www.wallbuilders.com/libissuesarticles.asp?id=63
7. Source: Wikipedia, Sec. Biblical Teaching, sec. Letter to the Hebrews para. 4, Turning Away,
http://en.wikipedia.org/wiki/Apostasy_in_Christianity
8. Source: Bible Study Tools Commentary, John Gills Exposition of the Bible, para. 1,
http://www.biblestudytools.com/commentaries/gills-exposition-of-the-bible/1-corinthians-2-13.html

Chapter Three: Keys for Unlocking Powerful Prayer

1. Source: My Jewish Learning, Article: Shabbat as a Sanctuary in Time, by Rabbi Abraham Joshua Heschel, para. 3, http://www.myjewishlearning.com/practices/Ritual/Shabbat_The_Sabbath/Themes_and_Theology/Sanctuary_in_Time.shtml

Key Three: Prayer for the Nation of Israel

1. Concordant Studies, Yahweh is the Only Elohim, para. 3
http://www.concordant.org/expohtml/GodAndChrist/onegod3.html

Key Five: Racial Healing

1. Research: Native Times Article, Apology to Tribes–US apologizes to American Indians for mistreatment, paras. 10, 11, http://www.nativetimes.com/news/tribal/3651-apology-to-tribes-us-apologizes-to-american-indians-for-mistreatment
2. Research: NPR, Senate Apologizes For Slavery, article by David Wellna, para. 1, http://www.npr.org/templates/story/story.php?storyId=105620620
3. Research: The Root, Article by Terrence Samuel, pg. 1, para. 5, 6; pg. 2, para. 1, http://www.theroot.com/articles/politics/2008/06/us_senate_apologizes_for_slavery.html

4. Source: Rev. Earl Carter's book: No Apology Necessary, Just Respect; Published by Creation House.

Key Six: Inheriting the Nations for Christ

1. Pentecostal Evangel Article: Faces of Hunger Journey into the Crying Slums of Nairobi, By Hal Donaldson, paras. 13, 14, http://pe.ag.org/Articles2006/4808_Hunger.cfm

Key Nine: How to Pray for the Middle East

1. Source: CBN Article by Chuck Colson, One Way Sympathy: Christians in the Muslim World, p.11, http://www.cbn.com/spirituallife/onlinediscipleship/understandingislam/Colson_Islam_Vatican0608.aspx
2. Source: Article: The Islamic Agenda and Its Blueprint, sec. Islam is socio-political, para. 2 http://answering-islam.org/Terrorism/agenda.html
3. Research: Clarion Project article: "Exclusive: Islamist Terror Enclave Discovered in Texas," by Ryan Mauro, paras. 1, 2, http://www.clarionproject.org/analysis/exclusive-clarion-project-discovers-texas-terror-enclave
4. Source: Christian Post article, Open Doors: Growth of Christianity in Iran Explosive, by Alex Murashko, paras. 1, 2, http://www.christianpost.com/news/open-doors-growth-of-christianity-in-iran-explosive-71946/
5. Source: Commentary: Loving Our (Muslim) Neighbors by Chuck Colson, paras. 9, 10, 11) http://www.cbn.com/spirituallife/OnlineDiscipleship/UnderstandingIslam/Loving_Our_Muslim_Neighbors.aspx
6. Source: Hajj–pilgrimage to Mecca, paras. 3, 4, http://www.tidenstecken.se/koranhaj.htm
7. Source: Am Israel Chair article: Islam–Peace or Terror?, Quote from the Hadith, paras. 3, 4, http://www.amisraelchai-eretz.com/peaceorterror.htm
8. Wikepedia, Temple Mount, sec. Management and Access, para. 1, http://en.wikipedia.org/wiki/Temple_Mount
9. Source: Prophecy Update: News and Information for the End Times, sec. Why Is The Temple Mount So Important? Paras. 1, 6; http://injesus.com/messages/content/173178
10. Ibid. paras. 4, 5.
11. Research: CBN Book Review: Crucified Again: The New Islamic War on Christians, by Raymond Ibrahim, article by Gary Lane, paras. 2, 3, 4, 5; http://www.cbn.com/cbnnews/world/2013/May/Crucified-Again-The-New-Islamic-War-on-Christians/
12. Research: CBN Article, Dreams and Visions: Revival Hits Muslim N. Africa, by George Thomas, sec. Along the Mediterranean, paras. 1, 2,

http://www.cbn.com/cbnnews/world/2014/April/Revival-in-Land-Once-Hostile-to-Christ/
13. Ibid. sec. A Profound Move of God, paras. 2, 4, 6.
14. Ibid. sec. What a Difference Technology Makes, paras. 2, 4.

Conclusion:
1. Opinion by Daniel Darling, special to CNN, Millennials and the false 'gospel of nice', para. 2;
http://religion.blogs.cnn.com/2014/04/03/millennials-and-the-false-gospel-of-nice/

Author's Bio

Rev. Ruth Schofield is ordained with the Assemblies of God. In 1995, she founded the *Embassy for World Peace* in Washington, D.C., which conducts a global mission protecting and defending religious freedom and an international prayer tower. Ruth is an ambassador to the nations, having traveled to the African Continent, India and Israel. She is frequently interviewed on television and for 16 years, she hosted her own award winning national television program, *The Washington Report,* from the U.S. Capitol. The *Washington Report* has received five *Angel Awards* for Excellence in Media. Her weekly Bible teaching program, *Daily Bread*, has aired on satellite radio across the 20/70 Window countries. As a Zionist, Ruth has produced numerous television documentaries for Israel that have aired via satellite around the world. She has continued the vital mission of representing religious freedom and human rights issues to the three branches of government at the nation's capital for 30 years.

Contact Information:

Embassy for World Peace
P.O. Box 5649
Washington, D.C. 20016
Email: info@embassyforpeace.org
Website: www.embassyforworldpeace.org
Blog: washdcreport.com

CPSIA information can be obtained at www.ICGtesting.com
Printed in the USA
BVOW06s1811230315

392917BV00002B/3/P

9 781498 406871

When a nurse is drinking out of a bottle slowly we say she is nursing the bottle.

When the doctor is sick he doesn't feel like playing doctor.

The doctor of the nervous system says some people are to nervous to see him. He works with two different people. Those who are are trying to get up the nerve to do something and those who have too much nerve. He said some people get on his last nerve.

The stomach doctor says he deals with people are real gusty and those that just went to spill their guys out. He said it is important to remember to trust your gut instinct.

The lumberman went to the doctor. He was shaking like a leaf.

The trainer goes to the doctor and says he is in pain. The doctor says don't you usually say "No pain no gain?"

The nurse took the patient's temperature. She told the other nurse that is was normal. She said that is the only thing normal about him.

The carpenter went to the foot doctor for an ingrown toe nail.

The foot doctor said "We will help you move forward this year."

I am getting my eyes checked. I am going to a must see movie.

The two statements most often said when visiting the ear doctor are "I can hear you" and What,"

The doctor says you don't want to speak ill of the dead.

A cold bone doctor is chilled to the bone.

Heart doctors say the worst condition of the heart is when someone has a cheating heart.

The doctor wrote a book on the difference between a healthy and a sick relationship.

Two psychologists were competing with each other. The one said he sees more patients with problems than you do. The other said that was okay because I help more people solve problems than you do.

The bone doctor said he would like to see more people do some leg work.

If you bend over backwards to help someone you will probably throw your back out.

A back doctor said that he and his friend go way back.

We use this sanitation worker's term who people are getting sick. We say some junk is going around.

He spent so much time with Tarzan in the jungle that has developed jungle fever.

When you get a health checkup you still live with a clean bill of health, but it is still a bill.

The banker is in the hospital Someone asked how he was doing. They said there has been no change in him.

A worker at the blood bank says he is going to try and trace his blood line.

Santa's doctor is named Doctor HO. His father was called Ho Ho and his grandfather was Ho HO Ho.

When the premed student got to his anatomy class he felt confident. He told his friend that he had been studying anatomy for years.

My first summer job was working at a hospital. I told everyone how exciting it was gong to be. When asked how my first day went I said I don't want to talk about it. I didn't want anyone to know my first job was cleaning bed pans.

A book by a lung doctor is called "As I live and breathe."

The heart doctors have seen their share of heartaches.

The tow truck driver was in the hospital. The other tow truck drivers sent him a card that says "We are all pulling for you."

Advice from a heart doctor. "Don't let your heart be troubled."

He asked the pilot how did he land up in the hospital?

The electrician is in the mental hospital. Last I heard he was receiving shock treatments.

A real estate worker had been very ill for a long time. Now he was recovering. He said it is like having a new lease on life.

At the mental hospital never ask anyone if they have lost their mind.

Both doctors and road workers are known to say the main artery is clogged.

The doctor has an infectious laugh.

When the ear, nose and throat doctor starts swimming he takes a nose dive.

The eye doctor said there is no excuse for a relationship not working out when you went into it with your eyes wide open.

Business has been slow for the bone doctor. He said he could sure use a break.

When the ear, nose and throat doctor reads a book he ear marks the pages he wants to go over again.

The heart doctor says he will be there in a heart beat.

At the metal hospital they call everyone nuts. But the main nut is called the big walnut. They say he is really off the wall.

When the dentist was having trouble to get the large man to open wide he said just pretend you are out eating and you want to get that big hamburger in your mouth. It works every time.

The man had hit his head hard in a car accident. The nurse was concerned that he had a concussion. She held up her hand and asked him how many fingers he saw. He said four. She said that is close enough.

Everyone in the family work in the medical field. You could say it is in their blood.

The worse thing a foot doctor can say to a store owner is that he is never gong to set his feet in his store again. The foot doctor says I am here to service your feet.

The man says his doctor acts like he is a teacher. He keeps wanting to give me tests.

When a heart doctor introduces his wife he says she is the one who captured my heart.

I asked the girl at the mental hospital if she liked the food. She said she wasn't too crazy about it.

One mental patient said to another mental patient that he has more days off than on.

One friend appeared to be upset. Carl asked Ben what is wrong with Jim? Ben said I don't know do I look like a doctor?

You are sick but just a little bit. We say we just have a touch of the flu.

An older man had to have his knee replaced. He had over the years done so many things wrong and been down on his knees begging his wife for forgiveness that he wore his knee out.

The emergency workers held a panic session.

The guy at the mental hospital said "How would I know what is going on I am delirious.

I asked an older doctor how his health was holding up. He said everything was good but his eyesight was failing but he was still operating.

The road worker had been ill for some time and had to be hospitalized. The doctor said his vital signs are still good.

When you go to a party with lots of doctors they always want you to circulate.

Giving shots seems to scare a lot of people from getting the shots. One clinic got around that by telling people they were giving away free samples.

The foot doctor said you have no idea of the trouble you can get into with one wrong step.

When you finally go you don't end up well.

If the vet got sick he would come down with the canine flu.

There is so much competition between operating doctors. One operating doctor has a shirt that says " I am your number one operator."

A sick trucker is all stopped up and is not going anywhere.

The worst thing a blood worker can say about someone is that they are cold blooded.

There are white cells and red cells so why did I have to get stuck having fat cells?

If you keep telling people it is all in their head, they will probably end up with a headache.

He was not feeling well, but it was the day of the office party and he hated to miss it. So he brings extra tissues with him and excuses his coughs and runny nose as he makes it through the day. He went home and collapsed in bed. He called in sick the next day. The strangest thing was that five others had called in sick too.

When a druggist gives advice he likes to put it in a capsule.

The lumberman is feeling better but he is not out of the woods yet.

The sanitation worker was so sick he was just wasting away.

The oil man says he is feeling well.

The nurse says she has some fluid moments.

The psychologist was getting anywhere with the patient. He could never see where his problem was. The psychologist gave him a mirror and told him to look into it. He told him he was now looking at the problem.

The medical team was gathered together with the patient and his wife. The doctor said our team is here to help and support you. The man took off his hat and passed it around. I could sure use the financial support.

Cleaners often suffer allergies from ragweed.

Heart doctors get really upset with heart breakers.

A young guy was in the heart hospital. He was a car racer. He said this one girl really got his heart racing.

The doctor always bragged that he never made a mistake. One day he was eating lunch with his wife in the cafeteria . A nurse asked another nurse if she had ever met his wife. She said she had and she is definitely his first mistake.

The heart doctor got after his patient for taking better care of himself. The patient said you cut me to the heart. The heart doctor says he always tries to get to the heart of the problem.

This year a lot of back doctors are making a comeback.

I told the dentist he should have been a builder when he said he wanted to build a bridge.

When the pirates took medicine it had a skull bone on the bottle.

The bone doctor said that was sure a lame question.

After the heart transplant the man just isn't sure what he wants to do. He has had a change of heart about many things.

You really want to pass the tests the doctor gives you.

It is difficult being a throat doctor and having people stick out their tongues at you all day.

The back doctor said he is not backing down for anyone.

The older man went to the doctor. In the doctor's office he noticed a file with his name on it. He had had some tests down to see what was wrong with him. When the doctor came in he asked him if he had found out what was wrong with him. So far the doctor all I have found out is that you are rude and grumpy.

The man had been encouraged to go to health clinic to learn how to live more heathy. Their motto was "We will have you live a healthy lifestyle and stay away for sickness." His wife went with him. They waited for a half an hour to meet with a counselor. Finally he went up to the desk. He told the secretary they had an anointed to see Jim who was to advise them about their health issues. The secretary said "Oh he called in sick about half an hour ago."

The former nurse now works at a grocery store. Before she starts work she likes to get the pulse of the store.

Asked how some patients were doing at the hospital.
I haven't seen any change in the banker.
The doctor asked the nurse if the artist had shown any color.
The doctor asked how the singer was doing. She isn't back to singing but a hear her humming awhile ago.
The doctor told the railroad man that he would soon be back on track.
The one nurse said to the other nurse. When I take care of the fireman my temperature sure goes up.
The highway man's vital signs are looking good. When he gets better nothing is going to stop him.

The bone doctor said his reaction was probably just a knee jerk reaction.

A bone doctor inviting someone to lunch says you can break bread with me.

Entertainment

The movie "The Waiting Game" is another movie about parents who have to wait for their children in activities that take place after school or on weekends. We have all been there so it is easy to identify with this movie.

The singing group "The Animals" all work at the zoo.

A dishwasher wrote the song "A Loving Spoonful."

The music teacher said if we are going to get along we need to learn to sing together.

The music group in high school was called "The Bad Boys." When they needed a drummer they asked Ken an excellent drummer if he wanted to play with the band. His mother said that Ken is a good boy and she won't let him play with the bad boys.

Who said "I am dying up here?" Many a comedian when no one is laughing at his jokes.

A music teacher told a student that she needs to be more in tune with what is going on.

The move "Grumpy old Men" is about older men who haven't had their coffee in the morning.

People say they can't sing. We know that is not true because most people sing in the shower.

The song "Walk on Bye" he is singing to all the girls he is not interested in to walk on bye.

The choir director said when he was through with them, they would be singing a different tune.

I asked the music teacher how she was doing. She said she was feeling kind of low key.

Children sing the song "I don't want to do it. I don't want to do it."
Parent sing the refrain "Just do it. Just do it."

I don't understand the movie "No Way Out." They just need to read the sings that say "This way out." There has to be exit or the movie wouldn't have an exit line.

They did the movie "Stand by Me." Now many years later the cast has gotten older the new movie is titled "Sit by Me."

The movie by a computer nerd is called "The Hard Drive."

The clockmaker says that years ago he was on the game show "Beat the Clock."

The movie "The Cutting Edge" is another movie about sewing.

The movie "License to Kill" is about deer hunting season.

They are remaking the movie "Sleepers." They are looking for some real lazy guys to play the parts.

The music teacher thought she had her boyfriend all figured out than he changed his tune.

The French horn player asked the band instructor something. He answered "Your darn tooting."

When rehearsing a play or a music number they always say let's take it from the top never the bottom.

The movie "Risky Business" has to be about a loan office.

The first soap opera stated at a laundry.
The main star got on her soap box at the beginning.
Than the drama began to unfold.
The hero was hot under the collar.
His wife said they were washed up.
He said we don't have any problems that can't be ironed out.
She said it is time for you to press on.
At this point her friends hung her out to dry.
She had caught her best friend hanging out with her husband.
He said we should stay together because we have been through so many cycles together.
Things were spinning out of control.
And to think this was just a dry run.

They are looking for some pests to play parts in the new bug movie.

Stupid movie name about five bank robbers. It is called "Takers." Well they couldn't be called givers now could they?

I saw the math movie "The Great Divide." It lasted so long because they used long division.

The movie "The Blood Bank" got an R rated. There was just too much blood for a G rating.

The movie "The Whisper" is about someone who has been going to too many games and has been doing too much yelling, so now he has to whisper.

The movie "The Hard Way" is about young people who don't listen to their parents so they have to learn the hard way.

The new movie "Let Their Be Blood" is about working in a blood bank.

An actor looking at the script says "I can't act on that."

The music teacher said she got it for a song.

The duet didn't go well. It sounded more like a duel.

The movie "Getting Lost" is told by five ladies who describe what happened when their husbands got lost. Now they have a squeal called "Lost in Space." It seems that the husbands are now lost in space.

I saw a movie about a bum but it turned out to be a bummer.

Songs by the demolition boys "Breaking up is hard to do." and "When you left me I fell to pieces."

The new mover song is "It's time for me to move on."

In the movie about a sky diver it is quite exciting. The one guy is always trying to get the jump on another guy.

The new movie by some electricians will leave you in for some shocks.

The musician was sick. They said he didn't sound good at a all.

Two music groups at the concert
The first group was young and immature. They were called the thumb suckers. They came out sucking their thumbs. They dedicated their first song to all the theme suckers out there. The next song they stuck out their thumbs and sang "Thumb a ride with us." Than they asked who was doing good and give us a thumbs up. The next group was from the pest control people. The group was called the "Swat Boys." They came out carrying big fly swatters. Their first song was "Where are you going to run to bug." They than sang "What you see a bug who do you call? You call the swat boys." They than asked if

someone was being pest around them. Now everyone was given small fly swatters. Get those swatters out and swat that pest. Everyone was swatting someone. It was a swatting good time.

The boss says he likes to go to action movies. It is because he doesn't see a lot of action in his work place.

The new song by the prison boys is "Born to be Free."

Hollywood tends to say they are for clean air, yet they pollute the air with their language everyday.

Often we say to people that we find them entertaining.

The dancing instructor told the man that he had never seen anyone dance like him. He later told his friend that he was that bad of a dancer.

The movie was about a man who had been in an accident and couldn't remember anything. The little boy said that sounds like grandpa.

When the choir agrees with the pastor there is a chorus of amens.

In looking back does anyone really remember what started all those Star wars?

The favorite movie in the apple growing country is "The Apple Dumpling Gang."

They are rehearsing a play. The one actor came on the stage and tripped over a chair. The director okay lets do this scene again. The actor says "I don't know if I can trip over a chair again."

Some actors are so vain. They think we don't see enough of them so they play a twin in the movie. Like we need to see twice as much of them.

In a movie when the movie star smiles those wide smiles, my husband the dentist says he should thank a dentist for that smile.

What a dumb movie "The Attack of the Killer Donuts." It is put out by some health conscious people who say if you eat too many jelly donuts they could kill you. During the movie they sell jelly donuts at the concession stand just to see how many are willing to tempt fate.

The actor was so bad that it was out of character for him to play a good guy.

The new song sang at many companies is "There is a whole lot of Nothing going on."

The song sang by selfish people is called "It's All About Me."

The new song of the postal workers is "Send Me."

They redid the movie "Grease." It all takes place in a garage where everyone gets really dirty.

The song of the hand doctors is "I Want to Hold Your Hand."

It turned out to be a low budget film. Earlier someone had told the director not to make such a big production out of it.

A little known fact is that the backstreet boys got their start in an alley.

It can be difficult being married to a rock star when he is an idol to his fans. He wants his wife and kids to worship him.

The music teacher was happy that he had harmony at home.

A scary movie is out for college students. It is called "The Student Who Knew too Little."

Movie out called "Stuck on You"
Famous lines
Stick with me and you will be okay.

I think we should just stick together.
Are you sticking around?
Don't be stuck up.
I promise to stick up for you.
There are lots of sticky situations

A move is out written by a vegetarian. It is about a meat lover who refuses to eat his vegetables.

They remade the movie "Twelve Angry Men." Now it is called "Eleven Angry Men. It was supposed to be twelve, but the one was only a little upset.

The movie "The Minus Man" is about a man missing so many numbers. He is never going to reach a O. He doesn't even have a plus side.

The ballet dancer was hoping to star in Swan Lake. She ended up starring in the "Ugly Duckling."

This battery was named for the Bruce Willis movies. It is the die hard battery.

Do you ever think that the reason teenagers have their music so loud is that they don't want to hear the words of the music?

I asked the electrician how the concert was. He said it was electrifying.

He wanted to play the part of the fool in a Shakespearean play. The director said you can't because I am not allowed to typecast.

The drama teacher always wants applause for everything she does.

The actor was so bad that he was asked to take his act somewhere else.

I know what the movie "Personal Shopper" is about. It has to be about buying underwear because nothing could be more personal than that.

At the amateur theater they were having a tryout. The one guy was really good. One of those trying out said he can't get the part because he is no amateur.

The singer at the belt shop can really belt out a tune.

Women walking sing this song "I am walking and I am talking."

New fireman song "Keep the home fires burning."

I like the line given the invisible man in the movie when he is out with a beautiful lady and he says "I can't be seen with you." He was afraid when he was going to be paid they would sign the check invisible ink. Frankly I couldn't see him in either one of his movies. The main character commits a perfect crime. Nobody saw him do it and no one can identify him.

The movie "In Hot pursuit" is about two girls chasing two guys around the country.

We know the music group by the Mammas and Papas must all have children.

The movie "The last Man standing" is about a man that was always standing over people's shoulders. Finally at the end someone says "Will someone please get that man a chair."

Those vegetable movies all seem to star Mr. Bean.

The movie "A Star is Born" is another movie put out by some astronomers.

The movie "Draw" is about two sketch artists.

The movie "Night Crawlers" only a fisherman can appreciate it.
Imagine a movie about worms.

They redid the song "Dead Skunk in the Middle of the Road." Now when they sing they say "What are you going to do?" You hold your nose and go phew.

Song of the astronauts is Goodbye World Goodbye."

The director says we need to leave out some of the blood in the scenes we have run out of ketchup.

The most famous line of the carpenter who was in a space movie. "Beam me up Scotty."

The theme song at the convention for little people is "It's a Small World."

Family

The hairdresser told her son that he needed to brush up on his homework.

My dad was a wine grower. He never wanted me to be one. When I was little he often told me to quit my winning.

Parents were not surprised when their son worked with air-conditioning. Even as a child he liked to hang around the cool guys.

Working with the royal family can be a royal pain.

The policeman called a mother and told her that her son and three other teenagers had been in a car accident. He cautioned her not to get too excited. There wasn't much damage to the car and they mostly suffered some cuts and bruises. But he wondered if her son had hit his head and suffered a concussion. He kind of talks nonsense, and we can't understand him. The mother says "Oh thank goodness he is all right. That is how he always talks."

Often her son's friend would be eating at their house. One day will taking a second helping he said to the boy's mom "Boy this food is rally good. Did you have it catered?"

My nephew is no longer a 90 pound weakling. He is now a 160 pound weakling.

I wanted a horse but can't have one. Now mom says dad's horse. What's up with that?

A travel agent says it is hard to keep the family together when they all go in different directions.

The baker tells his children not to get mixed up with the wrong crowd.

The daughter of a seamstress says she wants to pattern her life after her mother.

The first thing the electrician says to his children when he gets them up is "Rise and shine."

After a couple had their eyes checked they can see through the situation clearly.

To us children she was called mother, but to those who had to suffer through her English classes she was called many other names.

We all know how important the last words of a loved one are to the family. When the crusty old man died the family asked the nurse who last saw him if he had any last words. His last words to her were "Get out of here."

The two twin sisters always got after each other. One told the other she would give longer if she would only eat healthier. So how old was she when she died? She was ninety. But who knows she might have made it to 100 if she had only eaten better.

The mother's son was quite a handful for her. He didn't mind very well and was quite often getting into trouble. The grandmother called everyday to check on how things were going. One day when she called she heard the mother say "Good boy you have been a good boy." Relived the grandmother thought that at last her grandson was having good day. The grandmother asked if she was talking about Timmy. The mother said no she was talking to the dog.

My dad says try and try again and if that doesn't work ask mom.

When your teenage son reeks of cologne it probably means he needs to take a shower more often.

A trucker said his mother was always ready to go the extra mile for him.

I learned from my mother's knees. I didn't appreciate those spanking back than either.

My mother always said I was going to be going far away. She was so right. I became an astronaut.

The law man said he learned about law from his mother. She would lay down the law and tell me what would happen to me if I didn't obey the law.

Hop a along Cassidy's mother would tell him to get busy and hop along.

In cave days the children when they first learned to walk walked on stones. These stones were called stepping stones.

My mother always wanted me to come closer. That was so she could grab my ear to get my attention.

I told my son not to get so squirrelly and quit playing with those nuts in our neighborhood.

When a sister's clothes are all dirty and need to be washed and she is getting ready to go out it is time to visit her sister's closet.

College son says to dad "I am sorry I don't have any money to buy you anything for father's day. But if you want to give me ten dollars I can get you something, or if you want an more expensive gift give me twenty or more."

The parents looking at the grades of their college age son say you need a course of action.

The brother-in-law never does anything halfway. He is completely nuts.

A small boy points to a man with a large nose. He says Mom that man must have lied a lot.

A electrician is happy when his son finally sees the light.

Many a mother says she is out of breath after chasing after her children all day.

I was selling my joke books. A father of a ten year old said he wasn't sure his son would understand the joke book. He is like his Mother a little slow.

A banker worried that his son was worthless.

A hunter said his son had a clear shot at reaching his goal. He just wished that he would have aimed higher.

If we had only asked our children earlier about school and listened to them, we would know there was a problem with the schools. We asked them for years what they learned at school and they would answer "Nothing."

The boy asked his lawyer mom how things went in court. She said she lost her case. Well you can't win them all. No she set her case down and later couldn't find it anywhere.

An angry lady tells her mother to stay out of her affairs. The mother said she had never involved herself in her daughter's love life.

The runner often encourages his children to run around

It can be difficult having weatherman for a father.
When I am down and not in a good mood my father asks where is his Sunshine today.
When I am crabby he says boy are we in for a storm today.
When I have a sharp tongue, he tells people to watch out for the lighting coming out of my mouth. You don't want to get hit by lighting.
When I am not thinking clearly he says someone is sure in a fog today.
When I have a problem he says don't worry thing will clear up and the grey skies will go away.
When I am bragging he says it sure is windy today.

The favorite game of children in the old West was hangman.

The junkyard's mother said he was destined to collect junk. When he was growing up he was always bringing home junk and I would tell him to get rid of it. Unfortunately I said the same thing about his first wife.

My husband's brother is a bum. Unfortunately he is the inspiration for our sixteen year old.

The older sister tells her younger brother that he can be so irritating sometimes. See he says to his Mother "I am doing better she usually says I am irritating all the time."

A girl's parents were visiting and she was showing them her apartment. She had a roommate that worked nights and slept during the day. She knocked on her door and asked if she was decent. She yelled back "I am most of the time."

His daughter as a part of a musical program was going to singing her first solo. Unfortunately the father had a commitment at work and couldn't go to hear her. Later he asked how it went. She thought she did okay, but three different people gave her advice about what to do about her sore throat.

Granddaughter told grandpa that when he sings it sure is a joyful noise.

The older sister was talking about a boy that she thought was such a square. Her younger sister said you mean there are four sides to him.

Acting your age can be confusing for a child. He is twelve but thinks he should have the privileges of a twenty year old, and often acts like a six year old.

It can by difficult for the children when their mother is a judge. They do something wrong and appeal to her for mercy and instead get her judgment.

The PTA mothers were watching their children on a educational tv show set up at the school When the camera was on her son he was picking his nose. Another mom asked her "Now which one is your son?"

Grandpa had his teeth pulled. When he talked he would say well gum it all anyway.

A friend with her to church. When the choir sang her friend remarked with their robes on how the choir members all looked the same. The third one in the back robe I thought for sure with a woman, but than I noticed the mustache and knew it was a man. Later she texted her mother. "You need to shave your upper lip."

In Africa when children are running around they say that sound like a herd of elephants.

My dad said that I don't know the value of a dollar. I said I sure do that's why I always ask for ten dollars.

The carpenter's son said he wasn't built to do such heavy lifting.

Two brothers hated baseball from two different teams. They didn't get along. What can you expect when they are in two different leagues.

I wanted to be a wrestler when I was growing up. But every time I would practice and start a fight either my parents or another adult would break it up.

The mother asked the little boy how he got oil on his face. His dad works in a garage. When he was crying he gave him a rag to wipe away his tears. The rag was covered in oil.
His father is a cleaner. When he tells his dad a story he is always afraid that he is going to mess it up.

Dad had gone with a friend to play golf. Someone called for dad. His young daughter answered the phone and said he is gone. He has a play date.

A little by says he is not going over to Joey's house anymore. His mother said his dad is a monster.

A seamstress is telling stories about the family from the past to the present . She says they are the fabric that makes up the family.

Uncle Mike has been in prison for awhile but is now out. Dad thinks he will do okay. At least he is thinking straight.

The security man says that kids that aren't alert alarm their parents.

Widowed father remarried a lady thirty years younger. In a few years he died. The oldest son was sure he would be well taken care of because he was the manager of his dad's business and had helped build the business up. The second son was sure dad would leave something good for him in the will because he was dad's favorite. He wold stop by and visit him and take him out to lunch. The third son was a playboy. He and his dad never got along. He was good with the ladies. He was sure he could get the time and attention of the attractive widow.

My postman father always expected me to be letter perfect.

A disappointed farmer says he hasn't seen much growth in his kids.

Grandma and grandpa went to the Christmas concert with their family. Afterwards they went out to eat. Grandpa said he didn't know when he had enjoyed a concert more. Grandma said "You don't know what you are talking about. You slept through the first half."

A fruit growers child can get kind of saucy.

It can be difficult having a wrester for a father. When you got in trouble you were in for a smackdown.
The sail boat grandpa worried that he and his son were sailing apart.

Dad tells his daughter if you want more money you are out of luck because I am broke. She says "Please dad I don't want your money. I just want to borrow your credit card."

The older sister is home from college. She tells her mom that every time her younger sister is with Tim a family friend she is always bossing him around. Her mother said don't worry about it she is just getting ready for marriage.

The oil man's son plays the drums in the band.

The daughter asks dad why are they going to the mall to see Santa? Doesn't he still come to our house? "yes" the dad said "But I can't have the reindeer and sleigh on the roof, and if Santa falls off I just don't have roof insurance that will cover it all."

It can be difficult when both parents are professionals. They always say about their children that they were very unprofessional in their conduct.

The grandparents went on a senior trip with other seniors. When they got back the grandson asked grandpa what he saw the most of. He said bathrooms.

A child was called into the office for pushing another child. He said "What's the big deal? My dad said lots of people need a push."

Grandpa says he is only one yawn away from going to bed.

His two sons were slackers who wasted their time and money on gambling. The father was so disappointed in his boys, and they never had time for him. Finally as he got old he got cancer and knew he didn't have much longer to live. He told his boys what he wanted for his funeral. He had it all written out and told them to try and get one things right. After Dad died they said let's do what we want to do. They had a cheap casket and as cheap a funeral as they could have. Later they met with the lawyer for the reading of the will. The lawyer showed the pictures taken from the funeral. The will said that if my sons don't do what I said they should do for my funeral they get nothing.

His family was so small when they were looking it up they couldn't find a tree only a shrub.

It was a confusing time growing up. When the family would go somewhere his parents always told him not to get lost. His older brothers and sister always told him to get lost.

The teenage girl meant her mother at the door when her mother came home from work. You know that vase that has been passed on from generation to generation, well this generation just dropped it.

The parents had two daughters. The mother was beautiful and stayed that way even when she aged. The father was nice but never good looking. Some might even say he was homely. People and relatives would look at their beautiful mother and than they would look at her and say "You look so much like your father."

The thief said he had a good mother. Before he would he would go out at night she would say "Now don't get caught."

The kids go to the carnival with grandpa. There is one of the fastest and highest roller coster ride. Other rides are called death defying. There are many scary rides. When they got home the were busy telling their mother about the scary rides. She asked what was the scariest ride. Oh they said that was riding with grandpa. He is a terrible driver.

The trail guy's son was unhappy with his father. He said he wants me to follow in the path he has planned for me.

Four adolescent brothers were together. The youngest said life isn't fair. He said to Lee the oldest you have success with everything you do. You are good in school and are winner at sports. Tim as the second brother you are fun to be with. Everyone wants to hang around with you. Kevin I know you're not so smart but it looks like you got all the looks in the family. Girls want too be seen with you just because you are so good looking. So where does that leave me? What can I be best at? They said we will give you some of our chores and jobs and you can be known as the hard working brother.

Growing up he had its of problems. His mother told him that one day he would rise above the problems. " Did he?" "Yes later he became an airline pilot."

The older brother asked the younger brother if his softball team won. He said we must have because mom says we are all winners.

The forest ranger says he has deep roots on his mother's side.

When the magician explains how to do something to his children he ends up saying the trick is.

The electrician said his younger brother didn't know about all the problems his parents were having because they kept him in the dark.

The postal worker said the first things he teaches his children is how to address someone.

I couldn't believe I could do something so dumb. I felt like slapping myself. But than my younger brother came in the room so I slapped him instead. You know I did feel better.

Mother yelling for the third time at her son to get up. He says "I wish you wouldn't get so uppity with me."

The cowboy's sons were acting a little wild. He was told to reign them in.

A security man says when his daughter's boyfriend comes over, he is on full alert and all his alarms go off.

When a bone doctor tells his kids to get up he calls them lazy bones.

My Aunt couldn't read minds, but she could read faces.

It was not always a happy life for Tarzan. He said me Tarzan, you Jane but I don't know who boy is.

The railroad engineer is so proud that his son wants to work on the railroad too. He wants to follow in his tracks.

When all is said and done Aunt Julia comes in and says and does it all over again.

A plumber tells his kids before they go to bed to be sure and flush the toilet.

The photographer says he enjoys seeing the developing stages that his children go through.

In hog country the children were taught the value of money. All the children are given a piggy bank at an early stage.

Eat the dinner table the wife comments to the husband on how big the dog is getting. She doesn't understand because she just puts out so much food a day. The husband smiles. He knows the children are not fond of their mother's cooking and continue to feed the dog scrapes under the table.

There was a robbery at the malt shop. I was concerned because my daughter works there. I called her right away to see how she was doing. She said she was still shaking.

When the lady died they said she was the glue that held the family together. With her gone there was concern that the family would come unglued.

The man was a real brain. When he became a father he called his child, his brain child.
The masseur said he hopes that some of the good things he does will rub off on his kids.

The younger brother answers the phone. It's for his older sister. He yells it's Jim and he wants to talk to you. She tells back "Tell him I am not home.? He says "Jim she says she is not home."

The son of a waterman isn't sure what he should do. His dad told him to just go with the flow.

When the mother gets the boy up early for school. He tells her she needs to let him sleep long enough if he going to have any dreams to follow.

A younger brother showed his older brother a mark he had made in the wall. He said "See I am already making my mark in life."

The tow truck driver's son was working on his homework. He said "Dad I am stuck can you help me out?"

A sister going to a party invites her younger sister go go along.
Dad thinks it is nice that she is taking her sister. Mom says she is doing that so she won't be the dumbest one there.

He never had a chance to be an actor. Even as a child his parents didn't like the way he acted.

The electrician said it feels like he and his dad are light years apart.

The mother told her daughter she was going to find her roots. When dad asked where mom had gone to she said to the hair salon.

The caller said I would like to talk to the adult in the family. Girl "I will get my older sister."

The Thanksgiving dinner was at Aunt Jacky's. It was there because it was her turn even though she is a terrible cook. At the table everyone went around and said something they were thankful for. Little Timmy said he was thankful they only needed to eat her once this year.

It is difficult to be a parent and watch our child make a huge mistake. You feel like you need to try and not just be an innocent bystander who is watching a disaster happening.

The carpenter's son admitted that he really screwed up.

My Aunt was a psychic who could predict everything and know the future. I tried to ask her to predict what would happen in the next horse race and she said she had no idea.

Grandson called grandpa and asked him what he was doing. He said he wasn't doing anything. He couldn't find the "to do list" that grandma left for him when she had gone shopping.

The weatherman says when you have teenagers the often just breeze in and out of the house.

The elderly father's wife died. He had three children. Two lived in the same city as he did while the third lived in New York. Every night because he was lonesome he would show up at one of his kid's house. He was very opinionated about what he liked and what he didn't like. He always needed attention and would always show up at mealtime. For the first months they were okay with things, but after that the kids needed a break from dad. They knew he wouldn't go on a trip by himself, and they didn't feel like they could afford to send him on an expensive trip. Finally they found a cheap ticket to New York and sent him there to stay a month with the third child.

A guy was asked how he got to be a trucker. His dad told him that it is either my way or the highway.

The man from the water company couldn't be happier that for years his son has been the water boy for the football teams.

A boy yelled stupid at a younger boy in a yard. The boy yelled back that his name wasn't stupid. He said you must to talk to my older brother.

She works all day at a car park. When her children misbehave says tell them to park their butt over there.

A lawyer is proud that his family is a law abiding family.

Many a busy mother says she could be in a circus because she knows how to juggle things.

We were visiting relatives. They said their daughter worked at windows and we would see her that night. Sure enough when we went to a burger king she was working at the window.

The family we are told to keep up with was the Jones.

I got after my four year old for drawing on the wall. My wife said to leave him alone. He is just showing his creativity.

The carpenter got into trouble for giving his naughty child a pounding.

Growing up I was always looking up to my older brothers because they were always knocking me down.

Mother preparing for a family picnic. They are gong to a park about an hour away. She packs two different sandwiches to please everyone. She makes sure the drinks are cold. She remembers the mosquito lotion and the suntan lotion. She takes a freebie long for the kids and dog to play with. She even remembers to take a baseball bat so they can play baseball. She has everything covered. Later her mother asked how the picnic went. There was pouring rain so they ended up eating in the car.

A lawyer was getting ready for work. He yells at his wife that he can't find his case and asks if she has seen it. The son says to his mother "Dad hasn't even made it to court and he has already lost his case."

When the security man's children disobey they are placed in lockdown.

My dad is like a rocking chair. He goes back and forth on things.

A skydiver encourages his child to get a jump start on his day.

A mother can be compared to the life of a chicken,
When young you are called a chick.
Mother you are called a mother hen.
Worry about your children when they are teenagers. You are called a brooding hen.
Finally you get old you are called an old biddy.

A lot of middle age people are visiting the casinos to see where their parents spent their inheritance.

The words a cleaning lady tells her children
Don't make a mess.
Be sure and clean up for yourself.
Did you wash up?

A celebrity was in town. All the young people wanted to get his autograph The banker's son played it smart. He brought a check for him to autograph.

We use this bathroom term for a small boy. We call him a little squirt.

The twelve year old boy told his friend that he is maturing. Usually his boy says he acts like a four year old, but just the other day she said I act like a six year old.

He said his parent wonder if he is ever going to get smarter at school. He told his parents that just the other day the teacher told me I have a smart mouth.

When guys want their hair to look like a mop you can tell their mom is a cleaner.

The husband had always been mean. He was mean to his wife and his three children. When they were grown the children were happy to get away from him, but the problem was they always needed money or something from him that he could easily provide. He told them no. He said they had to earn everything on their own and as long as he was alive they were not getting anything. The wife would leave him, but she was afraid she would end up getting nothing. As he got older he developed some heart problems. She started to feed him fatty foods that were not good for the heart. The children saw him once in awhile afraid they would end up getting nothing out of his will if they didn't. Finally at 82 he had a massive heart attack and the children were called home. Later they were in a waiting room, waiting on the heart doctor to tell him the news. The doctor came in with a big smile on his face. He said we were able to fix the heart with a stint and he might even live for another ten years. So much for the happy news they had been waiting for.

The librarian told her child not to get buried in a book.

The man who worked at the water company said when his son cried it was like turning on the waterfalls.

The key maker's son is taught to lock in his answers.

It was Halloween night. Mother asked Timmy where he and his friends were going. He said they were going to Tom's house. He said his sister is a real witch, and she wouldn't be with her boyfriend if she hadn't cast a spell on him.

After church the little girl commenting on her dad who is a pilot. He must help a lot of people. At church people say help comes from above.

At a camping trip the girl says a nice warm feeling came over me. Her brother said your standing by the fire.

The two brother would go out to play. The one always came home with much more dirt on him than the other boy. The brother said he likes to play dirty.

It was going to be a difficult Christmas for the seven year old boy. He asked his teacher if they were going to write to Santa this year. She said due to global warming Santa has left the North Pole and hasn't left a forwarding address. He told his dad they should call him. His dad said he has an unlisted phone number.

The couple was divorced. It was the weekend they were going to say with dad. The little boy told mom that his dad really tells some good stories. Mom said she knows she has probably heard most of them.

The parents have the job of keeping their children in line.

When a mother divides things equally in three parts for her three children they always claim the other one got the bigger piece.

The skinny boy had three sisters. The sister and their friends are always teasing him about his underwear because he had trouble keeping his pants up. One day he told his mother he took care of the problem. He said he wasn't wearing any underwear.

The children were not listening to the teacher. The teacher asked them what do you do when your mother is talking to you? One boy put his hands over his ears.

The photographer's children did not turn out well. They had been overexposed to too many things.

Marriage

A lady left her reporter husband for not reporting in.

It is said that the lady vet keeps her husband on a short lease.

A young couple had just been married a few years. Because she cooked more and ate out with her friends she had put on a little weight. He was still quite thin and he through he was in good shape. He decided to run in a marathon. He was out running every day. One day he said he was going to run in the park. She said it was a beautiful day and she wold take her book and go along. He was running while she read her book on a park bench. The third time he waved at her as he ran bye her. He often heard runners behind him but didn't pay much attention to them. One runner came up to him and he looked over and to his surprise it was his wife. She said she was glad she had caught up with him. He thought you know maybe I am not quite ready to run in a marathon.

The husband complains to his too eager wife that he wished she wouldn't make the bed when he was still in it.

Wife tells jokes on the light side. Now she looks at her overnight husband and says now for some jokes on the heavy side.

She was so sweet. They said she wouldn't hurt a fly. She got married. On their honeymoon they stayed in a cabin in the mountains. When someone asked her how it was, she said everything was find until I got up one morning and caught him with a rolled up newspaper swatting flies.

A lady said her husband has invested thousand of dollars in the gambling casino without getting anything back.

A woman who was in counseling had to many problems. The counselor told her that she needed to find the source of all her problems. She thought for a moment and said okay. I will bring my husband along next time.

A crabby husband was buying an ice cream cone for his wife. The manager told the wife that he doesn't like the way her husbands treats her.

A retired man told another retired man that his wife wants him to go away for a few days, so she can miss me.

Someone asked a clumsy person how he met his wife. I just bumped into her.

Your house is a mess. It is a week before Christmas you have gifts yet to buy. You have baking to do and gifts to wrap. Your husband is on the phone talking to his fussy and critical mother. When he gets off the phone he says "Guess what mother is flying in tomorrow to stay a week." Now you have a desperate housewife.

The forest ranger was visiting with someone at the picnic area in the national forest. He pointed to an old man and said that last year he lost his wife. "Oh how did you die?" She didn't die he lost her in the woods.

It was not easy getting married to someone with bad allergies. At the the wedding instead of saying "I do" he said "ac choo." He sneezed all over her wedding dress.

The only size that matters for most women when getting married is that the husband has a sizable income.

A lady shopping with her husband had a mask on. When I asked her why she said her husband had not been taking as many showers as he needed to.

Many a wife has said her husband is nobody's fool. He is my fool.

A man is wearing a shirt with the S for superman. I asked if he felt like a super hero. He said no but as long as my wife buys the shirt and sees me as a superhero to her, that's all that matters.
The boss tells the secretary to call the manager into his office. Something very important has come up. She needs to hold all calls and don't let anyone into my office. Twenty minutes into the meeting the secretary interrupt him to say his wife is on line there and is quite upset. She doesn't know why he isn't answering his cell phone and she needs to talk to him. He tells the manager that he has to take the call. He doesn't want a second crisis.

The couple went on a trip laying to stay free in her husband's friend's cabin. When they arrived at the cabin and saw how dirty and dusty it was, there knew it had to be cleaned before they could stay here. It was than that she found out there was no running water. The husband said that fortunately there was a well down the hill where she could get water. He found her a pail and gave it to her. "You know I would love to help but you know I can't with my bad back." So hours later with at least three tips to well hauling water up the hill and cleaning and more cleaning. Her husband's role was to point out the areas that she missed where she needed to clean better. It now near night and they would need to build a fire, but there was no firewood. Fortunately the husband knew where they kept the firewood and he handed her an axe. He took book along to read while she chopped the wood. Finally he said "Couldn't you be quieter?' It was at this point that she hit him with the axe. Now do you think she was justified?

Many wives have said it isn't so bad that their husbands, don't know directions, but that they don't take directions.

The judge may be the law in court, but at home his wife last down the law for him.

The deer hunter fawns over his new wife.

The banker's wife left him. All he could talk was dollars and cents.

My wife would 't divorce me. She said she was staying in our marriage so I would suffer more.

An electrician getting back with his wife we can say he is reconnecting.

The customer asks the bartender to give it to him straight. "Is my marriage really on the rocks?"

I don't know who is losing more hair, my husband or the cat.

When two stars get married they have to share the spot light.

Someone came to see the pilot. His wife said "You just missed him. He just flew off."

When a trucker wife starts to bring up his past mistakes he says "Let's not go down that road again."

It is not easy to be married to a lady judge. You feel like you always have to defend her honor.

A couple was having a disagreement. The husband said he didn't think they should fight over it. The wife agreed. She said "Let's just go with I am right this time, and you are so wrong."

It can be difficult being married to a military man. You don't know if they do things out of love for you or they feel like it is their duty.

My husband and I have seen so many out of the way places. How did you find those places? We get lost quite a bit.

A lost of wives say their husbands are like statues. They don't move.

The wedding was going great until the ceremony. Than everyone heard loud sobbing and someone blowing their nose. She probably shouldn't have invited her former boyfriend to the wedding.

The husband came home from work and told his wife that he had lost his job. Today was his last day of work. His wife says well let's look at the bright side of things. We can spend a lot more time together. The next day he was out bating the pavement looking for a job. He just needed the right motivation.

My wife acts so immature. Fortunately she has he perfect job. She works at a daycare center.

A man had invited his boss and a couple of coworkers over to his house for a meal. While they were eating the appetizers he was telling funny stories about his wife's cooking. Once she cooked with the plastic wrapper still on. Another time what she fixed was raw in the middle. The last chicken she fixed bounced back on the bone. They are laughing hard at his stories. His wife came in from the kitchen sand said she was glad they are having a good time and dinner was ready. After they left his wife commented that they hardly touched their food. We are going to have enough leftovers to eat for the next two weeks.

The wife of a sanitation worker is concerned about her husband. He has been down in the dumps for so long.

The new chamber of commerce president was giving a talk. She went on and on. A man whispered to another man. "Do you think she will ever run out of things to say?" The guy behind them overhead them. He said "She is my wife. The talk will probably go on for a lot longer.

Husband complained that there house was too small. After his brother-in-law showed up with his five children, he complained that the house wasn't big enough.

The guests were coming to the party. It was a hot and humid night. The forecast was for a storm to come later. One man said to another "It is like the calm before the storm." The other guy said "You got that right. In another hour my mother-in-law will be here."

A man told the stewardess that there was a terrible smell coming from behind them. Another couple behind that told the stewardess they were noticing the smell too. In the seat behind them the wife said to her husband. "Frank, Frank quick wake up you need to out your shoes on right away."
Getting older isn't easy Two ladies that had been classmate met at a class reunion that was almost fifty years ago. The one was a widow. The other one was married but her husband wasn't with her. The other one asked if he was still active. "Oh no he hasn't been active for most of our married life."

The older man was sitting in the car waiting for his wife to get out of the beauty shop. He was getting impatient when she finally came out. She said she was sorry it had taken so long. He looked her over. He said you didn't need to hurry so much that they didn't have time to finish the job.

The sun is up. The birds are up and singing. Everything is up but my husband.

A friend tells a friend to have good day on his day off. He says it is too late for that because his wife has already given him a list of jobs for him to do that day.

When it comes to putting stuff together most men follow this rule "When all else fails read the directions."

My husband finally got a job. The other lady said so that means he is working. "Well I wouldn't go so far as to say that."

The couple had been married for just a short time. She was nervous about having his parents over for dinner. It was her first time cooking for them. The husband was on the phone talking to his mother. She asked so what his wife was cooking for them tonight. He was going to say baked chicken but than he saw the smoke coming out of the kitchen. He said smoked chicken.

You marry into a family of outlaws and now they become your in-laws.

When two sailors get married we say they tied the knot.

The pastor was comforting the grieving widow upon the death of her husband. He said some day you will see your husband again and spend eternity with him. She said "I don't think to pastor. I am quite sure when I die I will be going to heaven."

Many a wife should come with a tag that says "Handle with care."

The lawyer tells his client that his wife says he has a gambling problem. She says you bet on everything and never say no to anything. The client says "I bet you twenty-five bucks you are wrong."

The real estate man was showing a house to a couple. There was a crash. When they went to investigate they noticed the kitchen window was broke. The agent picked ups golf ball. Did I tell you how close the house is to the golf course? I hope you like golf.

A couple was having marriage problems. She took off to another state to visit her mother and family for a month. After only five days she called her husband. She said some problems had come up. He panicked asking her "your not coming home early are you?"

On a shopping trip with other women my wife gets very competitive. She always tries to outspend the rest of them.

When a couple introduce each other they have a problem deciding who is the better half.

The couple was going to a family gathering and a wedding. They hadn't seen the relatives for a long time. The wife got a makeover, her hair done and had brought some clothes that really made her look good. When she was all dressed up she asked her husband what he thought. He said "You don't look like my wife."

The mother of the bride talking about the groom says "Well I guess we have to take the bad with the good."

The husband called from the police station. His wife wondered how he could go to the bank to make a deposit and be arrested for a bank robbery. Unknown to him when he was making a deposit a bank robber was at another window two down from him. The robber handed the teller a note saying he had a gun and gather a bag to put money in. She did as she was told. He than pointed to the husband who was leaving the bank and said he is with me. When he ran out of the bank he yelled at the husband to hurry. Of course the guard arrested the husband.

All day long my husband worked in a toy store. At night when I would ask him to do some work he would say he was all played out.

The electrician said he was going to stay connected to his wife.

The older man was told by the doctor that he needed to do some exercising. Knowing he didn't like to do it the doctor suggested he have a goal in mind and reward himself for reaching it. He decided to walk. He would walk a mile and half and later come back so he was walking three miles a day. His wife was quite proud of him. After a couple of weeks she ran into her friend Madge. Madge said "You know my husband meets your husband everyday at the donut shop."

A math teacher should not marry a counselor. Together they have just too many problems.

The business owner got married. His wife had to teach him about the shared profit plan now that he was married.

When I got married I told my wife she was the one I was waiting for. Now after thirty years of marriage I still find myself waiting for wife day in and and day out.

Her husband is on a diet. He is eating healthier snacks but pigging out on his meals.

My husband is so childish. He refers to the den as his romper room.

They asked wives over the age of fifty what dwarf best described their husband. The majority said grumpy.

A health conscious couple promised each other that they work to lead a healthy lifestyle. If they felt nibbling they would only nibble on each other's ears.

The husband called his wife's best friend. He asked if she could help his wife find a project otherwise her project would be to change him.

A trail guide gets married.
The couple talk about how they met on a path and kept crossing paths with each other.
Vows
He promised to lead and guide her.
She promised to follow in his footsteps and let him be her guide.
Together they looked forward too discovering new paths.
She promised that every time she got upset with him she wouldn't beat a path to her mother's house.
There was a bonfire at the reception. We had s'more and roasted hot dogs. Everyone sang Kum Bah Ya. There wasn't a dry eye there.

Often someone sweet marries someone sour. The problem is you have to be careful that don't leave you with a sour disposition.

There is a little beast in most men. When they get hungry you can hear a l little growl from them.

The trail guide has good security in his marriage. His wife said she would be lost without him.

Husband and wife were at his 30th high school reunion. He said oh no there is Ted over there. Quick turn around and don't look at him. I and a couple of other guys were really mean to him in high school. Later while seated and eating Ted came by and poured is drink on his head. He turned to his wife and said "It looks like Ted recognized me."

I should have known how different it would be to be married to a man who was into sports all the time. Because he was watching a close game he was late to our wedding.

The guy went with the girl for many years. He would ask her to marry him and she would always turn him down. He told his friends if she ever says yes I will shout it from the rooftop. One day she said yes. Unfortunately on the way up to the rooftop he fell off the ladder and broke his leg.

I tell my wife I have been trying hard two keep my New Year's resolution not to worry. The problem is that my boss is always giving me things that he says I need to worry about.

The 37 year old lady was marrying a guy who was only twenty.
She said a good man is hard to find. Her friend said is that why you are marrying a boy.

The husband doesn't want to go to a dinner party. His wife feels like she has to treat him like a baby. She tells him to quit his fussing and be on your best behavior. I am sure a number of wives can identify with this couple.

A man said there would be no peace on earth form this year at Christmas. His mother-in-law is coming and she is going to stay a month.

A cattleman's wife left him for a richer cattleman. You could say the grass was greener on the other side of the fence.

Many people give up things for lent. My husband says he is giving up vegetables this year.

The man telling his sick neighbor that if he needs anything at all called him. It doesn't matter if it is night or day. I will send my wife over to check on you.

The lady asked "Is he housebroken?" No, he leaves his clothes all over and doesn't pick up a thing." The other lady said "I was asking about your new dog."

Wife comes home from work. Her husband says "You know those black shoes you love and kicked off in the living room. You aren't the only one who loves those shoes. It looks like the dog has been chewing on them most of the day."

The wife tells the couple leaving to come again. Her husband says "Be sure and call so you know we will be home." He is thinking so I have time to think of an excuse to be gone.

The first compliant during the stone age was when a lady about to get married demanded a bigger stone for her ring.

When a fruit grows didn't get married he said it was because the good ones were already picked.

When they say you aren't getting any younger that is not true for my wife. When we go out and meet people she always knocks a few years off her age.

It was a difficult wedding. Joe East was marrying Nancy West. The way the church was built you were either sitting on theEast or West side. It made people feel like they were choosing sides. The pastor was good. He said "Today I went to point you all in a new direction."

A guy at work was selling cookies for his daughter. The one man told him no he was good. A coworker overhearing him said that is not what your wife says.

I was showing houses to a sanitation worker and his wife. After seeing one the wife commented that it was a dump. The husband said "Don't you just love it?'

The doorman has not had good success in marriage. He says he keeps knocking at the wrong door.

It is hard being married to a math teacher. She sees problems everywhere and he doesn't see problems anywhere.

The realtor shows the master bedroom and point out the huge closet in there. The wife looks it over and says yes most of the clothes would fit in there, but her husband will still have to use the guest bedroom for his clothes.

Wife complained that her husband treats her like clay. He is always trying to mold her.

The librarian said her husband never shares his thoughts or feelings. He is like a closed book.

They say hard work never hurt anyone. They could be wrong. Many a husband has complained about a bad back going out because he working too hard.

The wife struggled and struggled to get into the pants she wanted to wear when the went out. She finally got them zipped. By this time she was sweating. She went out into the living room and asked her husband what he thought of her pants. He said "They look good on you if you could just take them out a couple of inches."

The couple had moved to a new address. Their nephew was coming to visit. Even though it was hard to find their home for most people he quite easily found their home. The wife said you must be street smart.

A couple was visiting another couple for a few days. The husband says to them to feel at home. The man puts his feet on the coffee table. His wife pushes them off. She said "Don't feel that much at home.

Worker tells lady boss that when she bosses him around she sounds so such like my wife.

When a man first got married he lost 15 pounds the first three months. He only ate his wife's cooking.

A young guy was telling another guy that he doesn't like anyone giving him orders. The other guy said you had better stay single.

A lady asked another lady if her and her husband would like to join them for a dinner out if her husband is not too tired from work. She said no her husband usually says he just stands around and looks busy.

Worker bees do all the work. The queen bee gets to just buzz around and give orders to all the workers. Some couples can identify with this situation.

An older couple was visiting a couple that were even older. The ladies were visiting. The older lady said that her husband's mind has been going for sometime. He doesn't remember things, and gets so mixed up. His mind is going downhill fast. On the way the husband told his wife how easy Carl is to visit with. He makes more sense then most meant half his age. What we have here is someone with half a mind that is still smarter than those with all their mind.

The husband of an older couple was in the hospital His wife's sister called her to ask how he was doing. She said they running some tests and everything seems to be okay, but he seems confused about things. The sister said "Oh than he is back to normal."

Three women were talking about how picky Helen was about just about everything. Well one woman said "She isn't picky about everything. You haven't met her husband yet."

The older lady died. Her husband said she was late to everything. He had told her that he hoped they didn't have to hold up choir practice in heaven waiting for you.

Three woman were talking at a party. One kept calling her husband a big baby. The other lady whispered to the other lady that she didn't think that was nice for her to call her husband a baby. Who is he anyway? Do you see him? The other lady looked around the room and said he is the one in the back by the window sucking his thumb.

A banker's wife in a divorce always wants a cash settlement.

When it comes to taking care of the horses the husband says he is the stable man.

It doesn't work out well when a cook marries a bartender. When sick she says it must be something I drank He says it must be something he ate.

A skydiver had been sick for awhile. His wife said she expected him to be well soon and landing on his feet.

The man says his wife is a plus in his life. The other guy asked him if he was talking about her clothes size.

A lady complained to the laundry worker that her husband had been acting like a stiff shirt lately. She said you have to quit putting so much starch in his shirts.

All morning he has been lifting heavy boxes and moving them around in the garage. His wife tells him what boxes to move and where to put them. He is sweating and sore from all the work. She gets a phone call. She tells them she can't talk because she and her husband are buys working in the garage. He looks at her and say "Maybe next time I can be the boss."

A lady who married a magician said that every time there is work for him to do he pulls his disappearing act.

The sanitation worker was proud that his wife wrote such a trashy novel.

The loan officer tells the young couple that there are many things they are going to have to learn to come to terms with.

Working at the airport and being married to my wife has similarities. In both cases I get lots of delays and we end up not going anywhere.

When a swimmer get married we say they took the plunge.

The salesman that went to the company was tired and hungry. He asked where he could get a decent meal. The manager said I will call my wife you can get at our house. A worker said to another worker "Well there goes the idea of a decent meal."

A book lover is having trouble with her marriage. She said we are not even on the same page.

Yesterday my problems seemed so far away but not anymore. My mother-in-law will be on the plane at two today.

His mother was a lawyer. He married his wife over her many objections.

A man introduced his third wife at a party. A lady commented to another lady that I am afraid she is his third mistake.

The older man says he doesn't have to remember his mistakes. His wife reminds him of them all the time.

It isn't easy to be married to a mountain climber. He is having another mountain top experience and you are down in the valley working hard to pay all the bills so he can have those mountain top experiences.

The lady said her husband is very creative. He can make mountains out of mole hills all the time.

A farmer says that after you have been married so many years you tend to grow on each other.

Wife to avid golfer husband asks him if he is just going to swing away another day.

A math teacher married a clock maker. They have to learn to divide up their time. The man married to a math teacher did something and she gave him a look of disapproval. He said "Do you have a problem with what I did?"

The railroad man said he really bettered his life when he married someone from the other side of the tracks.

An astronomer said his wife was the center of his universe. Now after twenty years of marriage, he says she is a little off center.

His wife and mother both testified in his defense. They both claimed that he was too dumb to pull of a complicated bank robbery.

It can be difficult being married to a guy in the mob. His sister asked her when she was going to have the whole mob over to eat.

A pilot says when he is home he likes to fly low under the radar. He does that so his wife doesn't find a project for him to work on.

A man's shirt says he is under new management. He has been divorced and is now remarried.

A wealthy man and his wife separated. A friend of his asked if he missed her. He said no what he misses is the money. When they got divorced she got most of it.

When the bride took her veil off they said it was unveiled love.

A laundry worker said that her and her husband have had a few wrinkles in their marriage, but it has been nothing that couldn't be ironed out.

I don't know what game my parents were playing, but I heard mom tell dad that two can play that game.

In the Old West when you got married they say you got hitched. It was like being hitched to a wagon and if you are gong to go anywhere you have to go together.

He wants to dance cheek to cheek. I told him not to get cheeky with me.

It can be difficult being married to a math teacher, because they see problems everywhere.

A housewife called her friend another housewife and asked what she was doing. She said the house is a mess. My company just left and the kids are finally back in school. I have several loads of laundry to do. I have to bake some brownies for my daughter to take to school tomorrow. I really have to go to the grocery store if we are going to have anything to eat. "Why did you ask." "Oh she said I probably should not have asked. I was wondering if you wanted to eat out and go to a movie." "Sure thing I can be ready in twenty minutes."

It was a tourist town. The shops were full of tourist items. One advertised projects that were unfinished. The man's wife finally figured out what to do with all his unfinished projects.

When my husband is stationary that means he is not going anywhere.

The man and his wife have different jobs but do the same thing as each other all day. She works in a daycare and he works at a discount tire shop. They both make many changes everyday.

A lawyer says when he knows he is going to be in trouble with his wife he always tries to build a good defense.

The couple was going to a party around Halloween time. After getting dressed the husband asked his wife what she thought about what he had on. She looked at him and said "Go change we are not going to a costume party."

Their marriage was not holding together. There was a heavy rain that flooded the neighborhood. He managed to get her to higher ground.
Than he left her. She said at least I am high and dry.

The cleaner said it wasn't so bad that her husband left her, but that he left her in a mess. It was a messy divorce.

I married a mover. I liked the way he moved. But after a divorce he has moved out. Now I am moving on.

The magician said it was going to take a little magic if he was going to impress his wife.

At work a guy took all the credit for a big project of which several others had helped on. One said he could have at least given some credit to his wife. If they hadn't been fighting so much he would not have spending so much time at the office.

A lady said when she married the magician all her money problems disappeared. The funny was though so did all her credit cards.

So how did you and your ex-wife get back together? I took one wrong turn and ended up back at her house.

The woman said if she dressed like her husband they would both be dressed like bums.

The chicken farmer's wife complained that she felt like she had been cooped up all winter.

My husband thinks he a radio. He wants me to tune into him. He doesn't want me to change the dail and listen to anyone but him. At times it is too much and I tell him I can't hear him because of the static.

My husband asked what was for supper. I said that I didn't have that much food, I think we should just eat out. He didn't want to eat out so he said he would look and see if he could find something for us to eat. After looking he said well I guess we need to go out for food. I was excited about eating out. Instead he took me to our local grocery store to buy food so when we went home I could fix us something to eat.

A judge takes his job home. When he comes to the table where his wife and five children are seated his wife says now all rise.

I was attending my thirty-fifth class reunion. I told my wife that Bill's eyesight was failing him. When he saw me he said I was looking good.

I was taking the bachelor coworker to my house for a meal. In the car I asked him if he was hungry. He said he was starved. I said that will help you when you eat my wife's cooking.

The magician was in trouble with the law. His wife disappeared and the law believed he had something to do with it.

The couple looking at a house to buy had different thoughts about the house. She looked at it and thought of all the possibilities. He looked at it and thought about about all the things he was going to have to fix.

When Tarzan married Jane he found out she was such a good cook. He ended up gaining weight. Unfortunately when he went swinging through the vines a vine broke and he broke a leg.

When they first got married she was like a breath of fresh air. When it didn't work out well she became like stale air and it became very stifling.

The woman that married Frankenstein later regretted it. She didn't know he would turn into a monster.

The bossy wife always told her husband that she didn't know what he would do without her. She has to tell what to do all the time. When things didn't work out and she left him, the first thing he did was throw a party.

The fisherman brought him a sting of fish that he caught. His wife said "If that isn't a fine kettle of fish."

Her husband worked at the Land Management company. When he died he left her a slough full of money.

The travel agent would talk to her mate about a trip somewhere. He would say "Don't even go there."

The doctor told her husband he needed to lose some weight and exercise. He hates doing both so he hasn't been doing either. They went to the grocery store together. When she was unloading the car, her neighbor saw her and came over and helped her carry the bags into the house. As they were putting away groceries and phone kept ringing. The neighbor asked her if she wasn't going to answer it. She said "No it's just my husband calling. I left him at the grocery store so he could get some exercise by walking home."

The lady had been losing so much weight. Some thought she was down to just skin and bones. When her husband backed over her with the car, and said he didn't see her it could be believed.

His wife worked at the radio station and had her own program. She told him to tune into her program. Instead he turned her off.

I can't get my husband to change his mind, or change his habits. or have a change of heart. I am lucky if I can get him to change his clothes.

An older man at the grocery was standing with his grocery cart looking around. I asked if he had lost his wife. He said not yet, but he was still trying.

The photographer recently got divorced. He said his wife is no longer in the picture.

It was a tough fight for the fighter. Finally it was over and he was declared the winner. He had suffered some bruises and had black eye. People were crowding around him and congraduahtioning him on winning the fight. His trainer told another trainer "He may won this fight but when he goes home and wife sees that black eye. He is in for another fight. I am not sure he will win this one."

The man and his wife were eating at a breakfast house. He went to pay the bill while his wife went to the bathroom. He run into an old friend who he hadn't seen for a long time. They both told each other how good they looked. His wife wife caught up with him and told him he better hurry he has an eye appointment in 20 minutes.

My husband is so lazy even when he hears disturbing news he takes it laying down.

Often wives try to change their husbands, while husbands try to change wives.

For Christmas cards the couple was going to send their picture. After looking at it she deiced it made her look fat. She wrote on the card that the photographer had the photo enlarged.

The unfaithful wife was married to a rich banker. When he died she was known as the merry widow.

The star war's hero got married. Now there is a new force in the universe.

The defendants wife was on the witness stand. She said I am not going to lie for him. He lies enough for both of us.

A carpenter was asked how his wife was doing. He said she is a work in progress.

The philosopher's wife claimed she understood her husband. Now you know that has to be a joke.

A lady was accused of poisoning another lady. In her defense her husband said that lots of people have gotten sick eating her food.

A wife attended a debt free seminar. On the third week the assignment for them all was to cut up their credit cards. Even thought they didn't want to they all signed a pledge to do it. The next week they went around the room and each shared their experience. One lady "Well you know when you are married you share everything. I just couldn't get myself to cut up my cards so I cut up my husbands."

A rich lady nearing sixty was getting married for the first time. The husband to be was fifteen years younger. All her friends told her he was just after her money. To satisfy them and herself she had him sign an agreement that is he left her he would get nothing. After a few years she began to suspect he didn't love her, and she started to fear that he might kill her. Her lawyer helped her to make a new will. If she died all her money would go to a pet rescue organization. She made sure that she left the will in a place where her husband would see it.

The man introduced his wife as his bossy half.

A gambler said it was time for him to take a chance on love.

Even robbers need vacations. The wife had complained about the family not going anywhere. The husband promises her a quick getaway. Their first stop was the bank. Dad said to leave the car running he was just going to stop off and get a little cash for the trip.

A couple was visiting another couple. The husband said what a good boss he had. The boss knew he had several projects to work on so he gave him time off to work on them. His wife told the other wife that her husband got laid off.

The gambler always had a card up the sleeve of his jacket. It was poker night so he went to put on the jacket. Wouldn't you know it his wife had sent it out to be dry cleaned.

The math teacher was getting married for the third time. She said she feels like she has leaned her lessons and made some corrections in her life.

The man tells his actress not to be so dramatic about everything.

My mother-in-law thinks she is really important. Everywhere she goes she rides in the front even in a cab. She says she is not taking the backseat for anyone.

Miscellaneous

A jumper was asked what he thought about something. he said nothing really jumps out at him.

If you think you are important you say "I don't take a back row for anyone.

The only thing we really want to lose is weight.

Sometimes a gambler can over play his cards.

A dog in a good mood is said to be howling with laughter.

For people who are afraid of getting germs they no longer shake hands on a deal but just shake their heads.

The celebrity was at a fair and was buying something from a vender and felt he was giving her a hard time. She said "Do you know who I am." He said "No, but it would help if you wore a name tag so you wouldn't forget."

The hair dressers says the girls that know how to have fun are those that let their hair down.

Did you notice that if most people are hot they are also bothered?

Money that changes hands quietly is called hush money.

When someone is really hip we call them a hipster.

When you take a stand, stand on the right side.

When a lumberman who had gone bad robbed a store he would say "This is a stickup."

The guy from the pickle factory was in a jam when the detective called him in to question him. He told him that I don't want you to go from sweet to sour while I am questioning you. I am going to be showing you some pictures to see if anything jars your memory.

I find there is always room for error.

An astronomer said it would nice to right once in a blue moon.

The police told the miner that when he did needed to be above ground.

When two people hug a third person that is called wrap around.

Most popular game at the North Pole is reindeer games.

Surf talk is when someone waves at you and you wave back you caught a wave.

I was getting medicine for my allergies. One bottle said 3.98 for a bottle of a hundred. Another bottle said 6.98 for a bottle of only twelve. They were the same brand. I couldn't find anything different about them. I asked the druggist what was the difference. She said three dollars.

The D.J. said what he was going to say had to be off the record.

The competition between tow truck drivers is called tug of war.

Tuck was a fry cook. His nickname was Friar Tuck.

The guy said the only thing he has outstanding are his bills.

Three girls were talking. The one girl asked "What has happened to your cousin that used to hang around us?" "You mean the one that is full of hot air? He has a job blowing up balloons for a party shop.

Photographers love flash dancing.

In Africa when they introduced a new chief they would say now let's hear a drum roll.

When asked how was the program he said it was six yawns too long.

In the Old West the calvary wasn't sure they could believe the scout. Than the scout would say "Scout's honor."

A sky diver lives at 20 Jump Street.

You want to keep your shoes tied so you don't have anything tripping you up.

A man got his fortune told. He was told he would soon be doing bigger things. Sure enough the next week he started making bigger mistakes.

When a soldier has to do something he says duty calls. A higher duty is when nature calls. That is when he has to go to the bathroom.

A young guy called an older lady and old bag. His friend said that he should remember not that many years ago she was a sack.

The mortician told the detective if he ran across any dead bodies to bring them to him.

A good hunter in the cave days could kill two birds with one stone.

A judge never says "I am not here to judge you."

There was a frog in the men's locker room. Nobody wanted to pick it up or do anything about it. Finally the trainer deciding to do his good deed for the day picked it up with some paper towels. He dropped it outside on the sidewalk. It jumped off the curb and got run over. That is a good deed gone wrong.

Never ask a pestimist what could go wrong.

When a sailor heard was some disturbing news he said "If that doesn't knock the wind out of my sail."

Around Halloween time at the magician's house a lot of hocus pocus
goes on.

Detectives look for solid evidence. Liquid evidence is too runny and difficult to follow.

A surprised hunter is shell shocked.

Christmas was late.
Santa didn't get his flight plan filed in time.
He got caught in a lot of turbulence.
It was a bumpy sleigh ride.
Lots of people complained about broken toys and gifts.

Santa's wife wrote a book called "Santa Baby."
At first she enjoyed the sleigh rides but later she could do without all the bell ringing which left a ringing in her ears.
She never would have guessed that Santa spent at least half of his time working with the reindeer. It got to be a problem choosing who would lead the sleigh and keep them happy.

Now you all know about the people who write to Santa about they want, but what about those who don't ask and have been good all year. Well that is where Mrs. Claus comes in and I am stuck picking out gifts for the rest of them. Isn't the wife always left picking out the gifts? And than there is Santa's weight problem. I have told him time after time to cut down on the cookies and milk.

The miner says we need to look out for the pit falls in life.

When you visit a city you may want to take a fireman with you. They know all the hot spots. The relator knows all the sites.

When it comes to coming up with ideas most people come up empty. It can be difficult asking people what they think about an issue only to find out that they haven't given any thought about the issue.

I don't believe in sit-down strikes. You need to stand up for something.

Getting it wrong is easy. Gettin it right takes more time.

It was difficult to be a court jester in King Arthur's days. He would try to entertain the people and they would comment on how he was making a fool of himself again. When the court jester was asked how he was doing he said he was just fooling around.

Around the senior center if someone is called by the initials F.C. it means avoid them. The initials stand for frequent complainer.

It is one thing to talk to yourself but do you really listen to yourself?

I thought I was wrong but I was only mistaken. Even at that it was little mistake.

In the Old West when they wanted to hear gossip they went to the listening post.

You work hard to throw a surprise party for someone. When she comes to the party she says "Why am I not surprised?"

What most people state is the obvious.

One counterfeit guy said to the other counterfeit guy that he makes more money than he does.

Someone was trying to sell a security system to the man. He was confused. His neighbor told him not to be alarmed.

Someone who is not sure about how they feel about something. We say they are still sorting their feeling out.

A landscaper says if you dwell too long on a problem it will develop roots in your brain and be a lot harder to pull up.

We call our helper in life our right handed man.

The three wife men were following the Christmas star in the program, but it wasn't hooked good and started to fall down. The one wise man that he was yelled "Watch out for the following star."

The baby playing baby Jesus was crying to loud. Finally one girl yelled out "Would someone give him his pacifier."

An honest card player has nothing up his sleeve but his arm.

When a weather man brags they call him a windbag.

An astronomer asked the other guy if everything was right with his world.

A farmer says if you sow seeds of doubt you will become very suspicious.

We need to thank a carpenter when we are playing on a level field.

The window man says as we get older we all turn various shades of gray.

Coffee for impatient people is instant coffee.

Asked the pilot what he had been doing. He said he had just been flying around.

At the county fair when someone wants too much attention we say they are grandstanding.

The astronomer was the star witness.

A fireman says when things don't work out it kind of backfires on him.

A skydiver tells another skydiver not to get so jumpy.

You can never reach your goal standing still.

Being a nun isn't easy. It has to be a daily habit.

The rancher said to the post hole digger "Be sure and keep me posted."

Many people are stuck on "Will call."

Signs your Christmas gift didn't go over well
"Well isn't this something. I never would have guessed."What they mean is they still are not sure about what it is or how they could use it.
"Well isn't this outfit colorful." Mean they would never wear those colors together.
"Well look at this. One size fits all." If I ever decide to wear a tent I will wear it.
"At what store did you buy it?" Hopefully I the tags are still on it and I can return it. Than your mother-in-law says "I hope it's big enough and you don't have to return it for a bigger size."

A dairy farmer that is not interested in something says he doesn't give a moo.

The road worker lost his job. Someone ran him off the road.

The clown was running for the office of mayor. The newspaper reported that he was not a serious candidate.

Closet must get kind of crowded. When someone is accused of something there are reports of people coming out the closets to testify against him.

The landscaper says at sometime everything grounds to a halt.

Superman says in an interview that people were always asking him to do the impossible.

In the fairy tale the young knight looks in the mirror and doesn't ask who is the fairest of all, but who is the coolest.

When you think you are about to die but get a second chance to live the clock maker that is called living on borrowed time.

An astronomer says we need to make a difference in our universe.

Why are some people called lefties but never righties? We often defend our hand. We say we didn't have a hand in it. Hand talk I really can't put my finger on what went wrong.

Life lesson. Treat your guests good, but not so good they want to stay longer.

A pointer likes to think they are so smart. They often tell people that is their point exactly.

A clockmaker says that this year a lot of people are trying to make up for lost time.

Is the smell of success the same as the smell of money?

The crossword guy couldn't get the word. He said it never crossed his mind.

You can have a party by yourself. When you go out to eat the hostess asked how many are in your party.

When people say you win some and lose some they are usually talking about their weight.

Two pointers are arguing. One makes point and the other one comes back with a counter point.

Most cooks after they had you try something new that they made they ask for your feedback.

The cave man's drink is always on the rocks. The caveman was the first to use the term stone walling. It was because the walls are made out of stones.

If you don't mind it doesn't matter.

The motto for the back doctor for the New Year is don't look back.

Don't you hate it when you eat out at a new restaurant and everything is good? When you wanted to complain, but couldn't find anything to complain about.

The clock maker was entertaining at a party. He said he was having the time of his life.

In beauty contests you don't have to just impress the judges but you have to wow them.

We don't always want to deal with reality. We need to leave something for our imagination.

He is not so tough he just looks tough. Some stay away from him because of the smell of fear, and other others stay away just because he smells bad.

A computer guy refuses to do something. He said he wasn't programmed to do that.

Some teenagers were running through the cemetery. The caretaker got after them. He said these people are here to rest in peace.

Lots of men have hair that is out of place. It is going in their nose, ear and on their face instead of on their head. That is called misplaced hair.

There was a conflict at the beauty contest. Things started to turn ugly.

The shoplifter lives by the motto "Take it easy."

Only a astronaut can say he never runs out of space.

Even vampire can learn to get along even when they are different blood types.

Use the word "Slammed" when a door has been slammed on you.

Some people say "ah" too much. You might say they are awe-struck.

Opting out can sometimes be the best option.

Sausage is really a confused meat that is all mixed up.

A reader was accused of reading too much into the situation.

The car salesman was asked how he met his wife. He said he knew a good deal when he saw one.

Many people want to rest their mind but usually they just end up putting it to sleep.

Finally we know what you don't want to leave home without it. It is your cell phone.

The problems the Indians had at their meeting was often that there were too many chiefs and not enough Indians.

At times when an Indian was acting crazy another Indian would ask him what he had been smoking.
The early settlers at times demanded squatter's right.

The shirt says "If you need help ask me." I said I needed help. He yells at another guy. "Frank could you help this guy?"

I wonder who came up with the idea of fat and jolly. Than I thought it must be Santa. If he can be overweight and jolly there is no excuse for the rest of us not to be jolly.

When we are young we are told the bogeyman is gong to come and get us. When we are older we are told the tax man is gong to come and get us.

The term we use for our apartment is taken from a frog. We say come over to my pad.

If you feel like you are joined at the hip you are going to have separation issues.

When someone who is not so smart wins something we say it was just dumb luck.

A lady complained about the sand in her hair. The other lady said that is what you get for putting your head in the sand.

The waterman knows so much. He is a fountain of information.

In Italy all roads lead to Rome.

There are lines everywhere. I just don't know where to go. Finally someone said a line is forming over here.

I know it is rude to ask people how old they are. I just ask them what year they were born in.

People demanding attention want to be the center of attention.

You notice robbers always want to get quick cash and make a quick getaway. It isn't good for you to want things so fast because you don't appreciate it if you don't work for it.

A clockmaker near death we say he has only a few minutes left.

What most of us want at the end of the line is a fish.

The sight most people are in need of is insight.

Notice that when something doesn't fit people often throw a fit.

The weather man can be kind of boring. He just wants to talk about the lows and highs of the day. The weather man says we need to learn to live on the sunny side of things.

As you get older the name of the rooms change. The living room is now called the sitting room.

Places where you go and have to wait on yourself seem to be so self-serving.

Dieters talk. They ask what is the skinny on that thing. Another time they say there is a slim chance of that happening.

You try to be nice and ask how you can help. You are told to get out of the way.

Some people talk farm talk. They say "hay." So I say "straw" in return.

The boy was called smarty pants. He thought now if it could only spread to the rest of me.

It isn't all bad when someone tells you, you got it all wrong. If you had only a small part wrong you would have to figure out what part you got right and what part you got wrong. This way you can just start out all over again.

The local AA chapter is sponsoring a dry run.

Dream the impossible but be ready to settle for something less.

There was a robbery at the plant. Someone asked if they didn't have a guard. They did. I guess he was just caught off guard.

The workers from the water plant when they go to their favorite bar they call it a water hole.

If you get too wound up you may not like where you wind up.

The gas station worker says that is fuel for thought. Fuel gets my brain going.

How can you lead from behind?

Unfortunately for most people the only thing that is expanding is their body.

A guy said that the only thing he has outstanding are his bills.

Turf wars are when two landscapers war over the turf.

The first beach in cave man days was called Pebble Beach.

A smart answer may not always be the right answer.

Back in the day the ladies were called "Ladies in Waiting." Now the ladies in waiting are in line waiting to use the bathroom.

If it is such a simple problem why does it have to seem so complicated for me?

The first sale in the cave man's day. The prices were at rock bottom.

A friend tells his friend that he doesn't think when people say to stop and smell the roses, that doesn't necessarily mean you should when are see them on a casket at a funeral.

If you are going to eat finger licking food make sure you have washed your fingers.

An astronaut says if you want to get closer to someone don't leave so much space between you.

If you don't read this it often gets you into trouble. You need to learn to read the fine print.

Young guy wears a t-shirt that says Navy. Old men wear a t-shirt that says Old Navy.

Whoever said money doesn't grow on trees never raised fruit trees.

He is like a crossword puzzle. The way he comes across can really bring you down.

Often the heaviest part of the body is the heart. People will say they have a heavy heart.

The cook has so much going on that he says he feels like a loaded baked potato.

It was in Greece where they first called someone a great pillar in the community.

Tell a fired doorman "Don't let the door hit you on your way out."

Often when people say "Leave it to me" nothing will get done.

A guy who has been gaining extra weight says "It looks like people will be seeing more of me next year."

What you say to a tall guy is that he is head and shoulders over the rest of us.

I have lots of convictions. Fortunately they are mostly for small crimes.

People complain about the high cost of living, but if you have even had to plan a funeral you would know dying doesn't come cheap either.

The director tells the actor before he goes on stage to try and get his act together.

When your days are numbered you still have to start with day l.

If pest control people get into a fight they usually slug it out.

Two young guys shared an apartment together. The one was taking a shower. The other one thought he heard yelling and screaming and thought he was yelling for help. He knocked on the door and yelled "Ken are you all right? Answer me Ken." Finally Ken shut off the shower. He said he was just singing in the shower. What you think of as your singing others see it as your screaming for help.

When someone tells you to "Get real", does that mean they thought you were a phony before?

Can most people explain themselves?

Remember it is supposed to be freely given not freely spent.

The time many seniors look forward to is nap time.

Even though most say it only half of the people really believe it. "Good Morning."

Do you know how hard it is to watch your back?

After working with UPS for twenty years he decided to go into politics. He thought that people would know he knows how to deliver.

The skill most people need to develop is their thinking skills.

If you can't get in the front door, you may try getting in the back door.

You want to be a positive force in your universe.

The number you dress for is the nines.

The trail guide said "If you don't learn to follow me consider yourself lost."

Some people have a personality like a snake. They slither around and hiss at people.

A short man complained every time he is involved in a deal he always gets the short end.

A basketball player doesn't roll out of bed. He bounces out of bed.

When a military men hears a burglar in his house he yells "Halt who goes there?"

When the clockmaker was having a good time, he lost track of the time.

When asked how the food is you don't want anyone saying it was just so and so.

Dentist says when it is your time to go don't leave with bad breath.

What do man have that reminds them of original sin? An Adam's apple.
The cook didn't know what to say. He had a deadpan look.

I asked if the cook was up. They said they hadn't heard him stirring.

Two heavy guys were weighing themselves. The one says to the bigger guy "It looks like I am gaining on you."

It is difficult to get close to people who value their personal space.

When you tell an older person to forget it, you can be pretty sure they will.

Most people are not good at living a double life. They have enough trouble living one life.

When it was a good day in the old West the sheriff would say "It is a good day for a hanging."

It is out of character when a neat girl messes up.

The wizard has been sick for awhile. He said he was getting over a bad spell.

The card player criticized the other card player. He said he doesn't know jack.

Two guys are building a fence. One tells the other guy that it is time to post it.

In the old West you wanted to learn to keep moving. You know it is harder to hit a moving target.

A man says he is out of breath. The other guy asked him if he didn't belong in a funeral home.

The state many people find themselves in is a state of confusion.

When someone says something to a Californian they say they are quaking in their boots.

Quite often when we get older the only thing that knocks is our knees.

You could store more in your brain if you could just get rid of some of the junk already stored there.

The time most people want is free time.

When someone chews you out using their tongue we say we got a tongue lashing.

If you keep circling the problem you will never solve the problem.

Scene in a men's bathroom. A man asks another man if he was Dunn. Meanwhile a man in the bathroom stall flushes the toilet and opens up the stall and says "I am done."

A tow truck driver says don't let yourself get pulled into too many directions.

In the Old West when someone was looking for you they would say "Carl is gunning for you."

When I told a joke to two concrete workers they both were cracking up.

They asked the man how he started to study planets and the solar system. He said someone told him that his world was too small.

When your life is spinning out of control you are likely to get dizzy.

To get ahead in life we are told to get up, stand up, and stand tall.

I feel like an old picture that has just been hanging around too long.

So I don't disappoint anyone I don't promise anything.

When a cheerleader hangs up her pom poms that is her last hurrah.

When twins bet they usually say double or nothing.

If you get too comfortable you are probably not going to want to move.

We need to learn the right way to wake up or we will have a bad day. Don't get up on the wrong side of the bed.

A man wrote a book called "My Brilliant Friend." Now he is gong back to his home town and at least five friends are convinced that he wrote the book about them.

A criminal without a defense attorney is defenseless.

When a hoodlum fools someone we say they are hoodwinked.

We need to remember the motto "Don't ask." When someone says it don't ask unless you want to get an ear full.

Just think if Colonel Sanders had been born in Tennessee we would be eating Tennessee fried chicken.

The ultimate insult to a celebrity is to say they are not worth gossiping about.

A prisoner told another prisoner he was gong to get off by pleading insanity. He said he was going to hire the dumbest lawyer. After the lawyer talked awhile everyone would realize that nobody in their right mind would hire him.

An astronomer says "They are no earthly good."

The book reader said it is a novel idea.

The reason you shouldn't be on needles and pins is because they are hard to sit on.

A cook likes to savor the good times.

A man says that this year he is going to try and be more like Santa. I asked if that meant he was going to learn to give more. He said no he was going to drink more milk and eat more cookies.

It is easy giving a speech at a prison because you have a captive audience. You hope they catch everything you say.

A fireman says he is like good piece of pottery because they have both been through the fire.

When a heavy guy is outside without a shirt on we can say he is showing off his weight.

For a crier it isn't just a shame but a crying shame.

When dieters have a meeting they call it a weigh in.

An unconscious cave man is said to be out stone cold.

It can be difficult knowing if a gambler is telling the truth when he wears a poker face.

Some people say they don't need to hear. They say they have heard enough.

We say to some people that they are standing tall, but to others we say they are falling short.

Sometimes we think there is only one way out, but remember there is a back door too.

A cattleman says it behooves me.

He was eating out alone. He thought about doing something nice for someone else. He noticed an attractive lady a few table over eating alone so he told his waiter to give him her bill. After that he didn't pay much attention to her. When he went to pay the bill a big guy came up to him and said "What's the big idea of buying my wife's lunch?"

The coffee man says when people are wrong about something we need to tell them to wake up and smell the coffee.

Only a bug man would say the place was crawling with police.

Now days when people are asked to go the extra mile they want to get paid for the milage.

There are lots of plans but few well thought out plans.

An AA member was giving his testimony. He said every time he ate he washed it down with alcohol. It got so bad he was spinning out of control. Now finally he is on the dry cycle.

Advice from a weatherman
Give everyone a warm welcome.
Don't leave anyone out in the cold.
Smile more so your face doesn't freeze up.
Remember you can be a shower of blessing.
Let your sunshine shine through you.

If you go to the center you can't be right and you will be left out.

The only flow most people want is a cash flow.

The Indians are computer savvy.

Remember in life it won't always be smooth sailing.

In order to reach his goal he had to move the goal post several times so it was closer.

He was a baby genius. What happened to him? He outgrew that stage.

One astronomer says to another one. You need to get over the moon and start looking at the stars.

If you are a slow talker don't expect fast results.

When you are asked to come to a pot luck it is good to bring fruit. It sounds so positive to say "I come bearing fruit."

The cook says everything is better in life with a little salt.

To have a good day postpone worrying. Leave it for another day.

It was in the cave day where they first said the famous statement "I am between a rock and a hard place."

Is it more important to make up your mind or to know when to change your mind?

Just because I made the error that doesn't mean that I am not going to look for someone else to blame.

When the weatherman comes into a lot of money it is called a windfall.

The telephone one operator says lots of people have missed their calling in life.

A ghost looking at his past call themes old haunts.

In the Old West when they had a surprise party and surprised you you could you were ambushed.

Many people wish they had a little magic in them when they want someone to disappear.

When all is said and done more is usually said than is done.

The best way to save time is to find someone else to do the job.

Your fingers can really get tired when you let your fingers do the walking.

It is one thing not to need someone's help, but it is something else when they say you are beyond my help.

A man says he was so smart in school when he did intellectual things was so far ahead of the others he only used half his brain.

This year there have been more disengagements than engagements.

It is disappointing for a guy who is into wires, when everything is going wireless.

In Idaho when someone has too much to drink we say they are mashed.

Don't go on a hike with a trail guide if you are not a follower.

I have been tackling so many problems head on that I now have a headache.

If they could talk who would say I have another mouth to feed? Definitely a bird.

Who says "I have a lot on my plate?" Most of the people at the end of a buffet line.

When a house falls down in California the owners say it was no fault of theirs.

The pastor says they have some redeeming qualities.

An upset vampire says that some things make his blood boil.

The astronaut says that when he was out in space he got a new prospective on seeing the world.

Learning is one thing. Applying what you learn is something else.

There was a contest at the prison. Every prisoner trimmed their cell. The winner was offered more free time.

The only vegetable we are told we can mess with. They say “spill the beans.”

When they someone is an old bat it is because they are always getting into your hair.

The customer asks the waiter to return his food. The waiter asks why. The food isn’t going to change.

The oil man says the trouble with a lot of people is that they need to be refined.

A monologue is when one person is talking and nobody else is listening.

The elevator guy is really feeling good. He says he really feels up.

Word of the day is “phooey.” You say phooey when you don’t want to do something.

The score keeper has an old score to settle.

Today Tarzan would not be allowed to swing through the vines because he might damage them.

The weather man was under a cloud of susipican.

When we say a well rounded figure a guy said you could be describing how I look.

When people do something wrong they often look for a cover story.

When people are busy they always say they are in the middle of something.

Don't you hate it when he says "I can find my own way out" and you wanted to show him the door?

The gambler say this year has been a year of hits and misses.

The shape of your face when you are feeling sad. You have a long face.

Boxer is willing to try something new says he will take a jab at it.

The tag in the store says 12.99 and underneath another tag says still 12.99 so you may as well buy it.

Oil workers like to bank at Wells Fargo.

Hands argue with themselves. One hand says on the one hand. The other hand says but on the other hand.

Indian terms
Long knife means they have a sharp tongue.
Twisted tongue they will change the story to suit them.
Talk with a forked tongue means they will lie.
Straight arrow they will give it to you straight.

China has to be one the busiest countries because it seems that most everything is made in China.

A counselor said don't give away free advice. Charge people for your advice so they will think it is more valuable.

The best compliment you can give a cave man is to say he is as solid as a rock.

A telephone operator says she is not close anymore to some of her friends. There has been some disconnect.

An apple grower says everyone needs core values.

The difference between a laugh and a giggle. A laugh goes Ha Ha and a giggle goes Hee Hee.

Some people have dark thoughts because they haven't been spending enough time in the light.

When someone is saying something that makes them seem smarter than you handle it by saying "Duh." This means what they said is simple and everyone knows it and you know more than they do. There is really nothing you can say to a duh if that doesn't work you can cross your arms and say "Oh Really." That means you doubt what they are saying is true. These are some real power words.

A fireman was in a fight but he said the other guy was no match for him.

We are supposed to learn to stand on our own two feet.

The name of the restaurant is called "Yum Yum." They say the food is really yummy.

In the days when there used to be elevator operators he loved telling the big guys he was going to take them down.

If you can't say anything nice about someone get together with your friends and gossip about them.

In Scotland when men can no longer fit into their pants they start wearing a skirt.

A landscaper in a fight with another landscaper tells him to get off his turf. When he swears he says "Oh sod it all anyway."

The guy's shirt says "I am not going to be a nice guy anymore." He said he was tired of finishing last.

My friend is like a turtle she always has a snappy comeback.

The skydivers have come up with their own dropout out program for young people.

The cook comments on a play she saw. There was a lot of raw talent. Sone of the lines were really in poor taste. It seems like the plot had been done too many times in the past. You could say it is overdone. It can be really difficult to digest everything that is going on. It did give me something to chew on. It definitely could be spiced up in part. They really need to cook up a new idea with lots of flavors that will appeal to the appetites of every one.

A plumber says you can tell when you are getting old. Your plumbing slows down. You are all clogged up, and your brain is leaking.

An upset vampire says that some things just make his blood boil.

If a dishwasher is in a fight and gets a black eye it is called shiner.

The club that most dishwashers belong to is the clean plate club.

When the news is big for the potato farmers they say it is one hot potato.

When someone says they have it in their pocket you know you are talking to a pool player.

It was at the cemetery where one worker called another worker a numbskulll.

The paper had to bury some news in the obituary section of the paper.

The circle most of us want to be is in the winner's circle.

Fruit growers say thanks a bunch.

Bill was always the life of the party. The party was in full swing with everyone laughing and having a great time. Than after a couple of hours it got very quiet. Several commented how dead everything had gotten. One said well Bill left several minutes ago.

I like the shirt that says "Don't wimp out on me."

When a tire man tells a story he likes to put a good spin on it.

When you get a call saying you owe money that is called a bad call.

The best compliment an oil worker can give someone is to say they are refined.

When they divide into small groups at the prison they are called break out sessions. The golfer died. He had one stroke too many.

When someone always feels the need to be one up on you we say they are being uppity.

Mongolia and China don't get along. Someone built a great wall between them.

When you go ghost hunting you need to get into the spirit of things.

A guy has his picture on his shirt that says "I love this guy."

An astronomer who is not feeling well says his world is spinning.

When you read a story backwards it starts out with the ending and ends with the beginning.

People who are part of a group don't want to be singled out.

The cook said it was terrible the way the mashed potatoes were assaulted.

During gladiator days when they beat the other team they say they got whipped.

Sanitation workers love to shop at the dump.

The young pilot was learning to fly. He took two of his friends with for a short trip. After an hour the friends said they really needed to go back to the airport because they had things to do. He said there was a problem. He knew how to take off but was still working on how to land.

Housing changed for the cave people. They started to live in rock houses. They would talk about things that happened back in their cave days.

What feeling we lose first is touch. People will say they lost touch.

The owner of a dog was accused of encouraging it to put the bite on someone.

A lot of people who call must go to alcoholic angnymous meeting because there is no name on the phone call we get.

When asked by the police who supplied his drugs he named the local druggist at the grocery store.

Talking scales don't work too well. A heavy man got on the scale and it said "Get that horse off of me." To a lady it said "No you haven't lost a pounds and your new diet isn't working." To another guy it said "You shouldn't of had that second desert."

In the Old West there were two bank robbers who ended up shooting someone. One got caught. Later he was sentenced to hang. There was a crowd at the hanging. He noticed the other robber there in a disguise. His last words were to him. He said "Don't leave me hanging."

Even if people are in a fog they often say "Do I make myself clear?

A skydiver said he would jump at the chance to do it.

The word of the day is "iffy." If certain conditions are meant or someone goes with me I might do it. Right now I am kind iffy about it.

I always try to keep an open mind when someone is trying to read my mind.

Two girls were talking about what to do about a problem. The one came up with an idea that the other girl thought was really stupid. The other girl said "You love the idea don't you?"

For people in a make believe world reality bites.

The butcher uses this term concerning losing weight. He says I have to trim off a little fat.

The deaf guy got in trouble. He was using bad hand signals.

When reading a mystery the real estate person is always interested in the plot.

A crafty person often asks if you are gong to make something out of it.

When an astronomer says he can't do something he says it is not in his sphere.

What light most people want to be in is the spotlight.

The fruit grows said he hoped to live to a ripe old age.

Word talk
Just say the word.
The word is out there.
I just need to find the right word.
They had words between them.

Just take my word for it.
I won't say a word.

In fruit country they say the pie was berry good.

When the weather man sang he left a lot of people misty eyed.

The tow truck driver was accused of pulling a fast one.

They played haunting melody at the cemetery.

The gas station owner says in life you need to step on the gas.
Don't run on empty.
If you are going to go further in life you can go further on a full tank of gas.

In the Old West there were outhouses. When a really bad bandit used the bathroom that is when the sheriff would grab him. That is where we get the slogan "He was caught with his pants down."

It is one thing to examine yourself and another thing to keep on reexamining yourself.

A gambler says that's another thing I can scratch off my list.

The miner is not a good eater. He just picks at his food.

If people are elbow to elbow it isn't too long before they start to elbow each other.

The pointer likes to be thought of as your point man.

Some people see everything in black or white while others think there is a little gray area in between. We know the gray cells are supposed to show wisdom.

We are told we need to bless others and not curse them. When a driver cuts in front of me, I say "Bless that stupid driver."

A nun who is no longer a nun says she has had a change of habit.

The weather man says we all have a dry spell, but if it lasts too long it is called a drought.

A gambler tells another gambler not to press his luck.
Some good New Year's Resolutions
Artist says this year he hopes to stay in line
I am going to keep my mouth full so I don't have to speak so much.
I am going to see more of a certain doctor that I have been dating.
I am going to go on more trips. Okay I might even take my family with me on a couple.
I am going to keep up appearances so no one will suspect that I am doing anything wrong.
I am going to eat my desert first so I will have room for it. When I get full I will say I just can't eat another vegetable.
I am going to spend more money wildly on me.
If I am going to be on the same page as my wife, I suppose I have to stop skipping pages.
Grow more and hopefully it won't be from a size 40 to a 42.
Quit thinking about the projects I haven't started and probably will never finish
Write more. I am going to put my complaints in writing.
I am tired of taking the blame for everything and than feeling bad. Next year I am going to look harder to see if I can find someone else to blame.
Learn to leave others alone. When my coworkers are busy and working on something I say leave them alone.

Some children's New Year resolutions
I am not going to annoy my sister so much. He have found two other people at school who are more fun to annoy.
I am going to tell on my brother and sister. There is no reason they should get by with so much.
I hope to get to the bottom of the cookie jar.

When your standing is so bad you often have to stand at the end of the line.

If you have too much going on you risk overdosing.

Oil men prefer distilled water.

The cave man always ordered his drink on the rocks.

The clockmaker had a grand time at the party.

Bathroom talk You think it is a good idea and than someone just poo poos the idea. You are tired we say we are popped. Call a little boy a squirt. We say someone's brain is so small they have a pea brain. Than there is the party pooper. Some people have a potty mouth.

Remember time doesn't stop for anyone and you are always on the clock.

The police brought the salvation army Santa Claus bell ringer in for questioning. They kept asking him "Does that ring a bell?"

A shoplifter just took small earring. She said she just needed a little pick me up.

People say they hate to brag when they really enjoy it.

A guy into dogs says at the end of the day that he worked his tail off. When his wife is after him about something he says he wish she would quit hounding him about it.

It is too bad his confidence doesn't match his abilities.

Remember if you are only part of the crowd you won't stand out and nobody will notice you.

The name of the dairy queen treat only people from up North can appreciate is Blizzard.

The alcoholic drink for blood workers is a bloody Mary.

Police talk. They say they captured it all on film.

At times the hog farmer can be kind of boorish.

Advice from a cook When you have to much to chew on cut in into smaller pieces.

When you are tall you find that many people will look up to you.

When the bee keepers break up into small groups they are called buzz groups.

A tire man gets into a fight. He knocks the air out of the other guys and lays him out flat.

Sign at vet shop shows a dog barking up a tree. If you keep barking up the wrong tree you won't get anywhere in life.

The pilot says if you want a soft landing in your life than you need to be just like the airplane, you need to be in control.

The fruit growers honored one of their own at the banquet. They say he had helped so many of them get out of a jam.

If a baker has an infection it is often a yeast infection from baking too much.

At the conference for the weather men they always have some ice breakers.

It is tough table talk when they say they are gong to turn the table on you.

The butcher says even if you don't think you know how to do something you should take a stab at trying.

Hand people try to finger things out.

To a electrician someone who isn't very bright is a dimwit.

The three ladies would go out together and eat a high calorie meal and discuss how they were going to go about dieting. One quit meeting with the other two. She eats alone, doesn't talk about dieting and has lost some weight.

Upset blood worker says doesn't that make your blood run cold.

The elevator man got sick. He was so down that he didn't know when he might feel up again.

People that love running egg yokes are called yokels.

When we are somewhere and we don't want to be there we find ourselves looking for the exit sign. It is a confusing world when half the people want in and the other half want out.

I love it when someone says stop what your doing when your not doing anything. When you get old the one part of your body that can stay young is your heart. You can be young at heart.

A hungry customer says he needs something to chew on.

Wills often end up splitting heirs.

An electrician says he hopes this year to see things in a new light.

In sailing a sailboat master you have to be able to unravel the knots.

Playground talk
I am going to let that slide.
I will swing by later.
We all need a push.
Get off that a merry-go-round and quit going around in circles.
I am just bettering on the edge of losing my temper.

The part of the body we favor when we travel is our legs. We always try to make sure we have leg room.

It is my turn to be right. You can be right tomorrow. The trick is to avoid seeing them tomorrow.

The air force pilot was in a talent show. They say he really bombed.

We are always going to be somewhere.

The customer was looking at boats. He said there was not a yacht to talk about.

The clockmaker says in life lots of people would like to turn the clock back.

What are face looks like when we are upset. We have a long face.

I am not engaged but my mind is engaged.

A vampire says you have to stick up for your family because they are blood relatives.

We use this seamstress term when someone doesn't have any clothes on. We say he doesn't have a stitch on.

When a lumberman talks small talk that means he is talking about twigs.

Several older men were talking about the good old days and what they missed most about them. They were talking about what they would like to see come back. The one man said I would like to see my hair grow back.

A guy always bragged that he had friends in high places. Finally his friend asked who they were. He said he was friends with a couple of pilots.

When everything is good to go, you need to go.

In a world of takers we need more givers.

A stock broker thought he was one hot commodity.

He doesn't want to be just right. He wants to be exactly right.

There is a fine line between showing up and showing someone else up.

What most people get is the obvious.

Remember you have to be in motion in order to get motion sickness.

The British talk in proper English. We say you need to just say it in plain English.

The customer at the ice cream sop said he's had his licks.
I asked the ice cream vender what is the latest scoop?

In Germany when you are tired they say the oomph has gone out of you.
I am in complete disagreement with you.

When offering peace in Greece you may want to offer an olive branch.

What part of your body suffers from taking on too much? Your shoulder.

In Panama when someone has mental problems we say they have going bananas day.

A tool man tries to teach others the tools of his trade.

What we would really like to see multiply is our blessings.

What number is close to an emergency number? 910

An advanced psychologist says he doesn't deal with simple problems, but with complex problems.

Only a burglar would ask another burglar what was his take on the day.

Lots of people hear but not that many listen.

I asked a farmer how he was doing. He said he was dragging all afternoon.

A lot of people can be very creative. They can make something out of nothing.

The clockmaker says you need to ask yourself what keeps you ticking.

The astronomer said "The world is not enough." That is when he begin to explore other planets. He tells his girlfriend that she means the world to him. Some accuse him of being too worldly. He say to a fellow worker "What in the world do you want now?"

Who said put the in your pipe and smoke it? An Indian chief trying to get another Indian chief to smoke the peace pipe.
The pilot says when you are having a good time, time flies.

The skinny kid lost another pound. He said "I have too much to gain to lose."

A fireman always likes his hamburgers charred.

When a tow truck driver is joking he says "I don't know if I can pull this one off."

The only drinks allowed at the energy company are drinks that will boost your energy.

When the magician deals with the IRS he is always trying to pull a few tricks.

If I make a mistake I don't want anyone referring to it as a dumb mistake. I want them to think of it as an honest mistake.

The end most people want to be on is the receiving end.

In cattle country often the young boys will have hair that is called a cow lick. Cattle men can be so bull headed.

Tarzan tells someone that he will swing by later.

Of course when two firemen are disagreeing it often leads to a heated argument.

Why do we often talk so much about ourselves? Because we have told not to talk about other.

The highway man wrote a mystery novel. It is full of curves, turns and dead ends.

Clockmakers have a lot of power because everything is timed.

A carpenter says you need to learn in life to smooth out your rough edges.

If someone has a vacant look it means there is a vacancy upstairs. No one is home upstairs.

I was in a different city going attending a convention at a hotel. In using the bathroom I noticed someone had written on the bathroom stall "For a good time call Rhonda" and than had left a phone number. I thought why not I am in a different city where nobody knows me. So that night I called Rhonda. "Oh" she said "My brother probably wrote that. He knew I have trying hard to get someone to go out with me to a polka festival"

Only in Arizona could a cleaner be late for work because she was caught in a dust storm.

You can be having a good day, but your hair is having a bad day.

Many people have problems inline because they don't learn to stay in line.

When the dairy farmer got into a fight he creamed his opponent.

People say that times are changing. The clockmaker says that's not true. We try to keep everything up to the minute.

I am not sure how you can catch your breathe.

It makes you feel important when you can say you have your papers.

A fireman says it is not okay to burn your bridges. You should never start a fire.

When sailors get a haircut it is called a crew cut.

When someone says "I am not taking any chances" you know they are not a gambler. Famous line of a gambler "It's all on the line." "It's all or nothing." It usually ends up to be nothing.

The guy said his friend's behavior is kind of kinky. He said he was going to help get the kinks out.

When you run out of words it is time to use the dictionary.

Shirt says "I may not be right all the time, but this time I am."

Growing up on a hog farm we were taught to save money. Everyone had a piggy bank.

When the butcher eats too much he develops a pot belly.

A guy from Poland says it is hard when he travels. People treat him like he is a pole. They walk around him and don't take to him or think he knows anything.

Some people see everything in black or white while others think there is a little gray area in between.

The clown takes his life to serious.

The drivers license worker hated it when the women would lie about their age. He was looking at a lady who said her age was 45 and he knew she hadn't seen forty-five for many years. He said we need to celebrate when we turn fifty and sixty. Now why don't you just correct your age and put down sixty. She yells "I won't be sixty for two more years."

If someone has long hair and large beard they are going to the shaggy dog look.

The skydivers offer new members one free fall.

When someone does something big we tell them that was big of them. When they do something small for you should we say that was small of you?

I asked for directions to Hidden Valley Ranch. The guy said I can't give them out. If I did it wouldn't be hidden anymore.

If you know some things that most other people also know that is known as common knowledge.

The landscaper says when he works with others, he tries to look for common ground.

A trucker who is still thinking says his wheels are still turning.

If something is apparent there is that hope that you will be able to catch on to what is going on.

When the cook hears the same ideas that she has heard many time before she says those ideas are over baked.

A carpenter doesn't knock on the door he pounds on the door.

In the fields of Bolivia where they grow opium when there is a police raid they are heard to say "Poppycot."

The older gardener says he really enjoys digging around in the dirt as he works in his garden. He doesn't appreciate that so many refer to him as a dirty old man.

A freudian slips is when someone tries to slip something in.

Pointer say get to the point.
Landscaper says don't beat around the bush.
The television man says you need to learn to be direct.
What part of your body has to do with values and problems? Your face. You take someone at face value and learn to face your problems.

A carpenter says to another carpenter we have the same build.

The skydiver says he is not gong to fall for that trick again.

A lumberman is at odds with another one lumberman. We say they are at logger heads with each other.

The pest control man and the skunk both use sprays to get rid of pests.

The road man says don't get ahead of yourself. Don't move ahead until you see the green light.

What did one priest say to the other priest? We are cut from the same cloth.

Someone said all I have to do is make an appearance. His friend said appearances are everything.

They said when my aunt died that she was the glue that held the family together.

The window guys is a shady guy who has been known to pull the blinds on others.

The road workers say their signs are just as vital as doctor's vital signs. You try going through a stop sign and see what happens.

At the vet place they call their emergency fund a kitty fund.

By the way if you are a scatterbrain that means your mind is not focused on one thing but on many things.

The two moves we all need to make is to move on and move up.

The fishermen were showing off heir catches of fish. A younger fisherman came in with an attractive lady. He said she was his catch of the day. You sit your way and I will sit my way.

Two guys were arguing at the mental hospital over who was the nuttiest. When one told where he used to work. The other worker said I give up you win. He used to work for the state of California.

They are having a mixer at the bakery.

I asked the ice cream vender what is the latest scoop?

In horse country the best compliment you can give someone is to say they have a lot of horse sense. The horse rider whispered to the horse "Let me take the lead next time."

I am in complete disagreement with you.

The demolition guy is the only person who knows what is going down.

The demolition guy said when you mess with you are messing with dynamite.

A waitress with lots of problems poured them to a counselor. He left her with several good tips.

When someone says things that don't make sense we say they are taking nonsense.

In Russia the ants are called red ants.

Overreach is when someone is trying to grab something that is yours.

A mind reader can't read your mind if you have a closed mind.

If you want to be noticed you need to look like a sharp pencil.

We can all be sharp. A clothing store manager says we may not all be sharp but there is no excuse for not dressing sharp.

It sounds so violent when someone says "I will grab you later."

When a judge gets it wrong we say he had a lapse in judgment.

I like to be in a line where there is a cashier. I like to have someone to complain to.

It can be difficult having man to man talk with someone when he is acting so childish.

If you keep on having stinking thoughts after awhile they will start to smell.

A man who has long hair and a large beard that style if called the "Shaggy Dog" look. You can be sure this person is not fond of barbers.

People who give advice often will say in their humble opinion. Anyone who gives advice all the time is not that humble.

Most people who are on the road never arrive at there they should be.

The candy maker admits that when it comes to telling the truth he fudges a little.

Many a grocery shopper has fun shopping and filling up the cart. They than lug it home and ask for help in putting everything away. Than they rest a little. Later they decide they are to tired to cook and say let's eat out. That is a very good shopping trip.

The man from the water department said that we need to learn to go with the flow.

The farmer raised chickens and geese. He was the first to come up with the term "goose bumps."

The glue maker was taken in for questioning. The are hoping he would come unglued. They couldn't get any of the charges to stick.

The detective said to try and hold the skydiver a little longer before he bails out.

They brought the air-conditioning guy in for questioning. Even thought they tuned up the heat, he played it cool.

The detective says life it not like a cookie. When someone steals a cookie all you have to do is follow the crumbs to find him.

The gas station owner said a lot of people think they are going somewhere, when if you run on empty you are not going anywhere.

The lady doesn't want anyone to know that she is using a little hair coloring to get rid of her grey hair. Now when she goes to work at least two women asked her if she liked her hair dye.

When a rancher doesn't want to hear something anymore he says that gate is closed.

A hog farmer was upset with another hog farmer because he squealed on him.

A lot of hog talk is just grunting.

The clockmaker was on the witness stand in court. He said he knew the exact moment it happened. He keeps everything up to the minute.

The man tells the trail guide that he won't be misled.

To dream something that can't happen is to dream the impossible dream.

It is hard to be a mediator when both sides want you to butt out of their business.

The clockmaker said when you are under too much stress it is good to call a timeout.

Man to psychologist says "You aren't just messing with my head are you?"

Two crooks were talking while waiting to get in line for a line up. The one said that he felt like most of his life he had been in lines starting with kindergarten. While the other one said "You would't be here if you had stayed in line."

A little girl was standing by the door of a store while waiting for her mom to finish shopping. A lady was standing there too. She asked what she was doing. The lady said she was waiting for somebody. The little girl looked up at the lady and said "You are waiting for me. My teacher told me that I am somebody."

When someone says they can't come over to help you because they are tied up, offer to send someone over to untie them.

When disgusted we say this letter "U."

I was talking to a guy at the grocery store. Finally he said he had to go. I told the bathrooms were in the back of the store.

Ken was a good guy. When he got older he was still a good guy.

You know what they say "He is an oldie but still a goodie."

There was a vote at the blood bank. The result was four negative and three positive.

An older man at the gym asked if I knew what his name was. I told another guy it is sad when someone can't even remember his name.

The mortician said "Well if that isn't putting the last nail on the coffin I don't know what is.

The magician asked the guy a question. The guy asked if this was another trick question.

An astronomer said his daughter went to Hollywood to become a star. Now how dumb is that.

If you bug the bug guy, he is going to zap you.

When you fix a steak you don't went people talking tough.

When someone is clumsy in their talking they keep dropping names.

Beggars should not to allowed to vote. You know the saying "Beggars shouldn't be choosers."

They sprang the mattress man from the jail.

Some people are like boxers they are always trying to get you into a corner.

The pilot says the way you approach things in life will effect where you end up at.

How you tackle your problems. You tackle them one by one.

A girl named Ivy isn't easy to get to know but she will grow on you.

He didn't like being in the military and taking orders. Now he is out and working as a waiter.

It is difficult when you live in a fantasy world and you have to have a reality check.

I went to a feminist church where instead of saying amen they say awoman.

A man having a lot of self-confidence wears a shirt they says "I am a Big Deal."

My dog is going to be a leader. When we got for a walk he always takes the lead.

When an artist has a close call it is called a brush with death.

It can be making a mistake to tell people to take their time.

In cave days the women had to wear fur coats to keep warm. When the women got into a fight we get the expression "You should see the fur fly."
In the Old West a cowboy using a mirror with his back to the object he was shooting at would shoot a shot glass off the head a dog. Some bragged about his good he was. One said "He isn't so good he shoot three dogs before he got it down."

The artist said that this year instead of drawing so many long faces he is going to draw more happy faces. He is also hoping to stay in line this year.

It was New Year's Eve. I asked the older lady what her New Year's resolution was. She said to be more organized and to be on time. Now get out of her so I can finish my Christmas cards.

A surveyor says before you make a decision you should get the lay of the land. It pays to get help from my Uncle Frank. He has a lot of pull. He is a tow truck driver.

Goldlilock had an overweight problem. She ate everyone's porridge.
She broke the chair. She was tired from over eating so she fell asleep in on the bear's beds.

You tell an accountant something and they say "That figures." They say that no account brother-in-law is worthless. We have problems when we don't take things into account.

When a farmer is in an accident he says the other car plowed right into him.

Life is like a large map. An X mark says this is where you are. A larger X on the other side of the map says this is where you should be.

It can be worse than being known as average Joe. You could be thought of as below average Joe.

The sailor likes to keep his opponents at bay. He is known as having a salty tongue.

The weather man says many people who are in a fog think they can talk themselves out of it. They say "Do I make myself clear?"

A bowler's' hair has a lot of splits ends.

When the submarine crew drink they say "Down the hatch."

A clocker maker says we don't always know what makes someone tick.

They knew the cat burglar had been on the prowl. Everywhere she went she left claw marks. They found out that her name was Kitty.
It was easy when they finally caught her. She was caught cat napping.

A loud thinker can hear himself think. When we don't have any thoughts we are said to be thoughtless.

Giving facials can be an in your face job.

A laundry working giving up says she is ready to fold.

Minnesota may brag about having the most lakes, but Wisconsin says they have the most fish.

The massager says "Now here is the rub."

A t-shirt to encourage girls says "You go girl."

At the campground the campers were to go to different focus groups. The one focus group was on "How to find a direction for your life." The head counselor asked the one camper how he found the group. He said he got lost and just stumbled into the group.

A horseman said his problems have been mounting. He has been in the hospital but he is in stable condition. When he is in a hurry we say he has been chopping at the bit.

Remember if you hang on too tightly you won't be able to receive anything.

A pastor acts like a weatherman when he is to long winded.
I think the pastor has been talking to my wife because they both of been to teach me the error of my ways.

An illusionist says things aren't always what they appear to be.

My sister-in-law is really into football. She is always trying to run inference in our lives.

At the fruit department of the grocery when you are really thankful you say you are grapefruit.

Someone asked the trucker if he would take a load for him. He said no You-haul it yourself.

Relationships

When a girl goes on a date her friends always want an update on how it went.

The lady said her boyfriend was financially sound, but the rest of him isn't so sound.

The UPS guy tells he girl he wants to be upfront with her.

A cleaner broke up with her boyfriend because when he came over he was always making tracks.

The girl dating a detective said he doesn't have a clue about what I think about him. He is so clueless.

The cook was not to excited about her daughter's prom date. She said I suppose in a pinch he will do.

The couple was at party. The man was rubbing his eye. He told his wife that something caught his eye. She said "I know and you need quit staring at her.

The seamstress warns her daughter not to be taken in by her boyfriend.

A guy had the word "Beast" on his shirt. When he asks a girl out he tells her that he is ape over her.

At the grocery store in honor of Valentine's day they are selling toilet paper that says soft and strong. It is what women want are men to be.

A man asked a girl if she wanted to go out with him for a walk on the wild side. They were going to the zoo.

The mortician's helper said the girl is drop dead goreages.

They say the judge is courting a certain lady.

The girl asked the rude guy to come closer to her. He said why. She said so she could slap him.

The delivery truck drive complained that his girlfriend is stalking him. She is always on his bumper.

A druggist is working on a book for valentine's day. It is called my Prescription for Love. He has daily capsules for each day.

A blood worker was dating another worker. Her friend asked her what type of guy is in. She said he is A positive.

An older road worker was dating again. When asked about his girlfriend he said she has has been a few miles down the road.

The skydiver in love really fell for the girl.

The guy was going to save a lot of money on taxes this year. He was dating a girl called Charity. He was going to deduct all the money in taxes that he gave to Charity.

The insecure football player always wanted to know if his girl was down with him.

U-haul driver says he has never gotten hitched.

The young man worked at service first. It was difficult for him to get a date because the girls always wanted to be first.

She complained that her landscaper boyfriend treats her like dirt.

A landscaper tells his girlfriend that he worships the ground she walks on.

A seamstress said when someone isn't attached to anyone they are a lose end.

It can be difficult dating someone who has so many weeds in their life. Even when you pick them out, you know how fast weeds grow back.

Guys who have trouble expressing themselves say they have a thing for a certain girl.

I asked the guy how got kicked out of his focus group. He said they claimed he focused too much on the girls.

The guy at the door factory said this one girl is always knocking on his door. His friend asked if he has let her in and he said not yet. His friend said if it is who I think it is she can knock on my door anytime.

A guy at his girlfriend's apartment says to her "All I see is you."
Her roommate said "That's for sure. Her pictures are up all over the place.

The baseball player was accused of hitting on the girls. He said it wasn't his fault. He is a big hit with the girls.

Sanitation workers have some of the best pickup lines.

The electrician said it didn't work well with his daughter when she dated a guy who had a dark past.

The dishwasher's girlfriend was very smart. He says she is a deep dish.

The guy worked at the carnival. The front of his shirt said "Go out with me for a thrill a minute." On the back is said "I will leave you screaming."

The science teacher described her relationship with her boyfriend as being solid.

A painter asked a girl out. He wanted to know if she wanted to paint the town with him.

A girl said her boyfriend makes her laugh. The other girl said when it comes to your boyfriend we all laugh at him.

When a fireman meets his match he gets a little fire going.

He was told he needed to improve himself so he has started to date smarter girls.

The artist said she wasn't sure what had drawn them together.

The advantage is dating an usher is when you go to events you get a front row seat.

New shirt for young guys on the front says "I am the best." On the back it says "Why settle for anything less."

She told her friend that her date was like a pig. You mean he stuffed his face with food? No, more like a male pig. You know a boar.

He had a little spat with his girlfriend. He had to go and take a test. He told his girlfriend that his mind wasn't on the test but on the argument they had. He said "Why don't you just say your wrong and sorry so I can concentrate on the test?" She told him not to blame her for his grades.

A girl was talking to her two girlfriends about how hard it was for her boyfriend when she broke up with him. He is having a difficult time getting over me. One girl said I think he is over you. I have seen him out twice with your sister.
The trail guide got in trouble. He was accused of leading a girl down the wrong path.

My boyfriend is really into nature. He took me with him on a camping trip with his family to get into touch with nature. I got in touch with poison ivy.

Two girls were dating a clockmaker. One said he likes me more than you because he is spending more time with me than you.

An older man was wearing a shirt with this pickup line "Help me I am lost please take me home."

A girl went out with a guy called "Greasy." When asked how the date was she said he was real slick.

The bee keeper's daughter was sweet on the candy maker's son. When they got together it was a very sticky situation.

Two dishwashers were dating. The one broke up with the other one. He said she just wasn't in sink with him.

The girl goes out with a guy who has a bad reputation. Her friends said he is not to be trusted and to watch out for him. She went out with him anyway. Her friend was worried about her. When she came back from the date she asked how it went. She said "He was a perfect gentleman. I was so disappointed."

A cleaner hates sloppy kisses.

A girl asked another girl why she dated so many losers. She said that when they go out with me they feel like they are a winner.

A hunter said he wanted a second shot at romance.

Some girls were gong to get together. Each one would bring something to snack on. One girl said she would bring the potato chips if you will bring the dip. Later when they got together the girl that brought the chaps said she had looked all over and she couldn't find the dip. She said Fred is over by the door.

The shirt says "I am a winner. Don't waste your time dating all those losers."

A girl asked another girl how her date with the new guy went. She said she had to slap him. Did he get fresh with you? No, he fell asleep on me.

The oil man was upset when he broke up with girlfriend after having sunk so much money into the well.

A cleaner in love is sept off her feet.

The boat captain said that the one lady really rocks his boat.

Two young women were discussing their boyfriends. The one said her boyfriend is into the dirty stage. Everything has to be dirty from dirty jokes or taking things the wrong way. The other one said he will get over that. My boyfriend is now into the mud stage. He is slinging mud at everyone.

At a party a guy was looking around. Someone asked him if he was looking for his wife. He said no that first had to look for a wife.

I have been helping my boyfriend save money. He has been taking me out on cheap dates.

Two girl cousins at a family gathering were bragging about their boyfriends. One said that her boyfriend was a part of the football team. Her younger brother overhearing that added that he was the water boy.

The relater's boyfriend told her he wasn't asking for a lot.

When an oil man really likes a certain lady he says she really gets his pump going.

Best pick up line at a juice bar is "You are just too squeezable."

A hunter was having some trouble in dating. He went to party hoping to find a girl he liked. First he scoped out the competition.
Than he saw a girl he liked and set his sights on her. Than he had to hunt her down and aim towards her. He wanted to make her the target of his affection. Then he blew it all by shooting off his mouth.

A gymnast flipped out for another gymnast.

The cleaner's boyfriend wanted to get back together with her. He told her that he knew he had really messed up. He wanted to pick up with her where they had left off.

A girl in a mental hospital asked another girl why she never went out with Ben who was also a patient. She said she may be crazy but she is not that crazy.

The oldest pickup line was a runner in the olympics in Greece. The runner told his girlfriend that he carries a torch for her.

A guy says to his girlfriend that she deserves the best. They end up eating out at a place that is cheap. He says I can't afford the best.

A girl getting dressed for a date asks her roommate what she thinks about an outfit that she has picked out to wear. She says "Do you want the truth or do you want me to lie again?"

The new look for bald guys is bald on top and than having a big beard. This pleases girls who think bald is beautiful, and the girls that want to put their fingers through your hair.

The man and the lady have been dating each other for five years and doing so many things together. Finally one day he asked her to marry him. She hesitated. She said "It just seems so sudden."

A gambler meet his girlfriend on a chance encounter.

The foot doctor knew she was the right girl for him when she threw herself at his feet.

A lonely number on valentine's day is one.

When a cook likes a guy she says he is yummy.

A money hungry man wanting to marry a rich lady when introduced to a rich lady he told her she looks like a million dollars.

A man dated two sisters. One was quiet and had nice things to say about everyone. The other one was very critical of others and liked to boss people around. He ended up marrying the on the one that reminded him of his mother. Now you do know which one reminds you of a mother.

Two girls were talking. The one said she knew he was trouble when she first meet him. The other one asked her why she still went out with him. She said maybe I like a little trouble.

Two gals were talking. One said I know you can't buy love but I do wish more guys would at least try.

Lots of guys in a relationship either take the slow road or the fast road with a girl. The guy said he is sort of a middle of the road guy.

A lot of girls aren't biting on the lines the guys have been giving them.

A girl started dating a guy who drove a fast sports car. At first the relationship just zipped along, and everyone was jealous of the good time she was having. Than after awhile he changed gears and things were not the same. She had to adjust to the changes he made, and the relationship slowed down. Her friend asked if she stayed with him. No, like a lot of relationships ours ran out of gas and ended.

The ticket taker told the girl she should go out with him. Together we could be the winning ticket.

The snobbish mother thought of his girlfriend as trash, but her son liked her. He asked if he could take the trash out.

The electrician's girlfriend was so happy. She was all aglow.

A cleaner's shirt says "Don't mess with those other guys."

A shirt says "This is Your Lucky Day I am available."

A guy said that Ken is going out with a girl who has a real high I.Q. The other guy said you have to be more specific. Most girls have a higher I.Q. than Ken. The third guy said "Most of them are smart enough not to want to go out with him.

I was dating a runner but she was too fast for me. I couldn't keep up with her. Later I heard that an old boyfriend caught up with her.

The college student and his girlfriend were very smart. They were always putting their heads together in working on a project or in planning something. Finally they got married. You know the saying "Two heads are better than one."

She finally got an engagement ring. The stone was so small. She took to having a magnifying glass in her purse so the ring could be seen.

Daughter asks her mother if she knows Max from down the street. "Oh course I do. He is a nice boy but extremely mentally challenged." "Well he wants to date my sister. I say it is like two peas in a pod."

Two girls were talking how their boyfriends were like birds.
The one said he is always tweeting me.
The other one said her boyfriend is cheap cheap.

Two musicians were dating. She knew something was wrong. His beat was off. They were having trouble staying in tune with each other. They were striking the wrong chords with each and were seldom in harmony anymore.

A man with a split personality had to date two different women. Each one had a different personality.

At a party a guy was going to talk to Carrie. His friends said don't bother. She is so stuck up. She won't even give you the time of the day. Later that evening he went over and talked with Carrie. When he came back to his friends he smiled and said it is 9:22.

I asked the young man how he got his black eye. He said he went to a party and had his eye on a girl. Unfortunately her boyfriend had his eye on me.

The lady dated a guy from discount tires. Her life had been flat before that and she just didn't have enough air to keep on rolling along. Than came Jack and he really helped to Jack her up and make a change in her life.

It was hard going out with an oil man. He is always pumping me for information.

Two people dating in a retail store. You could say they are an item. When they argue he says you are no bargain. She says I am going to mark down everything you say. He says I am going to discount that last remark you made. The way things are going I think there is going to be a price war.

Too much smiling can get you into trouble. A guy was told he needed to smile more. He went to a party and smiled at every pretty girl he saw. Their boyfriends weren't happy with him. He had to leave fast and in a hurry.

Why didn't the vampire date the rich girl? She was to rich for his blood.

Young man says he was working on getting more acquainted with his girlfriend. Than she got too learn too much about him from his friends. Thanks friends for telling on me.

The party shop employee finally popped the question to the girlfriend that worked with him. He hoped she would marry him. She didn't and ended up popping his balloon.

The plumber said what he told his girlfriend has not sunk in.

The fireman says if your girl is too hot for you to handle give her to me because I am used to playing with fire.

The salesman's girlfriend says don't sell me out.

The man had borrowed so much money from so many people. He felt bad when he went bankrupt. He sent all those he owed IOU's.

The tire man says when he goes out with his brother and his girlfriend he feels like a third wheel.

The front to the shirt says "When you don't know who to turn to" and on the back it says "You can turn to me."

A girl on a date tells her date that he is going to get a neckache if he does't quit turning around looking at the pretty lady that's sitting behind them.

A new shirt says "This is your lucky day. I am available."

Three guys were bragging about their girlfriends telling each other about the wonderful qualities they had. The intellectual guy said that his girlfriend has a beautiful mind.

A Librarian tale
Single girl checks out books on romance
Single guy checks out books on adventure
They meet and decide to start their life together
She can picture him on a mountain with his shirt off
He can picture her holding his hands while they climb a mountain
She is worn out with all the adventure, and most of the time he is too tired for romance.
Later they are looking for books on how to stretch your dollar and make your money last. All that travel has been expensive and kept them from having a

stable job.
Now they are into reading mysteries. They can't solve their own problems so maybe they can solve other people's problems.
He starts telling her he has to work late and go different places for work without her. She knows he is into reading fiction when he tells her those stories.
Finally she is reading books on how to be happy and single.

A guy told his girlfriend that she has a special place in his heart. His friend asked if that was where he had heartburn.

The doorman says his girlfriend is a real knocker.

The trainer liked the girl because she was in great shape.

A guy asked the girl if she was free to go out on Saturday night. She said she wasn't free any night. If she goes out with you it is going to cost you.

The young lady was on a date. Her boyfriend had his coat on and was sweating. She asked why he was wearing such a heavy coat. He said he was trying to look hot.

The pointer tells the girl that he doesn't see at any point where they will be together.

A guy had gone over to talk to a girl he was hoping to impress. His friend asked him how it went. He said "Not good. She told me she wanted me to be a stranger to her."

When the trail guide says something to his girlfriend he always asks her if she follows. The girl told the trail guide that he is like a thick forest. He asked why. She said because you are so dense.

Follow these signs and you will have a good relationship
Stop You need to stop some of the things you are doing
Yield Know when to yield so you you don't argue all the time.

Curves are okay at first, but later you need to get past their curves and get to know them.
Heavy load If they have to many problems they can drag you down.
Hazard You may want to stay clear of them or at least proceed with caution.
Speed limits signs. If you go to fast you may end up leaving them behind.

A mixed relationship is when she is sweet on him and he is sour on her.

Some girls want you to invest more money in them, while others want you to invest more time with them.

A runner and his runner girlfriend broke up. They just were't running in the same circles.

Date at a carnival
She really doesn't like carnivals and didn't want to go. She liked the guy and didn't want to disappoint him so she went. The first ride was the roller coaster. This is the ride where most people put their hands in the air screaming while they are having fun. She had her eyes closed and praying for the ride to end. She held on so tight act her knuckles were white. Her boyfriend looked at her and asked if she was alright because she looked so pale. Next they are on the tiltawhirl and similar rides where you spin around so much you can hardly walk afterwards. Her boyfriend bought her a drink. She was so dizzy she bumped into a stranger and spilled the drink all over him. Finally the last ride was the ferris wheel. She thought nothing can go wrong here. She didn't know how much her boyfriend liked to shake the car they were in. As the ferris wheel stopped to let some off she looked up at the car on top of them. At the same time a guy in the car above them leaned over and threw up. Yep all over her. Finally it was over. Her boyfriend said it was fun and we should do it agin. She was mentally crossing his name off her list.

A religious girl when she breaks up with a boyfriend she crosses his name off her list.

The boyfriend after meeting his girlfriend's mom tells her that she looks just like her mother. She said thanks I am thirty and she is sixty-five. I don't want to look like my mom.

The cook peppered her daughter's boyfriend with questions.

I didn't know if I had a chance with the baker, but the last that I heard I was still in the mix.

A runner had a hard nights sleep. In his dreams he was running after a girl that was playing hard to catch. He felt he had been running most of the night.

A friend asked her girlfriend who lives in an apartment where she got the big dog. She said she was out with a guy she wanted to impress. They stopped at his house and dog came up to them. She told him what a nice dog he has and that she loves dogs. He thought that was great because he was going to be gone for a couple of weeks and needs someone to take care of the dog. That was so dumb of me.

When my boyfriend says we are going to have a play date we usually end up playing golf.

My boyfriend is in the army. I think he works with tanks. Later I found out he cleans sceptic tanks.

She had a crush on the lifeguard. Unfortunately so did most of the young girls and nothing she did seem to get his attention. Finally she decided to pretend to drown so he could save her. She jumped into the deep part of the pool and started screaming for help. Unfortunately when she opened up her mouth she swallowed water and now found herself struggling. Finally the lifeguard reached her and pulled her out of the pool. She kept her eyes closed as he pumped her stomach and soon was giving her mouth to mouth resuscitation. She opened her eyes and to her horror it was the lady lifeguard that had saved her, and she didn't even like her. Now this was a moment she would remember for a long time.

A sailor said he and his girlfriend just sort of drifted apart.

He had been in a mental hospital for awhile. Now he was out and working at a business. He had a crush on a coworker. She told another worker that he is still delusional if he thinks he stands a chance with me.

The hunter set a target date with his girlfriend.

The young male customer was flirting with the clerk. He said you need to go out with me for a good time. Another clerk overheard the conversation and asked the clerk if she would really go out with him. She said you hardly know him. The clerk said "I know but you know the rules of our store. The customer is always right."

The potato farmer who likes a girl was talking sweet potato talk.

The guy's girlfriend lived alone in an apartment. He thought it would be nice to get her a cat for valentine's day to keep her company. Just before he gave it to her, her best friend told him she is allergic to cats. The next valentine's day he gave her flowers. She sneezed and sneezed and yelled get rid of them. He found out she wasn't allergic to chocolates so he got a double layer of chocolates this year. When he went to give them to her he found the wrapping was off, but when he looked the first layer looked fine. She had the chocolates and lifted up the first layer, but there was no second layer. Only a note from his brother that said "Love those chocolates."

Bill Hitchcock had a bad reputation with the girls. That is why he is called Wild Bill Hitchcock.

A girl who works at the malt shop has a crush on another worker there and follows him everywhere. He is having trouble shaking her off.

A guy from the glue factory broke up with his girlfriend. She was just too stuck up.

The diver told his girlfriend that he would go deep for her.

It can be very uplifting to date an elevator man.

She went with her boyfriend to a small party. When they got there, there was only one chair empty and he sat on it. She was upset he didn't even think of her. Than she decided to make the best of the situation. She came up with the famous song "He left me Standing at the Door." It became a number one country Western song.

The pool player said he had his girlfriend in his pocket.

At a romantic evening he wanted to split and appetizer and later split a desert. The girl found it quite romantic. Her friend told her he does that because he is too cheap to buy an extra one.

The guy asked the girl out. She hesitated not sure if she wanted to accept. He told her his offer was a limited time offer.

The basketball player didn't do well with the girls at the party. He said is game was off.

Girls want to hangout with cool guys. Guys want to go out with hot girls.

My boyfriend works at dairy queen. He tells me I am in for a treat he is coming over to see me.

The glue maker tells his girlfriend to stick with him. He said I am stuck on you.

The boyfriend asked the girl if he could be completely honest with her. She said sure go ahead. After that she had to break up with. She really didn't want to know all the things that he thought was wrong with her. She thought if only he had kept lying to me.

The girl wears a shirt that says "I love pink." All her clothes are pink and her bedroom is pink. Her boyfriend was getting jealous. He said to her next time you see me just call me pinky.

A guy at the gym was on the phone. This went on for about half an hour. I never heard him say anything. Finally when he hung up he said his girlfriend never lets him get a word in.

Sometimes guys on a date act like a horse. They can get kind of frisky. They need to reign in their emotions and quit horsing around.

The trainer says that her boyfriend is so bad that he needs to go back to basic training.

The boyfriend was upset with his girlfriend. "How did you happen to get fired on your fist day of work?" "Well I spilled some coffee."
"That shouldn't have gotten you fired." "Well I spilled it on the front of the boss's pants just before he had go and give a speech at a meeting."

You need to thank the eye doctor when you are dating someone. We say we are seeing someone.

I heard her boy friend was kind of wild. She said her boyfriend was everything she could ever imagine. So that is what happens when your imagination runs wild.

When fools fall in love they can act kind of foolish.

The butcher said he wasn't going to bust his chops to help his girlfriend anymore.

The clockmaker promised his girlfriend prime time if she went out with him.

The electrician broke up with his girlfriend. He said she just doesn't light up my life anymore.

Don't you hate it when she says you have a zero chance of getting a date with me.

A service station man said his girlfriend has been out of tune for so long she needs a major realignment.

Two girls are looking at pictures. The one asks the other one if she can see what is wrong with the one picture. Your ex boyfriend is still in the picture.

A stock broker said before he decided to marry the one girl he made sure he looked at all his options.

The guy said his girlfriend has a pouty mouth.

My boyfriend was a hair stylist. She broke up with him. She said that he was in her hair too much.

A girl tells her friend that she knows her boyfriend loves her. He is so sorry for his past mistakes and has begged me for forgiveness and to take him back. The other girl asked "How do you know he means it? You know he is an actor and he could be just putting on act for you?" "Oh I don't think so. I have seen him act and he just isn't that good an actor.

The salad maker said she tossed her boyfriend out. He wasn't a good mix.

A repair guy getting a date for his sister says he issuing to fix her up.

The guy asked his roommate at college who had gone out with so many girls how he kept track of all their names. He said he doesn't worry about it he calls them all honey.

A blind date if just like a package that you open and don't what is in it until you unwrap it.

A man had been dating several honeys, but he finally found the right one for him. He said she was pure honey.

The two truck driver is always trying to hook someone up.

When dating ballplayer we usually end up playing ball. I call that a play date.

A girl says be careful going out with a road worker. He has a temper and flares up. I should have paid more attention to the red flags he was holding. Even then he wanted me to follow him.

A golfer said if he and his girl friend are going to get close they both have o be on the same course.

If I am going to be smothered let me be smothered in kisses.

The mover tried to show his moves to two girls at a party. He was told to move over because there were two cute guys behind him.

She broke up with her football player boyfriend. She caught him making passes at the other team's cheerleaders.

A football player who is not ready to settle down we say he is playing the field.

Two woman were chasing the same heart doctor. When he finally choose one she told the other lady to eat her heart out.

She had a date with a magician. Her friend asked how it went. She said at first it was a night of magic. You could feel the magic in the air. Later when I got in his car and on the way to the restaurant rabbits kept coming out from the seat. I was relieved when we finally got to the restaurant. He took up his cap and two pigeons went flying around much to the annoyance of everyone there. He said with his magic wand he could make things appear or disappear. I asked to see it. When he showed it to me I waved it at him and said "Now disappear. He quickly told me that I shouldn't have done that and to give his wand back. Later when he went to pay the bill all his credit cards and money had disappeared and he blamed me.

A guy went out with a girl named Destiny. He liked to say he had a date with Destiny.

A baseball player gives instructions on how to find the right girl.
1. You have to forget the time you struck out and strike up a conversation with the girl.
2. Make sure she is willing to run the bases with you.
3. Make sure that her ideas are not to far off in left field that you have nothing in common.
4. Make sure that you doesn't distract you from your keeping your eye on the ball or your goal.
5. Hopefully she let you be the umpire and make the calls.
6. She will be a good catch.
7. Hopefully she will think of your home as her home plate.

The salvation army bell ringer broke up with his girlfriend because she just didn't ring any of his bells.

Two guys were studying in a library. The one looked at a girl and said to the other guy. "She sure has a great cover I would like to read the rest of the book" Remember if you don't like the cover you will never read the book.

The relator said it was love on site, but they didn't have a lot to talk about, but he still gave me his pitch.

A friend asked his friend why he didn't try to talk to Maria when he knew he liked her. He said he made an commitment not to interrupt others when they were talking and so far she hasn't shut up.

The date with the carnival worker didn't go well. She ended up telling him he was no prize.

The tv repairs men told his girlfriend that the time she spent with him was prime time. He said not too many girls want to go out with him because they are not ready for prime time.

It is around valentine's day and you need a date. The guy you agreed to date is crazy about you, but your only interest in him is a date for the day. You know he is going to try and kiss you. When you eat you order extra onions so he won't want to kiss you.

The repair man told his friend he would fix him up with a date.

Asked the stockbroker if he had asked his girlfriend to marry him. He said he was still trying to broker a deal with her.

Guys were always telling the librarian they wanted to check her out.

The weatherman said his relationship started out hot, and than after awhile got cool. It seems when they were together they had a few storms. He wasn't sure if their relationship could weather the storms.

School

At the professor's home students were busy putting in his garden. His wife says "I don't know how long you can offer them the class on earth science and offer them extra credit for putting in our garden"

The philosophy teacher told the logical student that if he was going to use logic he won't pass this class.

The student was close to passing the test. He sat right across from Michael who was very smart and go busy coping his test. Than Michael noticed him and covered up his paper. He said if I fail this test it is going to be your fault.

At college Amber was a pest. She was bossy and getting into everyone's business. When she showed up there was an Amber alert.

The teacher stressed how important the test was and he didn't want them to have any distractions. He noticed a number of boys starring at Carol Ann. He told Carol Ann to take a desk in the back of the room.

The lawyer's son can be very irritating in class. When his teacher says anything he always says "I object." The teacher has to spend so much time overruling him.

Don't you hate it when your professor has the motto "No excuses accepted?"

A college student told the professor that he should ask his dad to be guest lecture. He always gave me the best lectures.

A student told his geometry teacher that he has a parallel plan.

Some students in speech class worry about speaking out of turn. The speech teacher always gave her children a good talking to.

A couple of middle school students were having trouble with their homework. One said I can get my brother to help he always acts like he knows everything.

The English teacher can be so possessive and contradictory.

He failed creative writing. He as heard to say "I can't make this stuff up."

The professor told the student he protested too much.

The teacher told the students they wouldn't suffer so much from panic attacks if they actually studied for the test.

The math teacher really knows how to divide a pie.

The child was lining up all her friends. Mother asked what she was doing. We are plaything school. Everyone is lining up to go to class.

The speech teacher said I need to learn to talk. In speech class some students talk too much. We say they outspoken. The speech teacher is so different than the parents. She encourages us to talk back. Student says "What I didn't say anything." The teacher tells him that this is speech class and he is supposed to say something.

The kindergarten teacher was accused of telling tales out of school.

The biology teacher tells the student that she doesn't know where his ideas stems from. She told another teacher that the student is like fungus she can't get rid of.

The students were giving the substitute teacher a bad time. The teacher asked a student what should she do. She said I would say "Class dismissed."

In the teacher's lounge they were taking about a virus that was gong around that would make everyone who got it to act crazy. One teacher said it already happened at his last school. They asked what happened. Well he said everyone was already acting pretty crazy, so the virus really didn't affect anyone differently.

A science teacher can come up with a lot of solutions.

The math teacher teacher says you will have a good marriage if you always treat your mate as number one in your life. She says some things make zero sense.

The economics teacher tells the student that his answer is in the margin or error.

A student said the closest ever got to taking a foreign language was when he had to take geometry. He didn't understand anything about it.

In schools if you want the students to think more you need to feed them more. You heard the saying food for thought.

Colleges would do better if more professors would read the students the riot act.

The son of the zoning board president was asked to do something by his teacher. He told her that was out of his comfort zone.

Teachers can be very negative always trying to take points off your papers and pointing out your mistakes.

A teacher correcting a student's paper says you couldn't be more wrong.

The student in college said his professor could just as well been speaking French because he couldn't understand anything he was saying.

A nosy math teacher always wants to add to the conversation.

A teacher asked the student what he wanted to take away from the class. The student said an A would be nice.

Don't pay too much attention to the speech teacher because he is all talk.

The math teacher said you need to make each day count.

The student didn't do well on his paper getting a D-. He said at least it leaves lots of room for improvement.

The ditch diggers son did not do well in the story he wrote for his teacher. She said it was full of too many holes.

My grandson went to an agriculture college. Each semester they have a different field of study. He must be studying corn this semester. He is always sending me corny jokes, and he thinks he is hybrid.

The college student said he wished his grandfather would write more. His roommate asked if he meant more letters. No he said more checks.

An algebra teacher always signs her letter XXX.

Teacher asked "What is a fossil? Student answered that it is a study of old people.

Why study for the test when I sit by a very smart girl. When she got started on the test I copied her answers as fast as I could. After the test the teacher announced that there were two different tests. Each student by each other was given a different test. Boy am I sunk.

When the math teacher handed back the papers, she said we need to take some corrective action.

At a class reunion someone commented that he may not have been the smartest one in his class. Overhearing a former classmate says "You got that right. You weren't even close.

When called to the principal's office the music teacher always wanted another teacher to go with her. She didn't want to face the music alone.

A student pointed to his head and says "It is what is up here that counts." The teacher pointed to the paper and said "It is what is written here that I count."

At the middle school the visitor was looking for Mrs. Burke's room. The secretary told her to go down the hall and follow the noise and you will be at the right room.

It was the second semester of school. The student complained why do we have to take a final test. Last semester we were told the test was a final test.

Science teachers often feel they have to prove something.

There is a lot of traffic at the driving school.

Science teachers say we have to beware of foreign substances.

Only a science teacher feeling confident would say she has it all down to a science.

The college student told another student that the only thing he has been passing this year is gas.

The college student says he likes to psych out his psychology teacher.

The two chemistry teachers are involved in a chemistry warfare with each other.

The ditch digger's son wrote from college. He said he was proud that he got a hole in one at golf. He knows his grade are in the hole this semester and hopefully he can get them out of the hole next semester. His English teacher felt he left too many holes in his paper. Well I can't think of a hole lot more to say.

A farmer's son was going to college. The farmer asked what field he was going to study.

A science teacher said there were some liquid times in her marriage but now it is solid. The science teacher says he doesn't know what went wrong, but he has his theory.

The math teacher says we all like to be counted.

The science teacher said his child is finally beginning to evolve.

The student said he had only missed two days of class. After taking the test and doing badly, he said those two days must have been when they went over what was going to be on the test.

The earth and science teacher say love is in the air.

Story of three roommates. One roommate tells the other roommate he better miss the party and stay home and study because it counts one third of his grade and he needs to pass the class. The other roommate comes home and sees the roommate looking all sad and gloomy. He says you need to go to the party and cheer up.

The student willing to participate says to the math teacher that she can count me in.

A science teacher often asks what is the matter with others. She always wants to examine everything under a microscope.

The teacher said that one paper turned in didn't have a name on it. The student who wrote it said to another student "If you wrote a paper that poor you wouldn't want your name on it either."

A college professor asked a student why she was taking his chemistry class when she wasn't very good at chemistry. She said her last boyfriend broke up with her because there wasn't enough chemistry there.

The teacher tells a student he needs to quit feeling so dumb and thinking he can't do anything right. She said she has taught students in the past who were not very smart and they have turned out alright. One of them even married her daughter.

Student talk in cattle country
A student asked a question says his mind is like a calf who was wandering for a moment.
The students says it it is hard to always follow the herd.
They hope nobody steers him wrong.
Sometimes students feel like other other students are branding them.
When the student doesn't believe you he says that is a lot of bull.

In school it can be hard to write fiction, when your mother always told you to just stick with the facts.

The college professor is trying to get his dad declared insane. There is an insanity hearing and the grandson went to the hearing. His mother asked how it went. He said the judge thought grandpa was very sane, but he wanted to commit Dad. Dad had to talk real fast to convince him that all the professors take like he does.

The science teacher says that you have to watch out for too much exposure to the elements.

Sometimes professors go too deep. A student tells the professor that is is going to deep for the class. Most of the students are at best shallow thinkers. We can wade out a little but we can't go too deep or we will in over our heads.

The earth science teacher says some people don't realize the gravity of the situation.

The teacher asked Richard a question. Another student said "Richard doesn't know the answer." Richard said "Please I can speak for myself." "Okay Richard what is the answer?" "I don't know the answer."

The teacher was so excited about his plan he wanted to share it with the principal. Seeing him in the hall he caught up with him. The principal was on his way to a meet with some teacher who were already waiting for him in his office. He said you can come by but you can only have ten minutes to share your plan. Afterwards he went out and said to the secretary "I sure hope they liked my plan." The secretary had the intercom on. She said "It is difficult to tell because they are laughing so hard."

The teacher tells the student it is a make up test, but that doesn't mean I want you to make up the answers.

The teacher asked a student a question. The student said it looks like neither one of us knows the answer, so your guess is as good as mine.

The highway man's son tells the teacher you need to grade on the curve, pull out all the stops, bend the rules and give us a straight road to success.

The science teacher is good with babies. She knows her formulas.

The student complained not only can't he earn the best grades, he can't even get an honorable mention.

The student said all this talk about pie in my math class has really got me hungry.

The English teacher asked the students what was the main idea of the article on volunteering. One student said if you volunteer you will end up being stuck dong the most work.

The question was asked in history class why the period of time they were studying was called the Dark Ages. A student said it was before they had electricity.

A shirt is designed for student is not doing well in school. The shirt says "Don't fail me now."

A psychologist is smarter than a science teacher. You know the saying mind over matter.

The college student asked the other student if his parents were okay with him going to a sixth year of college. He said "Sure they have always told me I have a lot to learn."

The parents of a college age son watch him closely when he comes home on vacations. They are watching to see if they can see any signs that he is getting brighter. With all the money they are spending on him for college they don't want it be wasted.

In the craft class the student was told to paste a smile on his face.

What I am taught and what I learn are often two different things.

Students says to the teacher "You know about dry spells, well I am having a wet spell and need to use the bathroom again."

The geometry teacher says I went to offer you a square deal.

In English class in an elementary school the students are told to read the articles and find the mistakes in the article. One boy wrote that the first mistake the boy made was when he didn't listen to his dad and went off alone. His second mistake was petting the stray dog. He could have gotten bit.

The teacher asked Tom what day it was. He said "Why do I get all the hard questions?"

The student wanted his English teacher to know how much effort he had put into his test. He wrote on the paper that a lot of effort had gone into the test. When he got it back he had a D for a grade and underneath that she gave him an E for effort.

Two math teachers were arguing. One said she has it all figured out. The other one said you have it all figured out wrong.
In the science class there was mass confusion.

At a teacher's meeting the math teachers always want to divide everyone up in groups.

My professor and I need to come to a understanding so we can understand each other.

A geometry teacher was upset that her class wasn't getting what she was trying to teach. She said I guess we have to go back to square one.

In the pottery class the instructor asked the students how are things shaping up.

The drama student has a shirt that says "I have my act together."

The teacher asked the students what they wanted to be when they grew up. Most of them said bigger.

The students were taking a test. Ben looked up and looked around. Phil who sat ahead of him turned around and said "You are not trying to copy my paper are you?" Ben said "No, I want to pass the class."

There was going to be an physical abilities test in gym on Friday. One thing they were going to have to do was to climb a rope. Ray had never done that before and wasn't sure he could, but than he looked at his other classmates and thought if they can so can I. All week he kept giving himself positive thoughts like I can do this. I am able. By Thursday he was actually looking forward to doing the rope test on Friday. It was Friday and they were doing their physical abilities test. The coach looked at the rope and Ray and told him to climb the rope. Ray looked at the coach and said "I can't do this." This is a time where positive thinking and reality come together head to head.

A college girl said she was going on a journey of self-discovery. Her mother told her she could start by looking in the mirror and do something about her hair and make-up.

The teacher writes a note to a child's parents telling them that their boy has trouble following directions. She said he reminds her so much of her husband.

The teacher said your son is very argumentative. He wants to argue about everything. When I found out that both his parents were lawyers I understood.

The English teacher told the students to get ready for some action. Today we are going to study action verbs.

When it was Tom's turn to give a speech in class he motioned to Wayne. He said Wayne is my spokesman.

A teacher looking over a student's test said "You sure left a lot of unanswered questions.

A teacher before a test turns up the heat. She wants the students to sweat it out.

What goes on in the mind of a math teacher when she hears that someone has changed their shape. Do they look like a triangle now or are they shaped like a square?

The teacher tells the student she talks too much. The student says "Well this is speech class isn't it?"

In the cave days the students first learned to write using their stone tablets.

The music teacher told the student not to leave on a bad note.

When a speech teacher dies they are asked if they have any last words.

At the modeling school the students are posturing for a position.

The science teacher says if you are smart you have a lot of gray cells.

At the end of the day the math teacher always wants to say and in summation.

The teachers were working in groups at a workshop. The math teacher went to the one group and was told he was in the wrong group. They said they didn't have any problems in their group.

Girls usually try to talk themselves into something and boys try to talk themselves out of something.

Many people get into trouble with their finances because they didn't do the math first.

A college student told his roommate that next semester he is going to try and get more sleep. His roommate asked if that meant he would be going to bed earlier. He said no but that he would probably be sleeping through his first period class.

Don't mind the speech teacher. He is all talk.

The reading teacher told the students that they didn't do well answering the questions on the reading test. She said most of you need to give it a second reading.

When a football player takes a math test he always has to decide on what problem he is going to tackle first.

He asked his geography teacher how he was doing. The teacher looked at his grades and told him it was all up hill the rest of the semester.

They were going to dissect a frog in their biology class. A girl yelled she couldn't do it and ran out of the room. Another student told the teacher don't worry about her. She has been kissing so many frogs lately looking for her prince.

When the geometry teacher is teaching something new he tells everyone to circle around him.

This is a speech class I don't want you to be closed mouthed.

A elementary student was excited that his class won in their division.

He was going to the school for thought but got kicked out for doing something unthinkable.

Math teachers were remembering their former students. One a former football player was mentioned. The teacher said he was an outstanding number.

When the school of thought moved from the first floor to the fourteenth it was now called the school of higher learning. One worker complained about having to do all the thinking around there.
If the thought isn't good that is called "stinking thinking."

Did you ever notice that on the witness stand most criminals plead ignorance. That sure put our education system in a bad light.

The student was walking around the classroom. When the teacher asked him why he said "My dad says we shouldn't sit at a desk all day, but we need to get up and move around."

The teacher told the student that his behavior was questionable.

The math teacher said he was off just by a fraction.

The math teacher said we need to learn to divide our problems into smaller problems or our problems will be multiplying.

The teacher tells her students "When I tell you something it can go to your head. That is called head knowledge as opposed to being empty headed."

The student asked the teacher if they failed the test would something bad happen to them. He said his grandfather failed the test the doctor gave him and he had to go to the hospital.

Sports and Working Out

Nobody has more close calls than baseball players at a game.

A sign at a convention for baseball players says "Sluggers are Welcome."

Some baseball players like punishment. They say hit me again.

A happy basketball player is hopping it up.

A t-shirt for runners says "Sorry gotta run." On the backside it says "Eat my dust."

The pastor was on a church baseball team. He said his team was so good that the other team didn't stand a prayer.

The boxer was upset with his brother-in-law. He invited him over so could throw a few punches at him.

Two guys were attending a basketball game. The one said there sure is a lot of talent on the court. The other guy said it is too bad it is all on the other team.

Some people get upset with football players they can be so offensive.

The runner said to the other runner that he wanted him to run with him and not have you run ahead.

A runner says to another runner that he is sure he has ran into you before.

You don't get much sympathy when you have a problem around a trainer. They tell you to just work it out.

A guy complained that he didn't want to run with Jack. Jack has such a big nose, and you know he will win by a nose.

The workout club gets it all wrong when they say they will help you get in shape. We are all in a shape. They can only help reshape us.

When the twins come over and want to play tennis we always play doubles.

The workout slogan at the club says "Are you tied of being pushed around? Work out here and build your muscles up so you can push back."

A runner says guess who I ran into the other day.

When a swimmer is impressed with what some says he says that is really deep.

The high school wrestler was voted the most likely to take someone down.

It is easy to remember your place when you are in first place.

A runner asked another runner what he thought of his idea. He told him it sounds good and he would run with the idea.

When the mortician was in a race it ended up in a dead heat.

A skydiver into running hits the ground running.

The boy was teaching his younger brother to play softball. He told him to keep his eye on the ball. At the game the younger boy was playing outfield when the ball was hit and it came towards him. He watched it drop and roll towards him. Another player said you maybe should have told him about catching the ball.

The hunter looks at the sign "Deer Crossing Here." He says the buck stops here.

When a golfer is not doing well we say he is way off course.

It can be difficult to insult a basketball player. You insult them and it just bounces right off them.

Imagination getting a workout. We say that is a stretch of my imagination.

I am going to a party with a football payer. They really know how to get down.

The fighter named his dog fido.

When the UPS worker is through working out, he says it is all wrapped up.

Don't help someone when they are pulling weight. They have to learn to pull their own weight.

Several people were working out on a mat on the floor. They were going to start a new job and needed to learn things from the floor on up.

The first workout the foot doctor has people do is to touch their toes.

The pitcher was giving a speech. Someone in the audience yelled "Take it on home."

I think a personal trainer is getting to personal when they bring up your weight.

A swimmer says when you get new ideas you need to think about and if you like the idea let it sink in.

In golf you don't always want to keep your eye on your ball but the ball that comes closest to the green. Than when the other golfer comes down you point to the trees saying that is where his ball went.

An optimistic fisherman says there is always a catch.

The basketball team lost. The coach got the players together and asked them if any ideas bounced off their heads on what went wrong.

When a gymnast argues he always says and now on the flip side.

New workout is called "Twist and Turn."

Tough talk at the gym when someone says they are going to muscle their way in.

Runners who don't do good get shirts that say "I prarticipated."

The runner tells the other runners not to notice the cheerleaders who will be waving at them as they turn the corner.

The dad asked his daughter who is part of a track team how she did on her race. She said she placed. Her sister said she took last place.

He gave a strong talk to the weight lifters.

Hunters like to drink out of shot glasses. A hunter who is drunk is said to be loaded.

The swimmer wanted too make a big splash in the world. all he ended up doing was getting some people wet who complained about him.

We wish more people would run with us and not get ahead of us.

The track star was so happy when he passed his first hurdle.
I asked the boxer what he was doing. He said he was just knocking around.

Who claims to have had the most close calls. Many a baseball player.
When a runner is not beating his best time we say he is running a little late.

Sometimes a golfer just puts along.

At the gym you can work in with someone as long as you work out.

The soccer player doesn't want to play soccer anymore because it has been giving him too many headaches.

Many people feel like a washed up baseball player. We have more misses than hits in our life.

Because so many fishermen lie when they tell their stories. People often say to them that there is something fishy about their story.

The cleaners played another team in softball. The only reason they lost was because the other team played dirty.

My son is a basketball player and has been sick for awhile. I told my friend that I expect he see him bouncing back soon.

The mountain climber said he reached his peak early in life.

A smoker in a running race was huffing and puffing.

A hunter must have said "Hold on for deer life."

If you are ahead of the game are you still in the game?

Two cousins were going to work out at the gym. One got there earlier and had started working out. When the other cousin found him he asked if he could share a locker with him. He said sure go ahead. He asked how he could tell which locker was his. He said it was the one with the key in it.

A golfer says in life we all have different courses to play.

The name of its football team is very offensive to other football players. Really the New Orleans Saints. Does anyone really believe there team is made up of saints?

A trainer says his goal for this year is to leave the world in better shape.

A baseball player said he isn't too concerned about what the fans call him as long as the umpire doesn't call him out.

Running away from your problem won't help if you are the problem.

A guy at the gym said he was working out because he was off today. Overhearing it another guy said to another that the guy was off most days.

The fighter says to his opponent that he is going to treat him like a doormat and wipe his feet on him.

The baseball player's nickname for his son is slugger.

The air conditioner guy becomes a wrestler. His name in the ring is A.C. When he comes out you can feel a cool breeze in the ring. Some are shaking in their boots and others get cold feet and don't want to fight him. People yell "Chill out." The only way you can win this fight is to keep your cool.

The weather man went into wrestling. His name in the ring is Thunder. He wants all the applause. He doesn't want anyone stealing his thunder. He told his opponent that he was quick as lighting. He wouldn't know what hit him. He wanted to take him by storm. It seems to be working. His opponent was in the corner doing his Hail Mary's. The only way to win was to be calm in the midst of a storm.

A hunter says that at times things can really prey on his mind. A disgusted duck hunter says "Well if that isn't just ducky."

If you are going to get along with others you need to learn to play ball with them.

When shooting a cleaner usually waits for a clean shot.

A railroad man running in a race doesn't do well because he runs out of steam. The boy was so bad in sports. He played a game of basketball against himself and he still lost.

A football player at the end of his life is in the end zone.

The number on the locker was missing. A guy took it saying he didn't want anyone knowing his number.

I touched the boxer on his shoulder. He said that is still a sore spot for him.

I was at the park with my cousin. When asked what we did I said we played tennis. How did it go? It went back and fourth.

The golfer is said to be missing a few links.

Carpenter talk at the gym. We have the same build. You need to build up your muscles. You need to bench press more. You need to have some goals that you can measure. You need to nail your workout down.

The gas station attendant says when he is working out he is pumping iron.

The young runner is in trouble. He has been running with the wrong crowd.

At the gym a guy introduced to his girlfriend the guy he was with as his brother. She said "Oh is that the idiot brother you have been talking so much about?" To quickly save himself he said "No, that is my older brother."

A trainer's shirt says "Master Trainer." Before you workout with him you have to bow first.

The runner says he will relay the message. There is always hope for a runner as long as he is in the running.

Right before Valentine's day the boxer tells the other boxer that he is going to hit him in his kisser.

At the gym they never say "Don't get worked up."

A boxer tells someone who is bothering him to knock it off.

Unfriendly runner's shirt says You can run off now."

A guy was working out hard on his shoulder. He said lately he has had to shoulder a lot of responsibility.

The dog races are where one dog is tailing another dog.

The duck walk is when you waddle from side to side.

The guy was so good at archery because he had a bow finger.

Running isn't always fun so to encourage it to be fun often it is called a fun run.

When people from the power company go on a walk they call it a power walk.

A mountain climber is always trying to reach new heights.

A fisherman bragging says he has bigger fish to fry.

A football player complained he isn't used much. He is always on the sidelines.

A confident hunter says he is loaded for bear.

At the end of the wrestler's book it says they all went home and had a good fight.

A weight lifter told the pastor he had so much weighing on his mind, but that the pastor's powerful sermon really helped him.

The weight lifter uses tough love in dealing with his children.

Work Situations

Two bosses were talking. One commented how difficult it is to find good workers. The other said he has given up he just settles for workers.

At Victoria's Secret the workers have to be careful not to let any secrets slip out.

The worker at the clothing store said she fits right in.

The cook said remember there is a seasoning for everything.

The cook told her friend what she as making was a recipe for disaster. A cook says her problems have been mushrooming.

He works with bears at the zoo. He does some fuzzy thinking.

The plumber's helper was only one flush away from getting fired

When a cleaner is tired we say she is wiped out.

The undertaker told his helper that he likes his spirit.

The bee keeper said if your A plan doesn't work out always have a Bee plan.

If the place you work at runs a tight ship you can be sure the pay is low.

The man who works at a mental hospital on coming home from work his wife asked how his day was. He said it was another crazy day.

The umpire said he would have to call him out on the last remark he made

A dishwasher says when he goes out to eat he gets a table as far away as he can from the kitchen. He wants to be in a scrub free zone.

A sign at a gambling place says "We give everyone a chance."

The man was quite shy. He wanted to be noticed at work but nobody every paid any attention to him. One day the boss told him to give a report at the staff meeting. He was so nervous about it. Just before he was to give it, he went to the bathroom again. When he started his report the others started to whisper among themselves and laugh. He didn't have anything funny in his report. Finally he found out the problem. His zipper was down. He turned red in the face. He put his report over his zipper so he could pull it up. The zipper got stuck in his pants so he had to finish the report holding his report over his zipper. Now for months people noticed him. They would look at him and start laughing.

When the laboratory worker gets upset he says "Oh rats."
The lab worker got to work late. He said the traffic was terrible. He said it is a real rat race out there.

A cab driver can drive a hard bargain. The cab driver has a lot of drive and fares well.

The bartender said he was drafted to wait on you.

Even lame brains have ideas. The boss is heard to say "Whose lame brain idea is this anyway."

The sailor gives everyone in the sailboat a stern word.

A realtor with nothing to say often has a vacancy look.

I asked the florist how she was doing. She said she was just rosy.

Most clerks at the clothing store worry about fitting in.

The clock makers are the first to come up with the idea of timed tests. If you work at the clock factory you better be on time.

Often cattlemen think the grass is greener on the other side of the fence.

The cleaner says she will be there as soon she is finished her moping operation.

He said he can't get any higher up in the company because he already works on the top floor.

It is hard to be humble when you are a pastor and the choir is singing your praises.

A dishwasher with an attitude acts like he is fine china.

The general told his secretary that he was going to be at an important meeting and to hold all his calls. Later the secretary interrupted the meeting to tell him he had an important call. He said "I told you to hold all my calls." "But sir this person kind of outranks you." How can anyone outrank me when I am the general in charge of everyone?" "Sir it's your wife."

Around Christmas time the sentry says "Halt who goes there?" "The ghost of Christmas past." "Well go on in the general is probably expecting you."

A carpenter always tries to get his two bits worth of advice in.

When workers from the water plant go to a bar after work, they refer to it as their watering hole. The boss at the water plant said he hated to have to throw cold water on the worker's idea.

A sign at the belt shop says "Don't get caught with your pants down."

The boss told his secretary he felt like a good laugh. He asked her to find Robert's report so he could read it again.

The electric company keeps plugging their products. If you get a job at the electric company you can look forward to a brighter future. They let one guy go at the electric company because he just couldn't seem to connect with anyone.

The lawyer says his life has been on trial after another.
Sometimes defense attorneys can get so defensive.
The defense attorney told the judge that he thinks the charges against his client should be dropped. He has found two witness that will swear they saw a good looking man go into the store. Now judge and jury look closely at my client. You can see that in no way does he fit that description.

A lawyer loves it when no offense is taken.

When a lawyer says his time is valuable you better believe him.

A very angry fireman is inflamed.

When there is a meeting at the furniture store everyone is told to come to the table.

The banker likes people who make a lot of cents. The new slogan at the bank is "We are checking on you."

You are towards the front of the line hoping to get picked for the job. The employer looks one the line and says "And moving on down the line."

I was hoping the boss would be going us a big bonus for Christmas. When he talked to us at a meeting he said when it comes to the bonus you need to think small.

One realtor asks another realtor if there have been any recent developments.

Did you meet the cook's new helper. At least you can't say she is just another pretty face around here.

My uncle worked undercover in a bedding store. He said you should see some of the things they had been covering up.

The sign at the groomers says "Every dog has its day.

The cattleman saw the big bull. He said that is a lot of bull.

The boss tells a clumsy guy not to fall down on the job.

The undertaker's helper said to the undertaker "There are time you just suck the life out of me."

The dairy farmer said his business is his bread and butter.

It is difficult for the new cleaner because the past cleaner already knew where all the dust bunnies were.

When a weather man doesn't like someone he stands downwind from them.

Motto of the air conditioning company is "Things will always be better after you have a cooling off period."

At the feeling seminar they were told to express their feeling to each person in a circle. One guy punched Joe. He said he just felt like punching Joe. He said now that he expressed his feeling he feels so much better.

The best compliment you can give a butcher is to say you really butchered that last job.

It is difficult for small people. When one complained to her manager about a problem, the manager told her that was just a little problem.

A cleaner asks another cleaner if she can spot her a ten.

For those who are working to be an engineer on the railroad they have to go to training sessions.

A worker asked another worker where Henry was. He said he was helping a new worker by telling him what he knows about the job. Well I will just sit here and wait for him. It shouldn't take him more than ten minutes.

The banker doesn't make any allowances for mistakes.

The man asked the lady in charge of the zoning commission if he was right with his guess. She said you are in the neighborhood. Another guy was said to be a few blocks away. When upset the zoning commissioner calls one guy a blockhead and tells another one she is gong to zone him out.

Insurance people can be quite boring. They are always explaining what their policy is. They keep saying it is for your benefit.

You don't have to be insane to work here but it helps if you are.

The clockmaker worked for years with small clocks. Now he works with big clocks. You could say he has gone big time. The clockmakers say we think too small when we ask someone if they have a second or a minute. We should ask them for more time.

I asked the fireman what had got him all fired up.

A customer told the manager how helpful the one worker was. He gave him good advice and seemed to know what was going on. Another worker hearing this said, "If he knew what was going on he probably doesn't work here."

The gas station attendant was takin in for questioning. They kept pumping him with questions. He was afraid they were going to use the hose on him.

A banker says we all need to learn to make changes. We need to know how to make the exact change.

The motto at the taxi company is "Nobody gets a free ride."

Unfortunately the boss said when he talks most of it goes over the head of most of his workers.

The clerk at the gift shop said she just couldn't get her mind wrapped around the idea.

The dentist likes people with big mouths. When he is done he polishes you off.

The nickname for the old boss on the sheep farm is the old goat.

The workers at the party shop are taught to say to the customers "Are you ready to party?"

Sign on a mover's truck says "Says when you are ready to move for a smart move call us."

I asked the lifeguard why he decided to be a lifeguard. He said even when he was a child he wanted to be a whistle blower.

A door salesman says that everyone in life is going to have some hard knocks.

Looking at his body in a mirror the mortician's helper said I want a new body. His boss said be patient we have to take them as they come in.

A cleaner asks another cleaner it she is just going to mop around all day.

The massager said he sure hoped he didn't lost his touch with him customers.

Probably nobody has been around the block more than the local sanitation worker.

A confused pilot just flies around in circles.

He wasn't in good standing with the company. He was caught sitting down too much on the job.

A sign at the tire store says "Don't tread on me."

I went to a retirement party for another worker. One worker asked if we knew the former boss was in a home. They say he lost his mind. Anther worker said "I thought that happened twenty years ago."

At the malt shop they float some ideas to see if they are good.

You can't believe all the tomfoolery that goes on at the veterinary's office.

The man comes to work on Monday and tells everyone how hard he has worked in the garden all weekend. The boss overhearing said I wish he would save some of that energy for his job.

The nap room at the daycare is called the Z room. You know zzz.

I asked the bedding store manager about a problem they were having. He said he had it covered.

The boss had the lights changed at the company. He wanted his workers to see things in a different light.

A customer at the restaurant is shooting peas with a spoon at the waitress. The other waitress said "I believe someone is trying to get your attention."

In most workshops they use this cleaning term. They say before we get started we have to go over some housekeeping things.

It can be difficult being a guard when so many people try and catch you off guard.

The manager at the clothing store says he has one strong suit. Sometimes he will just skirt the issue.

The sergeant in the military said that some things have been brought to his attention. In the military they often speak in general terms.

The first thing workers at the land management office are taught to do is to establish boundaries.

If you work on a chicken farm you can expect to be pecked on a little.

At the glue factory they always use sticky notes.

The computer expert downplayed his achievements.

The highway patrolman told the other highway patrolman that he was all caught up.

At the weight and measurements building the manager has an upscale office.

The sandwich named for people who are looked up to is the hero sandwich.

Fruit growers can be kind of picky.

The boss told the worker that he thought had a bright future ahead of him. Unfortunately it would not be with their company.

For years he worked at the clock factory working on small clocks. Finally his manager asked him if he wanted to work on the grandfather clocks. He asked if he was ready for the big time.

You world think librarians were so smart. You ask them a question and they usually tell to go to some book and look up the answer.

The waitress wanted to discuss something with the manager. He says he will put it on the table at their next meeting.

Who said "Don't let the grass grow under your feet? A landscaper to his worker who wasn't working fast enough. The landscaper doesn't want to lose ground to another landscaper.

The motto at a small crisis center says "We can only handle one crisis at a time."

The cleaner has cleaned everything she can. Now she is working in a group working for clean air.

When a postman retires he is given a good send off.

The egg farmer told the other worker that he was acting like a cracked egg that is runny.

A sign at a store says we value your complaints. Later someone saw the managers in the break room laughing as they were reading the complaints.

Who said "What goes around comes around?" It had to be someone who works with tires. When a tire man tells a story he likes to put a good spin on it.

A butcher says there is a time when we just need to chuck it. He says I hate it when people are always ribbing me. Than there are those who have a beef with me. I feel like I am in my prime time. I know I have been eating too much and have developed a pot. Does anyone but me feel like it is roasting in here?

The manager at the door store told the new worker he would show him the ins and outs. Some workers work and leave and later come back. They are like a revolving door.

It is difficult to be bald headed barber and have to listen to all the hairy jokes.

A sign at the electric company says "We don't want to see so much negative energy.

When you work at a library and the head librarian wands a "Word" with you, you know you are in trouble.

The architect says he has the best laid plans.

The ambulance drivers and the 911 operators are called to a emergency meeting.

The worker got a promotion. Now he complains that the boss wants him to get to work on time.

The guy from the glue factory said many people have trouble because they don't learn to stick to anything.

The lady was on trial for stealing a purse. The lawyer said "Aside from both purses being red there was nothing the same about them. The purse you took was worth thousands and yours could not have been worth more than eight dollars." "Well you know they are making some good knockoffs these days" "Didn't you notice there was three thousand dollars in the purse?" "Well I told my husband I was gong shopping and needed some money and that he could just put it in my purse. I did think that was awful generous of him." Well folks is she guilty or not?

Unfortunately we don't have that many busy bodies at our work place.

The boss told the workers if they are going to build on success they must first have some success.

There was a workshop on making your dreams come true. Everyone had to write down their dream. One guy's dream was that one day his boss would be working for him.

The accountant showed the boss somethings that were wrong. The boss said "There must be some mistake." The accountant said there are lots of mistakes. The accountant said some things just don't add up.

On a cruise ship the entertainment director is often asked "What is on deck for tonight?"

A worker goes to see the manager. The manager says don't bother me now. The worker asks when could I bother you?

A lawyer used to wrestle in college. In court he says "Let me be brief. I am going to take you down."

Every day at the office the workers would take turns writing the word of the day on the blackboard. The workers tried to use the word during the day and really enjoyed learning a new word. One day it was the boss's turn. After he wrote the word everyone got busy and worked harder than they had for a long time. Nobody talked to each other about the word. The word he had written was "Fired."

The manager at the water plant told his worker that his excuse doesn't hold water.

They have a mutual feeling at the loan company.

The boss always talked while standing on a stool to his employees. He liked to talk down to everyone.

A military guy was discharged. He just couldn't seem to come to attention.

Giving a good job recommendation for a worker you want to get rid of.
He is very focused. Unfortunately it is mostly on the computer games and not his job.
He has skills that make money. Unfortunately they are betting skills that only make money for him.
He has leadership skills. Unfortunately he has a large following,
and with that happening he are getting less work done at the office.
He has listening skills. He listens to everyone but the manager and the boss.
He knows what is going on. Unfortunately none of this applies to his job.
He is quick on his feet. When you needed him, he can disappear quickly.

The tow truck driver got in trouble He was pulled over.

The digger wasn't very god at the job. He said he just couldn't seem to get a handle on it.

Salesman is like a baseball player
1. Need to know their bases or products
2. Need to have a good pitch
3. Need a catchy slogan
4. Need to be in the running for salesman of the year
5. Need to know how to score with the boss.

When they have special prices at the door company they are called door busters.

The boss told the worker that there is good news and bad news and asked him what he wanted to hear first. He said give me the bad news. The company is way behind on its bills and is in danger of going bankrupt very soon. The good news is that I am am giving you a promotion that you have wanted. You are now the president of the company.

Sign at a tie place says "Come on in and tie one on."

The young workers at the bedding store were always getting into pillow fights.

It is not easy working in a malt shop. Sometimes I feel like I am grasping at straws.

When they want you to hurry at the poultry place they tell everyone to scramble. The manager at the chicken farm wears his hair in a rooster tail. The helper at the chicken farm is referred to as the wing man.

What plan most bosses want to see is a plan of action.

The manager at the electric company was talking to a worker. He said some of the things that you have been doing have come to light.

The military is really into dogs. They were dog tags and sleep in pup tents. They chow down and the sergeant barks orders at them.

There was a sale at a tire store. They said it is a blow out.

The manager was giving a sales talk to his employees. He said you represent me and the company, so don't make me look bad. One employee said to another one "Now we are responsible for how he looks too."

He was a new guy at the company. He said "Hey Mr. Scatterbrain would you do something for me?" The man says "My name is not scatterbrain. He says "I am sorry. That is just what I hear everyone calling you."

The bartender is a little like a detective. He has to look for the proof.

The young man was stopped by the police for speeding. The police looked into the car and noticed a bag half covered up under the seat. They took it out and looked into and found drugs. They asked "How did that get there?" He said "Search me." A poor choice of words on his part.

The cleaner says she doesn't have any mob connections but she sure has mop connections and if you don't get out of her way she is going to mop you up.

What does a puzzle look, look like? Boss says it is the look on my worker's faces when I explain to them how to do something.

The boss said he doesn't worry or get concerned about how things are going to get done. That's what he pays the manager to do.

The pie maker says I don't want to mince words with you. I want you to roll out the dough. I know you have some rough edges, but you need to work on them so you can smooth them out.

The manager of the bedding shop was giving a pep talk. When he got done one worker said to another "I guess he just about covered everything."

The electrician corrects someone. The other guy tells him okay since you know what to do go ahead and enlighten me.

Many people at our company have college degrees, but I am not sure how many I would call professionals.

Many a lawyer wants to impress the bench.

They let the worker go at the weights and measurement place because he was just too overweight and didn't have an ounce of common sense.

The foreman at the company says that when people aren't too bright when he gives them instructions he goes by this saying "Keep it Simple.

The boss isn't in yet so everyone is busy playing games on their phone or computers. When he shows up the secretary announces over the intercom "Game Over."

A customer asked a clerk where Mary Jo was. Another clerk said she saw her in the backroom working. The other clerk said if she was working that couldn't be Mary Jo.

The line you don't want to be in is the line to be fired.

It can be annoying working at an air conditioning place. When anyone does something good the other workers all say "That's cool."

The astronaut got called into his superiors office before taking off on a mission. The supervisory said "I heard you have been been calling the mission, mission impossible.

The police are told not to touch the suspects. Their sergeant told them to wear gloves and it would be okay.

A lawyer tells the defendant that he doesn't have to worry about being honest. Nobody expects a lawyer to be honest.

At work the boss was hoping the animal the company would be like would be the beaver. He liked the idea of eager as a beaver. It turns out they way they work is more like a sloth. Slow as a sloth.

They were all assigned group to work in. After lunch when he went back to his group he could tell the others were unhappy with him. Than he remembered at lunch complaining to someone that he hated always being put in the slow group. Someone in the group must have overheard him.

A tired bartender says he is all tapped out.

A detective was supposed to tail a suspect. It didn't turn out well. He called his boss and said that the suspect, suspect's he is being tailed. He has bumper sticker that says "Get off my tail."

The vacuum guy was always hovering over me. He said he could suck up more than most guys. I don't know it is was true or he was just blowing hot air.

I asked how things were gong at the airport coffee shop. The waitress said they have been flying around all morning.

It takes the worker a long time to plan. Finally he has come up with a plan and submits it to his boss. The next day the boss says there has been a change of plans.

I asked the bread maker how the bread worker's convention was. He said there was a lot of toasting. He liked the songs. "No loafing around," and "It is the yeast that you can do." "The Yeast will help you rise to the occasion", "Don't forget your daily bread."

The weatherman says there is a freeze on hiring new workers at the weather station.

A man works undercover for Santa. This year he found more people who were naughty than nice.

To liven things up at the local grocery store the announcement comes over the loud speaker that says on aisle ten you can find horse meat for half price.

The trail guide says lots of people don't get to where they need to be because they don't follow through.

The one worker didn't last long working at the weight and measurements place. He got off balanced.

A worker told another worker at work that he hasn't made any mistakes yet today. He usually makes quite a few. His coworker says give it time you have only been at work for twenty minutes.

Are you confused we might just have the right job for you.

A worker says to another worker that if he had any skills he wouldn't be working here.

The rich pig farmer is accused of living high on the hog. The hog farmer said he had a swill time.

A banker tells the tellers that the job hangs in the balance.

The tire man said he was flat out of luck. The tire man said that hopefully this year he was gong to tread on some new roads.

The system analyst person was very positive. He said all systems are good to go.

The tobacco shop owner says that some people just aren't up to snuff.

The railroad man said he was grateful for his friend that helped him get back on track.

A sign at a spa says "We welcome challenges." Underneath that sign it says "But we don't do miracles."

A reporter says he hasn't been able to sniff out a good news story because he has had clogged up with a bad cold.

A depressed laboratory worker says he feels like his life has been going down the tubes.

At the sandwich shop one worker says he has too much to do and feels like he has been spread too thin. Another worker is accused of bragging too much and spreading it on too thick.

An employee wasn't working very hard at the shoe store. The manager said we don't want any loafers here.

I asked how the malt shop got started. First they had to float a loan. At first it didn't look good, it felt like they were a little nuts. Than he whipped up something for the top to sweeten the deal. We closed the deal on Sundae. Then of course we had to shake hands. Our boss is a real smoothie.

I am not sure what my new job involves but I know it is work related.

The manager at the retail store said that he was going to have to shelve that last project.

The worker was told he needed to take his thinking up to the next level.

A man likes to be in control. At work he controls the bathroom keys so everyone has to come to him.

The judge says don't rush into judgement.

Who says "I don't know what you are talking about?"
Unfortunately most of the workers at many companies.

The salesman had such a good idea, but he couldn't get his boss to buy it.

The worker at a retail store said his boss has sold him out.

The party shop is offering a blowout sale on balloons.

The sheep farmer has been having dreams about wool. He wakes up feeling hot and itchy.

The boss said you did it backwards. You tell him well anyone could do it forwards.

Man worked at the compliant department at the department store.
First customer approaches him. He says "Oh another complaint. That's all I hear all day long. Well I tell you I have a lot to complain about to but do I do it. My feet in these shoes are killing me. I have been on my feet all day. My wife has left me. My car got repossessed. My kids are failing at school and getting into trouble. I have a terrible cough that I can't get rid of. He coughs. So now what do you want to complain about? He looks up and he no longer has a line waiting.

The clockmaker says things aren't always good for him. He has had his moments.

The sign at the store says if you have any questions feel free to ask one of our workers. They will try to find someone who knows what is going on. Be patient it may take awhile.

The new worker in the fruit department has lots of fresh ideas. Now if the manager could only keep him from getting fresh with the girls.

I asked the dentist why he put so much water in my mouth when he was building a bridge. He said he wanted a bridge over troubled water.

An electrician says he has done well in life because he has the right connections.

The worker complained that he can't believe how dumb the foreman is. Overhearing this another worker asked if he can quote him when he has his meeting with the boss.

The oil worker says he has another worker over a barrel.

You can tell the waiter was in the military when he waits on you.
He says
Your wish is my command.
It has been an honor serving you.
The hear waiter outranks me.
I have to give marching orders to the bus boys.
Always pay attention to your food.
I am on kitchen duty.

The cashier had been working too long at the store. She starts cursing. She says "What do the beep beep you want?"

The mechanic is really into cats. He tells his customers that he will get their engine purring.

Two zoo workers were arguing. The one told the other one not to get cagey with him.

A criminal without a lawyer feels so defenseless.

The boss at the water plant wants all the ideas to filter through him. He told the one guy that his idea doesn't hold water.

It had to be a carpenter that came up with the term hangnail.

The forest rangers get a loan from the lending tree and they bank at the wood forest bank.

The company is offering focus groups to try and encourage the workers to focus on their jobs.

At the body shop there are a lot of busy bodies.

The undertaker wold the worker that when he works for him he needs to look alive so I don't bury you by mistake.

The judge doesn't like it when anyone questions his judgement.

The prison wardens wanted to get in good with the inmates. He asked them to vote on what they wanted most at the prison and he would try and make it happen. They said they wanted an open house.

The tow truck drive says in the morning he has to pull himself together.

I asked the bee keeper if had any good ideas. He said he has some things buzzing around his ear.

Even advice columnists can run out of advice.

I asked the guy at the electric company why he didn't work very hard. He pointed to the company saying "Save your energy."

A hairstylist often sees the world as cut and dried.

A waiter tells another waiter that her customer is so demanding. He demands I give him a good cup of coffee. Now you know we don't have good coffee here.

When they sell hub caps the salesmen are often heard saying hubs huba.

The clerk at the card shop says she should have been a magician. She always tells her customers to pick a card any card.

A worker yells at another worker who is standing up "Quick sit down. We are having a sit-down strike."

When the lobster fisherman was brought in for questioning he immediately clammed up.

There have been too many deaths. The funeral home director says the bodies are stacking up. The funeral home director told his workers that they needed to get into the spirit of things if they wanted to work here.

They let the worker at the flower shop go. They said he was too seedy.

No job is too big for people too do it, but many think the job is too small for them to do it.

A laundry worker says what holds things together is a clothes pin.

The clothing store is now handling children's clothing. They are down sizing.

The worker complained to his boss that he needed a raise. The boss said "I need some better workers. It looks like we are both going to be unhappy."

A small business in Idaho is said to just be small potatoes.

A worker says to another worker that you never hear me complaining. Another worker asked him if that was because he was still putting everything in writing.

At the dairy queen they keep a slush fund.

Our company has an open door policy. You never know what goes on behind closed doors.

Someone complained that there is too much swearing going on in court.

A guy at work says he usually gets everything right. He doesn't even know what it feels like to do something stupid. Another worker says "Oh you need to talk to Ben he does stupid things all the time."

The four workers were going over a report. Pete started sneezing. Mike says our report is nothing to sneeze at.

There was a rough situation at the air conditioning plant. The manager kept his cool during everything.

Three guys were working on a project at work. It was turning out great. Now the one guy said if we could just find some one with enough brains to run with it.

In order to work in a think tank you are required to have some thoughts.

I was having so much fun I lost track of time. I was working at my job and the minutes went by ever so slowly.

The only thing the UPS guy has to work on is his delivery.

A salesman in a shop that sells good China. He tells the customer that the piece they are looking is one of the best pieces of China. He says it is one of a kind. He said there were only two others like that. The customer asked what happened to them. He said I broke them so please buy this one before I break it too.

At the nail salon some women's nails are so bad because they watch too many shows that are nail bitters.

I was interviewing for a job at the juice shop. The manager says he doesn't have much time but he will try to squeeze me in.

At work the workers decided to stage a slow-down protest. The problem was nobody could tell it was a slow day because everything went the same way it did on a typical day.
The sergeant was 6 feet and eleven inches. He gave some tall orders.

Fishermen and salesmen talk alike.
Talk at a sales meeting
One worker said he had a nibble on the product.
Another one said he had some good bites.
A third one said he had to come up with a better line.
A fourth one said his bait wasn't working. If he was going to lure more customers he would have to change his bait.
A with said he had one one the line and was ready to reel him in.
The sixth said he was ahead of them all and had one already in the net.

A man was paying his bill at the store in cash. As he was counting out the money he said he was a little bit short. The clerk said don't worry about it honey I am not too tall myself.

It is not easy being a manager at a pet store. One worker I have to tell him to quit parroting me. Another worker is forever horsing around instead of working. Another one acts like a monkey climbing all over things. I have to bark orders at them all day.

A pet control truck had the sign"Mosquito Joe" on it. I asked how he got the name. They say he liked to take a bite out of others.

An impatient beer maker says he is just fermenting. If he gets too impatient he has got the hopps.

Who says it is not my job. Practically every worker who doesn't want to do any work.

A landscaper says in his business if you are going to get ahead you need to cover more ground.

In many places of work the Monday morning meeting turns into a yawning session and not much is accomplished.

The hair place slogan is "We will help you keep your hair." When they are done cutting your hair they sweep it up and put it in a bag for you to take home. They didn't say they would help you keep your hair on top of your head.

I get lots of exercise at work. I am told to walk the new worker through the days activities. Later I am told to give them a run down of what they need to know. Than I am told what areas I can skip. Finally I am told to jump ahead the end.

The insurance agent told the Californian that were you live there are too many earthquakes. I can't insure you. You are on shaky ground.

The loan officer has a good sense of humor. He turned down the man's loan for a house. He said the best I can loan you is ten dollars.

Two volunteers from different organizations were working together on a fund raiser. One person was supervising it. Fortunately some had on T-shirts with their names on them. On one man's shirt it said Mike. A couple of volunteers complained about Mike. They will tell him to do something or call his name and he would ignore them. The supervisor said he would talk to him. Maybe he was hard of hearing. He called Mike but he didn't pay any attention. Then the pointed to his shirt. Mike looked down. He said "Oh the shirt isn't mine I borrowed it from someone else. My name isn't Mike."

The worker for the taxidermist said it sure is getting stuffy in here.

In court the line that attorneys work on is the line of defense.

What a customer at a car dealership wants to hear. "This deal is too good to pass up."

The president of the company says if there is any problem too big for him to handle he gives it to his secretary.

The secretary asked the psychologist how the angry patient was doing. He said good. He is no longer mad at the world. He has narrowed it down to about 28 people.

It its tough being so smart when you try to help out the boss and tell him how the company should be run. I don't know why they don't appreciate this.
The drink in the bar for pest control people is called the grasshopper. The carpenter likes the screwdriver.

At the funeral home there was just a few workers there. The director says we just have skeleton crew today.

The worker at the ice cream shop was complaining to the other worker. There are all these exciting flavors of ice cream. They are exotic and all different colors and favors. I feel like in life I am stuck being just plain vanilla. The boss overhears. He said you do know that more people pick vanilla than any other flavor.

The news letter at the chicken farm is full of chicken nuggets.

The boss told the workers they all need to work on a major project. He assigned everyone a part. Cory asked "What about me?" You forgot to tell me what I need to do." The boss says "I am sending you on an extended vacation."

I asked the waitress what she would recommend. She said "Beans and franks. This is the only thing the cook can't mess up."

Two sailors used to sail together. They hadn't seen each other for a long time. When one ran into the other guy he said "Long time no sea."

They say the guy at the balloon shop can really blow things out of proportion.

The worker talked behind everyone's back. He had a bad word to say about everyone. Nobody liked him. The boss couldn't fire him because he did his work. He was killed in a car accident. The boss and his wife went to the funeral. It was a chapel where at least three or four funerals were held at the same time. The pastor started to tell stories of how kind he was and how much good he had done, and how everyone loved him. The boss's wife said "Are you sure we are at the right funeral because this doesn't sound at all like the guy you described." Now I ask you how many of you have felt like you have gone to the wrong funeral?

The best compliment you can give someone at the packing company is to tell them they can really pack it all in.

In Mexico the family had eight children. They had tacos for lunch everyday. The mother got tired of yelling at her children to come and eat so she hung a big bell outside the house and rang it when they were to come and eat. Later one child grew up and came to America where she was successful in business. She started her own chain of taco places and in memory of her mother she calls it taco bell.

My job at the clothing store is a good fit. I don't think a job could suit me better. When I work here I feel that I am wearing a tight t-shirt that hugs my body. With that I clothes.

I guy writing about his job at a bedding store.
I hate to lay this on you.
My paycheck doesn't cover my bills.
I hate to sound like a wet blanket.
At times I really feel short-sheeted.
I hope you are okay with my pillow talk.

The police brought the baker in for questioning. They wanted to know where he got all his dough from. They said he needed to roll out with some answers.

Finally he talked. He had been sitting so long on a hard chair. It was hard on his buns.

When questioning the doorman they had to wait for him to open up.

The cleaner says be good to me because I know all your dirty secrets.

The detective used to working with dogs says we need to collar the thief. We help take the bite out of crime.

We were all standing around at work and talking about a problem and deciding if we needed to make a stand. The boss came in and saw us standing around and said "Why are you all standing around? You need to get to work if you want to keep your jobs." So much for making a stand.

The conductor on a train says he likes telling people where to get off.

I worked for years on a chicken farm. I finally decided it was time to spread my wings and look for another job.

The slogan at the tie shop is "We will help you tie one on."

When they hire a cleaner they want someone who is not afraid to get down and get dirty.

What is a "ghost worker?" Someone you have never seen do any work or when you want to find hem to do some work you can't find them. You know they are supposed to work at the plant because you see a paycheck is made out to them every month.

The mover says "I am moving on up so you better move over. There isn't room at the top for the both of us.

A cement worker tends to glaze things over. He can be helpful when you are looking for someone to smooth things over.

The manager at the goodwill store was getting upset with his workers. He said there is a limit to my goodwill.

The large guy said to his coworker when I do something would you quit saying that is big of me.

During the winter up North the police don't have to tell robbers to freeze. They already are.

An agreeable attorney says to the other attorney there is no argument here.

When men go back to work over the weekend they usually discuss the latest sports event. The women want to catch up on the gossip.

Door workers get so tired of the knock knock jokes. If a doorman doesn't do much we say is dormant.

The cook's motto is "There is a season for everything."

He was a little older than the other firemen and couldn't get around so well, so he was their cook. The firemen were always teasing and making fun of him. One day they had soup for their first course. He came in from the kitchen. He was talking without his teeth. He says you guys are always giving me a bad time, and I got to laughing so hard I dropped my teeth in the soup. If you would all look in your bowl of soup to see who has been teeth, it would be much appreciated.

The manager of the dress store told her workers they need to dress it up a little more.

Often at work the plan that makes the most sense is the last one chosen.

The man says " I will have you know that our company has standards. Probably not high standards, but still standards.

At the land office where the deeds are, when the worker gives out a deed he feels like he has done his good deed for the day.

A cook at a famous hotel restaurant used to be a salad maker. He refers to those days as his salad days.

A lady waiting for the dentist remarked to another lady there about a poster of a beautiful lady smiling. She said she would smile more too if she looked like that.

The manager of the ticket booths got in trouble. He was accused of discrimination after he told a short worker who was a ticket taker not to be short changed.

The manager of the restaurant was in love with hiss girlfriend Patty. He said she melts my heart. In her honor he created the patty melt hamburger.

They always say that operators are standing by, but I am pretty sure they are sitting.

Ambulance drivers like to think of themselves as helpers. You know the operator tells the callers that help is on the way.

The worker at the clock factory asked the boss if he could work longer hours. The boss said no. We have to keep 60 minutes in each hour.

There was a raid on a house by the police looking for drugs. Later the sergeant called and asked one of the policemen if they found the dope. He said we sure did. He was hiding in one of he closets.

Bubbles is the name of the new manager at the bath shop.

The teams in the company were all assigned a letter of the alphabet. The one team was not doing well. Would you if you were assigned the letter the letter F?

A lot of people want to score points with the score keeper.

A man trying out for the job skills that would be helpful to the the job, but that he was good with people. The boss said he would put him down for a management position.

When a roofer has a party they can really rise the roof.

I told the boss that I am multitasked. I can chew gum walk, think, talk and blow bubbles at the same time.

He was really good working at the door factory. When he came in he really knew how to make an entrance.

The clockmaker said we all wait in life for our big moment.

She had a job doing facials.

A baggage handler was visiting a bar. He said he was going to case the joint.

A plumber sad he went on a vacation he always used his disposable income.

A cleaner said to another cleaner "You want the floor, you can mop the floor.

The customer was doing a trade in on his car with the salesman who was willing to give him what he thought he should get on the car. The salesman said "You sure drive a hard bargain."